1985
SEASON
THE COMPLETE HANDBOOK OF
PRO BASKETBALL

Super Sports Books from SIGNET

(0451)

☐ **THE ILLUSTRATED SPORTS RECORD BOOK by Zander Hollander and David Schulz.** Here, in a single book, are 350 records with stories and photos so vivid they'll make you feel that "you are there." Once and for all you'll be able to settle your sports debates on who holds what records and how he, or she, did it. (111818—$2.50)*

☐ **THE COMPLETE HANDBOOK OF THE OLYMPIC GAMES, LOS ANGELES, 1984 edited by Phyllis and Zander Hollander.** Here is the only guide you'll need to prepare for and follow the drama of the 1984 Olympic Games in person or on television. Legends, tips on viewing, best bets, records and rare photos will put you in the best seat for this exciting two-week sporting experience. (128850—$3.95)*

☐ **THE LEGEND OF DR. J: The Story of Julius Erving by Marty Bell.** An electrifying action-profile of the fabulous multi-millionaire superstar. "Graceful and admirable!"—*Dick Schaap* (121791—$2.95)

☐ **EVERYTHING YOU ALWAYS WANTED TO KNOW ABOUT SPORTS* *and didn't know where to ask by Mickey Hers-kowitz and Steve Perkins.** Here is the book that answers every question a sports fan ever had in the back of his mind and tells the truth about all the whispered rumors of the sports world. (124715—$2.75)

*Prices slightly higher in Canada

1985
SEASON

THE COMPLETE HANDBOOK OF
PRO BASKETBALL

EDITED BY ZANDER HOLLANDER

A SIGNET BOOK
NEW AMERICAN LIBRARY

ACKNOWLEDGMENTS

This is the season that will mark the coming of Akeem Olajuwon and the going of Kareem Abdul-Jabbar. Both are very much a part of this 11th edition of *The Complete Handbook of Pro Basketball*. So are Bernard King, the Celtics and all the others who make pro basketball the second-most exciting indoor sport of all.

We acknowledge with appreciation those who helped make this edition possible: contributing editor Howard Blatt, Fran Blinebury, Filip Bondy, Dan Shaughnessy, Joe Gergen, Kareem Abdul-Jabbar, Peter Knobler, Lee Stowbridge, Dot Gordineer, Beri Greenwald, Phyllis Hollander, Peter Hollander, Richard Rossiter, Fred Canty, Bob Rosen, Seymour Siwoff, Alex Sachare, Brian McIntyre, Terry Lyons, the NBA team publicity directors and Westchester Book Composition.

Zander Hollander

PHOTO CREDITS: Cover—Jerry Wachter (Focus on Sports); back cover—Noren Trotman; inside photos—Ira Golden, Michael Hirsch, Richard Reiss, Noren Trotman, AP/Wide World, UPI and the NBA team and college photographers.

SIGNET, SIGNET CLASSICS, MENTOR, PLUME, MERIDIAN AND NAL BOOKS are published by The New American Library Inc. 1633 Broadway New York, New York 10019

First Printing, October 1984

1 2 3 4 5 6 7 8 9

PRINTED IN THE UNITED STATES OF AMERICA

CONTENTS

Editor's Note: The material herein includes trades and rosters up to final printing deadline.

BIRD & McHALE: PRIDE AND POWER OF THE CELTICS

By DAN SHAUGHNESSY

Through the years, the Boston Celtic franchise has been blessed with some of pro basketball's most innovative, talented and successful players. Bob Cousy, Bill Sharman, Bill Russell, Tom Heinsohn, John Havlicek, Sam Jones and Dave Cowens all have won championships and earned a spot in NBA history.

Nothing has changed. The 1984-85 Celtics feature two star players in the prime of their careers. Together they have won two world championships in four seasons. They both earn at least $1 million per year, enjoy All-Star status and hail from middle America.

Meet Larry Bird and Kevin McHale, the pride and power of the Boston Celtics. Bird is a five-year veteran from Indiana State. He's probably the NBA's best-known player and won his first MVP award last season. McHale, meanwhile, settled for an All-Star invitation and the postseason honor of being named the NBA's best sixth man. There's no doubt he'd start on any other team. "He's already one of the top ten players in the league," says Chicago coach Kevin Loughery.

Bird and McHale are tall (6-9 and 6-11, respectively), white, and star in a hoop hotbed which has sold out over 170 consecutive NBA games. That's just about where the similarities end.

Boston's two superstars actually have little in common. Bird is a starter, single, extremely private off the court and uncomfortable with strangers. McHale is a reserve, married with a baby daughter and outgoing. He enjoys interviews and has fun con-

---

Dan Shaughnessy covered the Baltimore Orioles for the Baltimore Evening Sun *and was national baseball writer for the Washington* Star *before joining the Boston* Globe, *where he follows the fortunes of the Celtics.*

To the victors: Champ Celts' Kevin McHale and Larry Bird.

versing with strangers. During the playoffs last spring, McHale's teammates taped "411" to the back of his locker-room bathrobe. That's 411, as in "information." If you want information, you dial McHale.

Individually, they are two of the most-coveted talents in the NBA.

Bird came to the Celtics in 1979. He was drafted as a junior eligible. After leading his Indiana State team to the NCAA championship game (a game it lost to Magic Johnson's Michigan State team), Bird came to Boston and helped turn a 29-53 disaster into the NBA's best regular-season record (61-21) in one year. He played in his first NBA All-Star Game and was named Rookie of the Year. One year later, Bird led the Celts to their 14th world championship, beating Houston in six games. Bird finished runnerup in the MVP voting that season. He was runnerup again in 1982 and 1983.

The 1982-83 season ended badly for the Celtics. They were swept out of the Eastern Conference semifinals by the Milwaukee Bucks. It was the first time any Boston team had been beaten 4-0 in a playoff series. When it was over, Bird said, "This just makes me want to work harder than ever. I'm going to punish myself all summer and come back in better shape than ever so this doesn't happen again."

Bird built a regulation-size court behind his mother's house in French Lick, Indiana. He got the keys to the high-school gym and played there when the lights went down.

True to his word, Bird rebounded with an MVP award and a championship season. He averaged 24.2 points, 10.1 rebounds and 6.6 assists during the 1983-84 regular season. In 23 playoff games, he averaged 27.2 points and 11 rebounds. The 11 members of the voting committee unanimously named him MVP of Boston's classic championship series against the Lakers. After being unfavorably compared with Magic Johnson for four years, Bird proved to have much more impact than The Magic Man when the Celtics and Lakers jousted for the NBA title.

The numbers only begin to tell the story. Bird led the Celts with his work ethic and his selflessness. No one is quite sure how it happened, but somewhere along the line, Larry Bird became the ultimate teammate. Every move he makes on the court is designed with one goal: winning. He never takes a shot if a teammate has a better shot. He moves well without the ball and ranks as probably the greatest passing forward in the history of the game. He makes all of his teammates better. Bird's teammates are thankful for him, never jealous.

It should also be noted that Bird's best season came immediately

Encircled and undaunted, Bird emerged with MVP laurels.

after he signed a seven-year contract which pays him approximately $1.8 million per season.

"It made me feel good to have a good season after signing the big contract," Bird said when it was over.

McHale also responded with a big year after inking a multi-million-dollar pact.

McHale's contract situation proved much more distasteful than

Bird's. Unlike Bird, McHale spent a good deal of time talking about his contract before signing the new deal. The contract squabble was a source of some friction between McHale and his teammates throughout the stormy 1982-83 season.

The seeds of controversy were first planted when the Celtics drafted McHale No. 3 in the country overall in the spring of 1980. McHale didn't like the money the Celtics were offering and considered playing in Italy. Celtic coach Bill Fitch said, "Let him eat spaghetti," but McHale eventually came to terms with Boston.

The center-forward from Minnesota was never happy with his three-year deal. "I was picked third and at least seven or eight guys got more money than I did," McHale said when asked about his discontent.

Fitch proved to be another problem for McHale. Unlike Bird, who has an uncommon reverence for authority, McHale is the rebellious type. McHale didn't like Fitch's dictatorship and did everything he could think of to buck the system. When Fitch would say, "The bus leaves at 9:32," McHale would show at 9:33. If Fitch said, "Go left," McHale would go right, just to get a rise out of the tightly-strung coach.

Nevertheless, McHale established himself as one of the league's best players. He could come off the bench and create tremendous matchup problems for opponents. Few Celtic rivals had a 6-10 power-forward who could stop McHale's patented turnaround jumper.

The Celtics won a championship in McHale's first season. Boston lost to Philadelphia in the Eastern Conference finals a year later. Then came the final year of McHale's contract—which also proved to be Fitch's last year in Boston and the low point of McHale's pro career.

McHale talked about his impending free agency all season. The Celtics were unable to strike a deal and McHale verbalized his displeasure with some of the negotiating tactics employed by then-owner Harry Mangurian.

McHale's teammates felt that his contract talks were getting in the way of the job at hand. When the Celts were smoked by Milwaukee in four straight games, McHale said he could hold his head up high, but a lot of people blamed McHale's poor playoff on the contract talks.

The New York Knicks wanted McHale, but were boxed out when the Celtics signed Knick free agents Rory Sparrow, Marvin Webster and Sly Williams to contracts calling for a total of $1.4 million per season. That put New York near its salary cap. In mid-July, McHale signed a $4-million, four-year deal with the Celtics.

Meanwhile, Fitch had resigned under fire and K.C. Jones had

been hired to coach the Celtics. With a new contract, a new coach and a new baby girl, McHale came to camp a relaxed and confident player again. He wound up averaging 18.4 points per game off the bench, making his first All-Star team, winning the sixth-man award and his second championship ring. He also kept an impressive ironman streak alive. In four full seasons, McHale has never missed a game due to an injury.

Bird and McHale. McHale and Bird. They are successful, loved by Boston fans, and have a championship ring for each hand.

One might assume that Bird and McHale are best friends off the court, but this is not the case. They respect each other's game and lifestyle, but don't hang together much when the Celtics are at home or on the road.

Both are good friends of backup center Rick Robey, who was traded from Boston to Phoenix for Dennis Johnson in June 1983. Bird and Robey were like brothers. McHale and Robey were "Thumper and Bumper," according to Celtic radio legend Johnny Most.

With Robey gone, Bird is most likely to be seen hanging out with Indiana soulmate, Quinn Buckner, or playing backgammon with Scott Wedman. McHale spends all of his time at home with his wife Lynn and daughter Krysten. On the road, he catches up with some of his high-school buddies when the Celtics are playing in the midwest and spends a lot of free time with guard Danny Ainge.

Bird and McHale both like the outdoors. Bird loves to fish. McHale is a fisherman and a hunter. Both are extremely loyal to the people "who knew them when." Bird loves to seek out his high-school friends when he retreats to his summer home back in French Lick. McHale often leaves space on his hotel-room floor when his friends from Hibbing, Minn., catch up with him in Milwaukee.

They are extremely close to their families. Bird has been very generous to his mother and brothers. His mother often attends when the Celtics play in Indianapolis. McHale's father was a taconite miner for 40 years. Mr. and Mrs. McHale try to catch the Celtics when they come to Milwaukee. "Paul A. McHale, my dad, is my main man," McHale likes to say.

Both Bird and McHale possess a sharp wit, but Bird is more likely to save his best stuff for his teammates. McHale shows his sense of humor to everyone he meets. Bird is private and needs a sense of trust before showing his lighter side.

Bird is more likely to make fun of a Quinn Buckner airball, or one of Ainge's fights with the likes of Tree Rollins or Darrell Walker. Bird has had a lot of fun taunting Robey over the years.

When Robey said Bird might have to stand a few extra inches in back of the free-throw line because of his nose, Bird shot back with, "Yeah, but when Rick shoots a free throw he ought to get credit for a three-pointer because his butt sticks out all the way back to the three-point line."

McHale has fun with everyone and everything. He loved to poke fun at Fitch's seriousness. When Fitch refused to let out-of-town writers attend Celtic practices, McHale would say, "Yeah, you might get to see some of these plays we've been running here for the last 20 years."

When Fitch sent assistant coach Jimmy Rodgers to the top of Houston's Summit to check out a "spy," McHale laughed hardest when the spy turned out to be a maintenance man smoking a little weed during his lunch break. McHale remembered that scene when the Celtics had their first practice in the Summit, where Fitch now coaches, last winter. As the C's took the floor, McHale yelled toward the rafters, "Okay, Bill, we know you're up there. Come on out."

McHale has never been totally at ease with Eastern aggressiveness. "It's different here," he says. "Back home, if you see a car in a snowdrift, you just walk over and start pushing the guy. Here, you see a guy stuck and everybody says, 'Good, that's one less guy I'll have to worry about today.'"

Bird loathes the traffic and hostility of Easterners and can't bear to be bothered in public.

"I love baseball," he says. "But I hate going to Fenway Park because I end up signing autographs all during the game."

Bird has gotten to the point where he's cooperative, patient and analytical during postgame interviews. But he hates to be bothered away from the work place. A Boston TV station that sent a crew out to Bird's house the night he signed his contract is still paying the price. "Don't ever come out to my house," Bird says.

Bird probably enjoys the game more than McHale. He plays year-round, and is equally comfortable in the NBA All-Star Game or in a pick-up game with the high-school studs of French Lick. McHale is a frustrated hockey star who was forced into basketball when he grew to 6-10. He enjoys playing, but thinks of it as a job more than Bird. McHale said he'd rather go hunting when he was named for the All-Star Game last year and is the first Celtic to hit the golf course when springtime finally hits Boston. He golfed every day while the Celtics were in Los Angeles for the NBA finals last June.

Likes, dislikes, jokes and personal lifestyles are put aside when Bird and McHale patrol Red Auerbach's parquet palace.

Despite limited physical tools, Bird has made himself the NBA's best player. At a time when the game is dominated by mastodons, leapers, and roadrunners, Bird has more impact than any player even though he is slow afoot and not much of a jumper. But he is blessed with a 6-9 frame and great vision. He does the rest on his own.

Bird understands that only one of five players can have the ball at any given moment. He is a master of motion without the ball. When he gets the ball, he does the right thing. He keeps the sphere in the air most of the time.

Bird's shooting is feared, but he says he'd be even better if he hadn't broken a finger on his right hand playing softball in college. His "step-back" shot is ingenius. By stepping back before he shoots, Bird creates the space he needs to get his shot off. The step-back compensates for lack of quickness and vertical leap. If a defender anticipates the step-back, Bird is prepared to drive past his opponent.

Few 6-9 players have ever rebounded better than Bird. He follows the Paul Silas theory of rebounding: "It's not how high you go, it's how much space you take up while you're up there." Bird anticipates very well and grabs a lot of weak-side boards just by using his head and fighting for position.

McHale, meanwhile, has never been the rebounder people thought he might be, but possesses one of the game's unstoppable weapons: a turnaround, fallaway jumper. The shot is impossible to block because McHale is 6-11, has arms of a man 7-4 and releases the ball as he's falling away from the basket.

McHale's unusual build accounts for much of his success. He looks like someone who either cannot exhale or has a coat-hanger underneath his shirt. His shoulders are pinned back, his chest heaves forward, and his arms dangle down around his knees.

"I was blessed with this body for basketball," he says. "My parents aren't that tall and neither is my brother. It was me, so I have to use the gift to my best advantage."

McHale gives the Celtics a luxury that no other team has. He's a 6-11 bench player who creates severe matchup problems when he's on the floor simultaneously with Celtic center Robert Parish.

At the defensive end, McHale is one of the league's better shot-blockers. His timing and leap are above average, and the long arms take care of the rest.

Together, Bird and McHale give the Celtics two of the league's best players and top gate attractions. Both were under close scrutiny after signing for big money in the summer of '83, but they responded with their best seasons and helped bring championship flag No. 15 to the rafters of the Boston Garden.

BOOK BONUS

GIANT STEPS

By KAREEM ABDUL-JABBAR
and PETER KNOBLER

For 37-year-old Kareem Abdul-Jabbar, the end may be in sight. The 1984-85 season could be his last hurrah. The 7-2 veteran of 15 NBA campaigns has climbed every mountain, including Mt. Chamberlain last season when he surpassed Wilt Chamberlain to become the NBA's all-time leading scorer.

To some, there was a new Jabbar—"He seems to have a new inner peace that wasn't there before," said his Laker coach, Pat Riley.

Riley cited as contributing factors the fire which destroyed Jabbar's home a year-and-a-half ago, his nearing retirement and his autobiography, Giant Steps. *"After the fire, Kareem was showered with love and heartfelt concern for the first time in his entire career," Riley said. "The book is the end of a lot of self-examination for him."*

Excerpts from the book follow:

ON WILT CHAMBERLAIN

Wilt held his position in the pro basketball hierarchy with total seriousness. He fought for it the way he went for rebounds, with strength and intimidation. It was his only identity. Finally out from under Bill Russell's shadow, or at least no longer having to read the comparisons in every column and boxscore, he could have done without my interference.

It would have been pleasant for him to rule the roost for a few

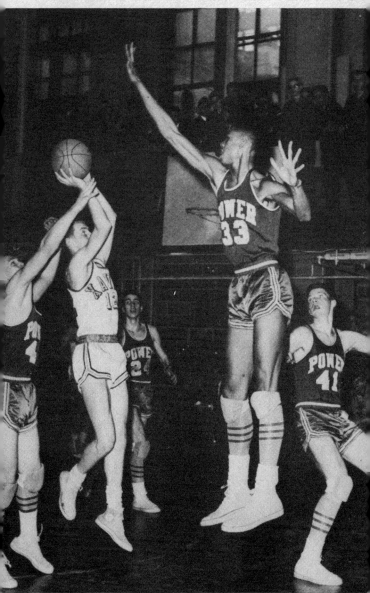

Kareem began as Lew Alcindor at Power Memorial Academy.

years before some new young guy knocked him out of the box. And why did it have to be me, the kid he'd taken under his wing? After all, I was the boy he'd loaned his records to, whom he'd shown the ropes. How could I possibly be threatening to take his place at the top? It took a special will to turn me into the demon threat to his kingdom who had to be defeated. But when the stakes are as high as identity itself, it's amazing what the mind can do.

Wilt had a lot to complain about because, from the start, he couldn't control me. Wilt's entire game was built on strength. He controlled the lane. He had great timing and excellent spring and he would routinely reject opponents' shots, either stuffing them while still in the guys' hands or batting them out of the air after they'd been launched. Nobody could move Wilt out of the pivot, and he was ferocious off the boards. He was the dominant guy in there, with a personality to match.

He personally made the game progress, brought the big man from clod to controlling factor. If it weren't for Wilt, people wouldn't believe some things were possible—100 points by one man in a single game, a 50-point-per-game average.

Wilt was not perfect, however. He wasn't the best competitor; he didn't have the most savvy as far as how to make his team win. Russell seemed to get the more crucial rebounds, and, though Wilt won all the scoring titles, Russell came away with 11 championship rings to Wilt's two.

More importantly to me, Wilt was stationary and I was mobile, and I found out fast that he could not handle me on offense. I was 11 years younger than he was, and quicker to begin with. I found my first time down the floor against him that if I let him stand in the pivot and didn't move before I got the ball, he would destroy me. The next time down, however, I saw that if I got even a little movement, I could either fake him left and go up the other way with all the time in the world for a hook, or fake the hook, get him up in the air and drive the other way for a stuff.

I never took Wilt for granted, however, You can't ever say that Wilt didn't give his best, or that his best wasn't superlative.

I think, though, that Wilt feels that beyond playing hard, I tried to embarrass him, somehow to build my reputation at his expense, pull him down from his greatness. Make him look small. And sometimes, on the court, I did embarrass him, though never intentionally.

Wilt and I have had our falling outs, however. I started to lose my reverence for him when he supported Richard Nixon for president in 1968. Harlem was in an uproar, black people were struggling for basic human rights and Wilt was throwing his weight behind an obvious crook who had no regard for us.

He became national figure at UCLA in mid-to-late '60s.

Our differences were also made perfectly clear when he published his autobiography and in it declared that black women were inferior sexual partners, were generally socially inferior because they were unsophisticated. I knew that was bullshit and though I should have assumed it would cause trouble, I said so in public.

ON OSCAR ROBERTSON

Oscar, in my opinion, is the best all-around player in the history of basketball. He was the epitome of the subtle, no-flash ballplayer. He had the game broken down into such fine points that if he got even a half-step on you, you were in big trouble. He kept the game very simple, which was his first secret. He didn't have blazing speed, and he didn't do a whole lot of pirouettes; all he did was score, rebound, and dish the ball off.

What the Big O did for me that gave a quantum jump to my game was get me the ball. It sounds simple, and it was—for him. Oscar had this incredible court vision and a complete understanding of the dynamics of the game. Not only did he see guys open on the periphery for a jumper, he knew when each of us would fight through a pick or come open behind a screen, and the ball would arrive and be there like you were taking it off a table.

ON WALT BELLAMY

Walt used to crack me up. He was a big, crazy center who would always be talking to himself whenever they called a foul on him. "You're always looking for me," he'd say to the referees, whether they were in earshot or not. "Never anybody else gets these fouls, just me, No. 8, got to give it to Dr. Bellamy." He wasn't slick, but he was a riot. Somebody would drive the lane, he'd slap him in the face, then pick him up off the floor and ask if he's hurt. Trip some guy on the way to the hoop, then bend down and ask, "You all right?"

ON WOMEN ON THE ROAD

Women don't have an easy time with ballplayers on the road. They make themselves available, which is always pleasant, then expect some commitment in return, which is unrealistic. Ballplayers are proud people, many to the point of egotism; that's how they become such good ballplayers. Women are attracted to the celebrity, the glamour, the wealth; what they often don't learn until it's too late is that there are 22 NBA cities and guys are in and out of them all year long.

The regard for womanhood in concept is very high around the NBA; in practice it's less than enlightened. Wives and girlfriends are not encouraged to tour with the teams. First, they could be a distraction from a player's concentrating on the game and, second, they might see some things they're not supposed to see and go report it back to the rest of the wives. That kind of team disruption is deemed not worth the risk. Divorce suits *will* detract from cohesive team play.

One of my teammates made himself a dubious reputation one evening when a prostitute trying to hustle him decided she would give him some of what he wouldn't pay for and then shame him out of the money on the other end. They had their time, and when he was done he said, "You gotta leave."

"Aren't you gonna pay me?"

"No."

She started to get loud, so he slapped her and threw her, half-naked, out into the hallway. The woman went and banged on Earvin Johnson's door. He opened it, looked at her and said, "Can't help you, baby," and as he was speaking, he saw the door down the hall open and the rest of her clothes come flying out. Earvin calls it "The Case of the Cash Bobos."

ON PLAYING TOUGH

I have a temper. I play the game hard and physically; I want to win every time I get on the court and when something or someone gets in my path, I am not unwilling to go right over it. I play within the rules, however, and I know them well enough to be aware when they're being broken. Because I am large and powerful and a significant force to be reckoned with, I am constantly the target of my large, strong opponents who will try almost anything to neutralize or undermine my effectiveness. I get banged around a lot.

It is the nature of the position of center in the game of basketball as it has developed that one has to almost literally fight for space under the boards or on the court. You know you're going to run into somebody's shoulder with your kidney. You can deal with that; it's part of the game. What I've had to contend with for as long as I've played the sport is my opponents' constant attempts to physically punish me and the referees' equally consistent refusal to permit the rules to protect me. Players either want to prevent me from playing successfully or prove themselves against me. Most can't do it within the rules. I take more abuse than anyone in the NBA. After a while, I started to dish it back.

At first it was annoying, being distracted from playing the game

Larry Bird's Celtics overcame Kareem & Co. in 1984.

by jabs to the ribs and shots to the head. Then it became painful. Then I began to expect it, got angry, even before the game began, at the crap I knew I was going to have to take. Finally, it developed into a matter of principle: if the rules will not defend me, I will defend myself; I will not be a punching bag.

There aren't many really hurtful players in the NBA. A lot of guys play hard—guys like Maurice Lucas, Elvin Hayes, Zelmo Beatty, Artis Gilmore, Paul Silas—but they're just doing their best. The only truly dirty player I've run into, a man who took real pleasure in viciousness, was Dennis Awtrey. Awtrey caught me with a blindside punch, very much on purpose, knocked me down, and was fined $50. He was great with the blindsider, but I never saw him go face to face. He was a mediocre player, and that one shot kept him in the league for several extra years.

I decked Kent Benson because I wasn't going to be abused. Benson was another white hope fresh out of college and looking to make a name for himself. The Lakers were playing in Milwaukee. It was two minutes into the first game of the season; Milwaukee had scored and I was jogging downcourt about to establish position to the left of the lane. Benson was going to show me that he didn't back down a step, that he was a man. I had gotten behind him and was ready for the ball when he glanced around, saw no one was looking, and threw a vicious elbow that caught me flush in the solar plexus. He knocked the wind right out of me.

Immediately, I was back in the streets. With no breath, I expected him to keep attacking me, because in New York that's exactly what would have happened. I was doubled over, on the playground, dealing with another beating. I hated it; I hated him. I kept saying to myself, if I can just get my breath back we *will* have a final confrontation.

I started to breathe again, in gasps like I was crying, and as soon as I could move, I ran out there and fired on him. I wanted to kill him. If I'd hit him a good shot in the temple, I believe I would have killed him. Fortunately, for all my training in the martial arts, when it came down to delivering a blow in anger I went with the roundhouse right and hit him in the orbit of the eye. His skull absorbed some of the impact. He went down as if he'd been shot, but I was yelling at him. I wanted some more. This was life and death for me and I was fully prepared to carry it through to its conclusion. Benson was a big man, 6-11, 245 pounds; he could have damaged me.

Benson was not getting up. My temper was fierce, but justified or not, there was no way a man should die over a basketball game. I was angry and confused. I had been attacked, had responded in my own defense, and once again had become the villain. My temper had gone out of control and taken my new-found relaxation with it. I knew I could count on even more public hostility now.

I had broken my hand against Benson's face and was sidelined again. The league couldn't suspend me because my hand was already in a cast, but they fined me $5,000. Benson, who had caused the initial injury, was neither fined nor reprimanded. (The official explanation was that since the referees had not seen Benson foul me, the league could not discipline him.) Typical NBA justice: discipline the nigger. All I see is white players being excused when attacking blacks, and black players who hit whites getting leaned on hard.

ON BLACKS AND WHITES IN BASKETBALL

Professional basketball is essentially a black sport being run as a white business. All the team owners are white, as are most of the general managers and coaches. (To the NBA's credit, however, it has accepted more blacks in significant management positions than any other major sport; baseball and football are still as white as a blank ledger.)

A great majority of the players are black, which more than anything else creates a marketing problem; the disposable income that pro sports needs in order to thrive is largely in the hands of white people. Blacks play the game in school and in the street, have refined its style and made it a cultural staple, but they haven't got the dollars to fill the arenas or support the television advertisers.

Pro basketball is a black game being sold to white people, and the owners, who have serious dollars sunk into the league, are all out to protect their investment. White players give white fans some faith; Larry Bird can be a white fan's fantasy alter ego a whole lot easier than Micheal Ray Richardson can. If they can compete with the black players, whites represent hope that America's athletic pride has not been totally usurped by strangers. If they outdo them, there is cause for joy. I've seen it.

Black players view fans with a reasonable amount of cynicism. Several years ago the entire 11-man squad of the Knicks was black, and you'd hear people grumbling about the "New York Niggerbockers." That will put you off your game.

ON EARVIN (MAGIC) JOHNSON

Earvin came out of college after his sophomore year as a 20-year-old kid with tremendous exuberance and outstanding basketball skills. In games, at practice, at pickup scrimmages, wherever he happened to be, Magic was very thrilled to be playing basketball. He was a boy living a dream and his enthusiasm was infectious. He was also a showman who was totally capable of playing the kind of intense winning basketball that I responded to and at the same time making the crowd feel like they were participating. And in some sense they were, because the more a place roared, the more he would make it roar. He would bring smiles to people's faces, mine included.

Earvin likes to make eye contact. He's got an expressive face and he enjoys the good challenge, so whenever possible he'll look right at a defender to let him know that not only is a basket and two points on the line but so is this guy's pride. He'll lock his opponent in a personal duel. When Earvin is going strong there is a real person out there for the fans to latch onto. He loves the attention and really basks in that public warmth.

Earvin broke into the league as a humorous fellow with basketball as his life. Even his style of play was humorous. He likes to have a laugh on the court and it's always at the opponent's expense. He keys everybody up: his teammates, because he's such an extraordinary passer that he's liable to get you the ball at any moment, and the other teams, because they don't like being the foil to some of his sleight of hand. He loves to fool someone, dash by, get the layup, not even look as the ball is going down, but beam downcourt and make some gesture that brings the crowd to its feet laughing and applauding while his defender seethes. Guys don't like having that done to them, so it raises the level of the game for all of us—we've got to deal with the other team coming back in our face—and puts a buzz on everyone who's watching.

Most important in what makes Earvin an outstanding ball-player, however, is his expertise. He's one of the great passers and, at 6-9, he's a guard who can crash the boards hard and often. He does his job well and consistently. That, more than anything, makes him a pleasure to work with.

ON JAMES WORTHY

The Lakers chose James Worthy as the No. 1 selection in the 1982 NBA draft. When he arrived at training camp it was immediately obvious that he was a player. He had size, speed, strength, quickness, agility, a good shot and the clear willingness to learn what he didn't already know. He also seemed like a nice guy and after a while we hit it off. I risked volunteering and he risked asking.

The NBA championship in '82 was Kareem's third team title.

There were definitely gaps. He was 16 years younger than I was, for starters. I'd begun to get used to that sort of thing, the longevity of my career putting more and more distance between me and the players. Worthy was drafted after his junior year in college, though, and was almost the youngest guy in the league. No way I could talk to him about Sandy Amoros' great catch against the Yankees in the 1955 World Series; it was five years older than he was.

We did talk basketball, though, and I found it satisfying to be able to put into words my pieces of personal information—subtle, specialized, valuable only to the very few people who could share in its benefit and understand the effort it had taken to gather and test it.

When I saw Worthy respond, by absorbing what I was telling him and thanking me, and by using it to play well, I got a private pleasure totally unlike anything basketball had offered me before. James Worthy is his own ballplayer and ought to succeed on his talents, but there was a continuity started that I was beginning to enjoy.

ON RETIREMENT

Sooner or later I will have to quit this game. The body will run down and, if the competitive desire never fades, the ability to do something about it is bound to. I like knowing I'm at the top of my profession; it's taken me a short lifetime and a good woman to appreciate it, but now I am aware of my position. I'd be surprised if I can attain the kind of dominance I've had over basketball in another field, but I'm definitely going to try. I'm considering going to law school; there's enough competition in that field to keep me interested. I want to resume my Islamic studies. I also want to lie on the beach in Hawaii for years on end. My children demand and deserve my attention.

BERNARD KING CAPTURES NEW YORK

By JOE GERGEN

Those were the days, my friend. There wasn't a tougher or more prized ticket in New York, on or off Broadway. In a town where it is widely assumed that the chic will inherit the earth, celebrities flocked to Madison Square Garden for a glimpse of the Knicks.

Woody Allen was a regular. So, too, was Dustin Hoffman. Robert Redford dropped by whenever he traveled East. The best and the brightest entertainers inhabited the courtside seats, less famous customers dressed as if attending the Metropolitan Opera and the energy level in the building, if harnessed, could have charged all the skyscrapers on the isle of Manhattan.

The Jets' hold on the city was as brief as a Joe Namath affair. And the Mets' magic lasted through one memorable season. Later, with the help of George Steinbrenner's manic drive to win, the Yankees would become the toast of the town. But in the early 1970s, only one team could be said to own New York. The Knicks not only played The City Game, but they played it with extraordinary skill and a special elan.

At cocktail parties and gallery openings, people exchanged sightings of The Open Man as if he had a face, a name and an American Express card. The favorite chant at the arena became so closely identified with the Knicks that, several years later, as Bill Bradley walked to the podium to deliver a commencement address, college students began shouting, "Dee-fense, dee-fense." It was a heady time for basketball in New York, and a lesson to anyone who harbored ambitions in the sport.

One such man was growing up tall and strong in the tough Fort

---

As sports columnist for Newsday, *Joe Gergen has been a close observer of the many bounces of Bernard King.*

Knick fans thrilled to Bernard King's 40-point machine.

Greene section of Brooklyn. Although the Garden was only a subway ride away, it was another world. And tickets were not only difficult to obtain but expensive. However, Bernard King had his dreams and his heroes. In high school, he asked to wear uniform No. 22 in honor of Dave DeBusschere, the Knicks' All-Star forward.

And then one day, King was invited to the Garden and introduced to the crowd as a member of the all-city high school basketball team selected by a New York newspaper. Part of his reward was a ticket in the blue seats, the mezzanine up near the ceiling. The Knicks overhauled the Bullets that night and King marveled at the sights and sounds of the famous arena on basketball night.

King went off to the University of Tennessee the following year and the sound was stilled. As the older players who had achieved two National Basketball Association championships in four years retired, management embarked on a disastrous open-checkbook approach to rebuilding. The Knicks signed every available player with marquee value, including Spencer Haywood, Bob McAdoo and George McGinnis (whose NBA rights, it developed, belonged to Philadelphia), without any consideration for how they would fit into a team concept. They even chased Wilt Chamberlain from coast to coast.

New York found another game. The Garden sat half-empty on basketball nights. The celebrities stayed away. That's the way it remained for the better part of a decade. Until the spring of 1982. Until that kid from Fort Greene who had worshipped at the shrine some 10 years earlier attracted a city's curiosity.

On consecutive midwinter nights in San Antonio and Dallas, the 6-7 King scored 50 points. The stars came for a closer look. Allen, Elliott Gould, Peter Falk, Pearl Bailey. The Garden became semi-fashionable again. In the first round of the playoffs, against the Detroit Pistons, the man stood up and demanded attention. He scored 36, 46, 46, 41 and 44 points, an unprecedented string of accomplishments in the postseason period, as the Knicks struggled to a five-game series victory. That set the stage for the night of May 4, 1984.

It marked the first home game of the second round of the playoffs. The Knicks hadn't won a second-round playoff game in 10 years and they already had lost the first two games of this series in Boston. But the opponents were the hated Celtics and the Knicks had King. The crowd at the Garden was at full throat 15 minutes before tipoff.

"I feel the history," King acknowledged. "I feel excited being part of it. It's a joy. It's exciting to be driving to the games. There's something special about this for me. To me, when you think about the NBA, you think about the Garden."

King was decked out for the occasion in uniform No. 30. The Knicks had long since retired DeBusschere's 22. Ironically, it was DeBusschere who, in one of his first actions as the new director of basketball operations for the Knicks, initiated the trade which brought King home from Golden State on the eve of the 1982-83 season. "I told Mr. DeBusschere I wanted to take his No. 22 down from the rafters and wear it," King recalled. "He just smiled."

And DeBusschere smiled again from a seat above courtside last May as King led the Knicks to a 100-92 victory over the Celtics. They were a team worthy of respect. Two days later, in a nationally-televised Sunday afternoon game, the Knicks won again, 118-113, as King scored 43 against physical defenders Kevin McHale and Cedric Maxwell, who had publicly vowed he

Bernard averaged 25.8 ppg at Tennessee.

had enjoyed his last 40-point game of the season. "I expected to rip off his shirt," McHale said in wonder, "and find a big red S."

The great forward would score more than 40 points (44) one more time in the series and the Knicks would take the Celtics to a seventh game before Larry Bird asserted himself. The full measure of that accomplishment wouldn't be felt for another month, until the Celtics completed their climb to a record 15th NBA title by overcoming the Los Angeles Lakers in the playoff finals. King, with a dislocated middle finger on each hand, had almost derailed the Celtics singlehandedly.

In the summer of 1982, Italian basketball officials sought NBA players and coaches for a national clinic in a resort town south of Milan. King spent a week at the camp, then took a tour of the country with his wife, Collette. He was enchanted.

A year ago, he went back. On that occasion, said Bill Pollak, his attorney and advisor, "I set him up with a car and said, 'Don't

With fingers mended, King should be even better this year.

tell me where you're going. Get lost.'" King did as requested,
developing a great appetite for Italian cooking in the bargain.

For his third engagement this past summer, he was accom-
panied not only by his wife, but his brother Albert and his wife.
Albert happens to play forward for the New Jersey Nets and their
relationship, hindered by an age difference which placed them in
separate basketball orbits, has blossomed since Bernard's home-
coming. The two men live in adjoining towns in northern New
Jersey and have struck a rivalry on the tennis court. King has not
pursued fame nor rushed to capitalize on the finest season of his
career. He limited his public appearances, which included a shooting session with Mayor Ed Koch to publicize the Big Apple Mobil
Games for New York youngsters. He prefers to do what he can
on an individual basis and the Knicks acknowledge that his char-
itable work is a secret even to them. No spotlights, thank you.

Others speak of his fondness for poetry, the most contemplative
of pleasures, but not King. On the road he lives a room-service
existence, preserving every bit of energy for the game he plays
at maximum intensity. The scowl he wears on court is more than
a mask. It is an attitude.

"Bernard is like a light switch," observed Ernie Grunfeld, who has known King since high school and played alongside him at Tennessee as well as with the Knicks. "Throw the switch; one second it's off and the next it's at 100 percent efficiency."

Basketball is serious business to Bernard King. It has not only been his career, but his salvation. "It's the way I am," he said during the playoffs last spring. "Isiah [Thomas] and Magic [Johnson], they smile all the time. That's the way they play best. I set into the scowl. If I was smiling, I'd miss half my shots."

The look and the manner are virtually impenetrable. King doesn't invite conversation from other players in the course of a game and he volunteers little himself. Bumps and elbows and even occasional manhandling elicit no special reaction. But names can and do hurt him.

Against the Pistons, late in the second game of the playoffs at the Silverdome, the Knicks were huddling around coach Hubie Brown when a heckler succeeded in getting under King's uniform. "Isn't it time you had a drink?" the man yelled. King started for the heckler but was restrained. Afterwards, despite a 46-point performance in the defeat, King declined not only to discuss the incident but even details of the game.

He regained his composure the following day but the obnoxious fan had picked at scar tissue. For now, King's past is a closed issue. The man has declined offers from book publishers and motion-picture producers. He has turned down first-person magazine articles and television interviews which would broach the subject. He has bottled it up inside.

King was an alcoholic. The only reason he is still playing basketball is that he admitted to the problem in 1980. A series of arrests—starting in college, proceeding to his rookie pro season with the Nets and culminating in charges of sexual abuse brought by a white woman in Salt Lake City while he was with the Utah Jazz—finally led him to a rehabilitation center and membership in Alcoholics Anonymous. "I was saving my own life," King said in the early months of treatment. "There's nothing more rewarding than that.

"I'd had a premonition for almost two years that I was going to die young. I was living very dangerously in the sense that I'd drive with a quart of alcohol in my system. I'd get in the car to drive home and I wouldn't remember the ride."

On one such occasion, in his second NBA season with the Nets, he was found slumped over the wheel while his car sat in the middle of a Brooklyn intersection at five in the morning.

He had started drinking, he said, as a social outlet in college, which was no place like home. The habit grew once he turned professional. "I was very unhappy my first year in the league," he said. "I'd have great games, score 30, 35 points and go home to an empty apartment. There was no one around to share the joy with."

The loneliness grew even more unbearable when the New Jersey Nets, his first pro team, decided he was beyond help and shipped him to Utah, a Mormon town with a tight social framework and few blacks. Although he started his rehabilitation process while with the Jazz, they, too, despaired of him and sent him to Golden State. It was in the Bay Area where King reclaimed his life and his talents, marrying a special-education teacher, establishing a home and growing into an All-Star. He played two seasons for the Warriors and, upon departing for New York, took out newspaper ads in Oakland and San Francisco to express his feelings: "To Bay Area fans. With gratitude and appreciation for your support. Thanks for the memories—Bernard King."

Despite the two championship teams in the early '70s, the Knicks have never had a player of King's ability. They were a total unit in their best seasons, five spokes in a wheel. The current Knicks, because of their own inadequacies and his remarkable presence, revolve around King. "He is," said Red Holzman, the coach of the great Knick teams and now an advisor to the club, "the greatest scoring machine I've ever seen."

In the Knicks' 180 playoff games prior to their meeting with the Pistons, only three players had scored 40 or more points— Cazzie Russell in 1968, Willis Reed in 1969 and King in 1983. In the next five games, with survival riding on the outcome, King topped 40 four times. "Not even Oscar Robertson, with all his greatness, ever dominated a team like Bernard," said Eddie Donovan, the Knicks' general manager in their glory years. "Once he gets out in the open floor, there is no stopping him."

"I've never seen any one player dominate a team like King has the Pistons this season," said Dave Bing, once a backcourt star in Detroit and now a team broadcaster. "He's just one great talent and there is really no way to stop him. His release is so quick that before you can even double-team him, his shot is in the air."

Although he often gives away a couple of inches to defenders, King likes to position himself down low, take a pass and hit a whirling baseline jumpshot. Half the time, it appears, he doesn't see the basket before he shoots. That's because half the time King relies on his feel for the basket. "I got the ball in the positions where I like to set it," he said after his 50-point performance against San Antonio, "and I felt all the seams. What I mean by that is that you don't always have to look to see where the defense is, you just feel it and go."

King is at his creative best on the fast break but coach Hubie Brown prefers a halfcourt game with set plays. The forward simply does his best within the system. "There are not enough adjectives to talk about Bernard King," Brown said. Suffice it to say that Brown appointed King captain for his dedication.

"People ask me where Bernard would play on those old teams," Holzman said, "and my only answer is, for a guy like that, you'd always find a place. What impresses me is how he shoots with such quickness and accuracy. Other teams overplay him, they try to deny him the ball, they double-team him and triple-team him. But he keeps scoring."

And he keeps improving. King has made a point each summer of going back to camp. After his vacation in Europe, he spent 10 days working on his game with Pete Newell at Loyola Marymount College in Los Angeles. He has always played with determination and intensity. But he continues to challenge his potential, even after being selected the NBA's Player of the Year by *The Sporting News* in a vote of league players.

His work habits, according to Brown, are the best he has ever seen. And that's fitting. When King returned to New York from personal and professional exile, he went to DeBusschere and told him he always wanted to be No. 22. "I emulated him," King said. "The way he worked, that's one of the things I like to think we have in common."

But DeBusschere, for all his effort, didn't have King's gift with the basketball. King and Bird, according to DeBusschere, "play on a different level. They have incredible talent."

To think, King's great talent almost was wasted. Certainly, the man thought about that himself as he wrestled with alcohol four years ago. "I know and realize now that I'm fortunate," he said at the time. "Fortunate that I wasn't arrested more in an automobile. Fortunate that I didn't kill anyone and that nobody killed me. I honestly believe that I should not be here, that I should have been gone long ago.

"But I think that God has left me here long enough to realize that I had a problem and that I had to deal with that problem. In terms of my career, I think this is my last opportunity, my last chance. But if I ever start indulging again, I won't have any chance. And so I can live if I want to live. I can play if I want to play. I've been given the chance to do that."

He has succeeded with that final chance, succeeded beyond anyone's expectations. King has forged a good life for himself back home and, in the process, given New York basketball the transfusion it desperately needed.

AKEEM OLAJUWON

The 7-Foot Nigerian Who Jumped To the Pros

By FRAN BLINEBURY

Just as it is hard to believe there was a time when Shakespeare couldn't write a sonnet or Beethoven couldn't scribble out a symphony, it is difficult to envision a time when Akeem Olajuwon was unable to dunk a basketball.

But if it took The Bard years to get a handle on iambic pentameter and if Ludwig von had to start by learning the musical scale, surely even the sergeant at arms of Phi Slama Jama didn't leap out of his cradle, latch onto a lob pass and throw down a rip-snortin' rim-rattler into his bowl of Cheerios.

Actually, the educational process began in December 1979, when a 16-year-old Olajuwon was playing goalie in a pickup soccer game right in front of his home in Lagos, Nigeria.

"I saw this car pull up and a guy got out to watch our game," Olajuwon recalls. "I guess it was because he saw this big, tall goaltender playing. Somebody in our game kicked the ball over near him and I went to get it. He said he was the basketball coach for the Nigerian national team.

"He asked me if I'd ever played basketball before. I told him no, but he asked me to go out and eat with him. But I didn't want to go. I was just mad that he had stopped our game. We had a pretty good game going that day."

But Richard Mills, an American who had been coaching in Africa for several years, was persistent.

As resident authority on the Houston Rockets for the Houston Chronicle, *Fran Blinebury is raring to follow the rookie Rocket.*

Akeem Olajuwon carried Houston to two NCAA title games.

"Anyway," Olajuwon says, "I told him I didn't like basketball. But we went out and ate and he took me to his office at the gym. He took me out on the court and gave me a basketball. I said I'd never seen anybody shoot a basketball. I didn't even know how to do it. When I shot my first free throw, I just pushed it and it didn't even hit the rim. But he told me to flick my wrist and I tried a few more.

"Then he told me to stand under the basket and dunk the ball. But I didn't know how. So he went and got a chair and got up on it. He jumped off the chair and dunked the ball. Then he told me to do it.

"So I tried to get on the chair and dunk the ball, too. But he told me I had to stand on the ground. I couldn't do it.

"The first time I dunked, it made my day. Nobody else in Lagos could dunk. The only other person in Nigeria who I knew could dunk was my idol, Yommy Sangodeyi. But he lived in another state."

Today, Akeem's dunking prowess is known in every state. Anyone with even a marginal interest in basketball who hasn't spent the last three years in suspended animation is aware of Akeem Abdul Olajuwon, the 7-0, 250-pound import who came to the United States in search of a college education and has wound up living out a modern-day version of the American Dream.

It is an unlikely story, to say the least. But this friendly young native of Nigeria with the charming British accent became the center of attention among fans and the media on the jivingest team in America at the University of Houston and was plucked No. 1 overall in the NBA draft by the Houston Rockets.

Just think how much has changed in the three years since the shy kid considered heading back to Africa after his plane landed in New York, because it was too cold. Then, he was the kid who was told by Houston coach Guy Lewis to take a cab in from Intercontinental Airport when he first arrived in Houston, because there were serious doubts about his ability. He was the kid who, because of his accent, told the cab driver he was going to the "University of Austin." He was the kid who took great delight in simple things like giving high fives and eating ice cream.

And now, he is suddenly Akeem Inc., a multi-million dollar enterprise that includes a Mercedes among its assets.

It's incredible that "That's Incredible" has never done his life story. His leap from backyard soccer player in a faraway land to the most sought-after basketball player in the U.S. ranks right up there with Bob Beamon's world-record long jump in the 1968 Olympics. It is almost beyond comprehension.

So, too, in the minds of many NBA officials, is the fact that

The dream continues as Akeem goes from Cougar to Rocket.

Olajuwon will now team up with 7-4 Ralph Sampson to give the Rockets one of the most potentially awesome frontlines in the history of the game.

In a span of just two years, Houston has gone from 14-68 to 29-53 to this. Just a short time ago the Rockets were doormats in the Midwest Division, but now they could be in line to rule the NBA roost for the next decade, particularly in light of the fact that Kareem Abdul-Jabbar is retiring after this season.

"Potentially, it could evolve into the greatest two-man combination that has ever played," said Detroit general manager Jack McCloskey. "I realize that is a strong, strong statement. But can you think of two players with the size, quickness and natural talent that those guys have?

Scouts have no doubt Olajuwon has the right stuff.

"Of course, I don't think the full dividends are going to come immediately because any rookie—regardless of his credentials—will have some difficulty adjusting to the program. I anticipate that Akeem will have some of the foul problems that Ralph went through last year. But when the indoctrination period is over, Akeem and Ralph are going to have a lot of fun for a number of years."

Rocket coach Bill Fitch is another one who expects the combination of Sampson and Olajuwon to mesh. He intends to use Olajuwon in the pivot, especially on defense, and move Sampson out to one of the forward spots, a position he has always been interested in playing.

"I don't know that there's any coach in the league who would say that Ralph and Akeem can't play together on the same team," Fitch said. "With the trend all around the league toward several big players in the lineup at the same time—Bill Cartwright and Marvin Webster in New York, Rick Mahorn and Jeff Ruland in Washington, Kareem and Bob McAdoo in Los Angeles—this pairing will enable us to match up with the competition."

In Sampson and Olajuwon, the Rockets have more than just the two preeminent young big men in the league, they have a pair of thoroughbreds whose specialty is running like the wind from baseline to baseline. The potential is now there to crank up as devastating a fast-break combination as the game has seen.

"You've got to build a team in bits and pieces to reach the level of a championship contender, and the Rockets still have some work to do," said Marty Blake, the NBA's director of scouting. "But Houston is way ahead in the building process with the two pieces that they've started with. The only problems I see in putting Ralph and Akeem together are all for the other team. Quite frankly, I don't know how a lot of people in the league are going to be able to match up with the Rockets.

"You know, I've heard all of the talk about how you're shifting an All-Star center (Sampson) out to a new position at forward. So he's 7-4 and nobody that tall has played the position before. But look at several years ago, before Magic Johnson came into the league. Nobody even thought of having a 6-9 point guard.

"Now everybody in the league is making the shift to the bigger guards. Ralph can handle the ball as well as most so-called small forwards in the league, so I don't anticipate any problem there. And he's fluid and has a good shot, plus he'll be able to take advantage of his size to go inside on the forwards.

"As far as Akeem is concerned, of course, it's far too early to say what he might develop into down the road. But all of the potential is there for him to turn into one of the best in the NBA. People look at potential as a bad word nowadays. But when you're looking at a young player, potential is all you can go on. And this guy has got as much as anybody I've ever seen.

"According to our records and statistics, we show that a team gets an opportunity to draft a top-flight center once every 15½ years. Centers are so hard to find. They're like strawberries in the winter. And now one year after they drafted Ralph Sampson, the

Houston Rockets turn right around and get a chance to grab Akeem Olajuwon.

"What are the chances of all this happening, not just to the Rockets, but to Akeem as well? The kid came here to go to school and look at everything that has happened. He's even been lucky enough that a flip of a coin allowed him to continue playing professionally in the city that he has made his adopted home. I'm just surprised that nobody from Hollywood has come along yet wanting to do his life story. It's a perfect movie script."

It's almost too hard to believe. And until this last year, when his younger brother also enrolled at the University of Houston and an older brother came to the U.S. for a visit, some of the biggest disbelievers of the entire Olajuwon fantasy were in his very own family. Akeem's parents own and operate a profitable cement company in Lagos and had always expected their son to return home after four years to help with the family business. They regarded Akeem's basketball career as a frivolous diversion, not a profession at which he could earn a living.

"They wrote to me all the time," Olajuwon says. "And their letters always talked about how I could eventually come back home and be with them. But I have said all along that I was going to surprise them."

It surely must have been a surprise to his family when, after a year during which they had heard only sketchy reports of Akeem's accomplishments, he blossomed into a hero on both sides of the Atlantic after being named the Outstanding Player of the 1983 NCAA Final Four. He capped his three-year collegiate career by averaging 16.9 points and 13.7 rebounds (tops in the nation) as a junior. Then, frustrated by the Cougars' failure to win the title and tempted by the high stakes and opportunity to play immediately in the NBA, he opted to go pro.

Out of the blue, the U.S. Information Agency in Washington, D.C., began to be deluged with requests from African newspapers and magazines, seeking the latest exploits of the one who has become known in his native land as "King Akeem."

"Everyone in my country is interested in America and what goes on here," Olajuwon said. "I've been thinking about coming to America since I was very little. Everybody dreams of coming to America. They say that if you don't come over here to go to school (college), you'll never make anything of yourself in life. But if you come to America, you'll be a big success."

Yet how much of Olajuwon's current success is due to luck? What if Mills had never been driving past his house on the day of the soccer game? What if Chris Pond, who works with the U.S. State Department and coached a team from the Central African

Republic, hadn't spotted Olajuwon in a tournament and convinced Lewis to at least give him a look? What if Olajuwon had turned right around and boarded a plane back to Nigeria? And, most importantly, what if Moses Malone didn't just happen to be playing in Houston for the Rockets at the time and didn't decide to take Olajuwon under his wing?

While much has been made of Akeem's great strides through each of his three collegiate seasons, it is more likely the sweating and working alongside Malone—the three-time NBA MVP—in the summers that has elevated his game to this level so quickly.

Olajuwon had first heard of Malone when he saw a poster of the then-Rocket center on Mills' office wall. When he arrived in Houston, Olajuwon attended several Rocket games and followed Malone's exploits in the newspapers.

Then Akeem received his baptism against Malone in pickup games at Fonde Recreation Center.

"I knew he was a big star and famous, but I never thought that I would end up being friends with him," Olajuwon said.

It's debatable who drives whom the hardest. During their very physical battles at Fonde, it's not unusual to see Olajuwon go up for a dunk, only to have Malone shove him out of the way or grab his shorts to hold him. When the NBA veteran tries to take it to the hoop, the kid is never afraid to go up and swat the ball back in his face.

Being around Malone and playing against him so much—Moses won't let Akeem be on his team—has taught Olajuwon excellent rebounding techniques and made him a ferocious inside player.

But the reason that Olajuwon is so special is not his bullish strength on the inside, but the grace and speed with which he can cover the entire court. It is his ability to block a shot at the defensive end, then get out on the wing to finish off a fast break at the other end that has had NBA scouts salivating and whispering comparisons to Bill Russell. He is also a good shooter from medium range when he's facing the basket. And now the faster-paced, more wide-open pro game is expected to bring out even more of his talents.

"I wish I could have won a championship in college, but I do feel that it is time for me to move on," Olajuwon said. "Since I first came here, I have always wanted to play in the NBA.

"All of the players that I would like to play against are in the NBA and they are the players who I believe are a challenge. The time has finally come, and I am looking forward to it. It is where I belong. It is where I believe I can succeed."

He won't even need a chair to stand on.

INSIDE THE NBA

By FRAN BLINEBURY and FILIP BONDY

PREDICTED ORDER OF FINISH

ATLANTIC	CENTRAL	MIDWEST	PACIFIC
Philadelphia	Detroit	Dallas	LA Lakers
Boston	Milwaukee	Utah	Portland
New Jersey	Chicago	San Antonio	Phoenix
New York	Atlanta	Houston	LA Clippers
Washington	Indiana	Kansas City	Golden State
	Cleveland	Denver	Seattle

EASTERN CONFERENCE: Philadelphia
WESTERN CONFERENCE: Los Angeles
CHAMPION: Los Angeles

Plunk down several million dollars for a franchise and you, too, can play the hottest new game in town. It's zanier than Pac-Man and more popular than Trivial Pursuit. It's the National Basketball Association draft lottery.

After nearly 40 years of a playoff system that has grown to include everyone except your local YMCA team, the wacky people who run the NBA have finally come up with a gimmick that just might keep your attention well past Memorial Day, while two teams are slugging it out under the hot summer sun for the right to call themselves world champions.

The draft lottery is so simple, it's brilliant. And it's so insane that you wonder why some geniuses in the league didn't come up with the idea years ago. It's based on a simple concept—share

---

Fran Blinebury lives the endless season as the pro basketball writer for the Houston Post. *Filip Bondy covers the New Jersey Nets for the New York* Daily News. *Bondy wrote the Eastern Conference, Blinebury the Western Conference and the introduction.*

the wealth. Why should on the league's two worst teams be the only ones with a chance to get the No. 1 pick in the college draft? In this age, where there's a Ralph Sampson, an Akeem Olajuwon or a Patrick Ewing coming out of college every season, why not let more teams have a chance at a piece of the pie?

Why not, indeed. And that's exactly what the league has done. From now on, all seven of the teams that do not qualify for the playoffs in any given season will have their names placed in a hat. Then commissioner David Stern will pull one out and that club will get the No. 1 choice.

It's the NBA's way of fighting the whispers that were rampant last season, alleging that several clubs were losing intentionally in order to try to gain a spot in the coin flip for the No. 1 pick. Of course, no one in the league wants to acknowledge that the same thing could happen this season if a borderline club decides that a one-in-seven shot at Ewing is better than gaining the No. 8 playoff berth and getting wiped out by the Lakers in the first round. At least, that's the worst of the NBA's problems these days.

Last spring's Championship Series between Boston and Los Angeles drew some of the largest TV ratings in league history. There were no changes of ownership during the off-season— though Utah's Sam Battistone sold one-half of his Jazz to Essam Khashoggi of Saudi Arabia—and only four teams hired new head coaches.

Of course, the big news in the player ranks is that Akeem Olajuwon and Michael Jordan are making their long-awaited pro debuts with Houston and Chicago respectively, while Kareem Abdul-Jabbar, the NBA's all-time leading scorer, is making his final swing through the league before a retirement that has been long awaited by the opposition.

The Jazz will play some more games in Las Vegas, Atlanta will play 12 home games in New Orleans and the much-discussed, little-understood salary cap will go into effect.

But when all is said and done and the NBA finals roll around again next spring—or summer—Magic Johnson won't choke in the final seconds and Kareem will go out a champ as the team that should have won last year—Los Angeles—comes through.

ATLANTA HAWKS

TEAM DIRECTORY: Pres.: J. Michael Gearon; VP/GM: Stan Kasten; Dir. Pub. Rel.: Bill Needle; Coach: Mike Fratello; Asst. Coaches: Brendan Suhr, Ron Rothstein, Bob Reinhart. Arenas: The Omni (15,900), Atlanta, and Lakefront Coliseum (10,000), New Orleans. Colors: Red and white.

SCOUTING REPORT

SHOOTING: The good news is the Hawks still have Dominique Wilkins (.479), so every kind of imaginable shot will still be on display at the Omni. The bad news is that Dan Roundfield is gone and departing with him is dependable, steady scoring from the power-forward spot.

In breaking up last year's mediocre team, Hawk management is hoping that NBA newcomer Antoine Carr and Cliff Levingston (.525) can provide some of the inside scoring for which Roundfield was famous. There is not much room for error. The Hawks were the lowest-scoring team in the league last year with a 101.5-ppg average and had a field-goal percentage of only .474.

Tree Rollins (.518) will never be aggressive with his shot and the backcourt is badly flawed. Mike Glenn (.563) has the shot, but no quickness, while Doc Rivers (.462) and Johnny Davis (.443) have quickness, but no shots.

PLAYMAKING: Coach Mike Fratello's systematic offense reduces his guards to distributors in a halfcourt offense. Eddie Johnson, Davis and Rivers are all adequate passers, but look a little uncomfortable operating at half-speed.

Up front, Rollins is as unselfish a player as they come. Sometimes he'll pass up an eight-footer to kick the ball out to a teammate much further away from the basket. Nobody has ever accused Wilkins of that. Not surprisingly, Atlanta had the fewest number of assists in the NBA with 1,827.

DEFENSE: The Hawks were second in the league in defense (102.8 ppg), which was as much a reflection of their playing style as it was a measure of any individual's effort. In any case, the Hawks will not be as effective in this department without Roundfield. Levingston is an aggressive shot-blocker, but has suffered from chronic foul problems. Carr is known more for his offensive abilities.

With all these question marks in the forecourt, Rollins stands as the rock in the paint. He was second in the league in blocked

No other Hawk can soar as high as Dominique Wilkins.

shots last season with 3.60 per game and is an intimidator extraordinaire. With Tree behind him, Wilkins can afford to make mistakes against the top small forwards in the game. Wilkins and Rivers are the chief gamblers on the club, accounting for the vast majority of the Hawks' steals.

REBOUNDING: The Hawks had big rebounding problems last year that figure to be worse without Roundfield. Atlanta spotted opponents 3.1 rpg, despite Roundfield's steady production of 9.8 rpg. Rollins (7.7 rpg) just isn't mobile enough to do the job. Besides, Tree is more effective a few steps away from the basket blocking shots. Wilkins acts as though there are more important things for him to do.

Rivers is the best rebounder in the backcourt, which isn't saying that much. Levingston should make up somewhat for Roundfield's absence, but look for the Hawks to spot opponents as much as four boards a game—a large handicap.

OUTLOOK: General manager Stan Kasten and owner Ted Turner know what they're doing. This team was going nowhere, despite

HAWK ROSTER

No.	Veteran	Pos.	Ht.	Wt.	Age	Yrs. Pro	College
31	Rickey Brown	F-C	6-10	215	26	5	Mississippi State
16	Johnny Davis	G	6-2	170	29	9	Dayton
34	*Mike Glenn	G	6-3	185	29	8	Southern Illinois
44	Scott Hastings	F-C	6-10	235	24	3	Arkansas
3	Eddie Johnson	G	6-2	190	29	8	Auburn
53	*Mark Landsberger	F	6-8	225	29	8	Arizona State
—	Cliff Levingston	F	6-8	210	23	3	Wichita State
5	*Billy Paultz	C	6-11	250	36	15	St. John's
25	Glenn Rivers	G	6-4	185	23	2	Marquette
30	Wayne Rollins	C	7-1	235	29	8	Clemson
21	Dominique Wilkins	F	6-7	210	24	3	Georgia
33	Sly Williams	F	6-7	215	26	6	Rhode Island
10	Randy Wittman	G-F	6-6	210	25	2	Indiana

*Free agent unsigned at press time

Rd.	Top Draftees	Sel. No.	Ht.	Wt.	College
1	**Antoine Carr	8	6-9	225	Wichita State
1	Kevin Willis	11	7-0	230	Michigan State
3	Bobby Parks	58	6-5	185	Memphis State
4	Dickie Beal	81	5-10	180	Kentucky
5	Terry Martin	104	6-9	225	NE Louisiana

**Drafted by Pistons in 1983, played in Italy last year and was traded to Hawks in June

Roundfield's presence, so why not stir things up and see what happens?

The Hawks are almost certain to finish down there with the Cavaliers and Pacers this season, but so what? They weren't drawing fans anyway. This way, the Hawks will get a decent draft choice next year. They already have the nucleus for their rebuilding job with Carr and Wilkins. It's going to be a long year at the Omni, but the long-range forecast isn't all that black.

HAWK PROFILES

DOMINIQUE WILKINS 24 6-7 210   **Forward**

Right man on the wrong team...He's a bird, he's a plane—unfortunately he's an Atlanta Hawk...Tries hard to tone down his act and fit into slow-motion offense, but has trouble hiding his physical talents...Still not among better defenders in league, but he can block shots...Has incredible body control, comparable to that of Elgin Baylor and Julius Erving...Led team in scoring (21.6 ppg) and minutes played

(2,961)...What would the Hawks draw without him?...Left Georgia after junior year to become one of top five dunkers in league...Born Jan. 12, 1960, in Sorbonne, France, where father was serving in Air Force...Hit only 41.7 percent of his shots against Milwaukee in five-game playoff series...Averaged 7.2 rpg over course of regular season, a remarkable figure for a small forward of his height.

Year	Team	G	FG	FG Pct.	FT	FT Pct.	Reb.	Ast.	TP	Avg.
1982-83	Atlanta	82	601	.493	230	.682	478	129	1434	17.5
1983-84	Atlanta	81	684	.479	382	.770	582	126	1750	21.6
	Totals	163	1285	.485	612	.735	1060	255	3184	19.5

RANDY WITTMAN 25 6-6 210   Guard-Forward

Didn't exactly burst on scene in rookie year, but will get second chance...Is a classic "tweener"—too slow to be a guard and too small to be a forward...A heady player who works well within Mike Fratello's system ...Doesn't make too many mistakes ...Had 17 turnovers in 1,071 minutes...On the other hand, he doesn't have much of an outside touch and can't hit from foul line...Moves well off ball and can penetrate...Hit 50.3 percent from field...Born Oct. 28, 1959, in Indianapolis...Drafted by Bullets as 22nd pick in 1983 draft, then was traded to Atlanta for Tom McMillen and a future draft pick...Led Indiana in scoring as a senior with 18.9 ppg.

Year	Team	G	FG	FG Pct.	FT	FT Pct.	Reb.	Ast.	TP	Avg.
1983-84	Atlanta	78	160	.503	28	.609	71	71	350	4.5

JOHNNY DAVIS 29 6-2 170   Guard

Nothing to write home about, but good enough to start in Atlanta...Not really a pure play-maker...Will take the shot...Won't always make it...One-third of Atlanta's poor shooting guard rotation...Started as rookie for Portland's 1976-77 world championship team...Very quick, but doesn't gamble much on defense and gets few steals...Smart enough to run coach Mike Fratello's set plays...Born Oct. 21, 1955, in

Detroit... His scoring average (12.3 ppg) was his lowest in six years... Deadly from the line, where he shot 84.8 percent ... Appeared more comfortable teaming with Glenn Rivers than with Eddie Johnson... Averaged 19.3 ppg in three-year career at Dayton... Ranks among Pacers' top 10 in career assists, scoring average, steals and free throws made.

Year	Team	G	FG	FG Pct.	FT	FT Pct.	Reb.	Ast.	TP	Avg.
1976-77	Portland	79	234	.441	166	.794	126	148	634	8.0
1977-78	Portland	82	343	.454	188	.828	173	217	874	10.7
1978-79	Indiana	79	565	.456	314	.793	191	453	1444	18.3
1979-80	Indiana	82	496	.428	304	.864	226	440	1300	15.9
1980-81	Indiana	76	426	.465	238	.796	170	480	1094	14.4
1981-82	Indiana	82	538	.467	315	.799	178	346	1396	17.0
1982-83	Atlanta	53	258	.455	164	.796	128	315	685	12.9
1983-84	Atlanta	75	354	.443	217	.848	139	326	925	12.3
	Totals	608	3214	.451	1906	.815	1331	2725	8352	13.7

EDDIE JOHNSON 29 6-2 190   Guard

His head is together, but his game is still slipping... Suffered through another injury-plagued season... Lost his starting job to Glenn Rivers... His 13.2-ppg scoring average was his lowest since his rookie season, in 1977-78... Has lost a couple of steps and can't get his own shot as easily as he once did... Averaged only 44.2 percent from the field... Was worse in playoffs against Milwaukee, when he hit only 35.2 percent from field and looked completely lost... Born Feb. 24, 1955, in Ocala, Fla.... Still does some things better than any other Hawk... Led team in assists and hit 16-of-43 three-point attempts... Licked drug problem, apparently for good... Two-time selection to All-Star Game... This season will tell whether it's time for this Auburn product to hang 'em up.

Year	Team	G	FG	FG Pct.	FT	FT Pct.	Reb.	Ast.	TP	Avg.
1977-78	Atlanta	79	332	.484	164	.816	153	235	828	10.5
1978-79	Atlanta	78	501	.510	243	.832	170	360	1245	16.0
1979-80	Atlanta	79	590	.487	280	.828	200	370	1465	18.5
1980-81	Atlanta	75	573	.504	279	.784	179	407	1431	19.1
1981-82	Atlanta	68	455	.450	294	.764	191	358	1211	17.8
1982-83	Atlanta	61	389	.453	186	.785	124	318	978	16.0
1983-84	Atlanta	67	353	.442	164	.770	146	374	886	13.2
	Totals	507	3193	.478	1610	.796	1163	2422	8044	15.9

GLENN RIVERS 23 6-4 185   Guard

Brightest discovery in Georgia...The 31st overall pick in 1983 draft, he forced his way into starting lineup...Explosive...A gambler on defense...The kind of player Mike Fratello needed to make traps work...Led team in steals with 127...His flailing hands led to 286 personal fouls and eight disqualifications...A good leaper who pulled down nearly three rebounds per game...Pushed Eddie Johnson to bench and Mike Glenn to fourth-guard spot...Hit 50.0 percent of his shots and 87.8 percent of his free throws in playoffs...Born Oct. 13, 1961, in Maywood, Ill....Came out of Marquette after junior year...Had 13.9-ppg career average as collegian...Looks durable, which is something most Atlanta players are not.

Year	Team	G	FG	FG Pct.	FT	FT Pct.	Reb.	Ast.	TP	Avg.
1983-84	Atlanta	81	250	.462	255	.785	220	314	757	9.3

WAYNE (TREE) ROLLINS 29 7-1 235   Center

The shot stops here...Blocked 3.6 shots per game, the second-best mark in the league ...First-team All-Defensive selection...Aptly nicknamed...Does nothing to hurt team... Hit 51.8 percent of his shots and led Hawks in rebounding (7.3 rpg)...Secret to his shot-blocking is definitely not his leaping ability ...It's strictly position and timing...Has very little range on offense, but then you can't have everything...Born June 16, 1955, in Cordele, Ga....Has reputation for having bad knees, but has missed only nine games in three years...Served out brief suspension for biting Danny Ainge's hand during playoff scuffle following 1982-83 season...Former star at Clemson was drafted 14th in 1977...Cousin of teammate Eddie Johnson.

Year	Team	G	FG	FG Pct.	FT	FT Pct.	Reb.	Ast.	TP	Avg.
1977-78	Atlanta	80	253	.487	104	.703	552	79	610	7.6
1978-79	Atlanta	81	297	.535	89	.631	588	49	683	8.4
1979-80	Atlanta	82	287	.558	157	.714	774	76	731	8.9
1980-81	Atlanta	40	116	.552	46	.807	286	35	278	7.0
1981-82	Atlanta	79	202	.584	79	.612	611	59	483	6.1
1982-83	Atlanta	80	261	.510	98	.726	743	75	620	7.8
1983-84	Atlanta	77	274	.518	118	.621	593	62	666	8.6
	Totals	519	1690	.530	691	.677	4147	435	4071	7.8

MIKE GLENN 29 6-3 185   Guard

What you see is all you'll get...Can bury the open jumper, but that's it...Lost his third-guard status when Glenn Rivers asserted himself... Hit career-high 56.3 percent from the field, the result of Mike Fratello designing plays to free him in corner...Can't make his own shot... A lumbering defender...Disappointed in playoffs, hitting only 5-of-14 shots against Milwaukee...Played in 81 games, but never started...Born Sept. 10, 1955, in Rome, Ga....Academic All-American at Southern Illinois...Knows sign language and runs basketball camps for the hearing impaired...One of the game's great gentlemen...Hit 80.0 percent from the line, but his non-physical game doesn't get him too many free throws...Nicknamed "The Stinger."

Year	Team	G	FG	FG Pct.	FT	FT Pct.	Reb.	Ast.	TP	Avg.
1977-78	Buffalo	56	195	.527	51	.785	79	78	441	7.9
1978-79	New York	75	263	.541	57	.905	82	136	583	7.8
1979-80	New York	75	188	.516	63	.863	66	85	441	5.9
1980-81	New York	82	285	.558	98	.891	88	108	672	8.2
1981-82	Atlanta	49	158	.543	59	.881	61	87	376	7.7
1982-83	Atlanta	73	230	.518	74	.831	90	125	534	7.3
1983-84	Atlanta	81	312	.563	56	.800	104	171	681	8.4
	Totals	491	1631	.540	458	.853	570	790	3728	7.6

CLIFF LEVINGSTON 23 6-8 210   Forward

Got more minutes, but never quite found niche with Pistons, who dealt him to Atlanta with rights to Antoine Carr and two future draft choices for Dan Roundfield during offseason...Was demoted from starting role after constantly getting into foul trouble defending against players who usually had an inch or two on him...Quickness makes him a good shot-blocker...Whenever Kent Benson was blown away by opponent, he came to the rescue...With all the shooters on the Pistons, he understandably limited his attempts from the field...Born Jan. 4, 1961, in San Diego...Averaged 6.8 rebounds per game in under 22 minutes per game, an outstanding ratio...Was disqualified seven times on fouls and drew 281 personals.

Year	Team	G	FG	FG Pct.	FT	FT Pct.	Reb.	Ast.	TP	Avg.
1982-83	Detroit	62	131	.485	84	.571	232	52	346	5.6
1983-84	Detroit	80	229	.525	125	.672	545	109	583	7.3
	Totals	142	360	.510	209	.628	777	161	929	6.5

SLY WILLIAMS 26 6-7 215   Forward

Back into the depths... Broke left thumb during first exhibition game in Gainesville, Fla. ... Didn't return until Dec. 13, then played just seven games before breaking right foot... Came back again March 6, then was suspended for four games by Mike Fratello for "improper bench conduct"... Foot started bothering him and he didn't play again... Has two years left on contract and Hawks may be wondering why they acquired this Rhode Island product from Knicks... Born Jan. 26, 1958, in New Haven, Conn.... Personal problems nearly destroyed him during 1981-82 season, but he bounced back with solid season for New York the following year... An instinctive, creative player when he is on his game... Rebounds well for his height... Always in the right spot for the garbage basket... One of 12 children.

Year	Team	G	FG	FG Pct.	FT	FT Pct.	Reb.	Ast.	TP	Avg.
1979-80	New York	57	104	.390	58	.644	121	36	266	4.7
1980-81	New York	67	349	.493	185	.690	416	180	885	13.2
1981-82	New York	60	349	.556	131	.757	227	142	831	13.9
1982-83	New York	68	314	.485	176	.680	290	133	806	11.9
1983-84	Atlanta	13	34	.298	36	.783	50	16	105	8.1
	Totals	265	1150	.486	586	.701	1104	507	2893	10.9

SCOTT HASTINGS 24 6-10 235   Forward-Center

Nobody calls him elegant... Basic backup banger... Started eight games when Dan Roundfield or Tree Rollins was out... Decent rebounder and shot-blocker... Plagued by foul problems, which comes with the territory ... Called for 220 personals in 1,135 minutes and was disqualified seven times... May have reached potential in second pro season... Born June 3, 1960, in Independence, Kan.... Acquired in February 1983 from New York for Rory Sparrow, if you can believe that... A smart, but not instinctive player... Drafted by the Knicks in the second round in 1982 out of Arkansas... Averaged 18.6 ppg for Razorbacks in his senior year... Has a surprising touch if left alone.

Year	Team	G	FG	FG Pct.	FT	FT Pct.	Reb.	Ast.	TP	Avg.
1982-83	N.Y.-Atl.	31	13	.342	11	.550	41	3	37	1.2
1983-84	Atlanta	68	111	.468	82	.788	270	46	305	4.5
	Totals	99	124	.451	93	.750	311	49	342	3.5

BILLY PAULTZ 36 6-11 250   Center

The ultimate survivor... Picked up by the Hawks as free agent after Spurs gave up on him... Played six seasons in the ABA, including one with 1973-74 Nets team that won title... His teams have made playoffs for 14 straight seasons, but he doesn't always have much to do with that... Used in limited role as back-up center... Slow as molasses... Smart player who knows the ropes... Born July 30, 1948, in River Edge, N.J.... "The Whopper"... Keeps a locker room loose... Still has fun... Looks back fondly at days in ABA... "You walked into one of those arenas, and you never knew what was going to happen to you," he says... Played just seven minutes in two playoff games last year... Attended St. John's.

Year	Team	G	FG	FG Pct.	FT	FT Pct.	Reb.	Ast.	TP	Avg.
1970-71	New York (ABA)	83	510	.524	201	.747	940	160	1221	14.7
1971-72	New York (ABA)	83	498	.488	207	.692	1035	128	1203	14.4
1972-73	New York (ABA)	81	532	.518	287	.709	1015	189	1351	16.7
1973-74	New York (ABA)	77	519	.494	222	.721	782	167	1260	16.4
1974-75	New York (ABA)	80	524	.485	214	.748	772	179	1262	15.8
1975-76	San Antonio (ABA) ..	83	566	.504	238	.735	862	340	1370	16.5
1976-77	San Antonio	82	521	.473	238	.744	687	223	1280	15.6
1977-78	San Antonio	80	518	.529	230	.752	675	213	1266	15.8
1978-79	San Antonio	79	399	.526	114	.588	625	178	912	11.5
1979-80	S.A.-Hou..	84	327	.486	109	.599	586	188	763	9.1
1980-81	Houston........	81	262	.507	75	.490	391	105	599	7.4
1981-82	Houston........	65	89	.394	34	.523	180	41	212	3.3
1982-83	Hou.-S.A..	64	101	.445	27	.458	200	61	229	3.6
1983-84	Atlanta..........	40	36	.409	17	.515	113	18	89	2.2
	Totals	1062	5402	.498	2213	.691	8863	2190	13017	12.3

MARK LANDSBERGER 29 6-8 225   Forward

May have worn out his welcome... Played only 335 minutes during regular season and made only cameo appearances in playoffs... Lakers dumped him when they realized they had better model in Kurt Rambis... Just not quick enough... Question is: How has he lasted so long?... Born May 21, 1955, in Minot, S.D.... A bruiser under boards, where he does more than his share of work... Can't shoot to save his career...Hit only 37.3 percent from the floor...A second-round pick by Bulls in 1977...Played at Minnesota for one year, then finished up at Arizona State...Pinnacle of career came in 1980, when he played modest role on title-winner in Los Angeles.

Year	Team	G	FG	FG Pct.	FT	FT Pct.	Reb.	Ast.	TP	Avg.
1977-78	Chicago	62	127	.506	91	.580	301	41	345	5.6
1978-79	Chicago	80	278	.475	91	.469	742	68	647	8.1
1979-80	Chi.-L.A.	77	249	.516	116	.523	613	46	614	8.0
1980-81	Los Angeles	69	164	.552	62	.534	377	27	390	5.7
1981-82	Los Angeles	75	144	.438	33	.508	401	32	321	4.3
1982-83	Los Angeles	39	43	.422	12	.480	128	12	98	2.5
1983-84	Atlanta	35	19	.373	15	.577	119	10	53	1.5
	Totals	437	1024	.481	420	.522	2681	236	2468	5.6

RICKEY BROWN 26 6-10 215   Forward-Center

Moved ahead of both Scott Hastings and Billy Paultz on depth chart by playoff time...Seems to have more talent than either of them...Played only 785 minutes during the regular season... A strong leaper and rebounder...Managed to get called for 161 fouls and was disqualified four times in limited playing time...Must learn to be a bit more subtle going up for the rebound...Born Aug. 20, 1958, in Madison County, Miss....A good shot-blocker...A bad ball-handler...Was drafted 13th overall in 1980 out of Mississippi State...Warriors picked him ahead of Larry Smith that year, but he ended up sitting behind Smith and became expendable.

Year	Team	G	FG	FG Pct.	FT	FT Pct.	Reb.	Ast.	TP	Avg.
1980-81	Golden State	45	83	.512	16	.762	166	21	182	4.0
1981-82	Golden State	82	192	.459	86	.705	364	19	470	5.7
1982-83	G.S.-Atl.	76	167	.479	65	.619	266	25	399	5.3
1983-84	Atlanta	68	94	.468	48	.738	181	29	236	3.5
	Totals	271	536	.474	215	.687	977	94	1287	4.7

TOP ROOKIES

ANTOINE CARR 23 6-9 225   Forward

This Carr was shipped out of Detroit without ever having played a minute for Pistons...Was drafted eighth overall by Pistons in

1983 after averaging 22.6 ppg and being named Co-Player of the Year in the Missouri Valley Conference in senior year at Wichita State...Contract dispute prompted him to play in Italy last season...Now he begins NBA career in Atlanta, which obtained him and former Wichita State teammate Cliff Levingston in Dan Roundfield deal...Will be battling Levingston for minutes at power forward with Hawks...Born July 23, 1961, in Oklahoma City, Okla....Failed to make Bobby Knight's U.S. Olympic team roster.

KEVIN WILLIS 22 7-0 230   **Center**

Hawks made him the No. 11 pick in the draft, gambling on his potential...His stock rose dramatically in final weeks before draft...Very quick for big man and has nice touch...Needs a lot of work before he can see regular minutes...Hawks hope he goes to school behind Tree Rollins for a couple of seasons... Averaged 11.0 ppg and 7.7 rpg in senior year at Michigan State ...Should have dominated Big Ten with that body and talent, but never did...Born Sept. 6, 1962, in Los Angeles.

COACH MIKE FRATELLO: "Little Hubie"...His team looked  like the Knicks South...Made the playoffs in his rookie season, but just barely...Finished at 40-42, which wouldn't have been good enough if playoffs weren't expanded...Team played methodical, boring offense and effective, trapping defense...Criticized by Gene Shue, who said he had taken a running team and forced them to walk...Under his reins, the Hawks became nearly unbeatable at home, but an easy mark on road...Born Feb. 24, 1937, in Hackensack, N.J....Chief assistant to Brown for three years in Atlanta and again in New York...Players seemed to respect him despite his small size, which had cost him the Chicago Bulls job a season earlier ...Hawks didn't quit at end of season and he may have had something to do with that...Attendance dipped sharply and he may have had something to do with that, too...Graduated from Montclair (N.J.) State College in 1969, worked his way through preps and assisted at Villanova...His connection with Hubie has boosted his career.

GREATEST FOUL SHOOTER

Since the Hawks moved to Atlanta in 1968, their top free-throw shooter has been Armond Hill. Hill, the elegant guard from Princeton, had an .840 percentage from the line during his four-plus seasons with the Hawks, from 1976-81. Other top free-throw shooters in Atlanta have included diminutive Charlie Criss (.890 in 1981-82) and giant Tom McMillen (a club-record .891 in 1978-79).

When they were still in St. Louis, the Hawks boasted two of the best and most durable foul shooters in the NBA—Cliff Hagan and Clyde Lovelette. Hagan was among the league's top 10 for four seasons and finished with a .798 career free-throw percentage. Lovelette was among the list of leaders three times, in 1958-59, 1959-60 and 1961-62, when his percentages were .820, .821 and .825 respectively.

Other standout foul shooters for the Hawks have included Lou Hudson, Mike Glenn and superstar Bob Pettit, a .761 career free-throw shooter.

ALL-TIME HAWK LEADERS

SEASON

Points: Bob Pettit, 2,429, 1961-62
Assists: Lenny Wilkens, 679, 1967-68
Rebounds: Bob Pettit, 1,540, 1960-61

GAME

Points: Lou Hudson, 57 vs. Chicago, 11/10/69
         Bob Pettit, 57 vs. Detroit, 2/18/61
Assists: Walt Hazzard, 19 vs. Cincinnati, 3/9/68
         Lenny Wilkens, 19 vs. Seattle, 3/7/68
Rebounds: Bob Pettit, 35 vs. Cincinnati, 3/2/58
         Bob Pettit, 35 vs. New York, 1/6/56

CAREER

Points: Bob Pettit, 20,880, 1954-65
Assists: Lenny Wilkens, 3,048, 1960-68
Rebounds: Bob Pettit, 12,851, 1954-65

BOSTON CELTICS

TEAM DIRECTORY: Chairman: Don F. Gaston; Pres.: Arnold (Red) Auerbach; VP/GM: Jan Volk; Dir. Pub. Rel.: Jeff Twiss; Coach: K.C. Jones; Asst. Coach: Jim Rodgers. Arena: Boston Garden (15,320). Colors: Green and white.

Robert Parish was Celtics' chairman of the boards with 857.

SCOUTING REPORT

SHOOTING: The Celtics have won two titles in four years without much perimeter shooting from the backcourt, so why worry about it now? Fact is, with Larry Bird's incredible accuracy from outside and the middle-range accuracy of Robert Parish and Kevin McHale, opponents can't afford to pack the lane.

The frontcourt rarely forces shots. No shot is a bad shot for regular-season and playoff MVP Bird (.492). Parish hit 54.6 percent of his field-goal attempts, while McHale bettered that at 55.6. Cedric Maxwell's twisting shots went in at a 53.2-percent clip. You don't need an Andrew Toney when your forwards are hitting like that. In fact, you may not want one.

Danny Ainge (.460) started burying jumpers in the playoffs, but don't count on him to do that often. Dennis Johnson (.437) is a streak shooter, while Gerald Henderson (.524) can knock down three-point shots with 35.1-percent accuracy. Rookie Michael Young, a sharp-shooting forward, hopes to offer what Scott Wedman (.444) was supposed to supply off the bench.

PLAYMAKING: Neither Johnson nor Henderson will ever be among the league leaders in assists, but together they form an unselfish backcourt that averaged a total of 8.0 assists per game last season.

On some teams that might not be enough, but the Celts boast the league's best-passing forwards. Bird averaged 6.6 assists per game and Maxwell also can hit the open man. Boston won the championship because its players were willing to give up the 18-foot jumper for the two-foot layup. That is a Celtic tradition that coach K.C. Jones helped cultivate as a player.

DEFENSE: The Celtics gave up 105.6 ppg last season and the only clubs with better defensive numbers were Milwaukee, Atlanta and New York. The Celtics, in other words, were the best defenders among the non-snails.

McHale and Parish are the intimidators underneath, blocking a total of 242 shots. Bird's sheer size gives smaller forwards some problems, even though he is not quick enough to defend against the likes of Bernard King. For that kind of thankless task, Maxwell gets the call.

In the backcourt, Dennis Johnson may still be the best defensive guard in the game. His work on Magic in the playoffs was stunning.

CELTIC ROSTER

No.	Veteran	Pos.	Ht.	Wt.	Age	Yrs. Pro	College
44	Danny Ainge	G	6-5	188	25	4	Brigham Young
33	Larry Bird	F	6-9	220	27	6	Indiana State
28	Quinn Buckner	G	6-3	205	30	9	Indiana
30	M.L. Carr	G-F	6-6	205	33	10	Guilford
40	Carlos Clark	G	6-4	209	24	2	Mississippi
43	*Gerald Henderson	G	6-2	175	28	6	Va. Commonwealth
24	Dennis Johnson	G	6-4	202	30	9	Pepperdine
50	Greg Kite	C	6-11	250	23	2	Brigham Young
31	*Cedric Maxwell	F	6-8	217	28	8	NC-Charlotte
32	Kevin McHale	F-C	6-11	230	26	5	Minnesota
00	Robert Parish	C	7-0	240	31	9	Centenary
8	Scott Wedman	F	6-7	233	32	11	Colorado

*Free agent unsigned at press time

Rd.	Top Draftees	Sel. No.	Ht.	Wt.	College
1	Michael Young	24	6-7	220	Houston
2	Ronnie Williams	47	6-8	239	Florida
3	Rick Carlisle	69	6-5	200	Virginia
4	Kevin Mullin	93	6-5	240	Princeton
5	Todd Orlando	116	6-10	215	Bentley

REBOUNDING: The Celtics outrebounded opponents by an average of 4.5 a game last season. Boston is simply too big and bulky to be pushed around in the paint.

The Celtics are a physical team and rely heavily on position and boxing out rather than quickness. A tightly-called game by the officials can destroy their rhythm and their effectiveness under the offensive boards. Only the Pistons collected more rebounds than the Celtics last season, so you know Boston got the calls most of the time.

OUTLOOK: Here we go again. Another championship team returning intact and facing the non-repeating jinx that has befallen every defending champion since the 1968-69 Celtics. Jones will be hard-pressed to get the same kind of day-after-day effort from his veterans—and the Sixers proved last season you can't just turn it on for the playoffs.

This is a great team, but it didn't really improve itself in the off-season and must face rugged playoff competition in the Eastern Conference. The Celts won't slip too far, thanks to Bird, but they'll be in trouble if they face Philly in the playoffs. Don't bet on Boston to beat the jinx.

CELTIC PROFILES

LARRY BIRD 27 6-9 220   Forward

MVP for season, MVP for playoffs, MVP for universe . . . His skills and sheer will lifted Celtics to title . . . Nothing he can't do . . . Incredible vision of the court . . . Killed the Lakers with his outside shot in Game 5 of finals, but relied on tireless work off the offensive boards during other games . . . His 24.2-ppg scoring average was his best as a pro, as was his assist average (6.58 per game) . . . A workhorse who logged 3,028 minutes . . . Swore at the end of 1983 season he would work harder on his game to help team and he did just that . . . Has ability to change the arc on his shot while retaining accuracy . . . Born Dec. 7, 1956, in French Lick, Ind. . . . Dropped out of Indiana and worked as a garbage collector before he found his way to Indiana State . . . Red Auerbach drafted him as a junior eligible and the franchise was saved . . . Has missed just 11 games in five years . . . In his rookie season, Celts improved from 29-53 to 61-21.

Year	Team	G	FG	FG Pct.	FT	FT Pct.	Reb.	Ast.	TP	Avg.
1979-80	Boston.	82	693	.474	301	.836	852	370	1745	21.3
1980-81	Boston.	82	719	.478	283	.863	895	451	1741	21.2
1981-82	Boston.	77	711	.503	328	.863	837	447	1761	22.9
1982-83	Boston.	79	747	.504	351	.840	870	458	1867	23.6
1983-84	Boston.	79	758	.492	374	.888	796	520	1908	24.2
	Totals	399	3628	.490	1637	.858	4250	2246	9022	22.6

CEDRIC MAXWELL 28 6-8 217   Forward

Saved his best for last . . . Scored team-high 24 points and had eight rebounds in Game 7 against Lakers . . . Became spiritual leader of Celtics this season and opened up with press . . . Before final game against Lakers, he told teammates, "Get on my back, boys, I'll take you home." . . . Did just that . . . His inside moves baffled Los Angeles . . . Was almost as good during regular season, averaging 53.2 percent from field . . . Rugged defender who makes you pay for every layup or rebound . . . Born Nov. 21, 1955, in Kingston, N.C. . . . Long reach allows him to outrebound taller opponents . . . He and Kevin McHale get almost equal minutes . . . Will make risky pass, which gives him plenty of assists and turnovers... A selfless ballplayer... First-round pick in 1977 out of UNC-Charlotte.

Year	Team	G	FG	FG Pct.	FT	FT Pct.	Reb.	Ast.	TP	Avg.
1977-78	Boston	72	170	.538	188	.752	379	68	528	7.3
1978-79	Boston	80	472	.584	574	.802	791	228	1518	19.0
1979-80	Boston	80	457	.609	436	.787	704	199	1350	16.9
1980-81	Boston	81	441	.588	352	.782	525	219	1234	15.2
1981-82	Boston	78	397	.548	357	.747	499	183	1151	14.8
1982-83	Boston	79	331	.499	280	.812	422	186	942	11.9
1983-84	Boston	80	317	.532	320	.753	461	205	955	11.9
	Totals	550	2585	.561	2507	.779	3781	1288	7678	14.0

DANNY AINGE 25 6-5 188   Guard

Finally meeting lowered expectations... Will never be the playmaking star he was tabbed to be, but is more than adequate as reserve ... Was more effective in playoffs than in regular season... Found his elusive outside shot against Lakers... Averaged just 5.4 ppg during season, hitting 46.0 percent of shots from field... Baby-faced whiner who has irritated his share of opponents and reporters... Born March 17, 1959, in Salt Lake City and attended Brigham Young... Turned ball over only 70 times... Have to wonder about scouts who once projected him as a top three pick... Was actually drafted 31st in 1981, because he was under contract to the Toronto Blue Jays... It appears he was as good an infielder as he is a guard—and he wasn't much of an infielder.

Year	Team	G	FG	FG Pct.	FT	FT Pct.	Reb.	Ast.	TP	Avg.
1981-82	Boston	53	79	.357	56	.862	56	87	219	4.1
1982-83	Boston	80	357	.496	72	.742	214	251	791	9.9
1983-84	Boston	71	166	.460	46	.821	116	162	384	5.4
	Totals	204	602	.462	174	.798	386	500	1394	6.8

KEVIN McHALE 26 6-11 230   Forward-Center

Best sixth man in game... Boston's leading shot-blocker (1.54 per game), third-leading scorer (18.4 ppg) and third-leading rebounder (7.4 rpg)... Hasn't missed a game in four years, but has started only 56... Looks like a stiff when he ambles upcourt, but his defensive timing is incredible... Seems to play much more effectively at Boston Garden... Had up-and-down playoff series against Knicks, Bucks and Lakers...Posted career bests in scoring average and field-goal percentage (.556)...Born Dec. 19, 1957, in Hibbing, Minn....Attended Minnesota...Talks as good a game as he plays...Makes $1 million a year, which sounds outrageous for a sub but isn't in his case...Everybody has matchup problems with him at power forward...Plays backup center to Parish, although coach K.C. Jones likes him better at forward.

Year	Team	G	FG	FG Pct.	FT	FT Pct.	Reb.	Ast.	TP	Avg.
1980-81	Boston	82	355	.533	108	.679	359	55	818	10.0
1981-82	Boston	82	465	.531	187	.754	556	91	1117	13.6
1982-83	Boston	82	483	.541	193	.717	553	104	1159	14.1
1983-84	Boston	82	587	.556	336	.765	610	104	1511	18.4
	Totals	328	1890	.542	824	.739	2078	354	4605	14.0

ROBERT PARISH 31 7-0 240   Center

"The Chief"...Another solid season...Team's leading rebounder (10.7 rpg) and second-leading scorer (19.0 ppg)...A mobile center in the mold of Kareem, not Moses Malone or Jeff Ruland...His aggressiveness gets him in foul trouble...Was nailed with 266 personals and was disqualified seven times last year...His outside touch can draw opposing centers away from basket and clear way for Larry Bird and Kevin McHale to grab offensive rebounds...Born Aug. 30, 1953, in Shreveport, La....Attended Centenary...Every time Celtics beat the Lakers, Parish held his own against Jabbar...Has made close to 55 percent of his shots since coming to Boston in 1980...Celtics stole him, along with pick that netted McHale, from Golden State for draft choice that became Joe Barry Carroll...Deep, intimidating voice goes with playing style.

Year	Team	G	FG	FG Pct.	FT	FT Pct.	Reb.	Ast.	TP	Avg.
1976-77	Golden State	77	288	.503	121	.708	543	74	697	9.1
1977-78	Golden State	82	430	.472	165	.625	680	95	1025	12.5
1978-79	Golden State	76	554	.499	196	.698	916	115	1304	17.2
1979-80	Golden State	72	510	.507	203	.715	783	122	1223	17.0
1980-81	Boston	82	635	.545	282	.710	777	144	1552	18.9
1981-82	Boston	80	669	.542	252	.710	866	140	1590	19.9
1982-83	Boston	78	619	.550	271	.698	827	141	1509	19.3
1983-84	Boston	80	623	.546	274	.745	857	139	1520	19.0
	Totals	627	4328	.524	1764	.703	6249	970	10420	16.6

SCOTT WEDMAN 32 6-7 233   Forward

Clunky... Not bad to have around in case of emergency, but the Celtic forecourt usually needs little help... Played only 916 minutes despite being generally healthy... Missed final playoff games with fractured fibula... Has nice touch for big man, but can't set up his own shot... Can step in against taller players and bump them off their game... Didn't come close to earning $700,000 salary he negotiated with former Cleveland owner Ted Stepien... Born July 29, 1952, in Harper, Kan.... Good sense of humor about his overpriced reserve status... Drafted sixth overall by Kansas City in 1974 out of Colorado... Reached his peak with Kings by averaging 19.0 ppg during his last two seasons there... Celtics got him from Cavs for a first-round pick in 1983 and Red Auerbach hasn't bragged about the deal.

Year	Team	G	FG	FG Pct.	FT	FT Pct.	Reb.	Ast.	TP	Avg.
1974-75	K.C.-Omaha	80	375	.465	139	.818	490	129	889	11.1
1975-76	Kansas City	82	538	.456	191	.780	606	199	1267	15.5
1976-77	Kansas City	81	521	.460	206	.855	506	227	1248	15.4
1977-78	Kansas City	81	607	.509	221	.870	463	201	1435	17.7
1978-79	Kansas City	73	561	.534	216	.797	386	144	1338	18.3
1979-80	Kansas City	68	569	.512	145	.801	386	145	1290	19.0
1980-81	Kansas City	81	685	.477	140	.686	433	226	1535	19.0
1981-82	Cleveland	54	260	.441	66	.733	304	133	591	10.9
1982-83	Clev.-Bos.	75	374	.475	85	.794	282	117	843	11.2
1983-84	Boston	68	148	.444	29	.829	139	67	327	4.8
	Totals	743	4638	.482	1438	.800	3995	1588	10763	14.5

DENNIS JOHNSON 30 6-4 202   Guard

Key reason Celtics went all the way... K.C. Jones put him on Magic Johnson starting with Game 4 of finals and the Laker star promptly disappeared... That was no coincidence... One of top defenders in league, he neutralized Andrew Toney and George Gervin during regular season... Celtics got "DJ" from Suns for Rick Robey and he cemented backcourt... Pepperdine grad showed surprising offensive ability during finals, burying jumpers usually considered out of his range ... Never a high-percentage shooter, he hit only 43.7 percent of his shots from the floor last season... Born Sept. 18, 1954, in San Pedro, Cal.... Phoenix coach John MacLeod didn't like his whining, but Johnson rediscovered his pride in Celtic uniform... Was also part of Sonic championship team in 1977-78, when he was voted playoff MVP of finals against Bullets.

Year	Team	G	FG	FG Pct.	FT	FT Pct.	Reb.	Ast.	TP	Avg.
1976-77	Seattle	81	285	.504	179	.624	302	123	749	9.2
1977-78	Seattle	81	367	.417	297	.732	294	230	1031	12.7
1978-79	Seattle	80	482	.432	306	.781	374	280	1270	15.9
1979-80	Seattle	81	574	.422	380	.780	414	332	1540	19.0
1980-81	Phoenix	79	532	.436	411	.820	363	291	1486	18.8
1981-82	Phoenix	80	577	.470	399	.806	410	369	1561	19.5
1982-83	Phoenix	77	398	.462	292	.791	335	388	1093	14.2
1983-84	Boston	80	384	.437	281	.852	280	338	1053	13.2
	Totals	639	3599	.444	2545	.779	2772	2351	9783	15.3

M.L. CARR 33 6-6 205   Guard-Forward

Better mascot than "The Chicken"... Keeps the Celtics loose on the bench and in the locker room... His on-court contributions have become minimal... He doesn't even get enough playing time any more to bother anybody ... Played just 585 minutes in 60 games... Fanned his teammates to keep them cool during sweltering heat of Game 5 against Lakers at Boston Garden... Can still play designated hit man when Celtics are being burned by an opponent... His defense isn't always clean, but it's usually effective... Once was a legitimate offensive threat with Pistons, for whom he averaged 18.7 ppg in 1978-79... Born Jan. 9, 1951, in Wallace, N.C.... Real name is Michael Leon.... Attended Guilford... Talks about retiring a lot and Celtics won't object anymore... Always a great interview, but his legs are now much slower than his mouth.

Year	Team	G	FG	FG Pct.	FT	FT Pct.	Reb.	Ast.	TP	Avg.
1975-76	St. Louis (ABA)	74	380	.483	137	.665	459	224	906	12.2
1976-77	Detroit	82	443	.476	205	.735	631	181	1091	13.3
1977-78	Detroit	79	390	.455	200	.738	557	185	980	12.4
1978-79	Detroit	80	587	.514	323	.743	589	262	1497	18.7
1979-80	Boston	82	362	.474	178	.739	330	156	914	11.1
1980-81	Boston	41	97	.449	53	.791	83	56	248	6.0
1981-82	Boston	56	184	.450	82	.707	150	128	455	8.1
1982-83	Boston	77	135	.429	60	.741	137	71	333	4.3
1983-84	Boston	60	70	.409	42	.875	75	49	185	3.1
	Totals	631	2639	.472	1280	.734	3011	1312	6609	10.5

GERALD HENDERSON 28 6-2 175   Guard

Silenced doubters with solid season as starter
...He's not flashy and he rarely wins games,
but he won't lose any, either...Plays either
guard spot, depending on identity of his partner...Gives up inches to opponents and gets
away with it most of the time because of quickness...His 117 steals were a career high
...Can penetrate and rarely forces shot...
When Lakers gave him outside shot in playoffs, he usually made
it...Not a great shooter, but he hit 52.4 percent from field last
season...Born Jan. 16, 1956, in Richmond, Va....Attended
Virginia Commonwealth...Drafted as the 64th pick overall by
San Antonio, then cut by the Spurs...Celtics, desperate for backcourt help, signed him as free agent in 1979...Challenged for
starting spot by Danny Ainge and Quinn Buckner, but held
fast...Had 300 assists, his best total ever.

Year	Team	G	FG	FG Pct.	FT	FT Pct.	Reb.	Ast.	TP	Avg.
1979-80	Boston	76	191	.500	89	.690	83	147	473	6.2
1980-81	Boston	82	261	.451	113	.720	132	213	636	7.8
1981-82	Boston	82	353	.501	125	.727	152	252	833	10.2
1982-83	Boston	82	286	.463	96	.722	124	195	671	8.2
1983-84	Boston	78	376	.524	136	.768	147	300	908	11.6
	Totals	400	1467	.489	559	.728	638	1107	3521	8.8

GREG KITE 23 6-11 250   Center

The latest in line of ineffective white backup
centers at Boston...Showed nothing in rookie
season to disprove cynics who figured him to
be too slow for pros...Doesn't have the shooting touch that can sometimes save this kind of
player...Saw only 197 minutes in 35 games,
though he started once when K.C. Jones was
obviously in a whimsical mood...Probably
shouldn't have been a first-round pick in 1983...Averaged only
6.0 ppg and 7.6 rpg at Brigham Young...Played with Danny
Ainge in college, watches him in the pros...Born Aug. 5, 1961,
in Houston...Collected 42 personals and just 65 total points...
Loves Willie Nelson and country misic...Earned bachelor's degree in physical education with honors...Nobody said he was
dumb, he just can't play this game.

Year	Team	G	FG	FG Pct.	FT	FT Pct.	Reb.	Ast.	TP	Avg.
1983-84	Boston	35	30	.455	5	.313	62	7	65	1.9

QUINN BUCKNER 30 6-3 205   Guard

Still can't find his place on this team... Fell back on the depth chart when Boston acquired Dennis Johnson, which should have told him plenty about his standing with Red Auerbach... Shooting percentage fell to dismal .427, but he rarely played long enough to establish touch... Saw only 1,249 minutes, and had career-low 324 total points... After running Milwaukee's offense effectively for six years, he looks lost on the Boston break... Born Aug. 20, 1954, in Phoenix, Ill.... Played for Bobby Knight at Indiana after giving up football... Was captain of gold-medal Olympic team in 1976... All parts of his game are giving him problems now, including once-solid defense ... Always had trouble on the free-throw line... At least he didn't cost the Celtics anything... Boston acquired him from Bucks for Dave Cowens in 1982.

Year	Team	G	FG	FG Pct.	FT	FT Pct.	Reb.	Ast.	TP	Avg.
1976-77	Milwaukee.	79	299	.434	83	.539	264	372	681	8.6
1977-78	Milwaukee.	82	314	.468	131	.645	247	456	759	9.3
1978-79	Milwaukee.	81	251	.454	79	.632	210	468	581	7.2
1979-80	Milwaukee.	67	306	.467	105	.734	238	383	719	10.7
1980-81	Milwaukee.	82	471	.493	149	.734	298	384	1092	13.3
1981-82	Milwaukee.	70	396	.482	110	.655	250	328	906	12.9
1982-83	Boston.	72	248	.442	74	.632	187	275	570	7.9
1983-84	Boston.	79	138	.427	48	.649	137	214	324	4.1
	Totals	612	2423	.463	779	.656	1831	2880	5632	9.2

CARLOS CLARK 24 6-4 209   Guard

Not the answer... They called him "Marques Johnson in miniature" during college days at Mississippi, but Johnson usually shoots better than 36.5 percent from the floor... His outside shot was a disappointment... If he couldn't crack Celtic backcourt, his future in league is not particularly bright... Played 127 minutes in 31 games, scoring 54 points... Born Aug. 10, 1960, in Somerville, Tenn.... Second on Ole Miss all-time scoring list with 1,882 career points... Survived arthroscopic surgery on left knee that almost ruined career and starred again as senior... Fourth-round choice who stuck after solid training camp... Seemed to lose confidence once season started and his role became significantly smaller.

Year	Team	G	FG	FG Pct.	FT	FT Pct.	Reb.	Ast.	TP	Avg.
1983-84	Boston.	31	19	.365	16	.889	17	17	54	1.7

TOP ROOKIE

MICHAEL YOUNG 23 6-7 220   **Forward**
Celts may have pulled steal by tabbing him No. 24 overall as last
pick on first round . . . Certainly did the job at Houston . . . Leading
scorer for NCAA runnerup with 19.8-ppg average . . . Good range
on jumper, but shot only 64.4 percent from line . . . Solid
body . . . Slipped in ratings because scouts don't know if he can
set up his own shot . . . Solid rebounder for his size . . . Born
Jan. 2, 1961 . . . Raised in Houston . . . Needs some coaching after
four years with Guy Lewis.

COACH K.C. JONES: Why wasn't this man given more Coach-
of-the-Year consideration? . . . Put the ball back
in the hands of players and the strategy netted
him 62 regular-season victories and a world
championship . . . Players wanted to win for him,
which is far more than was ever said about his
predecessor, Bill Fitch . . . Proved again he is a
winner . . . In four years as coach of the Bullets
and Celts, he has compiled a 217-111 rec-
ord . . . Paid his dues as assistant with Celtics under four coaches—
Tom Heinsohn, Satch Sanders, Dave Cowens and Fitch . . .
Quiet and dignified . . . When he was playing guard for Boston,
team won championship in eight of nine seasons . . . Born May
25, 1932, in San Francisco . . . Retained solid relationship with
players through season . . . Was criticized often for his deployment
of backcourt, but final results are what count . . . Came closest to
disaster when Larry Bird aggravated ankle sprain at end of blowout
victory over Knicks in playoffs . . . Will his low-key approach work
on defending champions?

GREATEST FOUL SHOOTER

True to their tradition of excellence, the Celtics have boasted
some of the greatest foul shooters in the game: Larry Bird, John
Havlicek, Sam Jones, Tom Heinsohn, Bob Cousy and Frank Ram-

sey. Their finest free-throw shooter of all, however, was Bill Sharman.

Sharman, now president of the Los Angeles Lakers, had an 11-year career mark of .883 from the line, the third-best in league history. During his days as a Celtic guard from 1951-61, Sharman led the league in free-throw percentage seven times. More impressively, Sharman compiled a .911 free-throw percentage during playoff games spanning those 10 years. During the 1959 playoffs, Sharman converted 56 straight free throws, still a postseason record.

"I used the one-hand push shot and free-throw shooting always reminded me a lot of putting in golf," Sharman said. "Whoever had the most confidence up there was the most effective.

"I tell the players today the only way to improve is to practice so much that your muscle memory gets locked in. It's obviously not something you want to be thinking about when you're on the line."

ALL-TIME CELTIC LEADERS

SEASON

Points: John Havlicek, 2,388, 1970-71
Assists: Bob Cousy, 715, 1959-60
Rebounds: Bill Russell, 1,930, 1963-64

GAME

Points: Larry Bird, 53 vs. Indiana, 3/30/83
Assists: Bob Cousy, 28 vs. Minneapolis, 2/27/59
Rebounds: Bill Russell, 51 vs. Syracuse, 2/8/60

CAREER

Points: John Havlicek, 26,395, 1962-78
Assists: Bob Cousy, 6,945, 1950-63
Rebounds: Bill Russell, 21,620, 1956-69

CHICAGO BULLS

TEAM DIRECTORY: Pres.: Arthur M. Wirtz; Managing Partner: H. Jonathan Kovler; GM: Rod Thorn; Dir. Pub. Rel.: Tim Hallam; Coach: Kevin Loughery; Asst. Coaches: Bill Blair, Fred Carter, Mike Thibault. Arena: Chicago Stadium (17,373). Colors: Red, white and black.

SCOUTING REPORT

SHOOTING: Now that they have the next Julius Erving in Michael Jordan, the Bulls need the next Kareem Abdul-Jabbar. This strikingly young and talented team can score from everywhere except the pivot—which will prove the Bulls' undoing again.

Jordan is an offensive dynamo who figures to be just as unstoppable in the pros as he was at North Carolina. Coach Kevin Loughery will probably swing Jordan between small forward and guard in order to keep players like Orlando Woolridge, Quintin Dailey and David Greenwood in the lineup. Jordan will hit from the perimeter and will penetrate. Woolridge, an inside threat, came into his own last season, averaging 19.3 ppg with a .525 shooting percentage.

Dailey is another potent scorer in the backcourt who averaged 18.2 ppg. He can penetrate or pull up for the jumper. Center Dave Corzine will try to get off his mid-range jumpers and fail most of the time again. Corzine is a perfect backup, but can't go up against the big guys. Addition from Houston of vet center-forward Caldwell Jones (9.9 ppg, .502 shooting percentage) could help.

PLAYMAKING: Ennis Whatley had a sensational rookie season at the point, averaging 8.3 assists per game and wowing the Chicago Stadium crowd with his passes. This guy does not just make the easy pass. Whatley is something of a liability when it comes to shooting, however, so Loughery will split his time with Dailey and Ronnie Lester.

In the forecourt, Corzine is a solid distributor from the top of the key. Woolridge and Greenwood, however, do not remind anybody of Larry Bird when it comes to dishing off. Jordan should be better.

DEFENSE: When Loughery benched and later exiled Reggie Theus last season, he got his point across. The coach wanted two-way players and he'd do whatever he had to do to get them. Perhaps as a result of Loughery's demonstration—but probably not—the

Ennis Whatley averaged 8.3 assists as a baby Bull.

Bulls did settle down to play decent defense for most of the season. They didn't harass or trap that much after the first month, but they were tough in the paint.

Corzine blocked 120 shots, a surprising number for someone so slow. Woolridge blocked 60 and Greenwood had 72. All in all, the Bulls ranked eighth in the league in blocks. And 7-foot Jones (80 rebounds at Houston) should add something in that department.

REBOUNDING: Like the Nets and Cavaliers, the Bulls are one of those odd teams that features a forward as its chief rebounder. Greenwood pulled down 10.1 rpg, while Corzine had only 7.0. Add Woolridge's solid rebounding stats, and you have one of the best-balanced rebounding forecourts in the league. Jordan could add rebounding to the backcourt, but would not be as effective as Greenwood in the forecourt.

The Bulls were narrowly outrebounded by opponents last season, chiefly because of the weakness at center. That weakness is still there and so are the problems.

OUTLOOK: The Bulls have been underachievers for the last three years, embarrassing more than one coach with their great individual talents, but sorry won-loss records. With Jordan in tow, the Bulls should at least pass the Cavs and Hawks and make the playoffs. In a way, that is a shame. With Patrick Ewing coming out this year and the NBA's new lottery system in effect for the draft, it might pay for Chicago to finish ninth in the Eastern Conference.

BULL ROSTER

No.	Veteran	Pos.	Ht.	Wt.	Age	Yrs. Pro	College
54	Wallace Bryant	C	7-0	265	25	2	San Francisco
40	Dave Corzine	C	6-11	260	28	7	DePaul
44	Quintin Dailey	G	6-3	180	23	3	San Francisco
21	Sidney Green	F	6-9	210	23	2	Nevada-Las Vegas
34	*David Greenwood	F	6-9	232	27	6	UCLA
22	Rod Higgins	F	6-7	204	24	3	Fresno State
27	Caldwell Jones	C-F	7-0	220	34	12	Albany State (Ga.)
32	Steve Johnson	C	6-10	245	26	4	Oregon State
12	Ronnie Lester	G	6-2	175	25	5	Iowa
33	*Jawann Oldham	C	7-0	215	27	5	Seattle
3	Ennis Whatley	G	6-3	177	22	2	Alabama
0	Orlando Woolridge	F	6-9	215	24	4	Notre Dame

*Free agent unsigned at press time

Rd.	Top Draftees	Sel. No.	Ht.	Wt.	College
1	Michael Jordan	3	6-6	197	North Carolina
2	Ben Coleman	37	6-9	225	Maryland
2	Greg Wiltjer	43	6-11	240	Victoria
3	Tim Dillon	49	6-8¼	210	Northern Illinois
4	Melvin Johnson	72	6-9	210	NC-Charlotte

BULL PROFILES

ORLANDO WOOLRIDGE 24 6-9 215   Forward

Took three seasons to develop, but it was worth the wait . . . As club's leading scorer (19.3 ppg) and floor leader, he shot 52.5 percent from the field . . . Survived a rookie season during which he didn't know what he was doing and an injury-plagued second year . . . Extremely quick . . . Good penetrating forward who uses his height to great advantage . . . Notre Dame product has occasional defensive lapses and is only adequate as a rebounder . . . Born Dec. 16, 1959, in Bernice, La. . . . Although Bulls were happy with his play, they asked the Nets if they were interested in acquiring him for Buck Williams. Nets said no, thanks . . . Cousin of former Knick great Willis Reed . . . Not much of a passer, he averaged just 1.8 assists per game.

Year	Team	G	FG	FG Pct.	FT	FT Pct.	Reb.	Ast.	TP	Avg.
1981-82	Chicago	75	202	.513	144	.699	227	81	548	7.3
1982-83	Chicago	57	361	.580	217	.638	298	97	939	16.5
1983-84	Chicago	75	570	.525	303	.715	369	136	1444	19.3
	Totals	207	1133	.539	664	.685	894	314	2931	14.2

QUINTIN DAILEY 23 6-3 180   Guard

Erstwhile villain finds acceptance... People of Chicago seemed to forgive him for involvement in much-publicized rape case during days at USF... Blossomed into a force at both ends of the court... Had to share off-guard spot with Mitchell Wiggins, starting 42 of 82 games he played... Was one reason why Kevin Loughery benched and eventually traded Reggie Theus... Several teams, including Knicks, tried to pry him from Bulls with no success... Born Jan. 22, 1961, in Baltimore... Was second-leading scorer on team (18.2 ppg)... Great quickness and leaping ability plus decent touch... An instinctive passer who averaged 3.1 assists per game... Most observers give him a wide edge in talent over Wiggins and can't understand why Loughery divided time so equally between the two players... Made 47.4 percent of his field-goal attempts and 81.1 percent from line.

Year	Team	G	FG	FG Pct.	FT	FT Pct.	Reb.	Ast.	TP	Avg.
1982-83	Chicago	76	470	.466	206	.730	260	280	1151	15.1
1983-84	Chicago	82	583	.474	321	.811	235	254	1491	18.2
	Totals	158	1053	.471	527	.777	495	534	2642	16.7

ENNIS WHATLEY 22 6-3 177   Guard

The next Tiny Archibald... Tremendous rookie season, starting 73 games at the point and averaging 8.3 assists per game, the eighth-best mark in the league... His playmaking moves range from good to spectacular... His shot remains suspect and the one flaw in his game... Shot a respectable 46.9 percent from the floor, but most of his baskets came on penetrating moves... Perfect complement to Quintin Dailey and Mitchell Wiggins in Bulls' promising backcourt... Born Aug. 11, 1962, in Birmingham, Ala.... Folks complain about Chicago GM Rod Thorn, but he stole this youngster from Kansas City for Mark Olberding and Larry Micheaux... Kings picked him No. 13 overall in 1983 draft after he had played two seasons at Alabama-Birmingham... Was the youngest player in the league in 1983-84.

Year	Team	G	FG	FG Pct.	FT	FT Pct.	Reb.	Ast.	TP	Avg.
1983-84	Chicago	80	261	.469	146	.730	197	662	668	8.4

ROD HIGGINS 24 6-7 204   Forward

From sleeper to disappointment in one season... Followed up surprising rookie season with a sophomore year that put him in danger of losing roster spot... Played in 78 games and saw plenty of minutes in reserve role, but posted lousy numbers... Born Jan. 31, 1960, in Monroe, La.... Rebound average went down from 4.5 to 2.6 per game... Scoring average dipped from 10.3 to 6.4 ppg... Remains a tough defender with plenty of speed... Was second-round draft pick out of Fresno State in 1982... Even lost his confidence at free-throw line, where he had been outstanding... Primarily played behind Orlando Woolridge at small forward.

Year	Team	G	FG	FG Pct.	FT	FT Pct.	Reb.	Ast.	TP	Avg.
1982-83	Chicago	82	313	.448	209	.792	366	175	848	10.3
1983-84	Chicago	78	193	.447	113	.724	206	116	500	6.4
	Totals	160	506	.448	322	.767	572	291	1348	8.4

DAVID GREENWOOD 27 6-9 232   Forward

Waiting for Godot... As former UCLA standout's scoring average keeps slipping from year to year, it has become clear he will never be an offensive force... Had best rebounding season in pros, finishing ninth in the league with 10.1 per game, the third-best average among forwards... Will never live down fact that Bulls chose him when they lost the coin flip and Magic Johnson to Lakers in 1979... Had career-best field-goal mark of 49.0 percent, but showed little interest in taking shots... Born May 27, 1957, in Lynwood, Cal.... Bulls were ready to peddle him, but a couple of trades fell through at the Feb. 15 deadline... Rebounding stats may be inflated a bit because he plays next to Dave Corzine, not Moses Malone.

Year	Team	G	FG	FG Pct.	FT	FT Pct.	Reb.	Ast.	TP	Avg.
1979-80	Chicago	82	498	.474	337	.810	773	182	1334	16.3
1980-81	Chicago	82	481	.486	217	.748	724	218	1179	14.4
1981-82	Chicago	82	480	.473	240	.825	786	262	1200	14.6
1982-83	Chicago	79	312	.455	165	.708	765	151	789	10.0
1983-84	Chicago	78	369	.490	213	.737	786	139	951	12.2
	Totals	403	2140	.476	1172	.772	3834	952	5453	13.5

STEVE JOHNSON 26 6-10 245   Center

About as subtle as a meat grinder... Had only 307 fouls called on him last season, as compared to a personal high of 372 in 1981-82. Those figures are even more striking when you realize he didn't play that many minutes ... Bulls settled for him at last minute when they realized they could get nothing better for Reggie Theus by Feb. 15 trade deadline ...Kings didn't hesitate to deal this Oregon State product ...Born Nov. 3, 1957, in San Bernardino, Cal....Left home after 11th grade because his family's religious beliefs forbade him from playing basketball on Friday and Saturday nights...Had field-goal mark of 55.9 percent for the season and 57.1 percent after coming to Bulls...All of his baskets come from inside...Kevin Loughery used him sparingly as backup to Dave Corzine.

Year	Team	G	FG	FG Pct.	FT	FT Pct.	Reb.	Ast.	TP	Avg.
1981-82	Kansas City	78	395	.613	212	.642	459	91	1002	12.8
1982-83	Kansas City	79	371	.624	186	.574	398	95	928	11.7
1983-84	K.C.-Chi.	81	302	.559	165	.575	418	81	769	9.5
	Totals	238	1068	.600	563	.598	1275	267	2699	11.3

RONNIE LESTER 25 6-2 175   Guard

By Chicago's backcourt standards, he is an aging veteran... Injuries again subverted his season, but this time the Bulls weren't depending on him...Played only 43 games, starting just three... His confidence appears totally gone after four disappointing seasons...Shot 41.5 percent from the field and averaged 5.4 ppg in limited minutes... Could be an insurance point guard for a desperate team, but Bulls aren't desperate—at least not at this position...Born July 30, 1959, in Chicago...Great things were predicted for him after he starred at Iowa, but he underwent knee surgery and was never the same...Understandably, he lists his four years in college as the best time of his life... Still can pass the ball.

Year	Team	G	FG	FG Pct.	FT	FT Pct.	Reb.	Ast.	TP	Avg.
1980-81	Chicago	8	10	.417	10	.909	6	7	30	3.8
1981-82	Chicago	75	329	.501	208	.813	213	362	870	11.6
1982-83	Chicago	65	202	.453	124	.725	172	332	528	8.1
1983-84	Chicago	43	78	.415	75	.862	46	168	232	5.4
	Totals	191	619	.471	417	.794	437	869	1660	8.7

SIDNEY GREEN 23 6-9 210   Forward

Looked like a poor man's David Greenwood in rookie season... Played in just 49 games, in part because of late-season injury... Proved he can rebound in the pros, pulling down impressive 174 boards in only 667 minutes... Didn't look like much of a scoring threat, however, hitting only 43.9 percent of his shots and demonstrating no range... Born Jan. 4, 1961, in Brooklyn, N.Y.... Couldn't pass Rod Higgins on depth chart... Led Nevada-Las Vegas in scoring (22.1 ppg) and rebounding (11.9 rpg) in his final season there... Considering he was picked No. 5 overall in 1983 college draft, he is a terrible disappointment.

Year	Team	G	FG	FG Pct.	FT	FT Pct.	Reb.	Ast.	TP	Avg.
1983-84	Chicago	49	100	.439	55	.714	174	25	255	5.2

CALDWELL JONES 34 7-0 220   Center-Forward

The quiet professional who came from Houston in trade for Mitchell Wiggins and two 1985 draft picks... Ralph Sampson gives him a lot of credit for his development as a rookie... Has submerged his own ego for most of his pro career... Ultimate role player... Started all 82 games at center in 1982-83, then started 73 as the Rockets' power forward last season ... Born July 4, 1950, in McGehee, Ark.... Played for Albany (Ga.) State... One of seven children, he comes from a long line of basketball players... Brother Major was a teammate in Houston for the last two seasons... Brother Wil played in the ABA... Not an overpowering rebounder, but he'll never shortchange you on effort... Age is beginning to become a factor... Knows how to enjoy life. Once listed his five best friends as: Miller, Miller Lite, Heineken, Budweiser and Michelob.

Year	Team	G	FG	FG Pct.	FT	FT Pct.	Reb.	Ast.	TP	Avg.
1973-74	San Diego (ABA)	79	507	.465	171	.743	1095	144	1187	15.0
1974-75	San Diego (ABA)	76	606	.489	264	.788	1074	162	1479	19.5
1975-76	SD-KY-St.L. (ABA)	76	423	.470	140	.753	853	147	986	13.0
1976-77	Philadelphia	82	215	.507	64	.552	666	92	494	6.0
1977-78	Philadelphia	80	169	.471	96	.627	570	92	434	5.4
1978-79	Philadelphia	78	302	.474	121	.747	747	151	725	9.3
1979-80	Philadelphia	80	232	.436	124	.697	950	164	588	7.4
1980-81	Philadelphia	81	218	.449	148	.767	813	122	584	7.2
1981-82	Philadelphia	81	231	.497	179	.817	708	100	641	7.9
1982-83	Houston	82	307	.453	162	.786	668	138	776	9.5
1983-84	Houston	81	318	.502	164	.837	582	156	801	9.9
	Totals	876	3528	.474	1633	.751	8726	1468	8695	9.9

DAVE CORZINE 28 6-11 260 Center

Could be one of best backup centers in basketball, but is one of worst starters instead ...Didn't ask for a $600,000-per-year contract, but he was sensible enough not to refuse it...Considering ample number of physical limitations, he didn't do all that badly ...Averaged 12.2 ppg and 7.0 rpg...A real workhorse who has not missed a game in four seasons...Born April 25, 1956, in Arlington Heights, Ill....A local boy all the way, having played his college ball at DePaul...Loves Chicago more than it loves him...Has lumbering style and is not much of a jumper, but makes you pay for your points...A legendary eater...Shot 84 percent from the line.

Year	Team	G	FG	FG Pct.	FT	FT Pct.	Reb.	Ast.	TP	Avg.
1978-79	Washington	59	63	.534	49	.778	147	49	175	3.0
1979-80	Washington	78	90	.417	45	.662	270	63	225	2.9
1980-81	San Antonio	82	366	.490	125	.714	636	117	857	10.5
1981-82	San Antonio	82	336	.519	159	.746	629	130	832	10.1
1982-83	Chicago	82	457	.497	232	.720	717	154	1146	14.0
1983-84	Chicago	82	385	.467	231	.840	575	202	1004	12.2
	Totals	465	1697	.487	841	.754	2974	715	4239	9.1

JAWANN OLDHAM 27 7-0 215 Center

Hanging in there, but not by much...Demoted from second to third string when Bulls acquired Steve Johnson in mid-February...Played in respectable 64 games, but logged only 870 minutes...Rarely embarrassed himself, but contributed almost nothing offensively...His rebounding average (3.7 rpg) nearly matched his scoring average (4.0 ppg)...Born July 4, 1957, in Seattle and attended University of Seattle...Drafted in second round by Denver in 1980, but was cut and played with Montana of CBA for the remainder of that season...Bulls signed him as a free agent in February, 1983 and he stuck...If nothing else, he tries.

Year	Team	G	FG	FG Pct.	FT	FT Pct.	Reb.	Ast.	TP	Avg.
1980-81	Denver	4	2	.333	0	.000	5	0	4	1.0
1981-82	Houston	22	13	.361	8	.571	24	3	34	1.5
1982-83	Chicago	16	31	.534	12	.545	47	5	74	4.6
1983-84	Chicago	64	110	.505	39	.591	233	33	259	4.0
	Totals	106	156	.491	59	.578	309	41	371	3.5

WALLACE BRYANT 25 7-0 265 Center

If he can't make it at center in Chicago, where does he go next?...Played only 29 games, showing more offensive potential than Jawann Oldham, but proving himself a liability on defense and under the boards... Too slow to stick with more mobile opponents... Bulls' second-round draft pick out of USF in 1982... Played in Italy in 1982-83... Born July 14, 1959, in Madrid, Spain... Hit just 14-of-33 attempts from the line, a dismal 42.4 percent... Wasn't any better from the floor, with a 39.1 percent mark... At least he wasn't scared of going to the hoop.

Year	Team	G	FG	FG Pct.	FT	FT Pct.	Reb.	Ast.	TP	Avg.
1983-84	Chicago	29	52	.391	14	.424	80	13	118	4.1

TOP ROOKIE

MICHAEL JORDAN 21 6-6 197　　　　**Forward-Guard**
Odds-on favorite to be Rookie of the Year... Only sure thing among entire rookie crop... Can do it all, brilliantly and gracefully... A great shooter who hit 55.1 percent of his field-goal attempts in senior year at North Carolina... With his quickness and instincts, he should have no problems swinging back and forth between guard and forward... Bulls will find a spot for him in starting lineup... Born Feb. 17, 1963... Raised in Wilmington, N.C. ... Will hit the three-point shot.

COACH KEVIN LOUGHERY: It was a banner year for Loughery haters, who claimed the coach could not mold a talented young team into a winner... Couldn't even manage the worst record in the league and a shot at the No. 1 draft pick, as Bulls finished a game ahead of Indiana at 27-55... NBA career coaching mark slipped to 246-394... Rumored to be in trouble despite two years left on $250,000-per-season contract, but probably won't be axed unless GM and close friend Rod Thorn goes with him... Showed questionable judgment in banishing Reggie Theus to bench long before trade could be worked out... Theus fans in Chicago taunted Loughery and his young backcourtmen with cries of "Reggie... Reggie..." every time they had problems... Born March 28, 1940, in The Bronx, N.Y.... His feud with Knick coach Hubie Brown continues, intensified by fact Loughery got the call over Brown to do playoff commentary on CBS... Played for Detroit, Baltimore and Philadelphia from 1962-73, averaging 13.3 ppg after starring for St. John's.

GREATEST FOUL SHOOTER

Long before Rod Thorn and any Artis Gilmore-for-Dave Corzine deals, the Chicago Bulls pulled off one of the best trades in NBA history. On Sept. 2, 1969, they sent Jim Washington to the Philadelphia 76ers for Chet Walker in a swap of forwards.

Walker starred for the Bulls for the next six seasons and was among the top 10 free-throw shooters in the league for five of those years. Walker's foul shooting was remarkably consistent: he hit .850 in 1969-70; .859 in 1970-71; .847 in 1971-72; .875 in 1973-74 and .860 in 1974-75. In a playoff game against the Milwaukee Bucks, April 18, 1974, Walker sank all 11 free throws he took in the final period.

Other top foul shooters who passed through Chicago during their careers have included Reggie Theus, Ricky Sobers, Jack Marin and Bob Love. During the 1970-71 season, Walker led the league and Love was ninth.

ALL-TIME BULL LEADERS

SEASON

Points: Bob Love, 2,403, 1970-71
Assists: Guy Rodgers, 908, 1966-67
Rebounds: Tom Boerwinkle, 1,133, 1970-71

GAME

Points: Chet Walker, 56 vs. Cincinnati 2/6/72
Assists: Ennis Whatley, 22 vs. New York 1/14/84
    Ennis Whatley, 22 vs. Atlanta, 3/3/84
Rebounds: Tom Boerwinkle, 37 vs. Phoenix, 1/8/70

CAREER

Points: Bob Love, 12,623, 1968-76
Assists: Norm Van Lier, 3,676, 1971-78
Rebounds: Tom Boerwinkle, 5,745, 1968-78

CLEVELAND CAVALIERS

TEAM DIRECTORY: Chairmen: George Gund III, Gordon Gund; VP/GM: Harry Weltman; Dir. Pub. Rel.: Harvey Greene; Coach: George Karl; Asst. Coach: Gene Littles. Arena: The Coliseum (19,458). Colors: Orange, blue and white.

SCOUTING REPORT

SHOOTING: How bad are the Cavs? Last season, they shot .465 from the field, by far the lowest percentage in the league. They averaged only 102.3 ppg, less than any club other than Atlanta. Their two leading scorers, World B. Free and Cliff Robinson, couldn't crack the 45-percent mark from the floor.

So, the Cavaliers decided to shake things up a bit, trading Robinson for rookie Mel Turpin. They weren't getting any scoring from the center position—starter Roy Hinson averaged a pathetic 5.5 ppg—and Turpin is going to get his points. He is a tough post-up player, whose shooting percentages at Kentucky during his junior and senior years were .593 and .591, respectively.

Unfortunately, new coach George Karl still faces a tremendous job coordinating a fledgling offense. Free (22.3 ppg) will always get his points from the perimeter, but Phil Hubbard (.511), Lonnie Shelton (.476) and Geoff Huston (.498) are not natural scorers. Without Robinson's 17.8 ppg, Turpin faces inordinate pressure to deliver in a hurry.

PLAYMAKING: Huston (5.4 assists per game) is a playmaker's playmaker, a smart point guard with good court sense and an unselfish nature. But former coach Tom Nissalke soured on him a bit last year because he lacked explosiveness and began starting the more erratic John Bagley in his place.

Other than these two players, the Cavs are a playmaking mess. They had 1,930 assists and 1,332 turnovers last season. That ratio stinks, and it won't get any better with Turpin replacing Robinson. Robinson wasn't much of a feeder, but he could finish the play off the break, leading indirectly to assists. Turpin is more likely to take the ball down low and set up his own shot.

DEFENSE: If Nissalke did nothing else, he somehow inspired players like Free and Robinson to play the best defense of their careers for a losing team. But the chemistry of last season's club is almost irrelevant now, because there is a new head coach and a new focal point in Turpin.

In college, Turpin was never known for his defense. He is big

When World B. Free, it's an automatic two points.

and should be able to stand firm against the dinosaurs. But nobody is sure whether he will be another Bob Lanier or merely another Clemon Johnson. He can't play a power forward's defense in the paint and expect to get anywhere in the NBA. Hinson will help out—he had 145 blocks last season—but Cleveland will get burned by the top small forwards in the league.

In the backcourt, Huston will continue to offer solid but conservative defense, while Free will do his best. No Cavalier had 100 steals last season.

REBOUNDING: This rag-tag outfit did all right for itself under the boards last season, grabbing 2.6 more boards per game than the opposition. But Robinson (10.3 rpg) was a major reason for their success and the Cavs will be hard-pressed to fill his shoes in the forecourt.

Turpin grabbed only 6.3 rpg at Kentucky, which is not a good sign. If Hinson (6.2 rpg) plays next to him, the Cavs won't be embarrassed or overpowered. But they may have sabotaged the strongest part of their game with the daring trade.

CAVALIER ROSTER

No.	Veteran	Pos.	Ht.	Wt.	Age	Yrs. Pro	College
5	John Bagley	G	6-0	185	24	3	Boston College
44	Jeff Cook	F-C	6-10	215	28	6	Idaho State
41	Geff Crompton	C	6-11	288	29	6	North Carolina
21	World B. Free	G	6-3	185	30	10	Guilford
55	John Garris	F	6-8	190	25	2	Boston College
10	Stewart Granger	G	6-3	195	22	2	Villanova
32	Roy Hinson	C	6-10	210	23	2	Rutgers
35	Phil Hubbard	F	6-8	215	27	6	Michigan
20	Geoff Huston	G	6-2	175	26	6	Texas Tech
50	Ben Poquette	F	6-9	235	29	8	Central Michigan
8	Lonnie Shelton	F	6-8	255	29	9	Oregon State
36	Paul Thompson	F-G	6-6	210	23	2	Tulane

Rd.	Top Draftees	Sel. No.	Ht.	Wt.	College
1	*Melvin Turpin	6	6-11	245	Kentucky
2	Ron Anderson	27	6-7	215	Fresno State
3	Ben McDonald	50	6-8½	210	UC-Irvine
3	Leonard Mitchell	60	6-7	203	Louisiana State
4	Art Aaron	73	6-7	200	Northwestern

*Picked by Washington and traded to Cleveland

OUTLOOK: Do you believe in Mel Turpin? That's what it comes down to. If you do, then figure the Cavs could beat out Atlanta and Indiana. If you don't, put them down for dead last. Either way, they're out of the playoffs again.

CAVALIER PROFILES

WORLD B. FREE 30 6-3 185　　　　　　　　Guard

Another year, another bushel of points . . . Played hard and even showed some interest in playing defense during the first half of last season, but seemed to lose edge when coaches passed him up for All-Star Game and Cavs' season wound down to its usual depressing finish . . . His average of 22.3 ppg was the third-best single-season scoring mark ever recorded by a Cavalier and was good enough for 14th place in the league last season . . . Shot only 44.5 percent from the field, an indication of how willing he was to launch his high-arcing bombs . . . He's essential on a team like the Cavs, but will he play on a winner again? . . . Born Dec. 9, 1953, in Atlanta, but grew up in Brooklyn, N.Y. . . . Attended

Guilford...Became the 46th player in NBA history to surpass 14,000 career points.

Year	Team	G	FG	FG Pct.	FT	FT Pct.	Reb.	Ast.	TP	Avg.
1975-76	Philadelphia	71	239	.448	112	.602	125	104	590	8.3
1976-77	Philadelphia	78	467	.457	334	.720	237	266	1268	16.3
1977-78	Philadelphia	76	390	.455	411	.731	212	306	1191	15.7
1978-79	San Diego	78	795	.481	654	.756	301	340	2244	28.8
1979-80	San Diego	68	737	.474	572	.753	238	283	2055	30.2
1980-81	Golden State	65	516	.446	528	.814	159	361	1565	24.1
1981-82	Golden State	78	650	.448	479	.740	248	419	1789	22.9
1982-83	G.S.-Clev.	73	649	.456	430	.738	201	290	1743	23.9
1983-84	Cleveland	75	626	.445	395	.784	217	226	1669	22.3
	Totals	662	5069	.458	3915	.750	1938	2595	14114	21.3

STEWART GRANGER 22 6-3 195   Guard

Disappointing rookie season...Villanova product was selected in the first round as the 24th pick overall in 1983 with Cavs' league-sanctioned bonus pick...Suspect shooting made him liability and he played only 738 minutes all season...Started 13 games, mostly in place of World Free when the off guard was hurt...Was touted above Paul Thompson after solid showing in California Summer League, but never put it together and fell back on depth chart...Born Oct. 27, 1952, in Montreal, but moved to Brooklyn, N.Y. when he was seven...Was eligible to play internationally for Canada and was member of 1981 Canadian World University Games team.

Year	Team	G	FG	FG Pct.	FT	FT Pct.	Reb.	Ast.	TP	Avg.
1983-84	Cleveland	56	97	.429	53	.757	55	134	251	4.5

LONNIE SHELTON 29 6-8 255   Forward

Still nowhere near the player he was with Seattle, but he got his act together a bit in the second half last season...Still a battler...Chased Buck Williams halfway down the court, knocked him down and punched him in Feb. 14 game at Richfield...Was suspended for two games because of the incident...When you've averaged eight rebounds per game for a world championship team, as he did in 1979, how can you get excited about putting on that orange uniform?...Averaged only 4.8 rpg last year, his worst mark as a pro...Born Oct. 19, 1955, in Bakersfield, Cal....Attended Oregon State...Was banished by Seattle for a measly second-round draft pick in 1983 . . . Took off some of his excess weight by the end of last season.

Year	Team	G	FG	FG Pct.	FT	FT Pct.	Reb.	Ast.	TP	Avg.
1976-77	N.Y. Knicks	82	398	.476	159	.707	633	149	955	11.6
1977-78	New York	82	508	.514	203	.736	580	195	1219	14.9
1978-79	Seattle	78	446	.519	131	.693	468	110	1023	13.5
1979-80	Seattle	76	425	.530	184	.763	582	145	1035	13.6
1980-81	Seattle	14	73	.420	36	.655	78	35	182	13.0
1981-82	Seattle	81	508	.486	188	.733	509	252	1204	14.9
1982-83	Seattle	82	437	.478	141	.754	495	237	1016	12.4
1983-84	Cleveland	79	371	.476	107	.764	381	179	850	10.8
	Totals	572	3166	.495	1149	.740	3726	1302	7484	13.1

GEOFF HUSTON 26 6-2 175   Guard

Became one half of Tom Nissalke's point guard platoon when John Bagley picked up his game . . . Had to learn to come off the bench again . . . The perfect role player . . . A 49.8 percent shooter last season . . . Plays tough defense and makes very few mistakes . . . Cavs know exactly what they'll get from Texas Tech grad every time he is on court . . . Has suspect shot, but can penetrate for the layup . . . Born Nov. 8, 1957, in Brooklyn, N.Y. . . . K. C. Jones has loved him since he broke into the pros with the Knicks in 1979 . . . Averaged 5.3 assists and only 1.8 turnovers per game last season . . . Somebody should rescue this guy and put him on a winning team . . . One of the most articulate, sophisticated players in the NBA.

Year	Team	G	FG	FG Pct.	FT	FT Pct.	Reb.	Ast.	TP	Avg.
1979-80	New York	71	94	.390	28	.737	58	159	219	3.1
1980-81	Dal.-Clev.	81	461	.489	150	.708	138	394	1073	13.2
1981-82	Cleveland	78	325	.484	153	.765	150	590	806	10.3
1982-83	Cleveland	80	401	.482	168	.686	159	487	974	12.2
1983-84	Cleveland	77	348	.498	110	.714	96	413	808	10.5
	Totals	387	1629	.481	609	.717	601	2043	3880	10.0

PAUL THOMPSON 23 6-6 210   Forward-Guard

Sometimes it pays to be drafted by Cavs . . . Was No. 50 overall pick in the 1983 draft, but got a shot with Cleveland and made it as a swingman . . . Played in all 82 games and was only Cav to do so . . . Patterns his game after hero Julius Erving and can match Doctor J in leaping ability . . . Born May 25, 1961, in Smyrna, Tenn. . . . Came off the bench to spell World

Free at off guard and got playing time behind Cliff Robinson at small forward . . . Averaged 9.0 ppg on 46.7 percent shooting from the floor . . . Had a spectacular alley-oop slam dunk basket off a bounce pass against Nets late in season . . . Holds Tulane's all-time scoring record with 1,851 points.

Year	Team	G	FG	FG Pct.	FT	FT Pct.	Reb.	Ast.	TP	Avg.
1983-84	Cleveland	82	309	.467	115	.772	312	122	742	9.0

JEFF COOK 28 6-10 215   Forward-Center

He'll give you six points, six rebounds and six elbows off the bench every night . . . Was called on to fill the void at center on many occasions and did his best . . . Really a power forward, where he can use his height and reach to throw opponents off their game . . . A physical player who learned that was the only way he could make the NBA while enduring two seasons with the Washington Lumberjacks of the WBA . . . Started 21 games last season, but is most effective coming off the bench . . . Born Oct. 21, 1956, in Pasadena, Cal. . . . Attended Idaho State . . . Second-leading rebounder for Cavs last season, which tells you something about Cleveland's front line . . . Cut out of the Kurt Rambis-Marc Iavaroni mold . . . There's a place in the league for him despite his lack of speed.

Year	Team	G	FG	FG Pct.	FT	FT Pct.	Reb.	Ast.	TP	Avg.
1979-80	Phoenix	66	129	.469	104	.806	241	84	362	5.5
1980-81	Phoenix	79	286	.464	100	.645	467	201	672	8.5
1981-82	Phoenix	76	151	.422	89	.664	301	100	391	5.1
1982-83	Phoe.-Clev.	75	148	.487	79	.760	335	102	375	5.0
1983-84	Cleveland	81	188	.486	94	.723	484	123	471	5.8
	Totals	377	902	.465	466	.715	1828	610	2271	6.0

JOHN BAGLEY 24 6-0 185   Guard

Was starting point guard by the end of last season . . . Tough to understand what Tom Nissalke saw in this Boston College product . . . Can be explosive penetrator at times, but usually does more harm than good with inconsistency . . . Shot 42.3 percent from the floor and had a low assist-to-turnover ratio (1.9) . . . Born April 30, 1960, in Bridgeport, Conn. . . . Has led charmed life with Cavs . . . Cavs ignored experts and picked him in first round in 1982 and he managed to pile up 1,712 minutes last season, despite his shortcomings . . . When he's teamed with

World Free, any semblance of order goes out window...If he's six feet, then Geff Crompton weighs 200 pounds.

Year	Team	G	FG	FG Pct.	FT	FT Pct.	Reb.	Ast.	TP	Avg.
1982-83	Cleveland	68	161	.432	64	.762	96	167	386	5.7
1983-84	Cleveland	76	257	.423	157	.793	156	333	673	8.9
	Totals	144	418	427	221	.784	252	500	1059	7.4

PHIL HUBBARD 27 6-8 215   Forward

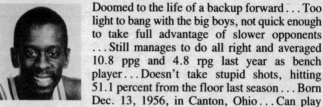

Doomed to the life of a backup forward...Too light to bang with the big boys, not quick enough to take full advantage of slower opponents ...Still manages to do all right and averaged 10.8 ppg and 4.8 rpg last year as bench player...Doesn't take stupid shots, hitting 51.1 percent from the floor last season...Born Dec. 13, 1956, in Canton, Ohio...Can play both forward spots adequately...Left Michigan with one season of eligibility left and was picked by Detroit in first round of 1979 draft...Has played for bad teams in his five pro seasons, but has managed to find his niche...Played in 80 games last season, starting six of them.

Year	Team	G	FG	FG Pct.	FT	FT Pct.	Reb.	Ast.	TP	Avg.
1979-80	Detroit	64	210	.466	165	.750	320	70	585	9.1
1980-81	Detroit	80	433	.492	294	.690	586	150	1161	14.5
1981-82	Det.-Clev.	83	326	.490	191	.682	473	91	843	10.2
1982-83	Cleveland	82	288	.482	204	.689	471	89	780	9.5
1983-84	Cleveland	80	321	.511	221	.739	380	86	863	10.8
	Totals	389	1578	.490	1075	.707	2230	486	4232	10.9

JOHN GARRIS 25 6-8 190   Forward

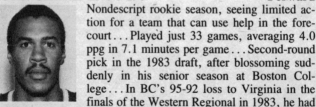

Nondescript rookie season, seeing limited action for a team that can use help in the forecourt...Played just 33 games, averaging 4.0 ppg in 7.1 minutes per game...Second-round pick in the 1983 draft, after blossoming suddenly in his senior season at Boston College...In BC's 95-92 loss to Virginia in the finals of the Western Regional in 1983, he had 25 points and 12 rebounds...A strong leaper, but he got lost in the shuffle when Paul Thompson asserted himself as an efficient swingman...Born June 6, 1959, in Bridgeport, Conn....Grew up in the same city as John Bagley and was his teammate for one season at Boston College.

Year	Team	G	FG	FG Pct.	FT	FT Pct.	Reb.	Ast.	TP	Avg.
1983-84	Cleveland	33	52	.510	27	.794	77	10	131	4.0

GEFF CROMPTON 29 6-11 288   Center

A rumbling tub of lard... Ordered by Tom Nissalke to lose about 40 pounds over the summer or not bother to show up for training camp ... Hard to believe he can't control his weight better... "Too many good times" is his only explanation... When he was with Milwaukee in 1981, he reportedly gained 20 pounds driving up to Wisconsin from his home in North Carolina... Born July 4, 1955, in Burlington, N.C.... Cavs gave him consecutive 10-day contracts, then signed him for three non-guaranteed years near the end of the season... North Carolina product has some talent beneath those layers of fat, having won the CBA MVP award last season by averaging 17 ppg and 10.2 rpg with Puerto Rico... Played seven games with Cavs last year and didn't show much.

Year	Team	G	FG	FG Pct.	FT	FT Pct.	Reb.	Ast.	TP	Avg.
1978-79	Denver	20	10	.385	6	.500	23	5	26	1.3
1979-80	Portland	6	4	.500	1	.200	18	2	9	1.5
1980-81	Milwaukee	35	11	.344	6	.400	41	13	28	0.8
1982-83	San Antonio	14	14	.412	3	.600	48	7	31	2.2
1983-84	Cleveland	7	1	.125	3	.500	9	1	5	0.7
	Totals	82	40	.370	19	.442	139	28	99	1.2

BEN POQUETTE 29 6-9 235   Forward

Broke a bone in his right wrist in late February and missed the rest of the season... Was expected to begin a conditioning program to rehabilitate the wrist starting in early May, when the cast was removed... A journeyman who didn't contribute much, even before his injury... Had a decent season in 1982-83 with Utah, but disappointed in early appearances with Cavs... Born May 7, 1955, in Ann Arbor, Mich.... Averaged about 16 minutes per game, posting 3.6 ppg average... Why would a team need both a Cook and a Poquette?... Central Michigan grad has a surprisingly good touch, but can't set up his own shots... One of the best free-throw shooters in the league.

Year	Team	G	FG	FG Pct.	FT	FT Pct.	Reb.	Ast.	TP	Avg.
1977-78	Detroit	52	95	.422	42	.700	145	20	232	4.5
1978-79	Detroit	76	198	.427	111	.782	336	57	507	6.7
1979-80	Utah	82	296	.523	139	.832	560	131	731	8.9
1980-81	Utah	82	324	.528	126	.778	629	161	777	9.5
1981-82	Utah	82	220	.514	97	.808	411	94	540	6.6
1982-83	Utah	75	329	.472	166	.751	521	168	825	11.0
1983-84	Cleveland	51	75	.439	34	.791	182	49	185	3.6
	Totals	500	1537	.486	715	.781	2784	680	3797	7.6

ROY HINSON 23 6-10 210   Center

The good news is he can play . . . The bad news is he can't play center . . . Suffered through one mismatch after another, throwing his gangly frame at opposing centers who were 50 pounds heavier night after night . . . Former Rutgers star could be a decent power forward . . . Was to work out on Nautilus equipment and try nutritional program to put on 15-20 pounds during summer . . . That still won't be enough . . . Born May 2, 1961, in Trenton, N.J. . . . Blocked 145 shots, showing good defensive timing for a rookie . . . Cavs pushed him for All-Rookie team, although Tom Nissalke was first to admit he wasn't much of a force in the pivot . . . Had a great night against Darryl Dawkins Feb. 18, grabbing 17 rebounds and getting five blocked shots while holding the Net center to five points and three rebounds.

Year	Team	G	FG	FG Pct.	FT	FT Pct.	Reb.	Ast.	TP	Avg.
1983-84	Cleveland	80	184	.496	69	.590	499	69	437	5.5

TOP ROOKIE

MEL TURPIN 23 6-11 245   Center

Cavs gambled it all on this Kentucky star . . . Gave up Cliff Robinson, their best player over past two seasons, and first-round pick Tim McCormick in three-team deal . . . Is he worth it? . . . Has a nice touch for a big man, but his rebounding, defense and overall quickness are question marks . . . Will start immediately and probably play 35 minutes a game . . . Cavs haven't had a real center for so long, they'll take anything . . . Born Dec. 28, 1960 . . . Raised in Lexington, Ky.

COACH GEORGE KARL: Upped in July from Cavs' post as

director of player acquisition, he's youngest coach in the NBA at age 33 . . . But figures to age fast . . . A strong motivator and evaluator of talent, Karl is in first NBA head-coach assignment, but proved himself as two-time Coach of the Year with Montana Golden Nuggets in CBA prior to joining Cleveland front office last season . . . Previously an assistant to Doug Moe with the San Antonio Spurs . . . Born May 15, 1951, in Pittsburgh

. . . Starred as guard at University of North Carolina and was an original Spur, a second-team ABA All-Rookie selection in 1973-74 . . . Played five years, all with Spurs, the last two in the NBA, before a knee injury ended career.

GREATEST FOUL SHOOTER

Considering they have already been in the NBA for 14 seasons—time flies when you're locked in the basement—the woeful Cavs have had few excellent foul shooters. The best of the lot was probably James Silas, who signed a big free-agent contract in 1981 and played just one season in Cleveland. Silas, always considered a clutch player at San Antonio, hit 246-of-286 free-throw attempts for a .860 percentage in 1981-82.

Other Cavs who have put together more-than-respectable seasons from the line have included Austin Carr (.856 in 1975-76); Dick Snyder (.852 in 1976-77); Walt Frazier (.850 in 1977-78); Dave Robisch (.842 in 1979-80); Dwight Davis (.840 in 1971-72); Roger Phegley (.839 in 1980-81); John Warren (.829 in 1970-71); and Lenny Wilkens (.828 in 1972-73). Only Snyder, who also had an .846 mark in 1974-75, was able to post two solid foul-shooting seasons for the Cavs.

ALL-TIME CAVALIER LEADERS

SEASON

Points: Mike Mitchell, 2,012, 1980-81
Assists: Lenny Wilkens, 628, 1972-73
Rebounds: Jim Brewer, 891, 1975-76

GAME

Points: Walt Wesley, 50 vs. Cincinnati, 2/19/71
Assists: Geoff Huston, 27 vs. Golden State, 1/27/82
Rebounds: Rick Roberson, 25 vs. Houston, 3/4/72

CAREER

Points: Austin Carr, 10,265, 1971-80
Assists: Foots Walker, 2,115, 1974-80
Rebounds: Jim Chones, 3,790, 1974-79

DETROIT PISTONS

TEAM DIRECTORY: Pres.: Bill Davidson; GM: Jack McCloskey; Dir. Pub. Rel.: Matt Dobek; Coach: Chuck Daly; Asst. Coach: Dick Harter. Arena: Pontiac Silverdome (22,366). Colors: Red, white and blue.

SCOUTING REPORT

SHOOTING: The Pistons had a field-goal percentage of .480 last season, which is dismal for a fast-breaking team. Isiah Thomas (.462), Kelly Tripucka (.459) and John Long (.472) were the worst offenders and they earned their low percentages by forcing up shots with plenty of time left on the shot clock. In the playoffs against the Knicks, undisciplined shot selection proved to be this club's eventual undoing.

Ex-Hawk Dan Roundfield (.485) will offer much more scoring punch from down low. He shouldn't get in the way of Bill Laimbeer (.530), since the Detroit center likes to operate from 10 feet and beyond. Thomas has tremendous range—he succeeded on 33.8 percent of his three-point attempts—but the jumper shouldn't be the dominant part of his game. Long can't do much except shoot, but when he's on a hot streak there are none better. Somehow, coach Chuck Daly must put the reins on Tripucka if Detroit is to contend.

PLAYMAKING: Thomas is, very simply, the best playmaking guard in the league. He was second in NBA with 11.1 assists per fame and there is no team—not even the Knicks, Bucks or Bullets—who can slow him down once he starts rolling.

Unfortunately, the Pistons are strapped for decent passers outside of Thomas. During the playoff series against the Knicks, Detroit had only one game plan: get the ball to Isiah. If it meant forcing a bad cross-court pass to get it there, the Pistons were willing. Cliff Levingston was probably the team's second-best passer and now he's in Atlanta.

As long as Thomas plays his usual 3,000-plus minutes, the Pistons will be all right during the regular season. But they better have some options ready for April and May.

DEFENSE: The Pistons were badly burned by power forwards with even a hint of mobility last season. Kent Benson was too slow and Levingston kept getting into foul trouble. All that should change this year with the addition of Roundfield, who is still one of the top defenders at his position.

Isiah Thomas launches Pistons' break into overdrive.

Roundfield's presence should do a couple of things for the Pistons on defense. A great deal of pressure will be lifted off Tripucka, who was often forced to match up against opposing scoring machines in the frontcourt. Also, Laimbeer's lack of speed and Long's occasional lapses in concentration may not prove as costly with Roundfield backing them up.

Thomas, as always, will create the defensive pressure in the backcourt. He was second in the league in steals with 2.49 per game.

REBOUNDING: The Pistons had the most rebounds (3,861) in the league last season. Now that they have Roundfield (9.9 rpg), they should get even more.

Laimbeer's rebound totals are bound to fall a bit with Roundfield's presence, but the center should be free to roam more defensively. The Pistons outrebounded opponents by three rebounds per game and almost all of that edge came on the offensive boards.

OUTLOOK: On paper at least, Roundfield is the missing link to a run at the championship. the Pistons won 49 games last season

PISTON ROSTER

No.	Veteran	Pos.	Ht.	Wt.	Age	Yrs. Pro	College
54	Kent Benson	F	6-10	235	29	8	Indiana
23	Earl Cureton	C	6-9	215	27	5	Detroit
9	*Lionel Hollins	G	6-3	185	31	10	Arizona State
15	*Vinnie Johnson	G	6-2	200	28	6	Baylor
40	Bill Laimbeer	C	6-11	245	27	5	Notre Dame
25	*John Long	G	6-5	195	28	7	Detroit
32	Dan Roundfield	F	6-8	205	31	10	Central Michigan
33	Walker Russell	G	6-4	195	24	3	Western Michigan
22	David Thirdkill	F	6-7	215	24	5	Bradley
11	Isiah Thomas	G	6-1	185	23	4	Indiana
24	Ray Tolbert	F	6-9	225	26	4	Indiana
7	*Kelly Tripucka	F	6-6	220	25	4	Notre Dame
41	Terry Tyler	F	6-7	220	28	7	Detroit

*Free agent unsigned at press time

Rd.	Top Draftees	Sel. No.	Ht.	Wt.	College
1	Tony Campbell	20	6-7	210	Ohio State
2	Eric Turner	32	6-3	175	Michigan
3	Kevin Springman	66	6-10	240	St. Joseph's (Pa.)
4	Philip Smith	89	5-10	165	New Mexico
5	Rick Doyle	112	6-10	250	Texas-San Antonio

and, in the relatively weak Central Division, they should be able to finish first.

But in this league, you're not great until you're great. Detroit has yet to show the cohesiveness of a title contender and it must improve its halfcourt offense to become a factor in the playoffs.

PISTON PROFILES

ISIAH THOMAS 23 6-1 185   Guard

None better, maybe ever...Point guard supreme...Played more than 3,000 minutes (3,007) for second straight year...Was second in league in assists (11.1 pg), second in steals (2.49 pg), 19th in scoring (21.3 ppg)...Got a $1 million-per-year contract in midseason, but could have had much more if he'd opted for free agency...Wanted to stay in Detroit... Selected as All-Star Game starter for third consecutive season...Born April 30, 1961, in Chicago...Pistons looked to him in every clutch situation and he usually delivered...Pistons might have beaten Knicks in playoffs if he hadn't fouled out in overtime of decisive Game 5, in which he had scored 35 points...Good range on jumper...Hit 33.8 percent of three-point attempts ...One of nine children...Second overall pick in 1982 draft after leading Indiana to NCAA title...All this and smiles, too.

Year	Team	G	FG	FG Pct.	FT	FT Pct.	Reb.	Ast.	TP	Avg.
1981-82	Detroit	72	453	.424	302	.704	209	565	1225	17.0
1982-83	Detroit	81	725	.472	368	.710	328	634	1854	22.9
1983-84	Detroit	82	669	.462	388	.733	327	914	1748	21.3
	Totals	235	1847	.456	1058	.717	864	2113	4827	20.5

KELLY TRIPUCKA 25 6-6 220   Forward

His stock is slipping...Complained his way through mediocre season in which he averaged 21.3 ppg, but shot only 45.9 percent from the field...His effort in final playoff game against Knicks said it all—he scored 23 points, but missed 15-of-23 shots and couldn't deliver in clutch...Was annoyed by Chuck Daly's substitution policies...Would love to return to New Jersey area...Born Feb. 16, 1959, in Bloomfield, N.J....Starred at Notre Dame, but was drafted only 12th overall because experts thought he might be too slow...Still hustles and still gets a lot of garbage baskets...Rebounding fell off, to 4.0 per game ...Doesn't miss many chances from the line...Contract negotiations fell through in midseason and his three-year pact expired in June.

Year	Team	G	FG	FG Pct.	FT	FT Pct.	Reb.	Ast.	TP	Avg.
1981-82	Detroit	82	636	.496	495	.797	443	270	1772	21.6
1982-83	Detroit	58	565	.489	392	.845	264	237	1536	26.5
1983-84	Detroit	76	595	.459	426	.815	306	228	1618	21.3
	Totals	216	1796	.481	1313	.817	1013	735	4926	22.8

BILL LAIMBEER 27 6-11 245   Center

A symbol of overachievement...He can't jump, he's slow and he doesn't scare anybody...But somehow, he more than does job...Finished fourth in the league in rebounding (12.2 rpg), third in free-throw shooting (86.6 percent), averaged 17.3 ppg and shot 53.0 percent from the field...Was selected as a reserve for the All-Star Game for the second straight season and excelled against the best...A physical player known for his sharp elbows and swiveling hips...A workhorse who played in all 82 games and averaged nearly 35 minutes...Born May 19, 1957, in Boston...Didn't look like he would make it when he first came into league with Cavs in 1981, but blossomed two years later with

Pistons... Has B.A. in economics from Notre Dame... An excellent golfer... Nicknamed "Incredible Hulk."

Year	Team	G	FG	FG Pct.	FT	FT Pct.	Reb.	Ast.	TP	Avg.
1980-81	Cleveland	81	337	.503	117	.765	693	216	791	9.8
1981-82	Clev.-Det.	80	265	.494	184	.793	617	100	718	9.0
1982-83	Detroit	82	436	.497	245	.790	993	263	1119	13.6
1983-84	Detroit	82	553	.530	316	.866	1003	149	1422	17.3
	Totals	325	1591	.509	862	.813	3306	728	4050	12.5

JOHN LONG 28 6-5 195   Guard

Quite a comeback... Nagging injuries had ruined his 1982-83 season, but he started every game last year and regained his touch from the floor and the line... One of the purest scoring guards around... Defense is still not his favorite part of the sport, but he'll retain interest in it for stretches... Finished second in the league in free-throw percentage (.884)... Getting married seemed to help his concentration and his commitment ... Doesn't have to handle the ball at all with Isiah Thomas around... Born Aug. 28, 1956, in Romulus, Mich.... Hasn't matched his 1981-82 season, when he averaged 21.9 ppg in the final year of his contract... Played college ball at Detroit.

Year	Team	G	FG	FG Pct.	FT	FT Pct.	Reb.	Ast.	TP	Avg.
1978-79	Detroit	82	581	.469	157	.826	266	121	1319	16.1
1979-80	Detroit	69	588	.505	160	.825	337	206	1337	19.4
1980-81	Detroit	59	441	.461	160	.870	197	106	1044	17.7
1981-82	Detroit	69	637	.492	238	.865	257	148	1514	21.9
1982-83	Detroit	70	312	.451	111	.760	180	105	737	10.5
1983-84	Detroit	82	545	.472	243	.884	289	205	1334	16.3
	Totals	431	3104	.477	1069	.846	1526	891	7285	16.9

KENT BENSON 29 6-10 235   Forward

A healthy, but erratic season... Was tried as a backup center, but when Cliff Levingston proved he wasn't ready to start, it was back to power forward... Slow, physical player who has terrible problems matching up against mobile forwards like Buck Williams... His return to starting lineup in midseason coincided with Pistons' winning surge... If he held his own against an opponent, Pistons usually matched up well enough everywhere else... Born Dec. 27, 1954, in New Castle, Ind.... Was terrible disappointment to Bucks after they made former Indiana star first pick overall in 1978 draft... Has been terrible disappointment for Pistons since they acquired him for Bob Lanier in 1981... Too slow for Detroit's running attack...Averaged 5.0 rebounds per game, his lowest mark since rookie season.

Year	Team	G	FG	FG Pct.	FT	FT Pct.	Reb.	Ast.	TP	Avg.
1977-78	Milwaukee........	69	220	.465	92	.652	295	99	532	7.7
1978-79	Milwaukee........	82	413	.518	180	.735	584	204	1006	12.3
1979-80	Mil.-Det........	73	299	.484	99	.702	453	178	698	9.6
1980-81	Detroit........	59	364	.473	196	.772	400	172	924	15.7
1981-82	Detroit........	75	405	.505	127	.804	653	159	940	12.5
1982-83	Detroit........	21	85	.467	38	.760	155	49	208	9.9
1983-84	Detroit........	82	248	.550	83	.822	409	130	579	7.1
	Totals..........	461	2034	.497	815	.748	2949	991	4887	10.6

VINNIE JOHNSON 28 6-2 200   Guard

Demoted to third guard, where he belongs ...Too small for off guard and on the wrong team to be a point guard...Chuck Daly used John Long ahead of him, reversing decision by former coach Scotty Robertson...A leaper and a penetrator with an erratic shot...Field-goal percentage dipped to .473...Can't possibly match up defensively against players like Sidney Moncrief...Born Sept. 1, 1956, in Brooklyn, N.Y....Had terrible steal-to-turnover ratio (44 to 135), indicative of bad hands...Can make things happen and is good to have around when Isiah Thomas gets into foul trouble...A solid rebounder and shot-blocker for his size...Played at Baylor after transferring from McLennon JC in Waco, Tex.

Year	Team	G	FG	FG Pct.	FT	FT Pct.	Reb.	Ast.	TP	Avg.
1979-80	Seattle..........	38	45	.391	31	.795	55	54	121	3.2
1980-81	Seattle..........	81	419	.534	214	.793	366	341	1053	13.0
1981-82	Sea.-Det....	74	217	.489	107	.754	159	171	544	7.4
1982-83	Detroit..........	82	520	.513	245	.778	353	301	1296	15.8
1983-84	Detroit..........	82	426	.473	207	.753	237	271	1063	13.0
	Totals..........	357	1627	.499	804	.772	1170	1138	4077	11.4

DAN ROUNDFIELD 31 6-8 205   Forward

Pistons figure they filled their biggest hole when they got this premier power forward from Atlanta for Cliff Levingston, the rights to Antoine Carr and two draft picks during offseason ...Not ready to slow down quite yet...In ninth pro season, he averaged 18.9 ppg and 9.9 rpg...Missed nine games in midseason with severe wrist sprain, but bounced back...You can bank on his consistency...An underrated ball-handler

...Second-team All-Defensive selection...Born May 26, 1953, in Detroit...Lost his four front teeth while playing for Central Michigan..."Rounds"...Works as stockbroker in offseason...Great mobility and anticipation under boards....One of the survivors of the ABA, where he played one season with Indiana in 1975-76 after being selected in first round of draft...Full name is Danny Thomas Roundfield.

Year	Team	G	FG	FG Pct.	FT	FT Pct.	Reb.	Ast.	TP	Avg.
1975-76	Indiana (ABA)	67	131	.427	77	.631	259	35	339	5.1
1976-77	Indiana	61	342	.466	164	.686	518	69	848	13.9
1977-78	Indiana	79	421	.489	218	.727	802	196	1060	13.4
1978-79	Atlanta	80	462	.504	300	.714	865	131	1224	15.3
1979-80	Atlanta	81	502	.499	330	.710	837	184	1334	16.5
1980-81	Atlanta	63	426	.527	256	.721	634	161	1108	17.6
1981-82	Atlanta	61	424	.466	285	.760	721	162	1134	18.6
1982-83	Atlanta	77	561	.470	337	.749	880	225	1464	19.0
1983-84	Atlanta	73	503	.485	374	.770	721	184	1380	18.9
	Totals	642	3772	.485	2341	.729	6237	1347	9891	15.4

TERRY TYLER 28 6-7 220   Forward

His role has diminished...Still played in every game, but was no longer the first forward off the bench and saw 800 fewer minutes than he did in 1982-83...His stats slipped accordingly, including scoring (8.8 ppg) and rebounding (3.4 rpg)...Seemed to lose some of the spark from his game, although he was still a tough defender...Born Oct. 30, 1956, in Detroit...A teammate of John Long at University of Detroit ...Vertical leap once measured at 45 inches...Like Cliff Levingston, his future role with team is in limbo if Antoine Carr arrives...Nicknamed "Thunder"...Blocked only 78 shots last year, less than half his previous low during five pro seasons.

Year	Team	G	FG	FG Pct.	FT	FT Pct.	Reb.	Ast.	TP	Avg.
1978-79	Detroit	82	456	.482	144	.658	648	89	1056	12.9
1979-80	Detroit	82	430	.465	143	.765	627	129	1005	12.3
1980-81	Detroit	82	476	.532	148	.592	567	136	1100	13.4
1981-82	Detroit	82	336	.523	142	.740	493	126	815	9.9
1982-83	Detroit	82	421	.478	146	.745	540	157	990	12.1
1983-84	Detroit	82	313	.453	94	.712	285	76	722	8.8
	Totals	492	2432	.488	817	.695	3160	713	5688	11.6

EARL CURETON 27 6-9 215   Center

Not your average season...Fled Philadelphia after championship year for Europe, but big contract blew up in a matter of days and he was back in America, searching for a job...Pistons signed him as a free agent and he played effectively as backup to Bill Laimbeer..."Earl the Twirl"...Born Sept. 3, 1957, in Detroit...Can surprise you offensively and is steady on defense against players two-to-five inches taller...Should be a power forward, but coaches can't resist his back-to-basket nature and throw him to wolves in pivot...Another Piston who played for University of Detroit...Chosen on third round as a a junior eligible by 76ers in 1980 and was minor role player in three seasons under Billy Cunningham...Averaged 3.9 rebounds per game in under 13 minutes per game.

Year	Team	G	FG	FG Pct.	FT	FT Pct.	Reb.	Ast.	TP	Avg.
1980-81	Philadelphia	52	93	.454	33	.516	155	25	219	4.2
1981-82	Philadelphia	66	149	.487	51	.543	270	32	349	5.3
1982-83	Philadelphia	73	108	.419	33	.493	269	43	249	3.4
1983-84	Detroit	73	81	.458	31	.525	287	36	193	2.6
	Totals	264	431	.456	148	.521	981	136	1010	3.8

DAVID THIRDKILL 24 6-7 215   Forward

Just doesn't have it...Was washout with Phoenix in rookie season after being tabbed as the 15th pick in 1982 draft...Did no better with Detroit, impressing nobody and earning very few minutes...Born April 12, 1960, in St. Louis...Starred at Bradley for three years, averaging seven rebounds and shooting 55.6 percent from the floor in his senior year...His game is penetration, not the outside shot, but he can't plow his way through the trees in the NBA...Hit just 15-of-31 free-throw attempts...His future is not with the Pistons and may not be in the league.

Year	Team	G	FG	FG Pct.	FT	FT Pct.	Reb.	Ast.	TP	Avg.
1982-83	Phoenix	49	74	.435	45	.577	72	36	194	4.0
1983-84	Detroit	46	31	.431	15	.484	31	27	77	1.7
	Totals	95	105	.434	60	.550	103	63	271	2.9

LIONEL HOLLINS 31 6-3 185   Guard

Hanging on by thread...Signed with Pistons as free agent after nobody else showed interest...Nothing more than backcourt insurance and there weren't any injuries to Detroit's guards last season...Once was one of smoothest, smartest guards in NBA...Played only 216 minutes last year, averaging 1.8 ppg...Had total of 59 points, which he used to score in a couple of good games...Best years were with Portland and he was integral part of Blazers' 1977 championship team...Born Oct. 19, 1953, in Arkansas City, Kan....Can still play defense against slower opponents, but has definitely lost a couple of steps...Played on four teams in five seasons.

Year	Team	G	FG	FG Pct.	FT	FT Pct.	Reb.	Ast.	TP	Avg.
1975-76	Portland	74	311	.421	178	.721	175	306	800	10.8
1976-77	Portland	76	452	.432	215	.749	210	313	1119	14.7
1977-78	Portland	81	531	.442	223	.743	277	380	1285	15.9
1978-79	Portland	64	402	.454	172	.778	149	325	976	15.3
1979-80	Port.-Phil.	47	212	.403	101	.721	89	162	528	11.2
1980-81	Philadelphia	82	327	.470	125	.731	191	352	781	9.5
1981-82	Philadelphia	81	380	.477	132	.702	187	316	894	11.0
1982-83	San Diego	56	313	.437	129	.721	128	373	758	13.5
1983-84	Detroit	32	24	.381	11	.846	22	62	59	1.8
	Totals	593	2952	.443	1286	.737	1428	2589	7200	12.1

RAY TOLBERT 26 6-9 225   Forward

Borderline talent who suffered indignities of nagging injuries last season...Simply too many forwards on this team...Can leap and has good quickness, but is too skinny to bang the boards and has very little to recommend his shot...Terrible at the free-throw line...Drafted in the first round by Nets in 1981, but New Jersey gave up on him and sent him to Seattle for James Bailey...Sonics didn't like what they saw, either...Born Sept. 19, 1958, in Anderson, Ind....Congenial fellow with great musical talent...Taught himself to play piano, guitar, and drums and once sang national anthem before game in Seattle...Decent defender.

Year	Team	G	FG	FG Pct.	FT	FT Pct.	Reb.	Ast.	TP	Avg.
1981-82	N.J.-Sea.	64	100	.495	19	.543	126	33	219	3.4
1982-83	Sea.-Det.	73	157	.500	52	.505	242	50	366	5.0
1983-84	Detroit	49	64	.529	23	.511	98	26	151	3.1
	Totals	186	321	.504	94	.514	466	109	736	4.0

TOP ROOKIE

TONY CAMPBELL 22 6-7 210   **Forward**
Scouts compare him to Mike Mitchell...That tells you great
things about his offense and casts aspersions on his defense...
Nobody doubts he can score...Averaged 18.6 ppg with Ohio
State in his senior year...Doesn't really complement Kelly Tripucka as backup small forward, since he also is an offensive
machine...Will give Piston fans their share of "oohs" and "ahhs"
...Born May 7, 1962...Raised in Teaneck, N.J....Outstanding
range on jumper.

COACH CHUCK DALY: Don't pinch him...Had dream season, winning 49 games—12 more than Scotty
Robertson did with same basic cast...Led
Pistons into playoffs for first time in seven
years...Well-liked by majority of players, who
felt closer to him than they had to Robertson...Listened to Isiah, which kept his point
guard happy...Great season rescued his career
from brink...Spent year of doing television
commentary with 76ers after a disastrous (9-32) fling as coach of
Ted Stepien's Cavaliers in 1981...Tells great Stepien stories.
Says that one time the Cleveland owner met with Daly's assistants
during practice to decide whether to fire him. Daly fined assistants
for missing practice...Suffered an attack of angina during preseason, but recovered nicely. Smooth season had to help...Was
Billy Cunningham's tutor at Philadelphia as an assistant coach
after serving as head coach at Boston College and Penn...Born
July 20, 1930, in St. Mary's, Pa....Pragmatic coach who holds
no grudges and is willing to admit mistakes when experiments
don't pan out.

GREATEST FOUL SHOOTER

The Pistons have a couple of solid free-throw shooters currently
on the team in Kelly Tripucka and John Long, but their all-time

best from the line is now coaching an Eastern Conference opponent.

Gene Shue, coach of the Washington Bullets, was among the NBA's top 10 foul shooters for four straight seasons, during his days as a Piston from 1957-62. He still holds the club record for the best free-throw percentage in a season—.872 in 1959-60. The former University of Maryland star later played for the Knicks and the Bullets. In his 10 years and 699 regular-season NBA games, Shue had an .806 free-throw percentage. In the playoffs, he shot at an .842 clip.

Shue says he does not get frustrated trying to teach foul shooting to players a bit less accomplished at the skill than himself. "It's really not something you can pass along," Shue said. "Either you have that ability, or you don't. Usually, a good field-goal shooter is a good foul shooter, but even that doesn't always hold true."

ALL-TIME PISTON LEADERS

SEASON

Points: Dave Bing, 2,213, 1970-71
Assists: Kevin Porter, 1,099, 1978-79
Rebounds: Bob Lanier, 1,205, 1972-73

GAME

Points: Kelly Tripucka, 56 vs. Chicago, 1/29/83
Assists: Kevin Porter, 25 vs. Phoenix, 4/1/79
　　　　　Kevin Porter, 25 vs. Boston, 3/9/79
Rebounds: Bob Lanier, 33 vs. Seattle, 12/22/72

CAREER

Points: Bob Lanier, 15,488, 1970-80
Assists: Dave Bing, 4,330, 1966-75
Rebounds: Bob Lanier, 8,033, 1970-80

INDIANA PACERS

TEAM DIRECTORY: Owners: Herb Simon, Melvin Simon; Pres./GM: Bob Salyers; Media Coordinator: David Paitson; Coach: George Irvine; Asst. Coach: Donnie Walsh. Arena: Market Square Arena (17,092). Colors: Blue and gold.

SCOUTING REPORT

SHOOTING: Four of the Pacers' top five scorers play in the forecourt, which tells you two things—the Indiana big men are potent and the Indiana backcourt is a joke.

New coach George Irvine will be faced with the same problem that eventually got Jack McKinney fired—a lack of versatility. The Pacers have four guys who would love to play power forward, but nobody who can shoot in the backcourt or can body his way past a hulking center.

Once again, the offense will rely heavily on Clark Kellogg (.519), who led the team with a 19.1-ppg average. Steve Stipanovich (.480) and Herb Williams (.478) can provide a variety of offensive moves against most players, using their mobility to good advantage. Guard Butch Carter came on in the second half, but he is a streak shooter who hit only 47.8 percent of his shots. Irvine hopes rookie Vern Fleming will help the backcourt, but the Pacers

Clark Kellogg was Pacer pacesetter at 19.1 ppg.

really need a point guard who is more of a threat than Jerry Sichting.

Indiana was 19th in the league in scoring last season, despite playing a relatively up-tempo game. This season, the Pacers should be just as bad.

PLAYMAKING: Sichting (5.7 assists per game) is the chief play-maker, until unseated. He rarely makes mistakes, but he's slow and can't penetrate to keep a defense honest. Kellogg, Williams and Stipanovich are all solid passers and ball-handlers at their positions.

Keep in mind one thing about the Pacers. They tend to handle the ball differently at the start of the game than at the end. At the finish of a tight game, there is chaos and every pass is a 50-50 proposition. Composure is not Indiana's strong suit.

DEFENSE: Opponents shot nearly 50 percent against the Pacers last season, because Indiana had no intimidators and gave up too much at center. Stipanovich can't possibly muscle up with the Dawkinses and Laniers of the world—and neither can his flawed backups. So teams usually beat the Pacers from the inside out, forcing Carter and Sichting to wear themselves thin trying to help out on the big men.

Sichting tries very hard on defense, but he's slow and gives up four or five inches in most matchups. Gone are the days when Don Buse could come off the bench as the stopper, but Carter is an effective pest and the Pacers led the league in steals.

REBOUNDING: The Pacers are probably the worst rebounding team in the NBA. Last season, they spotted opponents a 4.4-rebound-per-game edge, a significant handicap. The problems here are the same as in the other departments. They don't have a genuine center and the guards are too small to help out.

Kellogg (9.1 rpg) is by far the best rebounder, getting some help from Williams, George Johnson and Stipanovich. Center Granville Waiters probably rebounds better than Stipanovich, but he can't do anything else.

OUTLOOK: Not good. If the Pacers had only kept their own first-round draft pick instead of squandering it four years ago for Tom Owens, they could have had Sam Bowie at center and Stipanovich at power forward. Instead, they will field the same cellophane frontcourt and impotent backcourt.

As usual, gracious opponents will call the Pacers "scrappy," and "determined." As usual, the Pacers will lose 50 games, many of them in the fleeting moments.

PACER ROSTER

No.	Veteran	Pos.	Ht.	Wt.	Age	Yrs. Pro	College
12	Butch Carter	G	6-5	200	26	5	Indiana
34	Leroy Combs	F	6-8	210	23	2	Oklahoma State
24	*George Johnson	F	6-7	225	27	7	St. John's
33	Clark Kellogg	F	6-7	227	23	3	Ohio State
35	Sidney Lowe	G	6-0	197	24	2	NC State
25	Kevin McKenna	F	6-7	205	25	3	Creighton
11	Brook Steppe	G	6-5	200	24	3	Georgia Tech
40	Steve Stipanovich	C	6-11	245	23	2	Missouri
14	Jerry Sichting	G	6-1	175	27	5	Purdue
19	Jim Thomas	G	6-4	195	24	2	Indiana
31	Granville Waiters	C	6-11	220	23	2	Ohio State
32	Herb Williams	F	6-11	240	25	4	Ohio State

*Free agent unsigned at press time

Rd.	Top Draftees	Sel. No.	Ht.	Wt.	College
1	Vern Fleming	18	6-5	195	Georgia
2	Devin Durrant	25	6-7	201	Brigham Young
2	Stuart Gray	29	7-0	235	UCLA
5	Gene Smith	94	6-2	175	Georgetown
6	Clyde Vaughn	117	6-4½	210	Pittsburgh

PACER PROFILES

CLARK KELLOGG 23 6-7 227   Forward

Had solid second season after spectacular rookie year . . . Bouts with tendinitis in knees may have hampered him a bit . . . Already one of the premier swing forwards in league, he deserves better supporting cast . . . A perpetual motion machine on the floor, he works for every rebound he gets . . . Led team in scoring (19.1 ppg) and rebounding (9.1 rpg), but those numbers were down from previous season's output . . . Knicks kick themselves every time they realize they chose Trent Tucker ahead of him in the 1982 draft . . . Born July 2, 1961, in Cleveland . . . His success dwarfs that of young teammates Steve Stipanovich and Herb Williams . . . Ohio State product's rebounding totals can't be hurt by fact he is playing with the Pacers' odd assortment of centers.

Year	Team	G	FG	FG Pct.	FT	FT Pct.	Reb.	Ast.	TP	Avg.
1982-83	Indiana	81	680	.479	261	.741	860	223	1625	20.1
1983-84	Indiana	79	619	.519	261	.768	719	234	1506	19.1
	Totals	160	1299	.497	522	.754	1579	457	3131	19.6

HERB WILLIAMS 25 6-11 240 Forward

One of three natural power forwards the Pacers start in the forecourt... Great shot-blocker, good passer, fair rebounder... Doesn't assert himself as much as he could under offensive boards... Second-leading scorer on the Pacers (14.9 ppg)... Came off the bench in 16 games last season, as Jack McKinney experimented with his combinations... A lot of interest in him around league, but Pacers didn't move him despite crowd of talent at his position... Born Feb. 16, 1959, in Columbus, Ohio... Stayed close to home to star for Ohio State... Can play center if necessary and was used primarily at that position in his second pro season... Was 14th player picked in the 1981 draft.

Year	Team	G	FG	FG Pct.	FT	FT Pct.	Reb.	Ast.	TP	Avg.
1981-82	Indiana	82	407	.477	126	.670	605	139	942	11.5
1982-83	Indiana	78	580	.499	155	.705	583	262	1315	16.9
1983-84	Indiana	69	411	.478	207	.702	554	215	1029	14.9
	Totals	229	1398	.486	488	.694	1742	616	3286	14.3

GEORGE JOHNSON 27 6-7 225 Forward

Has shown slow but steady improvement... Had best scoring year with 13.0 ppg and averaged 5.5 rpg... Isn't the quickest player around, but is strong, smart reserve... Stepped in to start in 20 games last season, whenever Jack McKinney got fed up with Herb Williams or Steve Stipanovich... Solid free-throw shooter... Born Dec. 8, 1956, in Brooklyn, N.Y.... Stayed in area to play at St. John's... Played on three teams—Milwaukee, Denver, and Indiana—in first three pro seasons before blossoming into legitimate sub... Has missed only one game in last two seasons after suffering through three injury-plagued years... Sat out 30 games in 1980-81 with sprained left knee.

Year	Team	G	FG	FG Pct.	FT	FT Pct.	Reb.	Ast.	TP	Avg.
1978-79	Milwaukee	67	165	.482	84	.718	360	81	414	6.2
1979-80	Denver	75	309	.476	148	.783	584	157	768	10.2
1980-81	Indiana	43	182	.462	93	.762	278	86	457	10.6
1981-82	Indiana	59	120	.412	60	.750	217	40	300	5.1
1982-83	Indiana	82	409	.477	126	.733	545	220	951	11.6
1983-84	Indiana	81	411	.465	223	.826	460	195	1056	13.0
	Totals	407	1596	.467	734	.773	2444	779	3946	9.7

STEVE STIPANOVICH 23 6-11 245   Center

Rookie season wasn't as disastrous as some had feared, but wasn't as good as his boosters had hoped... Showed quickness and good court instincts, but was overmatched at center... Most opposing coaches agree his future is at power forward, but Pacers already have too many of those... Averaged 12.0 ppg and 6.9 rpg... Born Nov. 17, 1960, in St. Louis... Haunted by pressure that came with being No. 2 overall pick in 1983 draft... First-team all-league rookie selection... He's first to admit, "I'm not Ralph Sampson."... Missouri grad was plagued by foul problems, but he learned how to play with four or five personals... Was nailed with 303 fouls, but was disqualified only four times... Good passer.

Year	Team	G	FG	FG Pct.	FT	FT Pct.	Reb.	Ast.	TP	Avg.
1983-84	Indiana	81	392	.480	183	.753	562	170	970	12.0

KEVIN McKENNA 25 6-7 205   Forward

Another borderline player who managed to start in 13 games for Indiana... A decent passer and ball-handler who rarely turns the ball over... Can't run, can't jump, can't make his own shots, so he's a triple threat to Pacers on offense... Hit just 41.0 percent of his shots... Born Jan. 8, 1959, in St. Paul, Minn.... Signed as free agent after spending 1982-83 season with the Las Vegas-Albuquerque Silvers of the CBA... Originally drafted in fourth round by the Lakers, but saw limited action in 36 games with Los Angeles during his rookie season... Averaged 15.8 ppg as a senior at Creighton.

Year	Team	G	FG	FG Pct.	FT	FT Pct.	Reb.	Ast.	TP	Avg.
1981-82	Los Angeles	36	28	.322	11	.647	29	14	67	1.9
1983-84	Indiana	61	152	.410	80	.816	95	114	387	6.3
	Totals	97	180	.393	91	.791	124	128	454	4.7

JERRY SICHTING 27 6-1 175   Guard

One of only NBA players who can't dunk... Throwback to the prototypical playmaking guard of the '50s... Plays hard and intelligently, but makes nothing happen... Started 80 games last season and logged more minutes (2,497) than anybody on team except Clark Kellogg... Local product all the way... Born Nov. 29, 1956, in Martinsville, Ind.... Played at Purdue, where he showed steady, unspectacular style he later brought to pros...Reminds people a lot of Dave Wohl, now a Laker assistant...Excellent free-throw shooter (86.7 percent) who rarely gets to line...Led team in assists (5.7 per game) and hit 53.2 percent from the floor...Doesn't like to shoot unless he must, but he can stick the jumper if his man doubles up on someone else.

Year	Team	G	FG	FG Pct.	FT	FT Pct.	Reb.	Ast.	TP	Avg.
1980-81	Indiana	47	34	.358	25	.781	43	70	93	2.0
1981-82	Indiana	51	91	.469	29	.763	55	117	212	4.2
1982-83	Indiana	78	316	.478	92	.860	155	433	727	9.3
1983-84	Indiana	80	397	.532	117	.867	171	457	917	11.5
	Totals	256	838	.494	263	.843	424	1077	1949	7.6

BUTCH CARTER 26 6-5 200   Guard

Came into his own as a true scoring threat at end of season...A streak shooter who can turn a game around when he is graced by hot hand...Finally got playing time he needed to blossom, averaging 28 minutes per game...Born June 11, 1958, in Springfield, Ohio...Learned to be patient while spending three years as a reserve for Bobby Knight at Indiana...Second-round choice by Lakers in 1980 draft, but in rookie season, he had a strange sight problem that was diagnosed as a "transitory episode of one-eye blindness"...Sat out a season, then was acquired by Pacers for a third-round choice...A tough physical matchup for smaller guards.

Year	Team	G	FG	FG Pct.	FT	FT Pct.	Reb.	Ast.	TP	Avg.
1980-81	Los Angeles	54	114	.462	70	.737	65	52	301	5.6
1981-82	Indiana	75	188	.468	58	.829	79	60	442	5.9
1982-83	Indiana	81	354	.501	124	.805	150	194	849	10.5
1983-84	Indiana	73	413	.479	136	.764	153	206	977	13.4
	Totals	283	1069	.482	388	.781	447	512	2569	9.1

BROOK STEPPE 24 6-5 190   Guard

Best thing you can say is he knows how to shoot free throws...Slow, blue-collar guard who can hit open shot if it is given to him...Fact he played in 61 games and started 13 is proof enough of Pacers' sorry state...Came to Indiana in complicated three-way deal that sent Ray Williams to Knicks, Billy Knight to Kings and New York's first-round 1984 draft choice to Pacers...Led Georgia Tech in scoring his junior and senior years... Born Nov. 7, 1959, in Chapel Hill, N.C., but went to DeKalb Central Community College in Clarkston, Ga., after growing up in Atlanta.... Played less than 10 minutes per game in his rookie season under Cotton Fitzsimmons, who recognized lack of potential when he saw it.

Year	Team	G	FG	FG Pct.	FT	FT Pct.	Reb.	Ast.	TP	Avg.
1982-83	Kansas City	62	84	.477	76	.760	73	68	245	4.0
1983-84	Indiana	61	148	.471	134	.832	122	79	430	7.0
	Totals	123	232	.473	210	.805	195	147	675	5.5

SIDNEY LOWE 24 6-0 197   Guard

More fireplug than firebrand... Second-round draft choice in 1983 who was lucky to be picked by guard-hungry Pacers... Backed up Jerry Sichting at the point:... His shot isn't suspect. It's lousy... Can penetrate when defenses get lazy... Was all-time assist leader at North Carolina State, but didn't show that much imagination with the ball during his rookie year ... Born Jan. 21, 1960, in Washington, D.C.... Shot only 41.3 percent from the field... Started two games in place of injured Sichting... Can be a pest on defense and averaged more than one steal per game.

Year	Team	G	FG	FG Pct.	FT	FT Pct.	Reb.	Ast.	TP	Avg.
1983-84	Indiana	78	107	.413	108	.777	122	269	324	4.2

GRANVILLE WAITERS 23 6-11 220   Center

Looked and played like a 40-year-old rookie... Played in 78 games and started eight at center... Simply couldn't hold his ground against the league's dinosaurs... Acquired from Portland after Blazers had made him the 39th overall pick in 1983 draft... Born Jan. 8, 1961, in Columbus, Ohio... His greatest moment of glory came when his high school team defeated Clark Kellogg's school to win the Columbus city championship... Didn't disgrace himself against the smaller centers... Blocked 1.1 shots per game and committed few turnovers... But Ohio State grad averaged only 3.6 ppg and didn't really have to be guarded at the other end of the court... Took Brad Branson's place, so Pacers didn't lose much.

Year	Team	G	FG	FG Pct.	FT	FT Pct.	Reb.	Ast.	TP	Avg.
1983-84	Indiana	78	123	.517	31	.608	227	60	277	3.6

JIM THOMAS 24 6-4 195   Guard

For 40th pick, he had respectable rookie season... Former star for Bobby Knight at Indiana was used at both guard positions and started 15 games... Pulled down seven offensive rebounds in the Pacers' home opener last season, but never quite lived up to that debut performance... Has questionable shot, but worked hard on it with former Pacer star Roger Brown and shot 55.2 percent from the floor over the final 10 weeks of season... Had season-high 21 points vs. Chicago Nov. 19... Born Oct. 19, 1960, in Lakeland, Fla.... His father is a principal and his mother is an elementary school teacher... Must become better passer if he is to play the point for more than token minutes.

Year	Team	G	FG	FG Pct.	FT	FT Pct.	Reb.	Ast.	TP	Avg.
1983-84	Indiana	72	187	.464	80	.727	149	130	455	6.3

LEROY COMBS 23 6-8 210   Forward

Had tough switch to make from star center at Oklahoma State to reserve forward with the Pacers... A great athlete, but he showed few signs of possessing skills needed to make it in NBA... Couldn't find much playing time at crowded position and didn't shine when he got it... Averaged only 1.2 rebounds per game... Can get the easy basket... Shot only 61.5 percent from the free-throw line... Born Jan. 1, 1961, in Oklahoma City, Okla.... Drafted No. 26 overall by the Pacers in the second round of 1983 draft... Averaged 17.3 ppg in his senior year at Oklahoma State... Can't operate in open court... One of two Pacers—Brook Steppe was the other—with more turnovers than assists.

Year	Team	G	FG	FG Pct.	FT	FT Pct.	Reb.	Ast.	TP	Avg.
1983-84	Indiana	48	81	.497	56	.615	56	38	218	4.5

TOP ROOKIE

VERN FLEMING 22 6-5 195   Guard

Pacers hope he'll give boost to woeful backcourt... An all-around guard at Georgia, where he was the leading scorer in the SEC (19.8 ppg) and the all-time Bulldog leader in assists and steals ... "The only guy I know that can guard Vern Fleming is Vern

Fleming," said coach Hugh Durham...Averaged 7.0 rpg during NCAA tournament in 1983, so you know he can sky...Born Feb. 2, 1962...Raised in Long Island City, N.Y...Will get opportunity to start with Indiana, which made him the 18th pick overall.

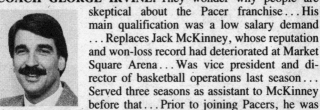

COACH GEORGE IRVINE: They wonder why people are skeptical about the Pacer franchise...His main qualification was a low salary demand ...Replaces Jack McKinney, whose reputation and won-loss record had deteriorated at Market Square Arena...Was vice president and director of basketball operations last season... Served three seasons as assistant to McKinney before that...Prior to joining Pacers, he was an assistant at Denver for three years...Spent five seasons as a guard in the American Basketball Association...Second-youngest coach in the NBA at age 36 (Indiana's George Karl is 33)...Born Feb. 1, 1948, in Seattle...Sure to be branded "a child" by Hubie Brown...Must have impressed owners Melvin and Herbert Simon along the way, as well as president Bob Salyers...Credited with scouting four rookies that made squad last season, which isn't really saying much...Will have to work with limited resources...At least he knows personnel.

GREATEST FOUL SHOOTER

Billy Keller, the former Purdue star who played seven seasons with the Pacers when the franchise was still in the ABA, was Indiana's most consistent foul shooter.

During his years with the Pacers, Keller strung together free-throw percentages of .850, .870, .879, .870, .870, .883 and a club-record .896 in 1975-76. That year, Keller hit 164-of-183 free-throw attempts.

Other top Pacer foul shooters of the past include Freddie Lewis, Dave Robisch, Johnny Davis and Ricky Sobers. Sobers hit 298-of-338 free throws in 1978-79 for an .882 percentage.

Sobers played for the Washington Bullets last season and was still remarkably accurate from the line, shooting .837.

"I don't think getting older affects foul shooting at all," said the 31-year-old Sobers. "It's a matter of concentration, repetition and, above all else, the ability to get yourself to the line."

ALL-TIME PACER LEADERS

SEASON

Points: George McGinnis, 2,353, 1974-75
Assists: Don Buse, 689, 1975-76
Rebounds: Mel Daniels, 1,475, 1970-71

GAME

Points: George McGinnis, 58 vs. Dallas, 11/28/72
Assists: Don Buse, 20 vs. Denver, 3/26/76
Rebounds: George McGinnis, 37 vs. Carolina, 1/12/74

CAREER

Points: Roger Brown, 10,002, 1967-74, 1975
Assists: Don Buse, 2,737, 1972-77, 1980-82
Rebounds: Mel Daniels, 7,622, 1968-74

MILWAUKEE BUCKS

TEAM DIRECTORY: Chairman of the Board/Pres.: James Fitzgerald; VP-Bus. Oper.: John Steinmiller; VP-Consultant: Wayne Embry; Dir. Pub. Rel.: Bill King II; Coach/Dir. Player Per.: Don Nelson; Asst. Coaches: Mike Schuler, Garry St. Jean. Arena: Milwaukee Arena (11,052). Colors: Forest green, red and white.

SCOUTING REPORT

SHOOTING: This team can score in every way imaginable and is almost impossible to defend against in a halfcourt game. How can you hope to stop the twisting drives of Marques Johnson (.502) and Sidney Moncrief (.498), the fadeaways of Bob Lanier (.572) and the bombs of Junior Bridgeman (.465) and Mike Dunleavy (.551)? When coach Don Nelson succeeds in breaking the game down to one-on-ones, the Bucks win 90 percent of the time.

If there is an offensive weakness, it may be at power forward. Alton Lister (.500) has a way of disappearing in some games, often because of his chronic foul problems. The Bucks can hope rookie Kenny Fields will complement Johnson as another scorer in the forecourt.

Sidney Moncrief led Bucks in scoring and assists.

PLAYMAKING: This category is almost irrelevant with the Bucks. How much playmaking ability is required to walk the ball downcourt and feed it—ever so slowly—to one of your scorers? Moncrief and Dunleavy are more than adequate for the job. Unselfishness and a sense of who has the hot hand are all that's required.

The Bucks had seven players with assist totals between 160 and 360 last season. That didn't include late-arrival Dunleavy, who also would have been in that range if he had played the full season. If injury-plagued Tiny Archibald can make another comeback, the Bucks would have more playmakers than they would know what to do with.

DEFENSE: A tight, switching defense is the hallmark of Nelson's Bucks. Nobody packs the lane better than these giants and nobody bodies teams off their game as well. The Nets ran the Sixers off the court in the first round of the playoffs, but Milwaukee would have none of that in the Eastern Conference semifinals.

Although Lanier remains the chief block of granite in the paint, Lister has developed into a top defender and shot-blocker (140). Opposing players who are driving the lane have to worry about the arc on their shots—and that's bound to cut into their field-goal percentages.

The Bucks gave up only 101.5 ppg, which was the stingiest mark in the league. Of course, their slow offense had something to do with that. But they have the ability to change the tempo of a game, to cut off the passing lanes and to force gazelles to play ugly basketball.

REBOUNDING: The Bucks had a very slight rebounding edge over their opponents (.4 boards a game), which is somewhat surprising. They don't possess a dominating rebounder, but have several contributors.

Lanier, whose slowness and advancing age has cut into his stats, gives a rebounding edge to opposing centers. Lister (7.4 rpg) is the top rebounder on the team and Moncrief (6.7 rpg) is second. Johnson, Bridgeman and Paul Pressey also contribute.

OUTLOOK: Opposing teams keep waiting for the Bucks to wither and die, but they won't go away. Foes dread their visits and harbor grudging admiration for their grind-it-out style.

For yet another season, their destiny appears to be linked with Lanier's. If he decides to hang it up as threatened, Nelson is left far short in the pivot. It's not so much what Lanier does, it's what he doesn't do—allow opposing centers to score lots of points.

BUCK ROSTER

No.	Veteran	Pos.	Ht.	Wt.	Age	Yrs. Pro	College
7	*Nate Archibald	G	6-1	165	36	15	Texas-El Paso
45	Randy Breuer	C	7-3	235	24	2	Minnesota
2	Junior Bridgeman	G-F	6-5	210	31	10	Louisville
42	Harvey Catchings	C	6-10	220	33	11	Hardin-Simmons
10	*Mike Dunleavy	G	6-3	180	30	9	South Carolina
35	Kevin Grevey	G	6-5	210	31	10	Kentucky
8	Marques Johnson	F	6-7	218	28	8	UCLA
16	*Bob Lanier	C	6-11	255	36	15	St. Bonaventure
53	Alton Lister	F	6-11	240	26	4	Arizona State
45	Paul Mokeski	C	7-0	250	27	6	Kansas
4	Sidney Moncrief	G	6-4	190	27	6	Arkansas
25	Paul Pressey	G	6-5	185	25	3	Tulsa
5	*Lorenzo Romar	G	6-1	180	25	5	Washington

*Free agent unsigned at press time

Rd.	Top Draftees	Sel. No.	Ht.	Wt.	College
1	Ken Fields	21	6-7	225	UCLA
3	Vernon Delancy	67	6-5	190	Florida
5	Ernie Floyd	113	6-8	216	Holy Cross
6	McKinley Singleton	120	6-5	175	Alabama-Birmingham
6	Mike Reddick	136	6-8	210	Stetson

BUCK PROFILES

SIDNEY MONCRIEF 27 6-4 190   Guard

One of the greatest players in game today, but when will he have a great playoff series?... The Bucks' leading scorer (20.9 ppg), leading assist man (4.5 per game), second-leading rebounder (6.7 rpg) and most consistent player ... Had more total rebounds than any other guard in league, including Magic Johnson... Shooting was off a bit, but he can still penetrate and leap for second and third chances... Couldn't solve Dennis Johnson's defense in Eastern Conference finals, so Celtics won easily... Born Sept. 21, 1957, in Little Rock, Ark.... A private sort who actually prefers Milwaukee to the larger media markets... Went to free-throw line amazing 624 times... Still holds scoring and rebounding records at Arkansas... "I don't know what you'd call me," he says. "I don't play the point and I'm not a traditional off guard because I don't shoot from way out."... Great athlete...Played 3,075 minutes...Picked in first round in 1979 behind Bill Cartwright, David Greenwood and Greg Kelser.

Year	Team	G	FG	FG Pct.	FT	FT Pct.	Reb.	Ast.	TP	Avg.
1979-80	Milwaukee.	77	211	.468	232	.795	338	133	654	8.5
1980-81	Milwaukee.	80	400	.541	320	.804	406	264	1122	14.0
1981-82	Milwaukee.	80	556	.523	468	.817	534	382	1581	19.8
1982-83	Milwaukee.	76	606	.524	499	.826	437	300	1712	22.5
1983-84	Milwaukee.	79	560	.498	529	.848	528	358	1654	20.9
	Totals	392	2333	.515	2048	.822	2243	1437	6723	17.2

MARQUES JOHNSON 28 6-7 218   Forward

Smooth as silk, yet he can muscle his way through a pack...His versatility makes him tough to defend against...Had strong post-season, excelling against Nets and Celtics ...Underrated passer who averaged 4.3 assists per game...Despite physical play, he is subtle and rarely gets nailed with the foul...Born Feb. 8, 1956, in Natchitoches, La....Raised in Los Angeles, where he was College Player of the Year for UCLA in 1977...Unlike Sidney Moncrief, he wouldn't mind a spotlight once in a while...Third player chosen in 1977 draft...Held out for 18 games during 1981-82 season until the Bucks gave him a new contract...Usually at his best for big games...Always a good interview.

Year	Team	G	FG	FG Pct.	FT	FT Pct.	Reb.	Ast.	TP	Avg.
1977-78	Milwaukee.	80	628	.522	301	.736	874	190	1557	19.5
1978-79	Milwaukee.	77	820	.550	332	.760	586	234	1972	25.6
1979-80	Milwaukee.	77	689	.544	291	.791	566	273	1671	21.7
1980-81	Milwaukee.	76	636	.552	269	.706	518	346	1541	20.3
1981-82	Milwaukee.	60	404	.532	182	.700	364	213	990	16.5
1982-83	Milwaukee.	80	723	.509	264	.735	562	363	1714	21.4
1983-84	Milwaukee.	74	646	.502	241	.709	480	315	1535	20.7
	Totals	524	4546	.530	1880	.736	3923	1934	10980	21.0

BOB LANIER 36 6-11 255   Center

He says every year is his last, then goes out and surprises himself...His knees held up for 72 games and 2,007 minutes...Ninth in league in field-goal percentage (.572)...As responsible as anyone for Bucks' successes and failures...Has limited mobility, but is an overpowering force when he's posted up...Boasts beautiful touch for a big man...Fouled out of eight games during regular season...Bucks will miss him when he goes...Did not have a strong series against

Robert Parish and Celtics...Born Sept. 10, 1948, in Buffalo...Attended St. Bonaventure...A proud man who wants nothing more than a championship ring...Would never endure another season with a bad club...Survived almost 10 seasons as the only bright spot on dismal Detroit teams...Stolen by the Bucks in 1980 for Kent Benson and first-round pick.

Year	Team	G	FG	FG Pct.	FT	FT Pct.	Reb.	Ast.	TP	Avg.
1970-71	Detroit	82	504	.455	273	.726	665	146	1281	15.6
1971-72	Detroit	80	834	.493	288	.768	1132	248	2056	25.7
1972-73	Detroit	81	810	.490	307	.733	1205	260	1927	23.8
1973-74	Detroit	81	748	.504	326	.797	1074	343	1822	22.5
1974-75	Detroit	76	731	.510	361	.802	914	350	1823	24.0
1975-76	Detroit	64	541	.532	284	.768	746	217	1366	21.3
1976-77	Detroit	64	678	.534	260	.818	745	214	1616	25.3
1977-78	Detroit	63	622	.537	298	.772	715	216	1542	24.5
1978-79	Detroit	53	489	.515	275	.749	494	140	1253	23.6
1979-80	Det.-Mil.	63	466	.537	277	.782	552	184	1210	19.2
1980-81	Milwaukee	67	376	.525	208	.751	413	179	961	14.3
1981-82	Milwaukee	74	407	.558	182	.752	388	219	996	13.5
1982-83	Milwaukee	39	163	.491	91	.684	200	105	417	10.7
1983-84	Milwaukee	72	392	.572	194	.708	455	186	978	13.6
	Totals	959	7761	.514	3724	.767	9698	3007	19248	20.1

MIKE DUNLEAVY 30 6-3 180   Guard

What a year...An unwanted free agent in October...A Wall Street broker in January...A Milwaukee Buck in March...A starter by April...Had given up hope of resuming basketball career when he got the call March 8...Don Nelson started him ahead of Paul Pressey because he was more dependable and offered the perimeter threat...Maybe the best three-point shooter in the league...Hit 19-of-45 bombs (42.2 percent) last season...Played in 17 games for Bucks, starting 12 of them...Born March 21, 1954, in Brooklyn, N.Y....Did remarkable defensive job on Micheal Ray Richardson in Eastern Conference semifinals...Can't find a slower point guard...There should be a spot for this South Carolina grad somewhere, but not in starting lineup of contending team.

Year	Team	G	FG	FG Pct.	FT	FT Pct.	Reb.	Ast.	TP	Avg.
1976-77	Philadelphia	32	60	.414	34	.756	34	56	154	4.8
1977-78	Phil.-Hou.	15	20	.400	13	.722	10	28	53	3.5
1978-79	Houston	74	215	.506	159	.864	128	324	589	8.0
1979-80	Houston	51	148	.464	111	.828	100	210	410	8.0
1980-81	Houston	74	310	.491	156	.839	118	268	777	10.5
1981-82	Houston	70	206	.458	75	.708	104	227	520	7.4
1982-83	San Antonio	79	213	.418	120	.779	134	437	613	7.8
1983-84	Milwaukee	17	70	.551	32	.800	28	78	191	11.2
	Totals	412	1242	.467	700	.807	656	1628	3307	8.0

ALTON LISTER 26 6-11 240 Forward

The only consistent thing about him is the way he spells his name . . . Brilliant in stretches, awful in others . . . Started 72 games and played in all 82, primarily at power forward and as a sub at center . . . Gets called for a lot of stupid fouls because he can't seem to control flailing arms . . . Was nailed with 327 personals and fouled out of 11 games while playing just 1,955 minutes . . . Nobody denies this Arizona State product can rebound, though, and he led team in that category (7.3 rpg) . . . Did decent job defensively against Nets' Buck Williams of Nets in second-round playoff series, but wilted under pressure of Celtic forecourt . . . Born Oct. 1, 1958, in Dallas . . . Best shot-blocker on team with average of 1.71 per game . . . Pays the price for his defensive aggressiveness with foul trouble and lethargic offensive play.

Year	Team	G	FG	FG Pct.	FT	FT Pct.	Reb.	Ast.	TP	Avg.
1981-82	Milwaukee.	80	149	.519	64	.520	387	84	362	4.5
1982-83	Milwaukee.	80	272	.529	130	.537	568	111	674	8.4
1983-84	Milwaukee.	82	256	.500	114	.626	603	110	626	7.6
	Totals	242	677	.516	308	.563	1558	305	1662	6.9

PAUL PRESSEY 25 6-5 185 Guard

Will never be floor leader that Don Nelson had hoped he would become . . . Error-prone, he led team in turnovers-per-minute . . . Started 18 games after Tiny Archibald was lost with injury, but sat at end of season, behind Mike Dunleavy . . . Not a great shooter, but can penetrate . . . Doesn't complement Sidney Moncrief, whose game is similar . . . Field-goal percentage (.523) was second-highest on club . . . When Dunleavy bruised muscle during second round of playoffs, he had another chance to prove himself in Game 5. But he didn't do much against Nets and Dunleavy was starting again in Game 6 . . . Born Dec. 24, 1958, in Richmond, Va. . . . Called for 241 fouls and disqualified six times . . . Didn't have enough steals to make those fouls worthwhile . . . Led Tulsa to NIT title in 1981.

Year	Team	G	FG	FG Pct.	FT	FT Pct.	Reb.	Ast.	TP	Avg.
1982-83	Milwaukee.	79	213	.457	105	.597	281	207	532	6.7
1983-84	Milwaukee.	81	276	.523	120	.600	282	252	674	8.3
	Totals	160	489	.492	225	.598	563	459	1206	7.5

JUNIOR BRIDGEMAN 31 6-5 210   Guard-Forward

Healthy again . . . Missed just one game all season and reestablished himself as dependable sixth man . . . Struggled with shot and from the free-throw line early in the season . . . May not be great anymore, but always a threat . . . Scored 19 points on 8-for-13 shooting and grabbed eight rebounds against Atlanta in second game of opening-round playoff series . . . Nine years with Bucks make him all-time club leader in games played . . . Only Seattle's Fred Brown has been with one NBA team longer . . . Born Sept. 17, 1953, in East Chicago, Ind . . . All-American for Louisville . . . Majored in psychology and was on dean's list all four years in college . . . Matchups determine how much forward he can play . . . There are more bruisers at small forward than when he first started with Bucks in 1975 . . . Streak shooter whose 46.5-percent shooting from the field was his worst mark since his second year in pros . . . Third-highest scorer on team (15.1 ppg).

Year	Team	G	FG	FG Pct.	FT	FT Pct.	Reb.	Ast.	TP	Avg.
1975-76	Milwaukee.	81	286	.439	128	.795	294	157	700	8.6
1976-77	Milwaukee.	82	491	.449	197	.864	416	205	1179	14.4
1977-78	Milwaukee.	82	476	.503	166	.810	290	175	1118	13.6
1978-79	Milwaukee.	82	540	.506	189	.829	297	163	1269	15.5
1979-80	Milwaukee.	81	594	.478	230	.865	301	237	1423	17.6
1980-81	Milwaukee.	77	537	.487	213	.884	289	234	1290	16.8
1981-82	Milwaukee.	41	209	.483	89	.864	125	109	511	12.5
1982-83	Milwaukee.	70	421	.492	164	.837	246	207	1007	14.4
1983-84	Milwaukee.	81	509	.465	196	.807	332	265	1220	15.1
	Totals	677	4063	.479	1572	.840	2590	1752	9717	14.4

KEVIN GREVEY 31 6-5 210   Guard

Strictly bench insurance these days . . . Slower than ever and not getting the minutes he needs to keep his shot sharp . . . Played in 64 games last season, but not many important minutes . . . Former Kentucky star still gets in streaks when he'll shoot the eyes out of the basket . . . His role diminished further when Bucks acquired Mike Dunleavy, who does everything he does and even shoots three-pointers better . . . Has problems defending against faster off guards in league . . . Born May 12, 1953, in Hamilton, Ohio . . . Played eight seasons with Washington before Don Nelson took him and his hefty salary off Gene Shue's hands . . . People are forgetting how effective he was at peak of career, when he started for Bullets' championship team in

1977-78 . . . His scoring average (7.0 ppg) was lowest since second season in league.

Year	Team	G	FG	FG Pct.	FT	FT Pct.	Reb.	Ast.	TP	Avg.
1975-76	Washington	56	79	.371	52	.897	60	27	210	3.8
1976-77	Washington	76	224	.423	79	.664	178	68	527	6.9
1977-78	Washington	81	505	.448	243	.789	290	155	1253	15.5
1978-79	Washington	65	418	.453	173	.772	232	153	1009	15.5
1979-80	Washington	65	331	.412	216	.867	187	177	912	14.0
1980-81	Washington	75	500	.453	244	.841	219	300	1289	17.2
1981-82	Washington	71	376	.439	165	.855	195	149	945	13.3
1982-83	Washington	41	114	.388	54	.783	49	49	297	7.2
1983-84	Milwaukee	64	178	.451	75	.893	81	75	446	7.0
	Totals	594	2725	.436	1301	.816	1491	1153	6888	11.6

PAUL MOKESKI 27 7-0 250   Center

He's not Kareem, he's not Cary Grant, but he stays in the league . . . When Harvey Catchings was hurt at the end of the season, he became indispensible as backup . . . May have found himself a home in Milwaukee after playing for four teams in his first four years . . . Don't count on it . . . Not as good on boards as Catchings, but he's more of an offensive threat . . . Has a decent touch around the key . . . Born Jan. 3, 1957, in Spokane, Wash. . . . Fifth-leading all-time rebounder at Kansas . . . Second-round pick by Houston in 1979, but the Rockets gave up on him after 12 games . . . Was ejected from playoff game against Nets after attacking Micheal Ray Richardson . . . Refs take one look at him and call the foul.

Year	Team	G	FG	FG Pct.	FT	FT Pct.	Reb.	Ast.	TP	Avg.
1979-80	Houston	12	11	.333	7	.778	29	2	29	2.4
1980-81	Detroit	80	224	.489	120	.600	418	135	568	7.1
1981-82	Det.-Clev.	67	84	.435	48	.762	208	35	216	3.2
1982-83	Clev.-Mil.	73	119	.458	50	.735	260	49	288	3.9
1983-84	Milwaukee	68	102	.479	50	.694	166	44	255	3.8
	Totals	300	540	.467	275	.667	1081	265	1356	4.5

RANDY BREUER 24 7-3 235   Center

First impressions weren't good . . . After great career at Minnesota, he was something of a bust in his rookie season . . . Averaged only 2.9 ppg and had a .384 field-goal percentage . . . If Don Nelson wants those stats, he'll look to Harvey Catchings . . . Showed some aggressiveness on offensive boards, so there's hope . . . Will require at least the standard three years it takes for gangly white centers to mature... Born Oct. 11, 1960, in Lake City, Minn.... Averaged 20.4 ppg in his senior year... Bucks made him No. 18 pick overall... Slipped behind Paul Mokeski on depth chart, which is no easy task... Played in 57 games, but Don Nelson went elsewhere when chips were down... Looks slow, even for a Buck.

Year	Team	G	FG	FG Pct.	FT	FT Pct.	Reb.	Ast.	TP	Avg.
1983-84	Milwaukee........	57	68	.384	32	.696	109	17	168	2.9

LORENZO ROMAR 25 6-1 180   Guard

Type of point guard you like to have on bench... Can do everything adequately, nothing spectacularly... Early-season acquisition from Golden State, after Warriors decided he couldn't crack guard rotation... Moved up a notch on depth chart in Milwaukee when Tiny Archibald went down... Left-handed shot ... Demotion in Oakland was swift and tough to take... He had led Warriors in assists previous season... Born Nov. 13, 1958, in Compton, Cal.... Don Nelson's decision to bring in Mike Dunleavy was another setback... A seventh-round pick who made it... Warriors tabbed him in 1980, after his successful career at University of Washington... Likes blues music.

Year	Team	G	FG	FG Pct.	FT	FT Pct.	Reb.	Ast.	TP	Avg.
1980-81	Golden State	53	87	.412	43	.683	56	136	219	4.1
1981-82	Golden State	79	203	.504	79	.823	98	226	488	6.2
1982-83	Golden State	82	266	.465	78	.743	138	455	620	7.6
1983-84	G.S.-Mil.	68	161	.459	67	.713	93	193	393	5.8
	Totals	282	717	.466	267	.746	385	1010	1720	6.1

HARVEY CATCHINGS 33 6-10 220   Center

Why does he even bother coming up the court?... A one-dimensional player throughout his career... He'll give you good rebounding and shot-blocking as a reserve, but defenders cheat on him like crazy... Injured his knee late in season and missed first nine playoff games... Shot only 39.9 percent from the field... Blocked 81 shots, second on team to Alton Lister... Born Sept. 2, 1951, in Jackson, Miss.... Attended Hardin-Simmons... Bucks use him when they already have built a lead... Once appeared on both sides of the same box score in 1979. Nets acquired him from Philadelphia and a protested game between the two teams was completed after he had changed uniforms.

Year	Team	G	FG	FG Pct.	FT	FT Pct.	Reb.	Ast.	TP	Avg.
1974-75	Philadelphia.	37	41	.554	16	.640	153	21	98	2.6
1975-76	Philadelphia.	75	103	.426	58	.604	520	63	264	3.5
1976-77	Philadelphia.	53	62	.504	33	.702	234	30	157	3.0
1977-78	Philadelphia.	61	70	.393	34	.618	250	34	174	2.9
1978-79	Phil.-N.J.	56	102	.420	60	.769	302	48	264	4.7
1979-80	Milwaukee.	72	97	.398	39	.629	410	82	233	3.2
1980-81	Milwaukee.	77	134	.447	59	.641	473	99	327	4.2
1981-82	Milwaukee.	80	94	.420	41	.594	356	97	229	2.9
1982-83	Milwaukee.	74	90	.457	62	.674	408	77	242	3.3
1983-84	Milwaukee.	69	61	.399	22	.524	271	43	144	2.1
	Totals	654	854	.432	424	.644	3377	594	2132	3.3

NATE ARCHIBALD 36 6-1 165   Guard

Can he come back one more time?. . . Respectable year with Bucks was snuffed out by injury. . . Bucks claimed him on waivers last August. . . Pulled his right hamstring Jan. 5 . . . Tried to come back too soon and tore the muscle March 2. . . Started 46 games before he was sidelined, but he finished season back at ground zero—and without a contract. . .
Once the premier point guard in the league and a model playmaker. . . Born Sept. 2, 1948, in New York City. . . Averaged 3.5 assists per game, which is less than half his career mark. . . Didn't seem to fit into Buck offense, where emphasis is on the move and not on the pass. . . Has played in 876 NBA games. . . People forget what a prolific scorer he was earlier in his career. . . Attended Texas-El Paso.

Year	Team	G	FG	FG Pct.	FT	FT Pct.	Reb.	Ast.	TP	Avg.
1970-71	Cincinnati	82	486	.444	336	.757	242	450	1308	16.0
1971-72	Cincinnati	76	734	.486	677	.822	222	701	2145	28.2
1972-73	K.C.-Omaha	80	1028	.488	663	.847	223	910	2719	34.0
1973-74	K.C.-Omaha	35	222	.451	173	.820	85	266	617	17.6
1974-75	K.C.-Omaha	82	759	.456	652	.872	222	557	2170	26.5
1975-76	Kansas City	78	717	.453	501	.802	213	615	1935	24.8
1976-77	N.Y. Nets	34	250	.446	197	.785	80	254	697	20.5
1977-78	Buffalo.		Injured							
1978-79	Boston.	69	259	.452	242	.788	103	324	760	11.0
1979-80	Boston.	80	383	.482	361	.830	197	671	1131	14.1
1980-81	Boston.	80	382	.499	342	.816	176	618	1106	13.8
1981-82	Boston.	68	308	.472	236	.747	116	531	858	12.6
1982-83	Boston.	66	235	.425	220	.743	91	409	695	10.5
1983-84	Milwaukee.	46	136	.487	64	634	76	160	340	7.4
	Totals	876	5899	.467	4664	.810	2046	6476	16481	18.8

TOP ROOKIE

KENNY FIELDS 22 6-7 225 **Forward**
Major talent who suffered from bad reputation ever since clashing with coach Larry Brown during freshman year at UCLA . . . Bucks took a chance on him at 21st pick, with nothing to lose . . . Probably will be used as reserve behind both Marques Johnson and Alton Lister . . . Played power forward at UCLA, but he's only 6-7 and may have problems getting his inside baskets in pros . . . Averaged 17.4 ppg and 6.9 rpg his senior year . . . Dangerous once he has the ball . . . Impressed people in college all-star games . . . Born Feb. 9, 1962 . . . Raised in Los Angeles.

COACH DON NELSON: Another season, another divisional championship, another near nervous breakdown . . . Nobody takes losing harder . . . Was disgusted with his club after bad start and pronounced it wasn't as good as previous teams . . . When new reserves plus Mike Dunleavy began to contribute, Milwaukee made solid run and won fifth straight division title . . . Got a break when the Nets knocked off the 76ers in the playoffs, but he couldn't perform magic to get by Boston . . . Wants a rest, but doesn't want to abandon coaching forever . . . Got along fine without the capable assistance of former aide and thorn-in-side John Killilea . . . Owns career mark of 374-264 . . . Born May 15, 1940, in Muskegon, Mich. . . . A terrible interview, but a genuinely nice guy off the court . . . Attended Iowa . . . Played forward for five world championship teams with Celtics . . . Learned the art of the psyche-out from the master, Red Auerbach . . . Uses his personnel perfectly . . . Bucks aren't pretty, but they break teams down to one-on-one contests at the end of close games and usually win with experience.

GREATEST FOUL SHOOTER

Flynn Robinson is probably most famous for being traded to Cincinnati with Charlie Paulk for Oscar Robertson in 1970. But by the time he left Milwaukee, Robinson had established himself as the Bucks' all-time greatest free-throw shooter.

Robinson, a 6-1 guard, ranks ninth in the NBA in career free-throw percentage at .849. He hit an amazing 439-of-489 foul shots during the 1969-70 season for a league-leading mark of .898.

Other top foul shooters for Milwaukee have included Junior Bridgeman, Sidney Moncrief, Jim Price and Brian Winters. Bridgeman entered last season ranked 10th in the NBA in career free-throw percentage with .845, but shot only .807 in 1983-84.

"I used to think of myself as one of the best, but don't even ask me about it after the way I was shooting at the start of the season," Bridgeman said. "When things are going right for you, it's so easy. It's just a matter of going up to the line and doing exactly the same thing over and over."

ALL-TIME BUCK LEADERS

SEASON

Points: Kareem Abdul-Jabbar, 2,822, 1971-72
Assists: Oscar Robertson, 668, 1970-71
Rebounds: Kareem Abdul-Jabbar, 1,346, 1971-72

GAME

Points: Kareem Abdul-Jabbar, 55 vs. Boston, 12/10/71
Assists: Guy Rodgers, 22 vs. Detroit, 10/31/68
Rebounds: Swen Nater, 33 vs. Atlanta, 12/19/76

CAREER

Points: Kareem Abdul-Jabbar, 14,211, 1969-75
Assists: Oscar Robertson, 2,156, 1970-74
Rebounds: Kareem Abdul-Jabbar, 7,167, 1969-75

NEW JERSEY NETS

TEAM DIRECTORY: Pres: Fred Lafer; Exec. VP: Lewis Schaffel; GM: Bob MacKinnon; Dir. Pub. Rel.: Jim Lampariello; Coach: Stan Albeck; Asst. Coaches: Herman Kull, John Killilea. Arena: Brendan Byrne Meadowlands Arena (20,149). Colors: Red, white and blue.

SCOUTING REPORT

SHOOTING: Although the Nets shot 49.8 percent from the field last season, they suffer from a lack of perimeter shooting. That problem became apparent in their playoff series against Milwaukee, when the Bucks shut down the Nets' fast break and forced them into a halfcourt game. Stripped of their transition layups, the Nets saw their shooting accuracy slip to 40 percent.

In coach Stan Albeck's offense, Darryl Dawkins plays low post and Buck Williams stays out on the wing. So Dawkins' field-goal percentage was a healthy .593, while Williams' dipped 53 percentage points, to .535. Albert King's stats (.492) don't reflect the peaks and valleys of his outside shot, while Otis Birdsong (.508) is the only Net guard who can consistently hit the 18-foot jumper.

The Nets hope that rookie Jeff Turner will add an outside touch off the bench, but it would help more if Kelvin Ransey (.434) regained his confidence.

And it would help, too, if the Nets can improve their foul

Blue-collar star Buck Williams is chief Net asset.

shooting. Their 70 percent in that department was the worst in the league last year and they spotted the opposition three successful free throws per game.

PLAYMAKING: Ransey led the team in assists last season with an average of 6.0 per game, but he was banished to the bench by playoff time. Micheal Ray Richardson may not be anybody's model of a point guard, but he can push the ball upcourt faster than most. It's his passing that's suspect, not his high dribble. Birdsong is an effective passer off the break, but tends to make only safe, uncreative passes in a halfcourt offense.

Dawkins and Williams are vacuums in the frontcourt. When they get the ball, they usually keep it. That leaves King and Mike O'Koren as the primary feeders in the forecourt, but O'Koren is at his best moving without the ball. Clearly, the Nets could use another playmaking forward.

DEFENSE: Under the guidance of assistant John Killilea, the Nets' defense improved steadily last season and reached maturity in the playoff upset of Philadelphia. There are a lot of mobile players on this team and they are all capable of doubling down low in a pinch.

The Nets blocked 499 shots, the fourth-highest total in the league. In individual matchups, the club has few problems at any position other than small forward and scoring guard. King is often dwarfed by more muscular forwards, so Albeck tries the slower O'Koren against the likes of Marques Johnson. That doesn't always work. Birdsong's defense has improved enormously, but he gives up some quickness. Richardson is a gambler who often gets burned by scoring guards. Darwin Cook (2.0 steals per game) is the stopper.

REBOUNDING: Williams is the best rebounding forward in the game and, largely because of him, the Nets are one of the better rebounding teams. They averaged 1.6 more boards than their opponents, despite getting little help in this category from their small forwards.

When Williams (12.3 rpg) leaves the game, the Nets are suddenly very vulnerable under the boards. Dawkins (6.7 rpg) and Mike Gminski (5.3 rpg) will get their share of rebounds, but they are not dominating centers. Richardson is the best rebounder in a smallish backcourt.

OUTLOOK: The Nets came on strong at the end of last season after a 26-29 start and are one of the league's most exciting teams

NET ROSTER

No.	Veteran	Pos.	Ht.	Wt.	Age	Yrs. Pro	College
10	Otis Birdsong	G	6-4	195	28	8	Houston
12	Darwin Cook	G	6-3	185	28	5	Portland
53	Darryl Dawkins	C	6-11	250	27	10	None
42	Mike Gminski	C	6-11	250	25	5	Duke
33	*Reggie Johnson	F	6-9	205	27	5	Tennessee
55	Albert King	F	6-6	190	24	4	Maryland
31	Mike O'Koren	F	6-7	215	26	5	North Carolina
14	*Kelvin Ransey	G	6-2	185	26	5	Ohio State
20	Micheal R. Richardson	G	6-5	190	29	7	Montana
14	Foots Walker	G	5-11	175	33	11	West Georgia
52	Buck Williams	F	6-8	215	24	4	Maryland
34	*Bill Willoughby	F	6-8	205	27	8	None

*Free agent unsigned at press time

Rd.	Top Draftees	Sel. No.	Ht.	Wt.	College
1	Jeff Turner	17	6-9	230	Vanderbilt
3	Yommy Sangodeyi	63	6-9	230	Sam Houston State
4	Hank Cornley	85	6-7	240	Illinois State
5	Michael Gerren	109	6-6	195	South Alabama
6	Oscar Schmidt	131	6-8	228	Brazil

to watch. But unless Albeck can do something about that inert halfcourt offense, New Jersey cannot compete with clubs like Milwaukee or Boston.

NET PROFILES

OTIS BIRDSONG 28 6-4 195   Guard

Cream finally rose to the top . . . After two injury-plagued seasons, he returned to his All-Star form of past and led team in scoring (19.8 ppg) . . . Was among top scorers in league until strained foot and pulled groin set him back . . . Came off the bench during 12-game stretch and didn't like it . . . Finally began to pay dividends on Nets' $1-million-per-year investment in him . . . Right knee has regained full mobility . . . Made a strong blend with Micheal Ray Richardson at end of season . . . Born Dec. 9, 1955, in Winter Haven, Fla. . . . Attended Houston . . . An odd psychological combination—very cynical, yet very religious . . . Underrated ball-handler (3.9 assists per game) and defender . . . A terrible free-throw shooter who refuses to try jumper from line... Had all sorts of trouble shooting in playoffs against Milwaukee. "Even the layups feel bad," he said.

Year	Team	G	FG	FG Pct.	FT	FT Pct.	Reb.	Ast.	TP	Avg.
1977-78	Kansas City.......	73	470	.492	216	.697	175	174	1156	15.8
1978-79	Kansas City.......	82	741	.509	296	.725	354	281	1778	21.7
1979-80	Kansas City.......	82	781	.505	286	.694	331	202	1858	22.7
1980-81	Kansas City.......	71	710	.544	317	.697	258	233	1747	24.6
1981-82	New Jersey.......	37	225	.469	74	.583	97	124	524	14.2
1982-83	New Jersey.......	62	426	.511	82	.566	150	239	936	15.1
1983-84	New Jersey.......	69	583	.508	194	.608	170	266	1365	19.8
	Totals	476	3936	.510	1465	.673	1535	1519	9364	19.7

ALBERT KING 24 6-6 190   Forward

A streaky, disappointing third year... Went cold in mid-December and was dropped from starting lineup... Got hot in January... Suffered ankle injury in February... Amazingly, he recorded highest field-goal mark of pro career (49.2 percent)... Claimed differently, but demotion to second unit, behind Mike O'Koren, seemed to kill his confidence... Always kills Philadelphia and did so again in playoffs... Disappeared against the Bucks in second round until it was too late... Born Dec. 17, 1959, in Brooklyn, N.Y.... Beautiful, fluid motion on jumper... Can't body up with the crop of bruisers at small forward and became defensive liability... Mild-mannered... Former teammate of Buck Williams at Maryland... Usually gets destroyed in battles with brother Bernard of Knicks... Scoring average dipped more than two points to 14.7 ppg.

Year	Team	G	FG	FG Pct.	FT	FT Pct.	Reb.	Ast.	TP	Avg.
1981-82	New Jersey.......	76	391	.482	133	.778	312	142	918	12.1
1982-83	New Jersey.......	79	582	.475	176	.775	456	291	1346	17.0
1983-84	New Jersey.......	79	465	.492	232	.786	388	203	1165	14.7
	Totals	234	1438	.482	541	.781	1156	636	3429	14.7

DARRYL DAWKINS 27 6-11 250   Center

A giant step closer to potential... His ninth NBA season was by far his best and most consistent... There were still nights when his mind wandered to Thunder Under, but he thrived operating out of Stan Albeck's low-post sets... Set a career high in scoring (16.8 ppg), leading the Nets 21 times in that department... Got to the free-throw line 464 times by slamming way to the hoop . . . Shot 59.3 percent from field . . . Albeck went on pre-season campaign to convince officials Darryl was being persecuted . . . Still was nailed with 386 personals and was disqualified 22 times . . . Born Jan. 23, 1957, in Orlando, Fla. . . . Jumped from high school to Philadelphia 76ers . . . Starting to climb out of financial abyss . . . Held own in playoffs against two nemeses—Moses Malone and Bob Lanier . . . His 6.7-rpg average was big improvement over his 5.2 mark in 1982-83 . . . A favorite in airports, he'll pose with anybody's grandmother.

Year	Team	G	FG	FG Pct.	FT	FT Pct.	Reb.	Ast.	TP	Avg.
1975-76	Philadelphia	37	41	.500	8	.333	49	3	90	2.4
1976-77	Philadelphia	59	135	.628	40	.506	230	24	310	5.3
1977-78	Philadelphia	70	332	.575	156	.709	555	85	820	11.7
1978-79	Philadelphia	78	430	.517	158	.672	631	128	1018	13.1
1979-80	Philadelphia	80	494	.522	190	.653	693	149	1178	14.7
1980-81	Philadelphia	76	423	.607	219	.720	545	109	1065	14.0
1981-82	Philadelphia	48	207	.564	114	.695	305	55	528	11.0
1982-83	New Jersey	81	401	.599	166	.646	420	114	968	12.0
1983-84	New Jersey	81	507	.593	341	.735	541	123	1357	16.8
	Totals	610	2970	.567	1392	.683	3969	790	7334	12.0

BUCK WILLIAMS 24 6-8 215   Forward

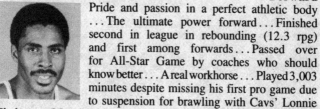

Pride and passion in a perfect athletic body . . . The ultimate power forward . . . Finished second in league in rebounding (12.3 rpg) and first among forwards . . . Passed over for All-Star Game by coaches who should know better . . . A real workhorse . . . Played 3,003 minutes despite missing his first pro game due to suspension for brawling with Cavs' Lonnie Shelton . . . Maryland product was not in top form at start of season . . . Let nagging contract problems affect him psychologically . . . Put troubles behind him in second half and became only ninth player in NBA history to get 1,000 rebounds in first three seasons . . . Reached that plateau by getting 14 boards in final regular-season game against Celtics . . . Born March 8, 1960, in Rocky Mount, N.C. . . . Shot an embarrassing 57.0 percent from line . . . Became tired during second-round playoff series against Milwaukee because Nets had no adequate reserves . . . Still a player to build a franchise around.

Year	Team	G	FG	FG Pct.	FT	FT Pct.	Reb.	Ast.	TP	Avg.
1981-82	New Jersey	82	513	.582	242	.624	1005	107	1268	15.5
1982-83	New Jersey	82	536	.588	324	.620	1027	125	1396	17.0
1983-84	New Jersey	81	495	.535	284	.570	1000	130	1274	15.7
	Totals	245	1544	.568	850	.603	3032	362	3938	16.1

MICHEAL RAY RICHARDSON 29 6-5 190   Guard

More plot turns in his 1983-84 season than in an Agatha Christie novel . . . Was dropped from roster after disappearing from Princeton training camp in October . . . Went through two drug rehab programs and was reinstated by skeptical Nets Dec. 21 . . . Sprained his ankle Jan. 13, a major setback . . . Became a starter at off guard when Otis Birdsong got hurt in late February . . . Switched over to the point when Kelvin Ransey faltered and excelled at his old position . . . His playmaking ability and sheer quickness turned Nets into contender . . . His play in series vs. Philadelphia was an inspiration . . . Born April 11, 1955, in Lubbock, Tex. . . . Teammates resented him upon his return, but he won them over and they voted him full playoff share . . . Still forces the jumper when it's not there and throws up a few too many finger rolls . . . Averaged 14.8 ppg in 25 starts . . . Averaged career-low 2.5 turnovers and tried to play a bit more under control . . . Quick hands create steals on defense, but he gets burned when matched against top scoring guards . . . First-round draft choice of Knicks in 1978 out of Montana.

Year	Team	G	FG	FG Pct.	FT	FT Pct.	Reb.	Ast.	TP	Avg.
1978-79	New York	72	200	.414	69	.539	233	213	469	6.5
1979-80	New York	82	502	.472	223	.660	539	832	1254	15.3
1980-81	New York	79	523	.469	224	.663	545	627	1293	16.4
1981-82	New York	82	619	.461	212	.700	565	572	1469	17.9
1982-83	G.S.-N.J.	64	346	.425	106	.650	295	432	806	12.6
1983-84	New Jersey	48	243	.460	76	.704	172	214	576	12.0
	Totals	427	2433	.455	910	.660	2349	2890	5867	13.7

DARWIN COOK 28 6-3 185   Guard

A perpetual pouter . . . Stock slipped last season and it showed in his decreased playing time (1,870) . . . Started first 25 games at point guard, where he was completely out of place . . . Demoted to third guard behind Kelvin Ransey and then Micheal Ray Richardson . . . Still a top defender who led Nets in steals for second year in row (2.0 per game) . . . Has missed only one game in four seasons with Nets . . . Has a remarkable way of sabotaging fast breaks . . . A streak shooter from the outside . . . No layup is a sure thing . . . Born Aug. 6, 1956, in Los Angeles . . . Has been trade bait for past three seasons . . . Plenty of teams interested in him as a defensive stopper . . . Got a $250,000-per-year contract and is no longer underpaid . . . Originally a fourth-round draft choice by Detroit in

1980 . . . Scotty Robertson, then coach of Pistons, dropped University of Portland grad and spent next two years insisting it wasn't a mistake.

Year	Team	G	FG	FG Pct.	FT	FT Pct.	Reb.	Ast.	TP	Avg.
1980-81	New Jersey	81	383	.468	132	.733	236	297	904	11.2
1981-82	New Jersey	82	387	.482	118	.728	156	319	899	11.0
1982-83	New Jersey	82	446	.449	186	.769	240	448	1080	13.2
1983-84	New Jersey	82	304	.443	95	.754	156	356	714	8.7
	Totals	327	1520	.461	531	.748	787	1420	3597	11.0

MIKE GMINSKI 25 6-11 250   Center

A man with a niche . . . The perfect backup, nothing more, nothing less . . . Fundamentally sound, but as graceful as a soda machine . . . Can't jump and has bad hands . . . Lost his shooting touch when he left Duke, but muscled up and has been able to hold his own under boards . . . Not very durable, yet he played in all 82 games . . . Averaged 5.3 rpg . . . Doesn't commit stupid fouls . . . Says he grew a beard because "black guys are scared of white guys with beards." . . . Born Aug. 3, 1959, in Monroe, Conn. . . . Had trouble at start of season adjusting to Stan Albeck's erratic substitution policies . . . Likes to know when he's getting into game instead of waiting for Darryl Dawkins to get into foul trouble . . . Picked seventh in 1980 draft, ahead of Andrew Toney.

Year	Team	G	FG	FG Pct.	FT	FT Pct.	Reb.	Ast.	TP	Avg.
1980-81	New Jersey	56	291	.423	155	.767	419	72	737	13.2
1981-82	New Jersey	64	119	.441	97	.822	186	41	335	5.2
1982-83	New Jersey	80	213	.500	175	.778	382	61	601	7.5
1983-84	New Jersey	82	237	.513	147	.799	433	92	621	7.6
	Totals	282	860	.466	574	.787	1420	266	2294	8.1

MIKE O'KOREN 26 6-7 215   Forward

If only he could shoot . . . Milks his other talents to the maximum . . . Moves well without the ball, can play defense against taller opponents, operates well in open court . . . Took over starting small forward role in February, when it looked like Stan Albeck had forgotten his name . . . Team immediately won 11 of 12 games . . . Can't leap and isn't much of a rebounder . . . Born Feb. 7, 1958, in Jersey City, N.J. . . . Albeck, like Larry Brown before him, gave up trying him at guard . . . An active social life . . . Loves pro wrestling . . . Attended North Carolina . . . Played effective defense against Julius Erving during playoffs, but didn't have much success against Marques Johnson in second-round disaster.

Year	Team	G	FG	FG Pct.	FT	FT Pct.	Reb.	Ast.	TP	Avg.
1980-81	New Jersey	79	365	.486	135	.637	478	252	870	11.0
1981-82	New Jersey	80	383	.492	135	.714	305	192	909	11.4
1982-83	New Jersey	46	136	.525	34	.708	114	82	308	6.7
1983-84	New Jersey	73	186	.483	53	.609	175	95	430	5.9
	Totals	278	1070	.492	357	.666	1072	621	2517	9.1

BILL WILLOUGHBY 27 6-8 205   Forward

The expectations finally match the performance... Will never be player they thought he'd be when he came to NBA straight out of high school in 1975, but he's an adequate spot player... Great leaper... A spectacular dunker, when he gets the chance... Doesn't follow playbook, which hurts his chances... Stan Albeck didn't trust him in the playoffs... Born May 20, 1957, in Englewood, N.J.... Played in 67 games, the third-highest total of his disappointing career... His 48.1-percent shooting mark was one of his best... A rarity as a Net who knows how to shoot free throws... Actually started at guard one night when injuries made Nets desperate... Plays it one year at a time... Has the athletic talent, but has never gotten it together.

Year	Team	G	FG	FG Pct.	FT	FT Pct.	Reb.	Ast.	TP	Avg.
1975-76	Atlanta	62	113	.398	66	.660	288	31	292	4.7
1976-77	Atlanta	39	75	.444	43	.683	170	13	193	4.9
1977-78	Buffalo	56	156	.430	64	.800	219	38	376	6.7
1979-80	Cleveland	78	219	.479	96	.756	329	72	535	6.9
1980-81	Houston	55	150	.523	49	.766	227	64	349	6.3
1981-82	Houston	69	240	.517	56	.727	264	75	539	7.8
1982-83	S.A.-N.J.	62	147	.454	43	.782	201	64	343	5.5
1983-84	New Jersey	67	124	.481	55	.873	193	56	303	4.5
	Totals	488	1224	.470	472	.750	1891	413	2930	6.0

REGGIE JOHNSON 27 6-9 205   Forward

Fodder for the bruisers... Nets picked up Tennessee product from Philadelphia for cash three days before start of season... Was used more early in the season... Started three games at small forward in December, averaging 11 ppg and 4 rpg in that span... Not really quick enough to play small forward, not strong enough for power forward... Born June 25, 1957, in Atlanta... Last season marked first time since his rookie year that he spent entire 82 games with the same team... Knows his place on the bench . . . Never complains about lack of playing time . . . Tough to pin down his game . . . A little of this, a little of that, not quite enough of anything.

Year	Team	G	FG	FG Pct.	FT	FT Pct.	Reb.	Ast.	TP	Avg.
1980-81	San Antonio	79	340	.499	128	.663	358	78	808	10.2
1981-82	S.A.-Clev.-K.C.	75	351	.530	118	.756	451	73	820	10.9
1982-83	K.C.-Phil.	79	247	.485	95	.731	291	71	590	7.5
1983-84	New Jersey	72	127	.496	92	.730	138	40	346	4.8
	Totals	305	1065	.505	433	.716	1238	262	2564	8.4

KELVIN RANSEY 26 6-2 185   Guard

Dallas coach Dick Motta was right . . . Just doesn't have it . . . Basketball people say it's his heart, but he also may not be as talented as folks said he was when he first came out of Ohio State . . . Hard-luck season . . . Father died right before season opener, so he missed first two games and didn't crack starting lineup until Dec. 22 . . . When Micheal Ray Richardson proved himself at the point, he was demoted from starter to fourth guard . . . Lost all confidence in playmaking skills by end of season . . . Born May 3, 1958, in Toledo, Ohio . . . Played only garbage minutes after embarrassing himself in first three playoff games . . . Nets weren't certain of his status at end of season, when he became free agent . . . A streak shooter who gives up a lot of points on defense . . . Religion has carried him through.

Year	Team	G	FG	FG Pct.	FT	FT Pct.	Reb.	Ast.	TP	Avg.
1980-81	Portland	80	525	.452	164	.749	195	555	1217	15.2
1981-82	Portland	78	504	.460	242	.761	186	555	1253	16.1
1982-83	Dallas	76	343	.460	152	.764	147	280	840	11.1
1983-84	New Jersey	80	304	.434	145	.792	127	483	760	9.5
	Totals	314	1676	.453	703	.765	655	1873	4070	13.0

FOOTS WALKER 33 5-11 175   Guard

Mascot and cheerleader . . . Rejoined team as free agent one day before opener . . . Nets had traded him along with first-round pick to Dallas for Kelvin Ransey in offseason . . . Stan Albeck kept raving about how smart he was, but used him only when desperate . . . Suffered strained ligaments in knee after collision with Dominique Wilkins in opener and missed 25 games with injury . . . During a nine-game stretch in January and February, he averaged 17.2 minutes and 4.0 assists . . . Then it was bench time again . . . Born May 21, 1951, in Southampton, L.I. . . . Nickname came from size-11 shoes he wore in elementary school... Has another year on contract, so Nets may find a place for him... Attended Vincennes JC and West Georgia College.

Year	Team	G	FG	FG Pct.	FT	FT Pct.	Reb.	Ast.	TP	Avg.
1974-75	Cleveland	72	111	.404	80	.684	146	192	302	4.2
1975-76	Cleveland	81	143	.388	84	.778	182	288	370	4.6
1976-77	Cleveland	62	157	.450	89	.774	160	254	403	6.5
1977-78	Cleveland	81	287	.448	159	.719	294	453	733	9.0
1978-79	Cleveland	55	208	.464	137	.783	198	321	353	10.1
1979-80	Cleveland	76	258	.454	195	.802	287	607	712	9.4
1980-81	New Jersey	41	72	.426	88	.793	102	253	234	5.7
1981-82	New Jersey	77	156	.413	141	.727	150	398	456	5.9
1982-83	New Jersey	79	114	.456	116	.779	136	264	346	4.4
1983-84	New Jersey	34	32	.356	24	.889	31	81	90	2.6
	Totals	658	1538	.435	1113	.762	1686	3111	4199	6.4

TOP ROOKIE

JEFF TURNER 22 6-9 230   Forward
Nets really stuck their necks out... Wasn't rated in anybody else's top 20, but they picked this Vanderbilt star No. 17 overall... His stock soared during Olympic tryouts, because of Bobby Knight's recommendation... Slow and not much of a ball-handler, but has nice touch and good court awareness... Left-handed shot... Will see some time behind Buck Williams... They say he's "Scott Wedman type"... Born April 9, 1962... Raised in Brandon, Fla.

COACH STAN ALBECK: Made it through rollercoaster season... The rest may be gravy... When Nets were struggling with 26-29 mark, his erratic substitution policies became focus of attacks from players and reporters... When team turned it around and beat Philadelphia in playoffs, all was forgiven... Took him a while to get adjusted to cynical fans in northeast... Another center—this time Darryl Dawkins—blossomed under his reins... Not an autocrat... Relies on input from assistants... Has two years left on $250,000-per-year contract... His even-tempered nature was welcome change from Larry Brown... Born May 17, 1931, in Chenora, Ill.... Paid his dues in 11 years as head coach at Northern Michigan and then as an assistant with four different pro teams... Roots against San Antonio and former boss Angelo Drossos... Has NBA career record of 235-175... One of the guys off the court, but won't talk about his basketball policies with players.

GREATEST FOUL SHOOTER

The Nets have had only two truly great free-throw shooters during their short history and both players were merely passing through in the midst of outstanding careers. While the club was still in the ABA, Rick Barry played two seasons with the Nets and posted free-throw percentages of .890 and .878.

The Nets' best free-throw shooter since joining the NBA in 1976 has been Mike Newlin, the somewhat flaky guard who played for the Nets during the team's "dark ages," in 1979-80 and 1980-81. Newlin averaged .886 from the line during those two years, despite some strange theories about the art of the free throw.

"I always know when I'm going to start missing, because that happens as soon as I start feeling too confident up there," Newlin once said. "When I start slumping a little and I'm forced to work on the shot again, I'm going to be all right."

Neither Newlin—stylistically conventional—nor Barry—an underhanded shooter—holds the club record for consecutive free throws. That honor belongs to one-time Rutgers star Bob Lloyd, who converted 49 straight during the club's inaugural season in 1968.

ALL-TIME NET LEADERS

SEASON

Points: Rick Barry, 2,518, 1971-72
Assists: Kevin Porter, 801, 1977-78
Rebounds: Billy Paultz, 1,035, 1971-72

GAME

Points: Julius Erving, 63 vs. San Diego (4 OT), 2/14/75
Assists: Kevin Porter, 29 vs. Houston, 2/24/78
Rebounds: Billy Paultz, 33 vs. Pittsburgh, 2/17/71

CAREER

Points: John Williamson, 7,202, 1973-77, 1978-80
Assists: Billy Melchionni, 2,251, 1969-75
Rebounds: Buck Williams, 3,032, 1981-84

NEW YORK KNICKS

TEAM DIRECTORY: Pres.: Jack Krumpe; Exec. VP-Dir. Basketball Oper.: Dave DeBusschere; VP-Dir. Player Personnel: Eddie Donovan; Dir. Communications: To be named; Coach: Hubie Brown; Asst. Coaches: Rick Pitino, Rich Adubato. Arena: Madison Square Garden (19,591). Colors: Orange and blue.

SCOUTING REPORT

SHOOTING: By the end of last season, the Knicks had become so dependent on Bernard King's scoring that the boxscores were incredibly skewed. And yet, the Knicks were winning. That's because King scores his 26.3 ppg within coach Hubie Brown's offensive system. Bernard doesn't force the drive or pull up for the shot when he doesn't have an opening. His remarkable 57.2-percent field-goal average attests to that.

Outside of King, the Knick offense is a bit of this and a bit of that. Bill Cartwright (.561) cannot be ignored or he'll burn you with his short fadeaways and mid-range jumpers. Ray Williams (.445) is a streak shooter, much like Trent Tucker (.500) and Rory Sparrow (.474). When Truck Robinson (.489) comes to play, he can still hit turnarounds and get his tip-ins. Unfortunately, he has become disillusioned with the King-oriented offense and rarely puts on his game face. Free-agent signee Pat Cummings, who shot .494 for the Mavs, can hit a mid-range jumper and should be a help.

PLAYMAKING: The chief job of a playmaker on the Knicks is to get the ball to King, preferably isolated on his man. Sparrow (6.8 assists per game) fulfills this role sufficiently, but brings little else to the point. Then again, he is under the close scrutiny of Brown, which is enough to dim any player's creativity.

For some strange reason, Williams is often given the ball to handle late in games. He can pass the ball, but he is just as likely to throw it away or force a shot. Darrell Walker may be the best point guard of the bunch, but Brown is planning to use him as much as possible at off guard.

King is probably the most natural passer of the forwards but, since he can't toss the ball to himself, he isn't an effective playmaker.

DEFENSE: While Brown's offensive sets and strategies may be questioned, the coach's defensive philosophy is redoubtable. The

Bill Cartwright used his soft touch to average 17.0 ppg.

KNICK ROSTER

No.	Veteran	Pos.	Ht.	Wt.	Age	Yrs. Pro	College
25	Bill Cartwright	C	7-1	240	27	6	San Francisco
42	Pat Cummings	C-F	6-9	235	28	6	Cincinnati
44	Len Elmore	F	6-9	220	32	11	Maryland
45	*Eric Fernsten	C-F	6-10	205	30	7	San Francisco
18	Ernie Grunfeld	F-G	6-6	215	29	8	Tennessee
30	Bernard King	F	6-7	205	27	8	Tennessee
55	Louis Orr	F	6-9	200	26	5	Syracuse
23	Len Robinson	F	6-7	225	33	11	Tennessee State
2	Rory Sparrow	G	6-2	175	26	5	Villanova
6	Trent Tucker	G	6-5	193	24	3	Minnesota
4	Darrell Walker	G	6-4	180	23	2	Arkansas
40	Marvin Webster	C	7-1	225	32	10	Morgan State
13	*Ray Williams	G	6-2	190	30	8	Minnesota

*Free agent unsigned at press time

Rd.	Top Draftees	Sel. No.	Ht.	Wt.	College
3	Curtis Green	64	6-1	175	Southern Mississippi
4	Bob Thornton	87	6-10	225	Cal-Irvine
6	Eddie Wilkins	133	6-10	210	Gardner Webb
7	Ken Bannister	156	6-9	230	St. Augustine (N.C.)
8	Ricky Tunstall	179	7-0	240	Youngstown State

Knicks ranked third in the league last season in points yielded (103.0 ppg), trailing only tortoise-like Atlanta and Milwaukee. The Knicks managed this despite the lack of a shot-blocker in the starting unit and a lack of size at forward.

Brown's trapping defense is the best in the league. It is run most effectively with kamikaze guards Williams (2.1 steals per game) and Walker (2.3 steals per game) on the court, but even Sparrow and Tucker are adequate for the task. The Knicks averaged exactly one steal more per game than their opponents last year, forcing other teams to eat up time on the 24-second clock while fighting their way past midcourt. Western clubs seem particularly bothered by the pressure.

Brown's teams can get away with pressing so hard for so long because the coach uses two complete units to give his players adequate rest.

REBOUNDING: Although nobody would quarrel with the fact the Knicks need a quality power forward, they did all right for themselves last season under the boards. They outrebounded opponents by 1.2 boards per game, despite giving up inches almost everywhere. Centers Bill Cartwright and Marvin Webster had a total of 1,015 rebounds, while Robinson, King, Louis Orr and

Williams all chipped in to keep opponents honest. Cummings is being counted on to be a force on the boards.

OUTLOOK: The Knicks are a team with a great deal of potential, because they would be so tremendously improved with the addition of that elusive power forward. For the time being, however, they remain the "Bernie and Hubie Show." King is in charge of the offense. Brown is in charge of the defense. There have been few changes. The Knicks should finish third or fourth in the Atlantic Division.

KNICK PROFILES

BERNARD KING 27 6-7 205   Forward

God at the Garden... Had a great first half of season, then dwarfed that effort with incomparable second half... Fifth-leading scorer in league, which is deceiving... Climbed from 21.5-ppg pace Dec. 18 to final average of 26.3 ppg... Began his tear after All-Star break, when he had back-to-back 50-point games at San Antonio and Dallas... Amazingly, he scores all those points within Hubie Brown's offense... The only reason the Knicks carried Boston to seven games... His baseline popper is unstoppable... Elected captain in midseason and took role to heart... Born Dec. 4, 1956, in Brooklyn, N.Y.... Wants teammates to contribute more on offense... Shot 57.2 percent from field in regular season... Dueled with Larry Bird for MVP award and in playoff series... Dropped out of Tennessee after junior year and was picked No. 7 by Nets in draft... Net ownership thought he was too risky and sent him to Utah, where his drinking problem caught up with him... Knicks got him from Warriors for Micheal Ray Richardson and obviously got better of deal... Scored 23 consecutive points for his team in Game 2 of playoff series vs. Pistons.

Year	Team	G	FG	FG Pct.	FT	FT Pct.	Reb.	Ast.	TP	Avg.
1977-78	New Jersey	79	798	.479	313	.677	751	193	1909	24.2
1978-79	New Jersey	82	710	.522	349	.564	669	295	1769	21.6
1979-80	Utah	19	71	.518	34	.540	88	52	176	9.3
1980-81	Golden State	81	731	.588	307	.703	551	287	1771	21.9
1981-82	Golden State	79	740	.566	352	.705	469	282	1833	23.2
1982-83	New York	68	603	.528	280	.722	326	195	1486	21.9
1983-84	New York	77	795	.572	437	.779	394	164	2027	26.3
	Totals	485	4448	.539	2072	.684	3248	1468	10971	22.6

BILL CARTWRIGHT 27 7-1 240 Center

"Mr. Bill"...Complain all you want, but only the elite post better numbers...Averaged 17.0 ppg and 8.4 rpg...Will never be the schoolyard bully, but he won't embarrass himself...Was only Knick who consistently gave Bernard King some help on offense...Scored careerhigh 38 points March 27 against Dallas...Led team in scoring 15 times...Has career fieldgoal mark of 56 percent, ranking him fifth among NBA's all-time shooters...Born July 30, 1957, in Folsom, Cal....One of the most boring interviews in NBA, but he has patience with hostile reporters...Dubbed "Invisi-Bill" because of his reluctance to take ball to the hoop...USF grad still prefers to pull up for five-foot pop instead of going over opponent and drawing a foul.

Year	Team		FG	FG Pct.	FT	FT Pct.	Reb.	Ast.	TP	Avg.
1979-80	New York		665	.547	451	.797	726	165	1781	21.7
1980-81	New York	82	619	.554	408	.788	613	111	1646	20.1
1981-82	New York	72	390	.562	257	.763	421	87	1037	14.4
1982-83	New York	82	455	.566	380	.744	590	136	1290	15.7
1983-84	New York	77	453	.561	404	.805	649	107	1310	17.0
	Totals	395	2582	.557	1900	.781	2999	606	7064	17.9

RAY WILLIAMS 30 6-2 190 Guard

Strap yourself in...The most frightening rollercoaster in the league...He and Hubie Brown are like oil and water...Free agent wants out of New York again...Played with first unit for 63 games, but probably was most effective with fellow kamikaze Darrell Walker on second team...Put on his usual playoff face, disappearing against Detroit and then giving up-and-down performance against Boston...Had 162 steals, but led team with 274 personals and 219 turnovers...Born Oct. 14, 1954, in Mt. Vernon, N.Y....Attended Minnesota...Good player to have around when you need a big lift...Bad player to have around when you're protecting a tight lead...Brother of Seattle's Gus...Hit

25 three-point shots, some of which he took under inadvisable circumstances.

Year	Team	G	FG	FG Pct.	FT	FT Pct.	Reb.	Ast.	TP	Avg.
1977-78	New York	81	305	.443	146	.705	209	363	756	9.3
1978-79	New York	81	575	.457	251	.802	291	504	1401	17.3
1979-80	New York	82	687	.496	333	.787	412	512	1714	20.9
1980-81	New York	79	616	.461	312	.817	321	432	1560	19.7
1981-82	New Jersey	82	639	.462	387	.832	325	488	1674	20.4
1982-83	Kansas City	72	419	.392	256	.769	327	569	1109	15.4
1983-84	New York	76	418	.445	263	.827	267	449	1124	14.8
	Totals	553	3659	.454	1948	.798	2152	3317	9338	16.9

LEN (TRUCK) ROBINSON 33 6-7 225   Forward

If he remains a Knick, nobody will be happy ...Wants out because he claims he's not part of offense..."I can still play, but I need more than two or three shots a game," he says...Got fed up and stopped playing around midseason...Hubie Brown had nobody else at power forward spot...Sat out a month with a mild ankle sprain in what appeared to be a protest...Season average of 10.8 ppg was nowhere near his old Phoenix marks...Born Oct. 4, 1951, in Jacksonville, Fla. ...Attended Tennessee State...Averaged 8.4 rpg but Knicks never knew on what nights he'd get them...Had one of his best halves of season in Game 7 against the Celtics, scoring 14 points and grabbing eight rebounds...Then, you guessed it, he disappeared in the second half...Hubie must wish he never gave up Maurice Lucas for him.

Year	Team	G	FG	FG Pct.	FT	FT Pct.	Reb.	Ast.	TP	Avg.
1974-75	Washington	76	191	.486	60	.522	301	40	442	5.8
1975-76	Washington	82	354	.454	211	.672	557	113	919	11.2
1976-77	Wash.-Atl.	77	574	.478	314	.730	828	142	1462	19.0
1977-78	New Orleans	82	748	.444	366	.640	1288	171	1862	22.7
1978-79	N.O.-Phoe.	69	566	.491	324	.701	802	113	1456	21.1
1979-80	Phoenix	82	545	.512	325	.667	770	142	1415	17.3
1980-81	Phoenix	82	647	.505	249	.629	789	206	1543	18.8
1981-82	Phoenix	74	579	.513	255	.687	721	179	1414	19.1
1982-83	New York	81	326	.462	118	.587	657	145	770	9.5
1983-84	New York	65	284	.489	133	.646	545	94	701	10.8
	Totals	770	4814	.483	2355	.663	7258	1345	11984	15.6

RORY SPARROW 26 6-2 175   Guard

Most overpaid player in league... He's not bad, but the guy makes $600,000 per season... His shot deserted him for stretches of games... Seemed to have trouble concentrating... Much steadier than backcourt mate Ray Williams and much less explosive... Started 74 games and averaged 6.9 assists per game ... Opponents could afford to play him dishonestly in order to double up on Bernard King... Quick-footed, but doesn't gamble much on defense... Born June 12, 1958, in Suffolk, Va.... Fourth-round pick by Nets in 1980, out of Villanova... Spent most of rookie year in the Continental League ... Was already making plans to become an engineer when Kevin Loughery gave him second life in Atlanta... Celtics made him the incredible contract offer and Knicks felt they had to match it.

Year	Team	G	FG	FG Pct.	FT	FT Pct.	Reb.	Ast.	TP	Avg.
1980-81	New Jersey	15	22	.349	12	.750	18	32	56	3.7
1981-82	Atlanta	82	366	.501	124	.838	224	424	857	10.5
1982-83	Atl.-N.Y.	81	392	.484	147	.739	230	397	936	11.6
1983-84	New York	79	350	.474	108	.824	189	539	818	10.4
	Totals	257	1130	.483	391	.791	661	1392	2667	10.4

LOUIS ORR 26 6-9 200   Forward

Gets most out of matchstick body... Overmatched at power forward, where he gives up as much as 40 pounds to opponents... Started 20 games, most of them when Truck Robinson was injured... A durable player who has missed just six games in four seasons ... Shot comes and goes... Born May 7, 1958, in Cincinnati... Part of "Louie and Bouie Show" at Syracuse, along with center Roosevelt Bouie... Gets almost half his rebounds at offensive end, where he gets excellent position... Scored season-high 25 points and had 10 rebounds against Phoenix Mar. 13... Shooting percentage of .458 was lowest in his four-year pro career... A smart, dedicated player who should be NBA reserve for seasons to come.

Year	Team	G	FG	FG Pct.	FT	FT Pct.	Reb.	Ast.	TP	Avg.
1980-81	Indiana	82	348	.491	163	.807	361	132	859	10.5
1981-82	Indiana	80	357	.497	203	.799	331	134	918	11.5
1982-83	New York	82	274	.462	140	.800	228	94	688	8.4
1983-84	New York	78	262	.458	173	.820	228	61	697	8.9
	Totals	322	1241	.479	679	.806	1148	421	3162	9.8

TRENT TUCKER 24 6-5 193   Guard

How long can director of operations Dave DeBusschere keep him in New York?... Hubie Brown wanted him out after 1982-83, but was overruled... Came on strong late last season, starting 21 games... In final nine games, he hit 67 percent from floor and averaged 12.8 points... A pure shooter who simply can't— or won't—drive to the hoop... Went to foul line only 33 times, an amazing stat that says it all... Born Dec. 20, 1959, in Tarboro, N.C.... Will always be remembered as the player the Knicks picked in the first round of the 1982 draft instead of Clark Kellogg... Decent hands... Hubie called him a "marshmallow" in his rookie year and he's never recovered ... Nobody cheats on this Minnesota grad defensively, except to overplay him.

Year	Team	G	FG	FG Pct.	FT	FT Pct.	Reb.	Ast.	TP	Avg.
1982-83	New York	78	299	.462	43	.672	216	195	655	8.4
1983-84	New York	63	225	.500	25	.758	130	138	481	7.6
	Totals	141	524	.478	68	.701	346	333	1136	8.1

MARVIN WEBSTER 32 7-1 225   Center

More of the same... One-dimensional reserve center who can play solid defense for stretches of about 10 minutes at a time... "The Human Eraser"... The constant criticisms of his offensive shortcomings have started to wear at him... Spent a couple of weeks in the hospital in March due to exhaustion... Had played in 333 consecutive games before that... Born April 13, 1952, in Baltimore... Led team in blocked shots for the third straight season, with 100... Has been with the Knicks longer than any other current player... Still isn't popular in New York... Ceded his captaincy to Bernard King... Had a bad season offensively —even for him— with .469 shooting percentage and 3.8-ppg average.

Year	Team	G	FG	FG Pct.	FT	FT Pct.	Reb.	Ast.	TP	Avg.
1975-76	Denver (ABA)	38	55	.458	55	.705	174	30	165	4.3
1976-77	Denver	80	198	.495	143	.650	484	62	539	6.7
1977-78	Seattle	82	427	.502	290	.629	1035	203	1144	14.0
1978-79	New York	60	264	.473	150	.573	655	172	678	11.3
1979-80	New York	20	38	.481	12	.750	80	9	88	4.4
1980-81	New York	82	159	.466	104	.638	465	72	423	5.2
1981-82	New York	82	199	.491	108	.635	490	99	506	6.2
1982-83	New York	82	168	.508	106	.589	443	49	442	5.4
1983-84	New York	76	112	.469	66	.564	366	53	290	3.8
	Totals	602	1620	.487	1034	.620	4192	749	4275	7.1

DARRELL WALKER 23 6-4 180 Guard

Check for your wallet... Had 127 steals, a rookie record... Doesn't lack confidence... Will gamble at the drop of a hat... Stole six passes from the 76ers Jan. 9, scoring 19 points in that game... A volatile player who had a couple of shouting matches with Hubie Brown during practices... Can leap with Bucks' Sidney Moncrief... Only disappointment was that his jumper wasn't quite as good as advertised... Born March 6, 1961, in Chicago... Had 15 assists against Spurs Jan. 31... Not coincidentally, Bernard King had 50 points that night... Brought the Knicks back from almost certain defeat in playoff opener against Detroit... Drafted 12th overall in 1983... Was Arkansas' seventh-ranked all-time scorer with 1,326 points in three seasons... Posted 18.2-ppg average in his senior year.

Year	Team	G	FG	FG Pct.	FT	FT Pct.	Reb.	Ast.	TP	Avg.
1983-84	New York	82	216	.417	208	.791	167	284	644	7.9

ERIC FERNSTEN 30 6-10 205 Center-Forward

Quintessential journeyman... Had to wonder why Knicks bothered with him, instead of carrying younger reserve... Hubie Brown seemed to forget about him by end of season and he rotted on bench during playoffs... Had strong preseason and a couple of strong games in regular season... Scored 11 points at Milwaukee Jan. 13 and had three steals, five rebounds and seven points Mar. 3 against Seattle... Born Nov. 1, 1953, in Oakland... Has hung on by skin of teeth after being picked in fourth round of 1975 draft by Cleveland... Played in Italy, averaging 17.6 ppg in 1977-78 and 15.1 ppg in 1978-79 for Siena... Won a championship ring with Celtics in 1980-81, when he appeared in 45 games... A banger on defense... Was Kurt Rambis type before it became fashionable... Attended USF.

Year	Team	G	FG	FG Pct.	FT	FT Pct.	Reb.	Ast.	TP	Avg.
1975-76	Cle.-Chi.	37	33	.384	26	.703	70	19	92	2.5
1976-77	Chicago	5	3	.200	8	.727	16	6	14	2.8
1979-80	Boston	56	71	.464	33	.635	96	28	175	3.1
1980-81	Boston	45	38	.481	20	.667	62	10	96	2.1
1981-82	Boston	43	19	.388	19	.633	42	8	57	1.3
1983-84	New York	32	29	.558	25	.735	86	11	83	2.6
	Totals	218	193	.445	131	.675	372	82	516	2.4

LEN ELMORE 32 6-9 220   Forward

His season never materialized...Knicks acquired him from Nets as insurance at power forward and center...Even he had to admit the legs just weren't there anymore...Played in 65 games, but logged only 832 minutes ...Started five games after Truck Robinson sprained wrist Jan. 7, but showed little...A distinguished eight-year career as solid reserve is about to end...Born March 28, 1952, in New York, N.Y....An ABA survivor who played with Pacers...Drafted by Indiana in first round of 1972 draft, he decided to finish his senior year at Maryland before starting pro career...Has a career in business all mapped out and ready to go...Had his best season in pros as starting center with Nets in 1981-82...Club intellectual...He'll do all right in life after basketball.

Year	Team	G	FG	FG Pct.	FT	FT Pct.	Reb.	Ast.	TP	Avg.
1974-75	Indiana (ABA)	77	218	.417	72	.774	395	35	509	6.6
1975-76	Indiana (ABA)	76	480	.402	152	.738	819	122	1112	14.6
1976-77	Indiana	6	7	.412	4	.800	15	2	18	3.0
1977-78	Indiana	69	142	.368	88	.667	420	80	372	5.4
1978-79	Indiana	80	139	.406	56	.718	402	75	334	4.2
1979-80	Kansas City	58	104	.430	51	.689	257	64	259	4.5
1980-81	Milwaukee	72	76	.358	54	.720	208	69	206	2.9
1981-82	New Jersey	81	300	.460	135	.794	441	100	735	9.1
1982-83	New Jersey	74	97	.398	54	.643	238	39	248	3.4
1983-84	New York	65	64	.408	27	.711	165	30	155	2.4
	Totals	658	1627	.410	693	.726	3360	616	3948	6.0

ERNIE GRUNFELD 29 6-6 215   Forward-Guard

Elegant, he ain't...Played fewest minutes of his NBA career, resulting in career lows in almost every statistical category...Slow as an ox and built that way, too...Has a way of hitting the big jumper coming off the bench...Can play off guard or small forward...Started season strong, scoring 13 points in opener against Cleveland and 16 points against San Diego Nov. 11...By end of the season, he couldn't crack the top two units at guard...Born April 24, 1955, in Romania...Signed in 1982 as free agent...Played with Bernard

King at Tennessee, where their act was known as "The Bernie and Ernie Show"... Sneaked into 76 games.

Year	Team	G	FG	FG Pct.	FT	FT Pct.	Reb.	Ast.	TP	Avg.
1977-78	Milwaukee........	73	204	.443	94	.657	194	145	502	6.9
1978-79	Milwaukee........	82	326	.493	191	.761	360	216	843	10.3
1979-80	Kansas City.......	80	186	.443	101	.771	232	109	474	5.9
1980-81	Kansas City.......	79	260	.535	75	.743	206	205	595	7.5
1981-82	Kansas City.......	81	420	.511	188	.821	182	276	1030	12.7
1982-83	New York........	77	167	.443	81	.827	163	136	415	5.4
1983-84	New York........	76	166	.459	64	.771	121	108	398	5.2
	Totals	548	1729	.482	794	.766	1458	1195	4257	7.8

PAT CUMMINGS 28 6-9 235   Forward-Center

Signed four-year, $2.5-million contract with Knicks as free agent... Is being overpaid by New York after being overmatched as a stop-gap center for the Mavericks the last two years... Didn't like it and club didn't like it—but he got the job done... Didn't score inside because of lack of height, but he did damage with a good perimeter shot... Mavs' leading rebounder (8.2 rpg)... Will thrive at power forward... Born July 11, 1956, in Johnstown, Pa.... Attended Cincinnati... A second-round draft choice in 1979 by Milwaukee, where he spent three very unheralded seasons... Very slow, but he's willing to do what's asked.

Year	Team	G	FG	FG Pct.	FT	FT Pct.	Reb.	Ast.	TP	Avg.
1979-80	Milwaukee........	71	187	.505	94	.764	238	53	468	6.6
1980-81	Milwaukee........	74	248	.539	99	.707	292	62	595	8.0
1981-82	Milwaukee........	78	219	.509	67	.736	245	99	505	6.5
1982-83	Dallas	81	433	.493	148	.755	668	144	1014	12.5
1983-84	Dallas	80	452	.494	141	.742	658	158	1045	13.1
	Totals	384	1539	.504	549	.742	2101	516	3627	9.4

TOP ROOKIE

CURTIS GREEN 22 6-1 175   Guard

Third-round choice will have to fight for roster spot... Knicks already deep at playmaking position... Best player on lousy Southern

Mississippi team...Averaged 16.0 ppg and 3.7 assists per game
in senior year...Quick and has good shot...Size could be a
problem..."I never thought I was good enough for the NBA. But
last year a few scouts began to watch me play and I began to
wonder," he said...Born June 30, 1962...Raised in Memphis,
Tenn.

COACH HUBIE BROWN: Fit another lifetime into a season...Kicked things off by infuriating fellow
coaches with *Sports Illustrated* interview
in which he called Billy Cunningham "a
child" and Stan Albeck "a washerwoman"
...Suffered attack of angina during preseason
that had everyone worried...Was told to take
things easy, which is like telling Moses Malone
to stop rebounding...Knicks made his season
in two stretches...From Jan. 24 to Feb. 18, they went 11-1...Then
in playoffs, they nipped Pistons and carried Celtics to seven
games...Utilizes two-unit system with traps on defense
...Alienated several players who claimed he went to Bernard
King too often on set plays...Born Sept. 25, 1933, in Elizabeth,
N.J....NBA coaching record is now 290-281, so critics no longer
can say he's a sub-.500 coach...Will his abrasiveness wear well
on players over the long term?...Not exactly a drinking buddy
of director of operations Dave DeBusschere...Took Kentucky to
ABA championship in 1974-75, then spent five years coaching
Atlanta...Came to Knicks for 1982-83 season...Most valuable
Knick next to Bernard King.

GREATEST FOUL SHOOTER

The Knicks have had an assortment of outstanding free-throw
shooters in their history, not all of them linked to their glory years.
During an otherwise disappointing 1981-82 season, Mike Newlin
managed to hit 85.7 percent of his foul shots. Henry Bibby hit 36
straight foul shots in 1973. Cazzie Russell, Howard Komives,
Richie Guerin, Willie Naulls, Kenny Sears and Carl Braun all

posted seasons in which they were among the league leaders from the line.

But the Knicks' greatest foul shooter is a player who contributed greatly to their championship seasons of 1969-70 and 1972-73. Forward Bill Bradley, now a U.S. Senator from New Jersey, was among the most proficient players from the line. Bradley finished among the league leaders in free throws for four consecutive seasons, averaging between .871 and .878 in free-throw percentage from 1972-76.

Bradley finished his career with an .840 career percentage during the regular season and .805 during the playoffs. The only reason those figures were not higher was that he took about five seasons to reach his peak.

ALL-TIME KNICK LEADERS

SEASON

Points: Richie Guerin, 2,303, 1961-62
Assists: Micheal Ray Richardson, 832, 1979-80
Rebounds: Willis Reed, 1,191, 1968-69

GAME

Points: Richie Guerin, 57 vs. Syracuse, 12/11/59
Assists: Richie Guerin, 21 vs. St. Louis, 12/12/58
Rebounds: Harry Gallatin, 33 vs. Ft. Wayne, 3/15/53

CAREER

Points: Walt Frazier, 14,617, 1967-77
Assists: Walt Frazier, 4,791, 1967-77
Rebounds: Willis Reed, 8,414, 1964-74

PHILADELPHIA 76ERS

TEAM DIRECTORY: Owner: Harold Katz; VP/GM: Pat Williams; Dir. Player Per.: Jack McMahon; Dir. Press Rel.: Harvey Pollack; Coach: Billy Cunningham; Asst. Coaches: Jack McMahon, Matt Guokas. Arena: The Spectrum (17,921). Colors: Red, white and blue.

After playoff failure, Moses begins another title mission.

SCOUTING REPORT

SHOOTING: You want the 20-foot jumper, you got the 20-foot jumper. Andrew Toney (.527) will be sticking the long bomb for his fifth pro season, while rookie guard Leon Wood drops in three-pointers like they were tip-ins.

You want the pull-up jumper and the drive? You got that, too. A fellow by the name of Julius Erving (.512) will do that for you and so will rookie forward Charles Barkley.

For mid-range jumpers, try Bobby Jones (.523) and Maurice Cheeks (.550). And finally, for the tip-in and the unstoppable fadeaway, there's Moses Malone (.483).

Barring last-minute trades or injuries, the 76ers bring the most potent team in the history of pro basketball into the 1984-85 season. There is nothing this team can't do with the ball and do better than any other contender. The Sixers can run and the addition of Barkley will greatly improve their attack in the halfcourt set.

PLAYMAKING: Cheeks has only one flaw—he is easily injured. He doesn't miss that many games, but he does play hurt and sometimes isn't as effective as he should be. When he's healthy, he can run the break as well as any player in the game.

Now that Wood has been added, Cheeks (6.4 assists per game) should get the rest he needs without worrying about costing his team games. In fact, he might be more worried about losing his job. If Wood's reputation at Cal State-Fullerton is anything close to the truth, he will be able to step right in behind Cheeks and work the break with the same kind of quickness and intelligence.

In the forecourt, Erving remains an excellent playmaker. He averaged 4.0 assists per game last season and his intuitions are seldom wrong.

DEFENSE: Last season, while the 76ers were suffering through an allegedly mediocre year, they led the league in blocked shots (653) and were fifth in defense (105.6 ppg). They also were fifth in steals and held opponents to a .480 shooting percentage. Shed no tears for this team.

Malone is a tremendous intimidator in the lane and gets help from the refs. He didn't foul out of a single game last year. Erving, Jones and Sam Williams are also tremendous shot-blockers in the lane. Maurice Cheeks and Jones are considered among the top two in defense at their positions. The rookies, Barkley and Wood, will learn by example.

76ER ROSTER

No.	Veteran	Pos.	Ht.	Wt.	Age	Yrs. Pro	College
10	Maurice Cheeks	G	6-1	180	28	7	West Texas State
14	*Franklin Edwards	G	6-1	170	25	4	Cleveland State
6	Julius Erving	F	6-6	200	34	14	Massachusetts
8	Marc Iavaroni	F	6-10	225	28	3	Virginia
45	Clemon Johnson	F-C	6-10	240	28	7	Florida A&M
24	Bobby Jones	F	6-9	212	32	11	North Carolina
2	Moses Malone	C	6-10	235	29	11	None
1	Wes Matthews	G	6-1	165	25	5	Wisconsin
11	Leo Rautins	F	6-8	215	24	2	Syracuse
3	Sedale Threatt	G	6-2	177	23	2	West Virginia Tech
4	Clint Richardson	G	6-3	195	28	6	Seattle
22	Andrew Toney	G	6-3	180	26	5	SW Louisiana

*Free agent unsigned at press time

Rd.	Top Draftees	Sel. No.	Ht.	Wt.	College
1	Charles Barkley	5	6-6	272	Auburn
1	Leon Wood	10	6-3	187	Cal State-Fullerton
3	James Banks	48	6-6	215	Georgia
3	Butch Graves	68	6-3	185	Yale
4	Earl Harrison	91	6-7	210	Morehead State

REBOUNDING: With Malone around, you'd figure the Sixers would kill everyone off the boards, but they edged opponents by an average of 1.1 rpg. Billy Cunningham is hoping that will change now that the "Round Mound of Rebound" is around.

Can Barkley play power forward? At 6-6 and 272, he is certainly wide enough, but what about his height? Intuition and his 9.5-rpg average at Auburn say he'll be able to do it. If he can't, he'll be teamed with Jones, Williams and Marc Iavaroni when Erving rests.

OUTLOOK: Rosy, to say the least. The Sixers will be hungry because of their playoff failure last year. Erving will be angry and inspired, because owner Harold Katz put him on the trading block in the off-season. And with two high first-round picks added to this all-star crew, Philadelphia has to be favored over the defending champion Celtics.

It has been three years since the Celtics and 76ers met in the playoffs. Hopefully, there will be no interlopers this season and the best rivalry in professional sports will be renewed.

Dr. J looks for another title in his 14th year as a pro.

SIXER PROFILES

JULIUS ERVING 34 6-6 200   Forward

Can he do it one more time?...Deeply disappointed by Sixers' playoff showing against Nets...Had another outstanding season, but didn't pick up his game in the playoffs...Nagging injuries may sap his resolve for second NBA ring...Still can soar when healthy, but is mortal when he is hurt or has played too many minutes...Wore his championship ring on bus to playoff game to inspire teammates against Nets, but the ploy didn't work..."We have to sit down and figure out what went wrong," he said. "I thought we were past that." ...Born Feb. 22, 1950, in Roosevelt, N.Y....Left Massachusetts early to sign with Virginia Squires...Three-time MVP in ABA and one-time winner in NBA..."The Doctor"...Very religious, very popular with other players...Always has time to answer questions...Never had a great shot, but his body control is best since

Elgin Baylor...Was 12th-ranked scorer in the league last season and averaged 4.0 assists per game.

Year	Team	G	FG	FG Pct.	FT	FT Pct.	Reb.	Ast.	TP	Avg.
1971-72	Virginia (ABA)	84	910	.498	467	.745	1319	335	2290	27.3
1972-73	Virginia (ABA)	71	894	.496	475	.776	867	298	2268	31.9
1973-74	New York (ABA)	84	914	.512	454	.766	899	434	2299	27.4
1974-75	New York (ABA)	84	914	.506	486	.799	914	462	2343	27.9
1975-76	New York (ABA)	84	949	.507	530	.801	925	423	2462	29.3
1976-77	Philadelphia.	82	685	.499	400	.777	695	306	1770	21.6
1977-78	Philadelphia.	74	611	.502	306	.845	481	279	1528	20.6
1978-79	Philadelphia.	78	715	.491	373	.745	564	357	1803	23.1
1979-80	Philadelphia.	78	838	.519	420	.787	576	355	2100	26.9
1980-81	Philadelphia.	82	794	.521	422	.787	657	364	2014	24.6
1981-82	Philadelphia.	81	780	.546	411	.763	557	319	1974	24.4
1982-83	Philadelphia.	72	605	.517	330	.759	491	263	1542	21.4
1983-84	Philadelphia.	77	678	.512	364	.754	532	309	1727	22.4
	Totals	1031	10287	.509	5438	.776	9477	4504	26120	25.3

MOSES MALONE 29 6-10 235   Center

Led league in rebounding (13.4 rpg) and led team in scoring (22.7 ppg)...That wasn't enough for Philadelphia owner Harold Katz, who labeled him a disappointment...Missed 11 games in midseason due to ankle injury and never recovered his form of championship season ...Stopped talking to the press late in the year for reasons unknown...Couldn't dominate offensively in playoffs against either Darryl Dawkins or Mike Gminski...Still a perpetual-motion machine under boards...Entering third year of $2.2-million-per season contract...Katz said he wasn't worth it last year...Born March 3, 1955, in Petersburg, Va....Jumped from high school to ABA Utah Stars...Has led NBA in rebounding five times in last six years...Rumors have him disenchanted with Philadelphia, but figure him to stay for length of contract...Still the best center in the game, though not by wide margin over three or four others.

Year	Team	G	FG	FG Pct.	FT	FT Pct.	Reb.	Ast.	TP	Avg.
1974-75	Utah (ABA)	83	591	.571	375	.635	1209	82	1557	18.8
1975-76	St. Louis (ABA)	43	251	.512	112	.612	413	58	614	14.3
1976-77	Buf.-Hou.	82	389	.480	305	.693	1072	89	1083	13.2
1977-78	Houston.	59	413	.499	318	718	886	31	1144	19.4
1978-79	Houston.	82	716	.540	599	.739	1444	147	2031	24.8
1979-80	Houston.	82	778	.502	563	.719	1190	147	2119	25.8
1980-81	Houston.	80	806	.522	609	.757	1180	141	2222	27.8
1981-82	Houston.	81	945	.519	630	.762	1188	142	2520	31.1
1982-83	Philadelphia.	78	654	.501	600	.761	1194	101	1908	24.5
1983-84	Philadelphia.	71	532	.483	545	.750	950	96	1609	22.7
	Totals	741	6075	.514	4656	.728	10726	1034	16807	22.7

BOBBY JONES 32 6-9 212   Forward

Can only play half a game now, but he's still effective when he's in there ... Averaged only 23.5 minutes per game during regular season and had lowest scoring average of career (8.3 ppg) ... When Billy Cunningham needed help in playoffs, he started him and hoped for best ... First-team All-Defensive selection for eighth straight season ... Looks tired and disinterested, but gets job done ... Like teammate Julius Erving, a very religious man ... Conquered epilepsy to play in NBA ... Born Dec. 18, 1951, in Akron, Ohio ... Never takes bad shot ... Hit 60 percent from the floor in college at North Carolina and shot 52.3 percent last season ... Grumbles a lot about length of season ... How much longer will he punish his body?

Year	Team	G	FG	FG Pct.	FT	FT Pct.	Reb.	Ast.	TP	Avg.
1974-75	Denver (ABA)	84	529	.604	187	.695	692	303	1245	14.8
1975-76	Denver (ABA)	83	510	.581	215	.698	791	331	1235	14.9
1976-77	Denver	82	501	.570	236	.717	678	264	1238	15.1
1977-78	Denver	75	440	.578	208	.751	636	252	1088	14.5
1978-79	Philadelphia	80	378	.537	209	.755	531	201	965	12.1
1979-80	Philadelphia	81	398	.532	257	.781	450	146	1053	13.0
1980-81	Philadelphia	81	407	.539	282	.813	435	226	1096	13.5
1981-82	Philadelphia	76	416	.564	263	.790	393	189	1095	14.4
1982-83	Philadelphia	74	250	.543	165	.793	344	142	665	9.0
1983-84	Philadelphia	75	226	.523	167	.784	323	187	619	8.3
	Totals	791	4055	.561	2189	.757	5273	2241	10299	13.0

MARC IAVARONI 28 6-10 225   Forward

May lose his starting job this season ... Was supposed to be a tough defender, but was burned often by more mobile power forwards ... A complete dud on offense ... Only adequate off boards (4.0 rpg) ... Benched during playoffs after being embarrassed by Buck Williams ... Born Sept. 15, 1956, in Bethpage, L.I. ... His career has been strange one ... Cut twice by Knicks, he bounced around Italy for three years before becoming starter on championship team ... Billy Cunningham may want more skills at power forward this time around ... Hustles and bumps, but couldn't beat a sloth up the floor ... Fourth-ranked rebounder in Virginia history.

Year	Team	G	FG	FG Pct.	FT	FT Pct.	Reb.	Ast.	TP	Avg.
1982-83	Philadelphia	80	163	.462	78	.690	329	83	404	5.1
1983-84	Philadelphia	78	149	.463	97	.740	310	95	395	5.1
	Totals	158	312	.462	175	.717	639	178	799	5.1

ANDREW TONEY 26 6-3 180   Guard

Was most consistent 76er during regular season and in playoffs . . . Still not Billy Cunningham's favorite . . . Had career highs in scoring (20.4 ppg) and field-goal percentage (.527) . . . Can get his own shot anywhere, anytime . . . Played more minutes than anybody on team other than Julius Erving and Moses Malone . . . Has matured into adequate defender . . . More than willing to take last shot . . . Born Nov. 23, 1957, in Birmingham, Ala. . . . Chosen eighth in 1980 draft, behind Mike O'Koren and Mike Gminski. Nets have kicked themselves ever since . . . Best free-throw shooter on team (83.9 percent) . . . Southwestern Louisiana product has nerves of steel . . . A perfect complement for Maurice Cheeks . . . Improved as passer, averaging 4.8 assists per game.

Year	Team	G	FG	FG Pct.	FT	FT Pct.	Reb.	Ast.	TP	Avg.
1980-81	Philadelphia	75	399	.495	161	.712	143	273	968	12.9
1981-82	Philadelphia	77	511	.522	227	.742	134	283	1274	16.5
1982-83	Philadelphia	81	626	.501	324	.788	225	365	1598	19.7
1983-84	Philadelphia	78	593	.527	390	.839	193	373	1588	20.4
	Totals	311	2129	.512	1102	.783	695	1294	5428	17.5

CLINT RICHARDSON 28 6-3 195   Guard

Great player to have on bench . . . A defensive stopper who can play either guard position . . . Can rebound, can pass, can block shots . . . Jumper isn't his bread-and-butter, but he can't be completely ignored . . . Started 12 games when Andrew Toney or Maurice Cheeks was injured . . . Strong enough to play forward at University of Seattle . . . Born Aug. 7, 1956, in Seattle . . . Borderline talent for three years before he worked his way up Billy Cunningham's depth chart in 1981-82 . . . His relations with media became strained by end of season . . . Wes Matthews started ahead of him at end of season, but he played while Matthews sat in playoffs.

Year	Team	G	FG	FG Pct.	FT	FT Pct.	Reb.	Ast.	TP	Avg.
1979-80	Philadelphia	52	159	.457	28	.622	123	107	347	6.7
1980-81	Philadelphia	77	227	.489	84	.778	176	152	538	7.0
1981-82	Philadelphia	77	140	.452	69	.784	118	109	351	4.6
1982-83	Philadelphia	77	259	.463	71	.640	247	168	589	7.6
1983-84	Philadelphia	69	221	.467	79	.767	165	155	521	7.6
	Totals	352	1006	.467	331	.727	829	691	2346	6.7

MAURICE CHEEKS 28 6-1 180   Guard

As he goes, so go the 76ers... Was walking wounded by playoff time, with sore knee and cut over eye... Missed seven regular-season games because of injuries and couldn't keep up with Micheal Ray Richardson in play-offs... Was fourth in league in steals (2.28 per game)... When healthy, he can penetrate better than anyone in league... First-team All-Defensive selection... Born Sept. 8, 1956, in Chicago... People forget he was only second-round pick in 1978 out of West Texas State... His jumper is good enough to keep everyone honest... Always among top guards in field-goal percentage (.550 last year)... Was underrated for about three years... Now everyone knows what he means to Philadelphia.

Year	Team	G	FG	FG Pct.	FT	FT Pct.	Reb.	Ast.	TP	Avg.
1978-79	Philadelphia.	82	292	.510	101	.721	254	431	685	8.4
1979-80	Philadelphia.	79	357	.540	180	.779	274	556	898	11.4
1980-81	Philadelphia.	81	310	.534	140	.787	245	560	763	9.4
1981-82	Philadelphia.	79	352	.521	171	.777	248	667	881	11.2
1982-83	Philadelphia.	79	404	.542	181	.754	209	543	990	12.5
1983-84	Philadelphia.	75	386	.550	170	.733	205	478	950	12.7
	Totals	475	2101	.534	943	.760	1435	3235	5167	10.9

CLEMON JOHNSON 28 6-10 240   Forward-Center

A journeyman clock puncher... Puts in his time, doesn't get embarrassed, hopes he leaves game with his team still leading... Was closest thing Philadelphia had to backup center... Managed to play in 83 regular-season games in 1982-83, when he was traded from Indiana to the 76ers late in season... Tough off offensive boards ... No shooting touch... Hit only 61.1 percent from foul line... Born Sept. 12, 1956, in Monticello, Fla.... Has bachelor's degree in economics from Florida A&M and spends offseasons working in banks... Averaged 21.5 minutes per game last season, nearly as much as Bobby Jones.

Year	Team	G	FG	FG Pct.	FT	FT Pct.	Reb.	Ast.	TP	Avg.
1978-79	Portland	74	102	.470	36	.486	226	78	240	3.2
1979-80	Indiana	79	199	.503	74	.632	394	115	472	6.0
1980-81	Indiana	81	235	.504	112	.593	468	144	582	7.2
1981-82	Indiana	79	312	.487	123	.651	571	127	747	9.5
1982-83	Ind.-Phil.	83	299	.515	111	.617	524	139	709	8.5
1983-84	Philadelphia.	80	193	.468	69	.611	398	55	455	5.7
	Totals	476	1340	.494	525	.609	2581	658	3205	6.7

SAM WILLIAMS 25 6-8 210   **Forward**

Jury's still out...76ers thought he might be their answer at power forward position, but he went out and had worst season in pros...Shot 52.6 percent from field with Golden State in 1982-83, but dipped to 47.3 percent last year ...Reputation as great rebounder didn't seem justified...Mistake-prone and Billy Cunningham gave him few minutes in playoffs...

Born March 7, 1959, in Los Angeles...Attended Pasadena City College and Arizona State...Warriors made him second-round choice in 1981...Became expendable at Golden State because of plethora of big forwards...Decent mid-range shooter...Started just 12 games and couldn't push Marc Iavaroni out of job...Many teams were interested in him when Warriors shopped him last November.

Year	Team	G	FG	FG Pct.	FT	FT Pct.	Reb.	Ast.	TP	Avg.
1981-82	Golden State	59	154	.556	49	.551	308	38	357	6.1
1982-83	Golden State	75	252	.526	123	.719	393	45	627	8.4
1983-84	G.S.-Phil.	77	204	.473	92	.657	339	62	500	6.5
	Totals	211	610	.514	264	.660	1040	145	1484	7.0

WES MATTHEWS 25 6-1 165   **Guard**

The party's over...Learned hard way he isn't the answer to every coach's dreams...Was cut after just six games with Hawks and didn't resurface until Sixers picked him up as free agent late in season...One of five quickest guards in league, but nobody trusts him...Started five games at end of season when Maurice Cheeks was hurt, but disappeared during playoffs...

Born Aug. 24, 1959, in Sarasota, Fla....Everybody knows he's talented...Branded a high-risk player ever since he was kicked off Wisconsin team just before NIT appearance...Can penetrate or make the pass, but his teammates are guessing along with opposition...Will have a tough time holding down roster spot ...Can't shoot.

Year	Team	G	FG	FG Pct.	FT	FT Pct.	Reb.	Ast.	TP	Avg.
1980-81	Wash.-Atl.	79	385	.494	202	.802	139	411	977	12.4
1981-82	Atlanta	47	131	.440	60	.759	58	139	324	6.9
1982-83	Atlanta	64	171	.403	86	.768	91	249	442	6.9
1983-84	Atl.-Phil.	20	61	.466	27	.750	27	83	150	7.5
	Totals	210	748	.458	375	.783	315	882	1893	9.0

SEDALE THREATT 23 6-2 177   Guard

Who knows?... Made the team on strength of remarkable preseason, then rarely demonstrated that spark again... Didn't get much playing time, averaging just 10.4 minutes in 45 games ... Wasn't supposed to have shot at making team... Was picked in sixth round of draft as 139th overall pick, out of West Virginia Tech ... Great name... Probably won a roster spot during preseason game in Atlantic City against Nets, when he went berserk and singlehandedly beat New Jersey in overtime... A pure shooter, but he'll have to do better than 41.9 percent from the floor to hold down job... Born Sept. 10, 1961, in Atlanta... Billy Cunningham showed lack of faith in him by signing Wes Matthews late in season.

Year	Team	G	FG	FG Pct.	FT	FT Pct.	Reb.	Ast.	TP	Avg.
1983-84	Philadelphia	45	62	.419	23	.821	40	41	148	3.3

LEO RAUTINS 24 6-8 215   Forward

Almost no chance... Rookie season sabotaged by early injuries, but that probably didn't matter... Whatever he had at Syracuse doesn't make it in NBA... Too slow to make his own shot, not enough of a leaper to establish himself as rebounder... Played in only 28 games, starting three... Shot 36.2 percent from the field... Born March 20, 1960, in Toronto... Known as a good passer in college... Was 17th pick overall in 1983 draft, which proves experts have a lot to learn... Played four years for Canadian National Team... Transferred to Syracuse from Minnesota after his freshman year.

Year	Team	G	FG	FG Pct.	FT	FT Pct.	Reb.	Ast.	TP	Avg.
1983-84	Philadelphia	28	21	.362	6	.600	33	29	48	1.7

TOP ROOKIES

CHARLES BARKLEY 21 6-6 272   Forward

Rich get richer... Can shoot, can rebound and has great quickness for his size... "Boy Gorge" must keep weight down to reasonable level... Long NBA season has a way of doing that... Sixers hope he'll be the answer at power forward, despite fact he'll give up several inches to opponents...That was never a problem at Auburn, but it might be different in pros...Came out early after junior year...Didn't get big money because he was drafted by Sixers, who couldn't offer much because of salary-cap problems...Born Feb. 20, 1963...Grew up in Leeds, Ala.

LEON WOOD 22 6-3 187   Guard

Unstoppable offensive machine at Cal State-Fullerton...Scouts question his defense...Perfect backup for injury-prone Maurice Cheeks...Can shoot and hit the open man...Loves working the fast break...Was MVP of Aloha Classic, averaging 12.0 ppg and 8.0 assists per game...Drafted 10th overall by Sixers, who owned Denver's pick...Averaged 24.0 ppg his senior year...Born March 25, 1962...Grew up in Santa Monica, Cal.

COACH BILLY CUNNINGHAM: Rough season for Billy C...Most coaches would love to win 52 games, but for defending champions the regular season and the early playoff exit were disappointments...Doesn't have much fun...Spent most of the season trying to cajole, coax and threaten his players out of post-championship lethargy...Has amazing 396-172 record in seven seasons, but then he's had some amazing teams...Owns 70-42 mark in playoffs...Made some mistakes against Nets, including his decision to put Julius Erving on Buck Williams in final three games. Erving was exhausted by end of series...Born June 3, 1943, in Brooklyn, N.Y....An ally of Kevin Loughery and Doug Moe in the anti-Hubie Brown conspiracy...Has two years left on $400,000-per-season contract, which makes him highest-paid coach...Appears ashen and incoherent after defeats...Really shouldn't take this so seriously...Came to Sixer job cold in 1977 after Gene Shue was fired and learned a lot from assistant Chuck Daly...A standout forward for Philadelphia, averaging 20.8 ppg from 1965-72 and 1974-76.

GREATEST FOUL SHOOTER

The Philadelphia 76ers probably have had the richest tradition of great, terrible and just plain weird free-throw shooters. Wilt

Chamberlain hit just 38 percent of his free throws during 1967-68, but others wearing the Sixers' uniform have been far more successful.

Hal Greer, shooting jumpers from the line, converted 81.5 percent in 1969-70. Larry Costello, shooting set shots, led the league at 87.7 percent in 1964-65. Dave Gambee, who threw underhanded and lifted his left leg to provide backspin, was often among the league leaders. The best of the lot, however, was Dolph Schayes, who led the NBA in free-throw percentage for three seasons and annually dueled with Boston's Bill Sharman for the top spot.

"We'd both push each other to greater heights," Sharman said. "Dolph would always say his set shot was the best and I would say the same thing about the one-hand shot."

Schayes, who played 15 years with the Syracuse Nationals and moved with the franchise to Philadelphia in 1963, had his best years in 1956-57 and 1957-58. In both those seasons, he shot .904 from the line. Schayes finished his remarkable career with a free-throw percentage of .844.

ALL-TIME 76ER LEADERS

SEASON

Points: Wilt Chamberlain, 2,649, 1965-66
Assists: Wilt Chamberlain, 702, 1967-78
Rebounds: Wilt Chamberlain, 1,957, 1966-67

GAME

Points: Wilt Chamberlain, 68 vs. Chicago, 12/16/67
Assists: Wilt Chamberlain, 21 vs. Detroit, 2/2/68
            Maurice Cheeks, 21 vs. New Jersey, 10/30/82
Rebounds: Wilt Chamberlain, 43 vs. Boston, 3/6/65

CAREER

Points: Hal Greer, 21,586, 1958-73
Assists: Hal Greer, 4,540, 1958-73
Rebounds: Dolph Schayes, 11,256, 1948-64

WASHINGTON BULLETS

TEAM DIRECTORY: Pres.: Abe Pollin; Exec. VP: Jerry Sachs; GM: Bob Ferry; Dir. Pub. Rel.: Mark Pray; Coach: Gene Shue; Asst. Coaches: Bernie Bickerstaff, Don Moran. Arena: Capital Centre (19,105). Colors: Red, white and blue.

Jeff Ruland was iron man with league-leading 3,034 minutes.

SCOUTING REPORT

SHOOTING: What a difference a year makes. Last season, the Bullets were 21st in the league in scoring and were about as explosive as molasses. But the acquisitions of Gus Williams and Cliff Robinson mean scoring dimensions heretofore absent in Landover.

On paper, at least, the new Bullets can do a lot of offensive damage. Jeff Ruland remains the chief post-up scorer and his 57.9-percent shooting mark shouldn't change. Rick Mahorn (.507) is another inside bruiser whose layups are nearly impossible to stop.

A backcourt of second-year man Jeff Malone and Williams should give the Bullets incredible perimeter shooting and an up-tempo look. Frank Johnson (.467) is more of a penetrator. Robinson (.450) operated most effectively in the running game at Cleveland, but is such a versatile scorer he may be able to adjust to the Bullets' traditional halfcourt style.

PLAYMAKING: The Bullets haven't been known for their passing in recent years. A typical Washington play started with Johnson dribbling down the clock, developed with a bounce pass inside to Ruland and ended with a five-foot banker by Ruland. With Williams on hand, things might be different.

Coach Gene Shue will have to decide whether to continue fitting the offense around Ruland or to encourage Williams, Johnson and Robinson to push the ball upcourt. Williams averaged 8.5 assists per game last season with the Sonics and knows how to operate on the run. Robinson is not a good passer, but is excellent at finishing off the break.

Ruland is an underrated ball-handler and has a knack for kicking the ball out to the right man. Greg Ballard is a better passer than Robinson, but can't do other things as well.

DEFENSE: The dramatic changes in the team are likely to have a detrimental effect in this department. Robinson's defense remains suspect after years of atrophy in Cleveland. Williams is a gambler who can create fast-break opportunities with his steals, but he won't give the Bullets the bread-and-butter physical defense the departed Ricky Sobers provided.

The Bullets still need another shot-blocker. They ranked dead last in that department last season with 320 and only Mahorn had more than 100. Robinson had only 32 blocks last season, so they can't look to him for help.

BULLET ROSTER

No.	Veteran	Pos.	Ht.	Wt.	Age	Yrs. Pro	College
42	*Greg Ballard	F	6-7	215	29	8	Oregon
23	Charles Davis	F	6-7	215	26	4	Vanderbilt
25	Darren Daye	F	6-8	221	23	2	UCLA
30	Mike Gibson	F-C	6-10	225	24	2	SC-Spartanburg
15	Frank Johnson	G	6-2	185	25	4	Wake Forest
31	Joe Kopicki	F	6-9	240	24	3	Detroit
44	Rick Mahorn	F-C	6-10	235	26	5	Hampton Institute
24	Jeff Malone	G	6-4	205	23	2	Mississippi State
54	Tom McMillen	C	6-11	200	32	10	Maryland
11	Cliff Robinson	F	6-9	225	24	6	USC
43	Jeff Ruland	C	6-10	240	25	4	Iona
13	Bryan Warrick	G	6-5	195	24	3	St. Joseph's
1	Gus Williams	G	6-3	180	31	9	USC

*Free agent unsigned at press time

Rd.	Top Draftees	Sel. No.	Ht.	Wt.	College
1	**Tom Sewell	22	6-5	191	Lamar
2	Tony Costner	34	6-9½	253	St. Joseph's
2	Fred Reynolds	44	6-7¼	205	Texas-El Paso
3	Ricky Ross	53	6-7	190	Tulsa
4	Jim Grandholm	76	7-0	228	South Florida

**Picked by Philadelphia and traded to Washington

REBOUNDING: Considering the Bullets' collective image as inside bruisers, one might expect their rebounding statistics to be among the best in the league. Instead, the Bullets did not even break even last season under the boards. They pulled down 3,414 rebounds, while their opponents grabbed 3,418.

Shue hopes that this problem has been corrected by the acquisition of Robinson, a 6-9 small forward who averaged 10.3 rpg. When Washington fields a frontcourt of Ruland (12.3 rpg), Mahorn and Robinson, it should dominate the boards. The backcourt, however, remains a smallish, non-rebounding corps. Williams will not add anything in this respect.

OUTLOOK: This team has become something of a wild card. The chemistry is questionable, but the talent is there. Will Ruland and Mahorn run? Will Robinson and Williams stop running?

Robinson's ability to play both forward spots and Mahorn's versatility at center and power forward give Shue all kinds of matchup options. Likewise, he can pair Williams with either Malone or Johnson in the backcourt. The Bullets just might be able to challenge the Nets and Knicks for third place in the Atlantic Division—if the pieces fall into place.

Awesome Rick Mahorn blocked 123 shots, drew 358 personals.

BULLET PROFILES

JEFF RULAND 25 6-10 240   Center

Not underrated anymore... Was legitimate MVP candidate... Without him, Bullets are fodder... Third in league in rebounding (12.3 rpg), 15th in scoring (22.2 ppg), sixth in field-goal percentage (.579)... Managed to elevate his game for playoffs, averaging 24.0 ppg and 12.8 rpg against bruising Celtics... A real workhorse... Led league in minutes played (3,082)... Born Dec. 16, 1958, in Bay Shore, N.Y.... Critics say he possesses only one move, but just try to stop it... Can't be budged when he plants himself in paint... Not a good ball-handler... Ineligible to play his senior season at Iona, he was drafted by Golden State in second round in 1980, then traded to Washington for second pick... Played in Spain for a year, then returned with vengeance... Still enjoys sticking it to people who doubted his ability.

Year	Team	G	FG	FG Pct.	FT	FT Pct.	Reb.	Ast.	TP	Avg.
1981-82	Washington	82	420	.561	342	.752	762	134	1183	14.4
1982-83	Washington	79	580	.552	375	.689	871	234	1536	19.4
1983-84	Washington	75	599	.579	466	.733	922	296	1665	22.2
	Totals	236	1599	.564	1183	.724	2555	664	4384	18.6

GREG BALLARD 29 6-7 215 Forward

Steady and durable...Scoring average dipped more than three points, but it wasn't his fault...Offense became more diversified with Ricky Sobers and Jeff Malone getting into the act, so he took 213 fewer shots...A deadly shooter behind screen, but can't get his own shot easily...Has missed only seven games in past six years...Born Jan. 29, 1955, in Los Angeles...Attended Oregon...Not the quickest forward in league, but he has worked on his defense and rarely gets embarrassed...Commands respect from teammates...Had solid playoff performances against Boston, hitting 12-of-13 free throws during four-game series...Was picked ahead of Walter Davis and fourth overall by Bullets in 1977 draft.

Year	Team	G	FG	FG Pct.	FT	FT Pct.	Reb.	Ast.	TP	Avg.
1977-78	Washington	76	142	.425	88	.772	266	62	372	4.9
1978-79	Washington	82	260	.465	119	.692	450	116	639	7.8
1979-80	Washington	82	545	.495	171	.753	638	159	1277	15.6
1980-81	Washington	82	549	.463	166	.847	580	195	1271	15.5
1981-82	Washington	79	621	.475	235	.830	633	250	1486	18.8
1982-83	Washington	78	603	.473	182	.781	508	262	1401	18.0
1983-84	Washington	82	510	.481	166	.798	488	290	1188	14.5
	Totals	561	3230	.473	1127	.786	3563	1334	7634	13.6

GUS WILLIAMS 31 6-3 180 Guard

There in the clutch...Struggled in 1982-83, turning in his worst shooting and scoring marks of any regular season since 1977-78 ...But he was the straw that stirred Seattle's drink and almost kept the Sonics alive in the playoff series against Dallas last season ...And now he's in Washington following trade for Ricky Sobers and rookie Tim McCormick...Born to run...One of the most effective open-court players at any position in the game...Set an all-time NBA playoff record by pumping in 23 points in one quarter against Dallas...Born Oct. 10, 1953, in Mt. Vernon, N.Y.... One of many to come out of that pro breeding ground, along with brother Ray and Scooter and Rodney McCray...Comeback Player of the Year in 1982, following a one-year hiatus due to a contract dispute...Loves to pull up and drill jumper on the transition...Range is unlimited, as evidenced by his 30-foot, three-point game-winner in Game 2 of the playoffs at Dallas...One of the many members of the Ex-Warrior Club, whose leading members are top-flight players who were allowed to get away by Golden State... Came out of Southern Cal as a second-round draft choice in 1975.

Year	Team	G	FG	FG Pct.	FT	FT Pct.	Reb.	Ast.	TP	Avg.
1975-76	Golden State	77	365	.428	173	.742	159	240	903	11.7
1976-77	Golden State	82	315	.464	112	.747	233	292	762	9.3
1977-78	Seattle	79	602	.451	227	.817	256	294	1431	18.1
1978-79	Seattle	76	606	.495	245	.775	245	307	1457	19.2
1979-80	Seattle	82	739	.482	331	.788	275	397	1816	22.1
1981-82	Seattle	80	773	.486	320	.734	244	549	1875	23.4
1982-83	Seattle	80	660	.477	278	.751	205	643	1600	20.0
1983-84	Seattle	80	598	.458	297	.750	204	675	1497	18.7
	Totals	636	4668	.470	1983	.763	1821	3397	11341	17.8

FRANK JOHNSON 25 6-2 185   Guard

Very quick, but out of sync with teammates ...Has lousy shot, which doesn't help... Averaged 6.8 assists per game during regular season and had solid playoff series...Like Ricky Sobers, he's not shy. But, unlike Sobers, he usually misses...Launches three-point shots with frightening regularity...Gives the appearance of being more out of control than he is...Committed respectable 2.3 turnovers per game...Born Nov. 23, 1958, in Weirsdale, Fla.... Attended Wake Forest... Seems to have reached potential, but he's not a championship-caliber point guard...Brother of Atlanta's Eddie...Tried playing off guard during rookie season, but couldn't cut it because of shot.

Year	Team	G	FG	FG Pct.	FT	FT Pct.	Reb.	Ast.	TP	Avg.
1981-82	Washington	79	336	.414	153	.750	147	380	842	10.7
1982-83	Washington	68	321	.408	196	.751	178	549	852	12.5
1983-84	Washington	82	392	.467	187	.742	184	567	982	12.0
	Totals	229	1049	.430	536	.748	509	1496	2676	11.7

TOM McMILLEN 32 6-11 200   Center

Has come full cycle...Once was a major disappointment in light of high expectations... Now surprises people with effectiveness when they forget he can play...A perfect backup for Jeff Ruland and Rick Mahorn...A tough defender with windmill elbows and excellent timing...Missed 20 games due to injuries...Has put off his political career for another year in order to compete . . . Keeps his name circulating in Washington circles with plenty of fund-raising appearances for Democrats . . . Born May 26, 1952, in Mansfield, Pa. . . . Was on cover of *Sports Illustrated* as schoolboy . . . Gray hair makes him look even more out of place on court . . . Tremendous tenacity . . . Maryland grad is one of the great cheerleaders on the bench.

Year	Team	G	FG	FG Pct.	FT	FT Pct.	Reb.	Ast.	TP	Avg.
1975-76	Buffalo	50	96	.432	41	.759	186	69	233	4.7
1976-77	Buf.-N.Y. Knicks	76	274	.487	96	.780	389	67	644	8.5
1977-78	Atlanta	68	280	.493	116	.800	416	84	676	9.9
1978-79	Atlanta	82	232	.466	106	.891	332	69	570	7.0
1979-80	Atlanta	53	191	.500	81	.757	220	62	463	8.7
1980-81	Atlanta	79	253	.487	80	.741	295	72	587	7.4
1981-82	Atlanta	73	291	.509	140	.824	336	129	723	9.9
1982-83	Atlanta	61	198	.467	108	.812	217	76	504	8.3
1983-84	Washington	62	222	.497	127	.814	199	73	572	9.2
	Totals	604	2037	.486	895	.803	2590	701	4972	8.2

BRYAN WARRICK 24 6-5 195   Guard

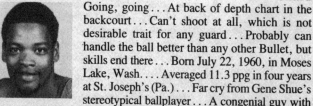

Going, going . . . At back of depth chart in the backcourt . . . Can't shoot at all, which is not desirable trait for any guard . . . Probably can handle the ball better than any other Bullet, but skills end there . . . Born July 22, 1960, in Moses Lake, Wash. . . . Averaged 11.3 ppg in four years at St. Joseph's (Pa.) . . . Far cry from Gene Shue's stereotypical ballplayer . . . A congenial guy with no past and almost as negligible talent . . . Didn't appear in play-offs . . . Will have tough time holding roster spot . . . Never was a scorer, but Bullets took him as 25th pick overall in 1982 draft . . . Had only 20 turnovers last season.

Year	Team	G	FG	FG Pct.	FT	FT Pct.	Reb.	Ast.	TP	Avg.
1982-83	Washington	43	65	.380	42	.737	69	126	172	4.0
1983-84	Washington	32	27	.409	8	.500	22	43	63	2.0
	Totals	75	92	.388	50	.685	91	169	235	3.1

RICK MAHORN 26 6-10 235   Forward-Center

Reputation obviously precedes him . . . Was disqualified from 14 games last season and was called for 358 personal fouls . . . People are afraid of this guy, for good reason . . . "He's crazy," says the Suns' Maurice Lucas, who knows about these things . . . Known for blind-side picks on point guards . . . Can pound the boards as well as the bodies . . . Averaged 9.0 rpg and shot 50.7

percent from the field... Like Jeff Ruland, this former Hampton Institute standout was a second-round pick who made good... Born Sept 21, 1958, in Hartford, Conn.... Grew up as a dumpy kid until he shot up during his 16th summer... He and Ruland were "The Beef Brothers" long before Wendy's stumbled upon its "Where's the beef?" advertising gold mine.

Year	Team	G	FG	FG Pct.	FT	FT Pct.	Reb.	Ast.	TP	Avg.
1980-81	Washington	52	111	.507	27	.675	215	25	249	4.8
1981-82	Washington	80	414	.507	148	.632	704	150	976	12.2
1982-83	Washington	82	376	.490	146	.575	779	115	898	11.0
1983-84	Washington	82	307	.507	125	.651	738	131	739	9.0
	Totals	296	1208	.502	446	.619	2436	421	2862	9.7

JEFF MALONE 23 6-4 205　　　　　　　　　　Guard

Bullets had hoped for a bit more versatility... A classic streak shooter who needs to become more consistent if he expects to start in NBA... Hit only 44.4 percent of his shots in rookie season, but went through stretches when he couldn't miss... Looks almost chubby, but has quick feet and can make his own shot... Sort of a slightly overweight Otis Birdsong... Looks a bit lost on the break, but experience should help... Born June 28, 1961, in Mobile, Ala., but grew up in Macon, Ga. and starred at Mississippi State... Tenth pick overall in 1983 college draft... Hit 24-of-74 three-point field-goal attempts... Gene Shue revealed a lack of trust in him by playing him only 71 minutes in four-game playoff series.

Year	Team	G	FG	FG Pct.	FT	FT Pct.	Reb.	Ast.	TP	Avg.
1983-84	Washington	81	408	.444	142	.826	155	151	982	12.1

CLIFF ROBINSON 24 6-9 225　　　　　　　Forward

Was wasting away in Cleveland and he came to Washington in a three-club deal on draft day involving five players, including the Super-Sonics' Gus Williams, now a Bullet as well ... Was eighth in the league in rebounding at 10.3 rpg and second on the team in scoring at 17.8 ppg... Still not the soul of consistency... Born March 13, 1960, in Oakland... An articulate player who would like to become a sportscaster when he leaves the pros and seeks exposure when he can get it... Became one of the youngest players in NBA history to surpass 6,000 career points... Entering sixth season in the pros after dropping out of USC... Retains the reputation of having low pain threshold, a tag laid on him by Hubie Brown while Robinson was still with Nets... Has missed 59 games in five seasons for three different clubs... Recent rebounding totals may be a bit deceptive because Cavs don't have a center.

Year	Team	G	FG	FG Pct.	FT	FT Pct.	Reb.	Ast.	TP	Avg.
1979-80	New Jersey	70	391	.469	168	.694	506	98	951	13.6
1980-81	New Jersey	63	525	.491	178	.718	481	105	1229	19.5
1981-82	K.C.-Clev.	68	518	.453	222	.709	609	120	1258	18.5
1982-83	Cleveland	77	587	.477	213	.708	856	145	1387	18.0
1983-84	Cleveland	73	533	.450	234	.701	753	185	1301	17.8
	Totals	351	2554	.468	1015	.706	3205	653	6126	17.5

JOE KOPICKI 24 6-9 240   Forward

You know this type... Reserve banger with no apparent skills but a lot of heart... Paid his dues in 1982-83 with Wisconsin of CBA... Picked up by Bullets as a free agent at the end of that year and played respectably behind the frontcourt bruisers last season... Started two games, but played in 59... Has surprising touch if left alone... Hit 81.3 percent from the line and has the ability to draw the foul... Originally a third-round draft choice by the Hawks... Waived in their training camp... Born June 12, 1960, in Detroit... Won award for excellence in athletics and academics at University of Detroit... Averaged 18.6 ppg and 10.5 rpg his senior year.

Year	Team	G	FG	FG Pct.	FT	FT Pct.	Reb.	Ast.	TP	Avg.
1982-83	Washington	17	23	.451	21	.840	62	9	6 7	3.9
1983-84	Washington	59	64	.485	91	.813	166	46	220	3.7
	Totals	76	87	.475	112	.818	228	55	287	3.8

MIKE GIBSON 24 6-10 225   Forward-Center

Strictly filler material... Played in only 32 games in limited reserve role and showed very little... Hit only 38.2 percent of his shots from the field... Didn't play enough to establish himself as a top rebounder, but showed promise in that department... Second-round draft choice in 1982 out of South Carolina-Spartanburg... Opted to play in the Philippines and then the CBA before signing a contract in June 1983... Born Oct. 27, 1960, in Williamsburg County, S.C.... Was a first-team All-American his senior season when Spartanburg won NAIA Tournament... Averaged 16.3 ppg and 9.2 rpg during his senior year.

Year	Team	G	FG	FG Pct.	FT	FT Pct.	Reb.	Ast.	TP	Avg.
1983-84	Washington	32	21	.382	11	.647	66	9	53	1.7

CHARLES DAVIS 26 6-7 215   **Forward**

Limitations doom him to minimal role . . . Can't shoot, can't hit the boards . . . Had more turnovers than assists for third straight season . . . Come to think of it, why is this guy around at all? . . . A good athlete who is effective in open court . . . No way he can challenge Greg Ballard or Darren Daye for playing time . . . Born Oct. 5, 1958, in Nashville, Tenn. . . . Second-leading scorer in Vanderbilt history . . . Drafted by Washington in second round in 1981 . . . Returned to college during offseason after rookie year to complete requirements for degree in recreation for the special education student . . . Played only 17 minutes in three playoff games.

Year	Team	G	FG	FG Pct.	FT	FT Pct.	Reb.	Ast.	TP	Avg.
1981-82	Washington	54	88	.478	30	.811	133	31	206	3.8
1982-83	Washington	74	251	.470	56	.629	213	73	560	7.6
1983-84	Washington	46	103	.472	24	.615	103	30	231	5.0
	Totals	174	442	.472	110	.659	449	134	997	5.7

DARREN DAYE 23 6-8 221   **Forward**

Depends how you look at it . . . Did well for a third-round draft choice . . . Didn't do as well as preseason hype had promised . . . Can't say he didn't have chance to show his stuff . . . Played in 75 games for total of 1,174 minutes . . . Shot only 44.1 percent from the field . . . Had nearly as many assists (176) as rebounds (188) . . . Great ball-handler in open court . . . Excellent instincts . . . Had trouble finishing plays . . . Born Nov. 30, 1960, in Des Moines, Iowa . . . Was second-leading scorer (15.7 ppg) and rebounder (6.0 rpg) during senior year at UCLA . . . Hit 55.5 percent of his shots during college career, but couldn't get the easy baskets in NBA.

Year	Team	G	FG	FG Pct.	FT	FT Pct.	Reb.	Ast.	TP	Avg.
1983-84	Washington	75	180	441	95	714	188	176	455	6.1

TOP ROOKIE

TOM SEWELL 22 6-5 191   **Guard**

Came to the right team . . . Bullets looking for a reserve guard to replace Ricky Sobers . . . Acquired from Philadelphia immediately after Sixers made him No. 22 pick overall in first round...Led Lamar to sixth league championship and was named Southland Conference Player of the Year...Led team in scoring (22.9 ppg) and posted .539 shooting percentage...Born March 11, 1962 ...Raised in Pensacola, Fla....His stock rose after an outstanding performance in Aloha Classic...Not noted for defense, but can hit the open shot and the open man.

COACH GENE SHUE: Stock remains high despite disappointing  season...His patience is reflected in team's attitude and style of play...Involved in more NBA games as a player and coach (2,239) than any other active player or coach in the league ...Owns career coaching mark of 685-689, but has had some dreadful teams...Faces tough decisions on revamping a club which appears to have reached its peak with current talent...His teams always play defense...One of very few coaches in league respected by Hubie Brown..."He wins everywhere he goes," Brown says. "The record speaks for itself."...Born Dec. 18, 1931, in Baltimore...We've been with him through the crewcuts, through the mismatched clothes, through some tough times in Philadelphia and San Diego...Makes up his own mind on players...Can be too trusting, as he was with John Lucas ...Was Coach of Year in 1981-82 for taking Bullets from the old-age home into the playoffs...His teams usually not noted for their explosiveness...As a player, he averaged 14.4 ppg for Philadelphia Warriors, the Knicks, Fort Wayne, Detroit and Baltimore after winning All-American honors at Maryland.

GREATEST FOUL SHOOTER

During six seasons with the Bullets, Jack Marin hit 1,619 foul shots in 1,932 attempts for an .838 percentage and the right to be called the club's all-time greatest free-throw artist. Marin, a big part of the Baltimore teams that challenged for the title in

1969-70 and 1970-71, led the club in free-throw percentage three times and led the league with a mark of .894 in 1971-72.

Other top Bullet foul shooters have included Kevin Grevey, who played eight seasons with the Bullets and posted an .812 percentage from the line; and Phil Chenier, Kevin Loughery and Bob Dandridge, all Bullets who shot over 80 percent for the team over a significant period.

Loughery, who struggled as coach of the Chicago Bulls last season, shot .830 with the Bullets in 1965-66 to lead the team. Despite a waistline that varies greatly from season to season, he is still capable of stepping to the line and beating most of his players in a free-throw contest.

ALL-TIME BULLET LEADERS

SEASON

Points: Walt Bellamy, 2,495, 1961-62
Assists: Kevin Porter, 734, 1980-81
Rebounds: Walt Bellamy, 1,500, 1961-62

GAME

Points: Earl Monroe, 56 vs. Los Angeles, 2/3/68
Assists: Kevin Porter, 24 vs. Detroit, 3/23/80
Rebounds: Walt Bellamy, 37 vs. St. Louis, 12/4/64

CAREER

Points: Elvin Hayes, 15,551, 1972-81
Assists: Wes Unseld, 3,822, 1968-81
Rebounds: Wes Unseld, 13,769, 1968-81

DALLAS MAVERICKS

TEAM DIRECTORY: Pres.: Donald Carter; GM: Norm Sonju; Dir. Player Personnel: Rick Sund; Dir. Communications: Allen Stone; Dir. Media Services: Kevin Sullivan; Coach: Dick Motta; Asst. Coach: Bob Weiss. Arena: Reunion Arena (17,007). Colors: Blue and green.

Mark Aguirre was second in league in scoring at 29.5 ppg.

SCOUTING REPORT

SHOOTING: Did Zorro need fencing lessons? Should William Tell have enrolled in an archery course? Should the Dallas Mavericks have drafted more good shooters at the forward and guard positions? Isn't this overkill? The skeptics claim that sharpshooting Dallas will never advance deep into the playoffs until it gets that one high-percentage shooter where he's needed most—in the middle.

Rookie Sam Perkins, the fourth player chosen in the draft, will be playing the pivot this season, but, at only 6-9, he is certainly not going to find shooting as easy in the NBA as it was at North Carolina. Still, Perkins is a proven scorer and so is guard Terence Stansbury, who was taken with the 15th pick. Neither of the top two draft picks will hesitate the shoot the ball with the game on the line.

Add them to veteran Maverick marksmen Mark Aguirre (.524), Rolando Blackman (.546), Brad Davis (.530) and Dale Ellis (.456) and you can see why the Mavs should once again be among the handful of NBA clubs to shoot 50 percent from the floor.

PLAYMAKING: This is another area where the Mavericks appear to be very solid. Who can doubt the outstanding job that Davis (6.9 assists per game) has done since coming in from out of the cold of Anchorage in the CBA? He can hit the perimeter shot if needed, but concentrates on getting the ball into the hands of scorers like Aguirre, Blackman, Ellis and Jay Vincent. Coach Dick Motta's offense has been drummed into his head and it shows.

And, despite his faux pas in the playoffs against Los Angeles, Derek Harper has proven himself to be a very capable backup. Again, these guys just need the big guy in the middle so they can practice their alley-oop passes.

DEFENSE: Every direction you turn, the lack of a center keeps popping up to haunt the Mavs. Put a top-flight 7-footer in the middle on defense and Dallas' opponents would have a much tougher time shooting 50 percent. The Mavs need that shot-blocker.

Ellis is capable at one forward spot, but you can pretty much forget about Aguirre. Blackman has the size and the speed to harass opponents in the backcourt, but the Mavs' biggest defensive weapon is Harper. Once he became comfortable in the lineup last season, he began to show his aggressiveness and wound up as the club leader in steals.

REBOUNDING: Remember that big man the Mavs don't have? Of course you do. Well, where else would you expect his absence

MAVERICK ROSTER

No.	Veteran	Pos.	Ht.	Wt.	Age	Yrs. Pro	College
24	Mark Aguirre	F	6-6	229	24	4	DePaul
22	Rolando Blackman	G	6-6	200	25	4	Kansas State
15	Brad Davis	G	6-3	182	28	8	Maryland
14	Dale Ellis	F	6-7	200	24	2	Tennessee
20	Bill Garnett	F	6-10	225	24	3	Wyoming
12	Derek Harper	G	6-4	185	23	2	Illinois
40	Kurt Nimphius	C	6-11	220	26	4	Arizona State
21	*Roger Phegley	G	6-6	205	28	7	Bradley
34	*Jim Spanarkel	F-G	6-5	190	27	6	Duke
33	*Elston Turner	G	6-5	200	25	4	Mississippi
31	Jay Vincent	F	6-7	230	25	4	Michigan State
45	Mark West	C	6-10	225	23	2	Old Dominion

*Free agent unsigned at press time

Rd.	Top Draftees	Sel. No.	Ht.	Wt.	College
1	Sam Perkins	4	6-9	234	North Carolina
1	Terence Stansbury	15	6-5	170	Temple
2	Charles Sitton	38	6-9	215	Oregon State
2	Anthony Teachey	40	6-9	210	Wake Forest
2	Tom Sluby	41	6-4	190	Notre Dame

to be felt more than in the rebounding department? Dallas ranked 21st out of 23 teams. Perkins, the successor to the departed Pat Cummings, can leap, but he's not going to change the picture dramatically. Houston's Ralph Sampson and Akeem Olajuwon will be able to play volleyball against the glass during their meetings with the undersized Mavs.

OUTLOOK: In the beginning, the Mavericks had a grand five-year scenario that would eventually land them a spot in the playoffs. Well, Dallas grew a little faster than expected, winning 43 games, finishing second in the division to Utah and earning its first playoff berth last year.

The problem is that to take that next step up the ladder—and going from 43 to 48 wins is a big jump—Dallas needs a center. By passing up Kentucky's Melvin Turpin in the draft, the Mavs are obviously rolling the dice again in hopes of coming up with Georgetown's Patrick Ewing in 1985. Keep in mind the Mavs own the No. 1 pick of Cleveland and Denver in the upcoming draft. This season, Dallas will be fortunate to repeat last season's accomplishments and is not likely to get past the first round of the playoffs until that big man arrives in Big D.

MAVERICK PROFILES

MARK AGUIRRE 24 6-6 229   Forward

No more bad attitude... Met with coach Dick Motta before the season to clear the air, then went on to have his finest NBA season... Ranked second in league in scoring (29.5 ppg) behind Adrian Dantley... When he has got it going, he can't be stopped... Will take it to the hole or pull up for a jumper from the outside... Has one of the quickest releases of anyone in the game... Earned his first selection to the All-Star Game... Shoots well over 50 percent... With his shaped-up body and attitude, he is the team leader... Spent much of his first two pro years in Motta's doghouse... Born Dec. 10, 1959, in Chicago... Starred for three years at DePaul, but he and team failed in NCAA Tournament play... Mavs made him No. 1 overall pick in the 1981 draft... Used to be known as "The Pillsbury Doughboy" and "The Muffin Man"... Now he has one of the lowest levels of body fat in league.

Year	Team	G	FG	FG Pct.	FT	FT Pct.	Reb.	Ast.	TP	Avg.
1981-82	Dallas	51	381	.465	168	.680	249	164	955	18.7
1982-83	Dallas	81	767	.483	429	.728	508	332	1979	24.4
1983-84	Dallas	79	925	.524	465	.749	469	358	2330	29.5
	Totals	211	2073	.497	1062	.729	1226	854	5264	24.9

ROLANDO BLACKMAN 25 6-6 200   Guard

The other half of the Dallas one-two punch... The best thing to come out of Panama since Roberto Duran... Broke through to the star level in third pro season and gained respect around the league... Should have made the All-Star team... Can handle the ball, play defense and shoot... In short, he does it all... Born Feb. 26, 1959, in Panama City, Panama... Started sports career as soccer player in his native land, then took up basketball after his family moved to Brooklyn when he was seven... A portrait in persistence, he was cut from basketball teams in the seventh, eighth and ninth grades... Led the Mavs in field-goal percentage (.546) and holds the all-time record at Kansas

State ... A first-round 1981 pick with the choice acquired from Denver in the Kiki Vandeweghe trade ... Will excel for years.

Year	Team	G	FG	FG Pct.	FT	FT Pct.	Reb.	Ast.	TP	Avg.
1981-82	Dallas	82	439	.513	212	.768	254	105	1091	13.3
1982-83	Dallas	75	513	.492	297	.780	293	185	1326	17.7
1983-84	Dallas	81	721	.546	372	.812	373	288	1815	22.4
	Totals	238	1673	.520	881	.790	920	578	4232	17.8

JAY VINCENT 25 6-7 230   Forward

His address is the doghouse ... His stock dropped dramatically from his first two years and his scoring average fell more than seven points to 11.0 ppg ... Partly a victim of the overcrowded situation at forward and partly a victim of his own grumbling ... Born July 10, 1959, in Kalamazoo, Mich. ... Was a high-school rival of Magic Johnson, then became his teammate at Michigan State and won an NCAA title in 1979 ... Mavs scooped him up on the second round of the draft in 1981 ... Burst into prominence when Mark Aguirre went down with a broken toe and continued to play strong in his second year ... Shot poorly last season and frequently asked to be traded ... Lost much of his playing time to rookie Dale Ellis ... Aguirre calls him "Big Daddy" ... A businessman ... Owns several record stores that feature home delivery ... Carries briefcase on the road ... Plays the drums, sings and jogs.

Year	Team	G	FG	FG Pct.	FT	FT Pct.	Reb.	Ast.	TP	Avg.
1981-82	Dallas	81	719	.497	293	.716	565	176	1732	21.4
1982-83	Dallas	81	622	.489	269	.784	592	212	1513	18.7
1983-84	Dallas	61	252	.435	168	.781	247	114	672	11.0
	Totals	223	1593	.483	730	.755	1404	502	3917	17.6

BRAD DAVIS 28 6-3 182   Guard

At long last, somebody wants to keep him ... Has got more mileage on his odometer and more dents in his fenders than a used car, but he certainly has proven to be valuable ... Scrappy, tough ... Runs the offense the way Dick Motta wants it run ... Born Dec. 17, 1955, in Rochester, Pa. ... Set an NBA record for guards in 1982-83 by shooting .572 from the field ... Scores mostly on the break, but is capable shooter from perimeter ... Drafted on the first round in 1977—ahead of Norm Nixon—by Lakers ... Bounced around to Indiana and Utah, then to the CBA before reluctantly signing with Dallas in 1980...Played under Lefty Driesell at Maryland...A baseball fanatic, he had a tryout with the Pittsburgh Pirates...Texas Rangers fan who worked with their TV crew during off-season.

Year	Team	G	FG	FG Pct.	FT	FT Pct.	Reb.	Ast.	TP	Avg.
1977-78	Los Angeles	33	30	.417	22	.759	35	83	82	2.5
1978-79	L.A.-Ind.	27	31	.564	16	.696	17	52	78	2.9
1979-80	Ind.-Utah	18	35	.556	13	.813	17	50	83	4.6
1980-81	Dallas	56	230	.561	163	.799	151	385	626	11.2
1981-82	Dallas	82	397	.515	185	.804	226	509	993	12.1
1982-83	Dallas	79	359	.572	186	.845	198	565	915	11.6
1983-84	Dallas	81	345	.530	199	.836	187	561	896	11.1
	Totals	376	1427	.538	784	.817	831	2205	3673	9.8

DALE ELLIS 24 6-7 200   Forward

The hits just keep on coming...Latest of the forwards who were drafted by the Mavs and shined as rookies...First-round 1983 choice out of Tennessee, he was a surprise pick ...Quickly earned time in the lineup, displacing Jay Vincent...Very capable shooter from the perimeter...Will also play some defense...Born Aug. 6, 1960, in Marietta, Ga....Averaged more than 22 ppg his senior year in college...While playing for the Volunteers, he had such varied defensive assignments as 7-4 Ralph Sampson and 6-4 Jeff Malone...Twin brother Darryl is a Marine.

Year	Team	G	FG	FG Pct.	FT	FT Pct.	Reb.	Ast.	TP	Avg.
1983-84	Dallas	67	225	.456	87	.719	250	56	549	8.2

BILL GARNETT 24 6-10 225   Forward

A flop...How else can you describe a guy who was the No. 4 pick in the 1982 draft and averaged only 5.1 ppg last season?...Mavs had choice between him and LaSalle Thompson and obviously went wrong...Born April 22, 1960, in Kansas City, he grew up in Denver...Nothing special in high school...Went to Wyoming and attracted attention by hitting 60 percent from the field...Father Shad was a defensive tackle at Kansas and was drafted by the San Francisco 49ers...Has been squeezed out of Dick Motta's playing rotation...Scores nothing more than garbage points and hits an occasional jumper...Can't play defense . . . When he was student-teaching third-graders, one youngster summed him up perfectly when he said, "The best thing about Mr. Garnett is that he can change lightbulbs without using a ladder."

Year	Team	G	FG	FG Pct.	FT	FT Pct.	Reb.	Ast.	TP	Avg.
1982-83	Dallas	75	170	.533	129	.741	406	103	469	6.3
1983-84	Dallas	80	141	.472	129	.733	331	128	411	5.1
	Totals	155	311	.503	258	.737	737	231	880	5.7

KURT NIMPHIUS 26 6-11 220   Center

Who? . . . Just when you start to wonder what he's doing in the league, he'll come off the bench to hit a key bucket, grab a crucial rebound or swat a shot back in somebody's face . . . Fans on the road may laugh, but he has been a very valuable backup and has allowed the Mavs to get away without a true NBA center the last three years . . . But, with Pat Cummings gone, the heat will be on him and rookie Sam Perkins now . . . Born March 13, 1958, in Milwaukee . . . Played on Arizona State team that included NBA players Alton Lister, Sam Williams and Lafayette Lever . . . Drafted on the third round by Denver in 1980, then cut . . . Played in Italy and the CBA . . . Mavs signed him as a free agent in 1981 and have never regretted it . . . Married his wife Susan while playing in Italy . . . Likes to tour the country during the off-season.

Year	Team	G	FG	FG Pct.	FT	FT Pct.	Reb.	Ast.	TP	Avg.
1981-82	Dallas	63	137	.461	63	.583	295	61	337	5.3
1982-83	Dallas	81	174	.490	77	.550	404	115	426	5.3
1983-84	Dallas	82	272	.520	101	.623	513	176	646	7.9
	Totals	226	583	.496	241	.588	1212	352	1409	6.2

DEREK HARPER 23 6-4 185   Guard

Ooops! . . . That will likely be everyone's memory of this guy for a long time . . . Dribbled away the final seconds of Game 4 of Dallas' playoff series with Los Angeles, thinking his team was ahead by a point. Actually the score was tied and Mavs lost in overtime . . . Single biggest mistake of the NBA season . . . Born Oct. 13, 1961, in New York City, he grew up in West Palm Beach, Fla. . . . The third guard selected and the No. 11 pick overall in 1983 draft . . . Before his big playoff blunder, he had come on strong to have a good second half of the season...An enthusiastic defensive player and a capable shooter...A psychology major at Illinois...Tough-minded...Will have to be after his big blunder.

Year	Team	G	FG	FG Pct.	FT	FT Pct.	Reb.	Ast.	TP	Avg.
1983-84	Dallas	82	200	.443	66	.673	172	239	469	5.7

ELSTON TURNER 25 6-5 200   Guard

A scrapper...A hustler...Came along in the same 1981 draft treasure chest that included Mark Aguirre, Rolando Blackman and Jay Vincent...Made the team by playing defense and making the sacrifices...His playing time has diminished, but he's valuable to have in a pinch...Born July 10, 1959, in Knoxville, Tenn....Tennessee did not recruit him, so he went to Ole Miss and helped the Rebels gain an NIT berth in his junior year...Mavericks plucked him with 43rd pick in the draft...Will always be fighting for a job.

Year	Team	G	FG	FG Pct.	FT	FT Pct.	Reb.	Ast.	TP	Avg.
1981-82	Dallas	80	282	.441	97	.703	301	189	661	8.3
1982-83	Dallas	59	96	.403	20	.667	152	88	214	3.6
1983-84	Dallas	47	54	.360	28	.824	93	59	137	2.9
	Totals	186	432	.421	145	.718	546	336	1012	5.4

MARK WEST 23 6-10 225   Center

A project...Taken on the second round in the 1983 draft with a pick obtained from Utah for Billy McKinney...Was on the roster all season, but played only 202 minutes in 34 games...Slow and no real threat at either end...Born Nov. 5, 1960, in Fort Campbell, Ky., but grew up in Petersburg, Va., the home of Moses Malone...Played at Old Dominion...College basketball's third-leading shot-blocker of all-time, behind Ralph Sampson and Tree Rollins...Has a degree in finance and is likely to be making a fortune on Wall Street rather than in the NBA.

Year	Team	G	FG	FG Pct.	FT	FT Pct.	Reb.	Ast.	TP	Avg.
1983-84	Dallas	34	15	.357	7	.318	46	13	37	1.1

ROGER PHEGLEY 28 6-6 205   Guard

Travelin' man...Has been with five teams in six NBA seasons...There's no reason to think that Dallas will be his last stop...Signed as a free agent late in the season and played only 76 minutes in 10 games...Born Oct. 16, 1956, in Peoria, Ill....Stayed at home and went to Bradley...Set seven school records there and was 14th player taken in 1978 draft, by Washington...Went to college on a baseball scholarship and had a tryout with the Cincinnati Reds...Best weapon is an outside shot...But he has never hit 50 percent from the field or averaged more than 14.4 ppg...His other NBA stops were in New Jersey, Cleveland and San Antonio...Could have a career on NBA benches.

Year	Team	G	FG	FG Pct.	FT	FT Pct.	Reb.	Ast.	TP	Avg.
1978-79	Washington	29	28	.359	24	.828	22	25	80	2.8
1979-80	Wash.-N.J.	78	350	.477	177	.872	185	102	881	11.3
1980-81	Cleveland	82	474	.491	224	.839	246	184	1180	14.4
1981-82	Clev.-S.A.	81	233	.460	85	.780	154	114	556	6.9
1982-83	San Antonio	62	120	.449	43	.768	84	60	286	4.6
1983-84	S.A.-Dallas	13	11	.314	4	1.000	11	11	28	2.2
	Totals	345	1216	.470	557	.834	702	486	3011	8.7

TOP ROOKIES

SAM PERKINS 23 6-9 234   Forward-Center

Most polished player in the draft...Should be a long-time star... Will be asked to play center in Dallas...Lacks height, but has a 77-inch wing span, the equal of somebody much bigger...Born June 14, 1961, in Latham, N.Y....Has a fine outside touch ...Motivation is the only question mark...Three-time All-American at North Carolina...Averaged 17.6 ppg and 9.6 rpg in final season as Tar Heel.

TERENCE STANSBURY 23 6-5 170   Guard

Solid all-around game...Can handle the ball and hit the outside shot...Many scouts liked him...Born Feb. 27, 1961, in Los Angeles...Passed Guy Rodgers to become the all-time leading scorer at Temple with 1,811 points...Third-team All-American...His 25-footer at the buzzer beat St. John's in NCAA Tournament...Averaged 18.6 ppg as senior after posting 24.6-ppg mark in 1982-83.

COACH DICK MOTTA: Has gotten the job done in Chicago, Washington and now Dallas... Used stern hand to bring this fourth-year expansion franchise home with its first winning record (43-39) and first playoff berth... Enjoys the challenge and, though he probably won't admit it, this is probably the most fun he has had coaching... Bringing along young talent like Mark Aguirre and Rolando Blackman perfectly ... Born Sept. 3, 1931, in Medvale, Utah... Son of an Italian farmer... Was cut from his high school and college teams ... Attended Utah State... One of the first college coaches to make transition to NBA ranks... Led Weber State to three straight Big Sky titles, then turned expansion Bulls into playoff contenders... Won NBA title with Washington in 1977-78 ... Operating on a handshake basis with Mavs' owner Donald Carter... Loves the wide-open spaces... Spends the off-seasons in Fish Haven, Idaho... The fifth-winningest coach in league history with 665 victories, against 647 defeats.

GREATEST FOUL SHOOTER

Having been in existence for only four NBA seasons, the Mavericks don't have much of a history. But they have had a couple of fine free-throw shooters.

Jim Spanarkel still sits at the top of the club list in percentage (.857 in his four years in Dallas) and that is only fitting since he was the only member of the original expansion team to be with the franchise during 1983-84. Still, Spanarkel spent all but seven games of the season on the injured list following a wrist injury.

Meanwhile, Brad Davis continued to establish himself as one of the league's finest point guards and one of Mavericks' top free-throw shooters. Davis' .836 mark last season left him second on the club in foul-shooting accuracy with an .822 percentage during his four years as a Maverick and he will surely move to the head of the class in the near future.

Not bad for a guy who just four seasons ago was ready to give up basketball after finishing the year in the CBA.

ALL-TIME MAVERICK LEADERS

SEASON

Points: Mark Aguirre, 2,330, 1983-84
Assists: Brad Davis, 565, 1982-83
Rebounds: Pat Cummings, 668, 1982-83

GAME

Points: Mark Aguirre, 46 vs. Denver, 3/24/84
Assists: Brad Davis, 16 vs. Los Angeles, 3/17/81
       Brad Davis, 16 vs. Kansas City, 2/26/81
       Mark Aguirre, 16 vs. Denver, 1/14/83
Rebounds: Pat Cummings, 20 vs. Seattle, 3/2/83

CAREER

Points: Jay Vincent, 3,041, 1981-83
Assists: Brad Davis, 1,459, 1980-83
Rebounds: Jay Vincent, 1,157, 1981-83

DENVER NUGGETS

TEAM DIRECTORY: Owner: Red McCombs; Pres.: Vince Boryla; GM: Paul Phipps; Asst. GM: Paula Hanson; Dir. Pub. Rel.: Tom Hohensee; Coach: Doug Moe; Asst. Coach: Allan Bristow. Arena: McNichols Sports Arena (17,251). Colors: White, blue, green, yellow, red, purple and orange.

SCOUTING REPORT

SHOOTING: Coach Doug Moe's Nuggets have always operated under the hand-grenade theory of offense—if you throw up enough of them, you're bound to hit something. Actually, the motion offense has produced some very good open shooting opportunities—and Denver has always had plenty of very good open shooters.

Dan Issel (.493) and Alex English (.529) are still around, but, with Kiki Vandeweghe now in Portland, the Nuggets will be a little more conventional on offense. They will look to work the ball inside to newly-acquired center Wayne Cooper, a .459 shooter. The Vandeweghe deal also brought forward Calvin Natt, who ranked fifth in the league last season with a .583 mark, despite taking most of his shots from the perimeter. Once again, there's no shortage of people to put the ball into the little round hole in the Rockies.

PLAYMAKING: There are those who will tell you that a playmaker is a fifth wheel in Moe's offense. Actually, everybody on the floor has to be a playmaker, since the motion offense relies calls for players to pass the ball until it reaches the hands of an open man. And, based on the frequency with which the Nuggets take shots, it seems to work.

Still, when you get to the playoffs and want to work the ball inside, you do need a real point guard. And considering that the Nuggets spent the off-season trying to peddle Rob Williams and Howard Carter, it's probably safe to say they didn't have one last season. Lafayette Lever (4.3 assists per game), the other player obtained for Vandeweghe, will probably step right into the starting lineup. While splitting the duties with Darnell Valentine the last two years in Portland, he has given every indication he is going to be a good one.

DEFENSE: Are you kidding? This club lost to Detroit, 186-184, last season. Denver lives by that old motto: the best defense is a

Nuggets' Alex English shot .824 from foul line.

good offense. The Nuggets try to stop the opposition by wearing them out with the breakneck pace and it's very effective at the high altitude in Denver. When you bring them down to sea level—or into the more controlled atmosphere of the playoffs—the Nuggets are defenseless. Lever is very capable in the backcourt and is probably their best defensive player. Nobody here will ever win the Olivia Newton-John "Let's Get Physical Award."

REBOUNDING: The Nuggets have been known to get their fair share of rebounds, ranking in the middle of the NBA pack. The

NUGGET ROSTER

No.	Veteran	Pos.	Ht.	Wt.	Age	Yrs. Pro	College
35	*Richard Anderson	F	6-10	243	23	3	UC-Santa Barbara
32	Howard Carter	G	6-5	220	23	2	Louisiana State
42	Wayne Cooper	C	6-10	230	28	7	New Orleans
23	*T.R. Dunn	G	6-4	192	29	8	Alabama
10	Keith Edmonson	G	6-5	203	24	3	Purdue
2	Alex English	F	6-7	190	30	9	South Carolina
5	Mike Evans	G	6-1	170	29	6	Kansas State
24	*Bill Hanzlik	G	6-7	200	26	5	Notre Dame
44	Dan Issel	C	6-9	240	36	15	Kentucky
12	Lafayette Lever	G	6-3	170	24	3	Arizona State
33	Calvin Natt	F	6-6	220	27	6	NE Louisiana
34	Danny Schayes	C	6-11	245	25	4	Syracuse
21	Rob Williams	G	6-2	175	23	3	Houston

*Free agent unsigned at press time

Rd.	Top Draftees	Sel. No.	Ht.	Wt.	College
2	Willie White	42	6-3	205	Tenn.-Chattanooga
4	Karl Tilleman	79	6-2	180	Calgary
5	Prince Bridges	103	6-1½	165	Missouri
6	Willie Burton	125	6-7	210	Tennessee
7	Mark Simpson	149	6-8	225	Catawba

problem is the opposition usually gets more. Denver allowed opponents to pull down more rebounds than any other club in the league last season and that is not likely to change because Cooper is in town. When your frontline people like Issel and English are busy putting up jumpers from 10- to 20- feet away, they're not going to be in very good position to grab their missed shots. The best rebounder on the club is T.R. Dunn (7.2 rpg). Considering he's a 6-4 guard, that's not saying very much.

OUTLOOK: The front office is obviously going for a new look. That's why they were willing to trade the popular Vandeweghe. Statistical studies showed that English was a more effective all-around player—translation: Kiki don't play D—and that's why he stayed in Denver. Anyway, this is a transition year for the Nuggets. Problem is, they have already traded away their No. 1 draft pick in 1985 to Dallas.

The Nuggets figure to be a team that still runs a lot, but without the same results. For Denver fans tired of seeing their team make an early exit from the playoffs, this season will offer a change—Denver won't even qualify. And Moe is the early favorite to be the first coach fired this season.

NUGGET PROFILES

ALEX ENGLISH 30 6-7 190   Forward

Poetry in motion... It's a thing of beauty to watch him shoot his unorthodox jumper from the baseline... Hardly looks like he's breaking a sweat... Just seems to pop open at different spots on the floor... Makes his defender pay by scoring right in his face... Has been on the trading block forever... After leading the NBA in scoring two years ago, he dropped to fourth last season... Led the Nuggets in minutes played (2,870) and field goals (907) and was second in assists (406)... Born Jan. 5, 1954, in Columbia, S.C., and attended South Carolina... Before the Nuggets traded Kiki Vandeweghe in the off-season, he and English formed one of the greatest one-two scoring punches in the history of the league... Sensitive and introspective... Published a book of his own poems three years ago.

Year	Team	G	FG	FG Pct.	FT	FT Pct.	Reb.	Ast.	TP	Avg.
1976-77	Milwaukee	60	132	.477	46	.767	168	25	310	5.2
1977-78	Milwaukee	82	343	.542	104	.727	395	129	790	9.6
1978-79	Indiana	81	563	.511	173	.752	655	271	1299	16.0
1979-80	Ind.-Den.	78	553	.501	210	.789	605	224	1318	16.9
1980-81	Denver	81	768	.494	390	.850	646	290	1929	23.8
1981-82	Denver	82	855	.551	372	.840	558	433	2082	25.4
1982-83	Denver	82	959	.516	406	.829	601	397	2326	28.4
1983-84	Denver	82	907	.529	352	.824	464	406	2167	26.4
	Totals	628	5080	.518	2053	.815	4092	2175	12221	19.5

DAN ISSEL 36 6-9 240   Center

King of the mountains... The only things missing from this guy are his front teeth and maybe a couple of inches in height... Has spent his entire career doing battle with the giants in the middle... And somehow he gets the job done... Developed a great touch from outside when he was killing spare time during his University of Kentucky practices under coach Adolph Rupp... Born Oct. 24, 1948, in Geneva, Ill.... Played for the ABA Kentucky Colonels until the year before the league folded in 1976... Has been a fixture in Denver for the last nine seasons... The only time he has played alongside a real pro center, Artis Gilmore, they won an ABA title in Kentucky... When a defender comes out to guard against the jumper, he'll drive to the hoop with surprising quickness... Owns a stable of thoroughbred horses.

Year	Team	G	FG	FG Pct.	FT	FT Pct.	Reb.	Ast.	TP	Avg.
1970-71	Kentucky (ABA)	83	938	.470	604	.807	1093	162	2480	29.9
1971-72	Kentucky (ABA)	83	972	.486	591	.785	931	195	2538	30.6
1972-73	Kentucky (ABA)	84	892	.513	485	.764	922	220	2292	27.3
1973-74	Kentucky (ABA)	83	829	.480	457	.787	847	137	2118	25.5
1974-75	Kentucky (ABA)	83	614	.471	237	.738	710	188	1465	17.7
1975-76	Denver (ABA)......	84	752	.511	425	.816	923	201	1930	23.0
1976-77	Denver..........	79	660	.515	445	.797	696	177	1765	22.3
1977-78	Denver..........	82	659	.512	428	.782	830	304	1746	21.3
1978-79	Denver..........	81	532	.517	316	.754	738	255	1380	17.0
1979-80	Denver..........	82	715	.505	517	.775	719	198	1951	23.8
1980-81	Denver..........	80	614	.503	519	.759	676	158	1749	21.9
1981-82	Denver..........	81	651	.527	546	.834	608	179	1852	22.9
1982-83	Denver..........	80	661	.510	400	.835	596	223	1726	21.6
1983-84	Denver..........	76	569	.493	364	.850	513	173	1506	19.8
	Totals	1141	10068	.499	6334	.792	10802	2770	26498	23.2

LAFAYETTE LEVER 24 6-3 170   Guard

"Fat" is his nickname—not because he's overweight, but because that's the way his younger sliblings pronounced his name when he was growing up... Had two productive seasons in Portland before moving to Denver in the Kiki Vandeweghe trade... But he was never going to reach full-time status running the offense as long as Darnell Valentine was breathing ... Plays solid defense, is quick and could really blossom with the Nuggets... Born Aug. 18, 1960, in Pine Bluff, Ark., he grew up in Tucson, Ariz.... Trail Blazers picked him first in 1983 ... Starred at Arizona State... Doesn't score big, but Denver doesn't need points from him... Will spread the ball around.

Year	Team	G	FG	FG Pct.	FT	FT Pct.	Reb.	Ast.	TP	Avg.
1982-83	Portland	81	256	.431	116	.730	225	426	633	7.8
1983-84	Portland	81	313	.447	159	.743	218	372	788	9.7
	Totals	162	569	.439	275	.737	443	798	1421	8.8

CALVIN NATT 27 6-6 220   Forward

When the Portland Trail Blazers traded him to the Denver, they probably informed him by phone or mail... You don't mess with Calvin... He's rough, he's tough and he likes to mix it up... His size is what's kept him from reaching superstar status in the league... Plays a power forward's game with a small forward's body... Has a good touch from the outside

...Born Jan. 8, 1957, in Bastrop, La....The son of a Baptist minister...The Nets' top draft choice in 1979, but he didn't last out his rookie season there...Spent the last four-plus years in Portland...Hit at a .583 clip last season from the field last season, but his scoring average dropped more than four points...Attended Northeastern Louisiana...Younger brother Kenny had a brief career with Utah and now plays in the CBA.

Year	Team	G	FG	FG Pct.	FT	FT Pct.	Reb.	Ast.	TP	Avg.
1979-80	N.J.-Port.	78	622	.479	306	.730	691	169	1553	19.9
1980-81	Portland	74	395	.497	200	.707	431	159	994	13.4
1981-82	Portland	75	515	.576	294	.750	613	150	1326	17.7
1982-83	Portland	80	644	.543	339	.792	599	171	1630	20.4
1983-84	Portland	79	500	.583	275	.797	476	179	1277	16.2
	Totals	386	2676	.532	1414	.757	2810	828	6780	17.6

DANNY SCHAYES 25 6-11 245   Center

It's doubtful he'll follow father Dolph into the Hall of Fame...But his size alone is likely to keep him in the league for a long time...A smart player with a degree in chemistry from Syracuse...But he doesn't bang around under the boards enough to make full use of his body...Prefers to shoot jumpers from the perimeter...May be a white version of Darryl Dawkins...Born May 10, 1959, in Syracuse, N.Y....Has not yet proven he can be a consistent offensive threat...Still strictly a backup to 36-year-old Dan Issel and may have to move out to forward with the acquisition of Wayne Cooper...Plays the trombone.

Year	Team	G	FG	FG Pct.	FT	FT Pct.	Reb.	Ast.	TP	Avg.
1981-82	Utah	82	252	.481	140	.757	427	146	644	7.9
1982-83	Utah-Den.	82	342	.457	228	.773	635	205	912	11.1
1983-84	Denver	82	183	.493	215	.790	433	91	581	7.1
	Totals	246	777	.473	583	.775	1495	442	2137	8.7

WAYNE COOPER 28 6-10 230   Center

On the road again...Playing for his fifth team in six pro seasons...Obtained from Portland with Lafayette Lever, Calvin Natt and two draft picks for Kiki Vandeweghe...Became expendable in Portland when the Blazers drafted Sam Bowie...Make no mistake about it, he's a journeyman...But he is competent and has been improving since working with hoop guru Pete Newell at his summer camp...Started 38 games for the Blazers last season...Tied Natt for the team lead in rebounds

...Never has been a serious offensive threat, but that could change in Doug Moe's motion offense...Born Sept. 16, 1956, in Milan, Ga....Played under Butch van Breda Kolff at University of New Orleans...Has made other pro stops at Golden State, Utah and Dallas.

Year	Team	G	FG	FG Pct.	FT	FT Pct.	Reb.	Ast.	TP	Avg.
1978-79	Golden State	65	128	.437	41	.672	280	21	297	4.6
1979-80	Golden State	79	367	.489	136	.751	507	42	871	11.0
1980-81	Utah	71	213	.452	62	.689	440	52	489	6.9
1981-82	Dallas	76	281	.420	119	.744	550	115	682	9.0
1982-83	Portland	80	320	.443	135	.685	611	116	775	9.7
1983-84	Portland	81	304	.459	185	.804	476	76	793	9.8
	Totals	452	1613	.452	678	.738	2864	422	3907	8.6

BILL HANZLIK 26 6-7 200   Guard

Who says that attributes like hustle and willingness to sacrifice your body aren't appreciated anymore?...They're the only reasons this guy's pro career has lasted four years...Came over from Seattle in July 1982 as part of the David Thompson trade...If it's possible, his shooting had actually gotten worse over the last two seasons...You'd almost think he shoots with his eyes closed...Born Dec. 6, 1957, in Middletown, Ohio...Has been a jack of all trades with the Nuggets...Missed only two games in the last two years...A member of the 1980 Olympic team after a successful career at Notre Dame.

Year	Team	G	FG	FG Pct.	FT	FT Pct.	Reb.	Ast.	TP	Avg.
1980-81	Seattle	74	138	.478	119	.793	153	111	396	5.4
1981-82	Seattle	81	167	.468	138	.784	266	183	472	5.8
1982-83	Denver	82	187	.428	125	.781	236	268	500	6.1
1983-84	Denver	80	132	.431	167	.807	205	252	434	5.4
	Totals	317	624	.449	549	.792	860	814	1802	5.7

ROB WILLIAMS 23 6-2 175   Guard

On the edge...What once looked like a very promising pro career could come to an abrupt end if he doesn't turn it around quickly ...Reported late to camp as a rookie and was branded "a fat little hog" by coach Doug Moe...In his second year, he was repeatedly late for practices, buses and planes, always blaming robberies at his home..."What do they want, his gold tooth?" asked Moe...Has shown flashes of ability, but hasn't been able to maintain any consistency...Shoots a hor-

rible-looking flat jumper...Born May 5, 1961, in Houston...
Was a star for the University of Houston before leaving in igno-
miny after an 0-for-8 shooting performance in the Final Four
finished his junior year...Denver took him reluctantly as the 19th
selection in the 1982 draft and has never really been happy with
him...Faces the real possibility of losing his job to Lafayette
Lever.

Year	Team	G	FG	FG Pct.	FT	FT Pct.	Reb.	Ast.	TP	Avg.
1982-83	Denver	74	191	.408	131	.753	136	361	515	7.0
1983-84	Denver	79	309	.461	171	.818	194	464	804	10.2
	Totals	153	500	.439	302	.789	330	825	1319	8.6

T.R. DUNN 29 6-4 192   Guard

Has never averaged in double figures in seven
NBA seasons, yet is indispensable...Plays the
good defense and is the best rebounding guard
in the NBA...Initials T.R. stand for Theodore
Roosevelt...Born Feb. 1, 1955, in Birmingham, Ala....Had a solid-but-unspectacular
college career at the University of Alabama
...Was a second-round draft choice by Port-
land in 1977...He's no threat at all from the outside...But he
knows his role and picks up all of his points by sneaking inside
for garbage baskets...Very durable...A knee injury forced him
to miss two games last season, the only time he's been sidelined
in four years with the Nuggets.

Year	Team	G	FG	FG Pct.	FT	FT Pct.	Reb.	Ast.	TP	Avg.
1977-78	Portland	63	100	.417	37	.661	147	45	237	3.8
1978-79	Portland	80	246	.448	122	.772	344	103	614	7.7
1979-80	Portland	82	240	.436	84	.757	324	147	564	6.9
1980-81	Denver	82	146	.412	79	.653	301	81	371	4.5
1981-82	Denver	82	258	.512	153	.712	559	188	669	8.2
1982-83	Denver	82	254	.482	119	.730	615	189	627	7.6
1983-84	Denver	80	174	.470	106	.731	574	228	454	5.7
	Totals	551	1418	.458	700	.722	2864	981	3536	6.4

KEITH EDMONSON 24 6-5 203   Guard

Living proof that so many of those post-season
basketball tournaments are just scam vacations
for NBA scouts...His stock soared in the spring
of 1982 and the Atlanta Hawks made him their
first-round draft choice...Played only 309
minutes as a rookie...Made intermediate stop
in San Antonio last season before being dealt
to Denver for a third-round draft choice...Born

Sept. 28, 1960, in San Antonio...All-time San Antonio high school scoring champ...Established himself as a decent scorer in last two years at Purdue...Holds a degree in radio-TV and will probably have to put it to use soon.

Year	Team	G	FG	FG Pct.	FT	FT Pct.	Reb.	Ast.	TP	Avg.
1982-83	Atlanta	32	48	.345	16	.593	39	22	112	3.5
1983-84	Denver	55	158	.492	94	.746	88	34	410	7.5
	Totals	87	206	.448	110	.719	127	56	522	6.0

HOWARD CARTER 23 6-5 220   Guard

The Nuggets' second straight first-round draft choice with a questionable future...Billed as an outstanding shooter and scorer coming out of college, he made only 45 percent of his shots as a rookie...Born Oct. 26, 1961, in Baton Rouge, La....Became a legend in Louisiana schoolboy history...The third-leading scorer on the LSU all-time list, behind Pete Maravich and Rudy Macklin...Credits the wife of an assistant coach at LSU with making him a better shooter...Would probably be wise give her a call again.

Year	Team	G	FG	FG Pct.	FT	FT Pct.	Reb.	Ast.	TP	Avg.
1983-84	Denver	55	145	.459	47	.770	86	71	342	6.2

RICHARD ANDERSON 23 6-10 243   Forward

Someday, when he tells his grandchildren he played in the NBA, they won't find it any easier to believe than we do today...Stuck as a 1982 second-round draft choice of the San Diego Clippers, partly because the lowly franchise needed bodies...Hustles and runs the floor, but he's no threat to score and doesn't play defense...Born Nov. 19, 1960, in Anaheim, Cal....Went to college at Santa Barbara...Plays volleyball...Majored in sociology...Typical California boy...Nuggets traded Billy McKinney to the Clippers for him to add some bulk to the frontline...Will be gone soon.

Year	Team	G	FG	FG Pct.	FT	FT Pct.	Reb.	Ast.	TP	Avg.
1982-83	San Diego	78	174	.404	48	.696	272	120	403	5.2
1983-84	Denver	78	272	.426	116	.773	406	193	663	8.5
	Totals	156	446	.417	164	.749	678	313	1066	6.8

MIKE EVANS 29 6-1 170   **Guard**

Speed and quickness . . . Without them, he'd be out of the league . . . Has no other exceptional talent . . . Can only dream about shooting 50 percent from the field, but is not shy . . . The best three-point shooter on the team . . . Has been with Denver for the last two years and that's practically a lifetime, considering he made three stops—San Antonio, Milwaukee and Cleveland—in his first three seasons . . . Born April 19, 1955, in Goldsboro, N.C. . . . A first-round draft choice of Denver in 1978 after a solid career at Kansas State . . . Nuggets promptly traded him to Kings, who cut him . . . Bounced around in the CBA before getting another shot with the Nuggets via a 10-day contract . . . Always in danger of losing his job.

Year	Team	G	FG	FG Pct.	FT	FT Pct.	Reb.	Ast.	TP	Avg.
1979-80	San Antonio	79	208	.448	58	.682	107	230	486	6.2
1980-81	Milwaukee	71	134	.460	50	.781	87	167	320	4.5
1981-82	Mil.-Clev.	22	35	.407	13	.650	22	42	83	3.8
1982-83	Denver	42	115	.473	33	.805	58	113	263	6.3
1983-84	Denver	78	243	.431	111	.847	138	288	629	8.1
	Totals	292	735	.446	265	.777	412	840	1781	6.1

TOP ROOKIE

WILLIE WHITE 22 6-3 205   **Guard**

Tenth-leading free-throw shooter (.867) in the nation as a senior . . . Showed good touch from perimeter and was an above-average passer at Tennessee-Chattanooga . . . Southern Conference Player of the Year in 1983 . . . An all-around athlete, who was offered football scholarship and drafted by Montreal Expos . . . Born Aug. 20, 1962, in Memphis, Tenn. . . . Averaged 18.5 ppg in final season.

COACH DOUG MOE: Is his act beginning to wear thin in the

thin air of the Rockies? . . . After three years of keeping the natives excited with his run-and-gun brand of basketball, there was definitely disenchantment last season . . . For the first time in his eight-year pro coaching career, his team finished below .500 . . . Admittedly, he's been handicapped by the lack of a dominating big man in the middle . . . But he whacked his own thumb with the hammer when he attempted to tamper with the success formula of Dan Issel, Alex English, Kiki Vandeweghe on offense... By the time he went back to the system, the Nuggets were out of the playoff picture... Has been taking grief for his high-scoring style for years, but winning most of the time... Known for his loud laugh and outgoing personality... Born Sept. 21, 1938, in New York City... Played under Dean Smith at North Carolina... For the first time since arriving in Denver in 1981, he's on the hot seat with the Nuggets... His overall NBA record at San Antonio and Denver is 332-277.

Calvin Natt now blazes trail to the Rockies.

GREATEST FOUL SHOOTER

Kiki Vandeweghe was asked how a kid growing up in Southern California could manage to not have a tan. "The sun doesn't shine in the gym," he replied.

Indeed, the gym is where Vandeweghe has spent so much time through the years working on the fundamental aspects of his game, including his foul shooting.

Vandeweghe is proficient from anywhere on the court, but he's especially tough from the line (.857 in a four-year career). If you give him an opening, Kiki will burn you, and if you give him a free trip to the line, he'll make you pay.

But even without Kiki, the Nuggets remain the best foul-shooting team in the NBA. Dan Issel, Alex English, Bill Hanzlik, Rob Williams and Mike Evans all shot better than 80 percent from the line.

Issel is a .792 career foul shooter who has made more free throws and has attempted more (3,960-of-4,958 for .799) than any other Nugget during his nine-year career in Denver. Issel also owns the second-longest consecutive free-throw streak in NBA history with 63, trailing only Calvin Murphy's 78.

ALL-TIME NUGGET LEADERS

SEASON

Points: Spencer Haywood, 2,519, 1969-70
Assists: Al Smith, 619, 1973-74
Rebounds: Spencer Haywood, 1,637, 1969-70

GAME

Points: David Thompson, 73 vs. Detroit, 4/9/78
Assists: Larry Brown, 23 vs. Pittsburgh, 2/20/72
Rebounds: Spencer Haywood, 31 vs. Kentucky, 11/13/69

CAREER

Points: Dan Issel, 15,605, 1975-84
Assists: Ralph Simpson, 1,950, 1970-76, 1977-78
Rebounds: Dan Issel, 6,299, 1975-84

GOLDEN STATE WARRIORS

TEAM DIRECTORY: Pres.: Franklin Mieuli; Exec. VP: P.K. Macker; GM: Al Attles; Dir. Media Services: Joe Dearborn; Coach: John Bach; Asst. Coach: Bob Zuffelato. Arena: Oakland Coliseum (13,335). Colors: Gold and blue.

Warriors' Joe Barry Carroll swatted away 142 shots.

SCOUTING REPORT

SHOOTING: Larry Smith and Russell Cross, take a bow. Also, take a shot. Please. That's what Warrior coach John Bach must be thinking, because Smith and Cross were the only two Golden State players who finished with shooting percentages above .500. Of course, the bruising Smith (.560) is never going to be confused with Adrian Dantley as far as scoring ability is concerned and, until he loses some weight, Cross (.571) won't be confused with anybody other than The Cookie Monster.

In short, the Warriors were the worst-shooting team in the NBA last season. There's no reason to think that will change dramatically this time around, unless center Joe B. Carroll bounces back from his .477 effort. Guard Steve Burtt from Iona, picked up on the second round of the draft, should add some scoring punch. The Warriors' problem is definitely not shyness. Purvis (Moonball) Short (.473), Sleepy Floyd (.463) and Mickey Johnson (.421) aren't bashful.

PLAYMAKING: The Warriors have Lester Conner (4.9 assists per game) and that's about all the good things you can say about the playmaking situation. Floyd has been entrusted with those duties from time to time, but is more preoccupied with putting up unconscionable jumpers than working the ball inside. The backup duties fall to Mike Bratz and that is quite a fall.

DEFENSE: Maybe the Warriors went for a weekend visit and left their defense in San Francisco. Or maybe they never had any. The latter is more likely to be the case, since 1983-84 was the second straight season in which the opposition hit more than 51 percent of its shots from the field. The Warriors ranked dead last among the 23 NBA teams in this category and that explains why they have been watching the playoffs on television since the days before Rick Barry needed a hair-weave.

Conner is the best defender of the lot, showing a willingness to stick his nose in there. But this is a very curious team. Five Warriors—Conner, Short, Johnson, Floyd and Carroll—had more than 100 steals apiece. Apparently they are more interested in gambling for the steal and an occasional breakaway layup than playing solid, straight-up defense.

REBOUNDING: The Warriors are all out there trying to make the steal and nobody is packed in guarding the hoop. They are

WARRIOR ROSTER

No.	Veteran	Pos.	Ht.	Wt.	Age	Yrs. Pro	College
23	*Mike Bratz	G	6-2	185	29	8	Stanford
2	*Joe B. Carroll	C	6-10	235	26	5	Purdue
18	*Don Collins	G-F	6-6	205	25	5	Washington State
15	Lester Conner	G	6-4	180	25	3	Oregon State
40	Russell Cross	F	6-10	245	27	2	Purdue
55	Chris Engler	C	7-0	240	25	3	Wyoming
21	Eric Floyd	G	6-3	170	24	3	Georgetown
43	Mickey Johnson	F	6-10	190	32	11	Aurora
20	Pace Mannion	F	6-8	190	24	2	Utah
45	Purvis Short	F	6-7	210	27	7	Jackson State
13	Larry Smith	F	6-8	225	26	5	Alcorn State
22	Darren Tillis	C	6-11	215	24	3	Cleveland State
33	Jerome Whitehead	C	6-10	220	28	7	Marquette

*Free agent unsigned at press time

Rd.	Top Draftees	Sel. No.	Ht.	Wt.	College
2	Steve Burtt	30	6-2	185	Iona
2	Othell Wilson	35	6-0	193	Virginia
2	Gary Plummer	45	6-9	210	Boston University
3	Lewis Jackson	55	6-6	205	Alabama State
5	Steve Bartek	101	6-8	230	Doane College

outrebounded by wide margins almost every night on the defensive boards and there is really no excuse for that with a player of Carroll's size playing in the middle. The best rebounder-per-minute is, of course, the underrated Smith (9.0 rpg). But his offensive skills are so limited that, even when Smith picks a ball off the offensive glass, he can't consistently put it in the basket.

OUTLOOK: The Warriors are always catching the bouquet, but never walking down the aisle themselves. The last seven years, they've cried about how they just missed out on the last playoff spot. Well, the NBA expanded the playoff field last season and they still missed out.

Things are not likely to change this year unless the Warriors can somehow be convinced—perhaps with a big, spiked stick— to give up their laid-back attitude and begin taking this game seriously.

WARRIOR PROFILES

PURVIS SHORT 27 6-7 210   Forward

Rarely short on points...One of those guys who seems to have his own built-in radar device...Mr. Outside on offense...Tosses up his shots with a rainbow arch...Tenth-leading scorer in the NBA last season...His 57 points vs. San Antonio Jan. 7 was highest single-game total in NBA last season...Born July 2, 1957, in Hattiesburg, Miss....Taken by Warriors on the first round in 1978...Started out on the bench, but they couldn't keep that deadly shot there for long...A small-college All-American at Jackson State...Brother Eugene was drafted by the Knicks...Says most memorable moment was the birth of his son...The little guy probably came out shooting, too.

Year	Team	G	FG	FG Pct.	FT	FT Pct.	Reb.	Ast.	TP	Avg.
1978-79	Golden State	75	369	.479	57	.671	347	97	795	10.6
1979-80	Golden State	62	461	.503	134	.812	316	123	1056	17.0
1980-81	Golden State	79	549	.475	168	.820	391	249	1269	16.1
1981-82	Golden State	76	456	.488	177	.801	266	209	1095	14.4
1982-83	Golden State	67	589	.487	255	.828	354	228	1437	21.4
1983-84	Golden State	79	714	.473	353	.793	438	246	1803	22.8
	Totals	438	3138	.483	1144	.801	2112	1152	7455	17.0

JOE B. CARROLL 26 6-10 235   Center

Who really knows what goes on inside that head of his?...It's been said the initials J.B. stand for Just Breathing, but he's had his share of standout performances over the course of his four-year career...Plum of the offseason free-agent market, because enough coaches around the league think they can be the one to make him breathe fire on the court...Born July 24, 1958, in Pine Bluff, Ark., the hometown of Denver's Lafayette Lever...Established himself as a force in the middle at Purdue, where he was named an All-American and never missed a game in four years...Has sat out only 11 in four pro seasons...Shooting percentage dipped to .477, his NBA low...Not a very aggressive rebounder, but he can dominate on offense...It's just a myth that he never talks to the media. He just picks his spots...When he opens up, he proves to be articulate and intelligent...Fans usually get on him for seeming more interested in chewing his ever-present wad of bubble gum than in playing defense.

Year	Team	G	FG	FG Pct.	FT	FT Pct.	Reb.	Ast.	TP	Avg.
1980-81	Golden State	82	616	.491	315	.716	759	117	1547	18.9
1981-82	Golden State	76	527	.519	235	.728	633	64	1289	17.0
1982-83	Golden State	79	785	.513	337	.719	688	169	1907	24.1
1983-84	Golden State	80	663	.477	313	.723	636	198	1639	20.5
	Totals	317	2591	.499	1200	.721	2716	548	6382	20.1

ERIC FLOYD 24 6-3 170   Guard

"Sleepy" . . . Opponents can't snooze against this aggressive, gambling defensive player . . . Shot .463 from the field, but isn't shy about putting the ball up . . . A first-round choice of New Jersey in 1982 . . . Traded to Golden State along with Mickey Johnson in exchange for Micheal Ray Richardson halfway through his rookie season . . . Born March 6, 1960, in Gastonia, N.C. . . . A key member of the Georgetown club that finished as the NCAA runnerup to North Carolina in 1982 . . . The Nets didn't seem to give him much of a chance . . . Though Richardson seemed to resurrect his career late last season, the Nets may still live to regret giving up this guy.

Year	Team	G	FG	FG Pct.	FT	FT Pct.	Reb.	Ast.	TP	Avg.
1982-83	N.J.-G.S.	76	226	.429	150	.833	137	138	612	8.1
1983-84	Golden State	77	484	.463	315	.816	271	269	1291	16.8
	Totals	153	710	.452	465	.822	408	407	1903	12.4

LESTER CONNER 25 6-4 180   Guard

"Lester The Molester" . . . Earned reputation for his tough defense at Oregon State, where he played under Ralph Miller . . . The only Warrior to start all 82 games last season . . . Could be a very good one at the point guard spot . . . Assist-turnover ratio is better than 3-to-1 . . . Born Sept. 17, 1959, in Memphis, Tenn., he was raised in Oakland, the home of the Warriors . . . An avid tennis player, he's not afraid to hustle on any court . . . Spent two years at Los Medanos JC in Antioch, Cal. before going on to OSU . . . Voted the best defensive player in the 1982 Aloha Classic . . . Led Golden State in steals (162) last season.

Year	Team	G	FG	FG Pct.	FT	FT Pct.	Reb.	Ast.	TP	Avg.
1982-83	Golden State	75	145	.479	79	.699	221	253	369	4.9
1983-84	Golden State	82	360	.493	186	.718	305	401	907	11.1
	Totals	157	505	.489	265	.712	526	654	1276	8.1

MICKEY JOHNSON 32 6-10 190   Forward

Will never be voted the most popular guy on any team . . . It doesn't have as much to do with the way he plays the game as with how much griping and complaining he does . . . Also has a reputation for laying down in big games . . . Spell it D-O-G . . . Born August 31, 1952, in Chicago . . . Played college ball at Aurora and has always said he gets no respect because of his small-college background . . . Fourth-round draft choice of Portland in 1974 . . . Nobody has ever doubted his ability to score . . . Many doubt his willingness to play defense . . . Then-coach Larry Brown traded him from New Jersey to Golden State, along with Eric Floyd, just days after he had been named NBA Player of the Week in 1983 . . . Warriors are his fifth NBA team, after stops in Chicago, Indiana, Milwaukee and New Jersey . . . Will probably play in several more cities before his career is over and will complain in all of them . . . Wallace Edgar is his real name . . . Knits in his spare time.

Year	Team	G	FG	FG Pct.	FT	FT Pct.	Reb.	Ast.	TP	Avg.
1974-75	Chicago	38	53	.449	37	.638	94	20	143	3.8
1975-76	Chicago	81	478	.463	283	.786	758	130	1239	15.3
1976-77	Chicago	81	538	.446	324	.796	828	195	1400	17.3
1977-78	Chicago	81	561	.462	362	.812	728	267	1484	18.3
1978-79	Chicago	82	496	.449	273	.830	627	380	1265	15.4
1979-80	Indiana	82	588	.463	385	.799	681	344	1566	19.1
1980-81	Milwaukee.	82	379	.448	262	.789	545	286	1023	12.5
1981-82	Milwaukee.	76	372	.491	233	.801	454	215	978	12.9
1982-83	Mil.-N.J.-G.S.	78	391	.425	312	.821	494	255	1097	14.1
1983-84	Golden State	78	359	.421	339	.785	518	219	1062	13.6
	Totals	759	4215	.452	2810	.799	5737	2311	11257	14.8

LARRY SMITH 26 6-8 225   Forward

"Mr. Mean" . . . Seemed to have lost some of the raw edge off his game in fourth pro season . . . Warriors picked him up as a steal in the second round of the 1980 draft and his first two seasons were outstanding . . . No offensive threat . . . Quickly established himself as one of the league's ferocious and tireless rebounders . . . Would knock you down as soon as look at you . . . But injuries marred his third season, limiting him to just 49 games . . . Was healthy last season, but didn't put the same impressive numbers on the board in the rebounding department . . . Born Jan. 18, 1958, in Rolling Fork, Miss. . . . Was the leading rebounder in the nation as a senior at Alcorn State . . . Well-rounded individual . . . Enjoys billiards, reading and boxing, though not necessarily in that order . . . Also spends a great deal of time working out with Nautilus machines, giving him muscles on top of muscles.

Year	Team	G	FG	FG Pct.	FT	FT Pct.	Reb.	Ast.	TP	Avg.
1980-81	Golden State	82	304	.512	177	.588	994	93	785	9.6
1981-82	Golden State	74	220	.534	88	.553	813	83	528	7.1
1982-83	Golden State	49	180	.588	53	.535	485	46	413	8.4
1983-84	Golden State	75	244	.560	94	.560	672	72	582	7.8
	Totals	280	948	.542	412	.567	2964	294	2308	8.2

DON COLLINS 25 6-6 205   Guard-Forward

Three teams in four years . . . No wonder the guy thinks the world is against him . . . Couldn't cut it at all with one coaching extreme—Hubie Brown—in Atlanta or the other—Gene Shue— in Washington . . . May fit in with Warriors and the easy-going John Bach . . . Born Nov. 28, 1958, in Toledo, Ohio . . . First-round choice of Hawks in 1980 out of Washington State . . . Has always had a reputation as a bad apple . . . His wife has worked hard to help him get the chip off his shoulder and enjoy life . . . Led the Pac-10 in scoring and was named Player of the Year as a senior . . . Can swing down to the small forward position . . . A good player in the open court . . . A gambler on defense, he will get burned.

Year	Team	G	FG	FG Pct.	FT	FT Pct.	Reb.	Ast.	TP	Avg.
1980-81	Atl.-Wash.	81	360	.444	211	.776	268	190	931	11.5
1981-82	Washington	79	334	.511	121	.716	196	148	790	10.0
1982-83	Washington	65	332	.523	101	.743	210	132	765	11.8
1983-84	Golden State	61	187	.483	65	.730	129	67	440	7.2
	Totals	286	1213	.488	498	.748	803	537	2926	10.2

MIKE BRATZ 29 6-2 185   Guard

Traveling man . . . As long as he's healthy enough to put on a uniform, he'll always have a job, because he's willing to sit quietly on the bench . . . Drafted by Phoenix in 1977, he stayed there for three seasons . . . But now there have been five different addresses in five seasons . . . A decent playmaker . . . Born Oct. 17, 1955, in Lompoc, Cal. . . . His niche in the league is as a designated three-point shooter. His percentage on bombs (.294) was among the top six in the league last season, but he didn't have enough attempts to qualify for the statistical lead . . . The player Dallas palmed off on Cleveland in order to come up with the No. 4 pick in the 1984 college draft . . . An economics major at Stanford, so he's smart enough to put the money in his pocket and not complain.

Year	Team	G	FG	FG Pct.	FT	FT Pct.	Reb.	Ast.	TP	Avg.
1977-78	Phoenix	80	159	.403	56	.824	115	123	374	4.7
1978-79	Phoenix	77	242	.454	139	.818	141	179	623	8.1
1979-80	Phoenix	82	269	.392	141	.870	167	223	700	8.5
1980-81	Cleveland	80	319	.390	107	.811	198	452	802	10.0
1981-82	San Antonio	81	230	.407	119	.783	166	438	625	7.7
1982-83	Chicago	15	14	.333	10	.769	19	23	39	2.6
1983-84	Golden State	82	213	.409	120	.876	143	252	561	6.8
	Totals	497	1446	.406	692	.830	949	1690	3724	7.5

RUSSELL CROSS 27 6-10 245   Forward

Ouch!... John Bach wanted him badly and spent the No. 6 overall pick in the 1983 draft to get him... So, of course, he holds out, reports to camp late and overweight and has injury problems all year long... Played only 354 minutes in 45 games, averaging 3.7 ppg... Joined fellow Purdue alum Joe B. Carroll on the Warriors... Played center for the Boilermakers and was supposed to make the transition to the forward spot at Golden State and provide some inside scoring punch... Says he'd like to play facing the basket... Warriors would just be happy to have him play, period.

Year	Team	G	FG	FG Pct.	FT	FT Pct.	Reb.	Ast.	TP	Avg.
1983-84	Golden State	45	64	.571	38	.418	82	22	166	3.7

PACE MANNION 24 6-8 190   Forward

Maybe they had a spare uniform lying around the Golden State training camp... Or maybe he's one of those guys who looks a lot better in practice... Let's hope so... Other than the fact that he doesn't shoot well, rebound well or pass the ball with any exceptional skill, his game is just fine... There must be something about him that appeals to the average fan, because at least one hard-core group in Houston brought banners to the games and cheered wildly whenever he touched the ball—even in warmups—during each of the Warriors' three visits... A second-round draft choice out of Utah... Enjoy him while you can—he won't be around long.

Year	Team	G	FG	FG Pct.	FT	FT Pct.	Reb.	Ast.	TP	Avg.
1983-84	Golden State	57	50	.397	18	.783	59	47	121	2.1

DARREN TILLIS 24 6-11 215   Center

Former stringbean has gained considerable weight in the two years he has been in the league . . . Can't shoot, can't rebound and can't play defense . . . So, of course, he was the first-round draft choice of the Boston Celtics in 1982. Maybe coach Bill Fitch and Red Auerbach were hallucinating that day . . . Born Feb. 23, 1960, in Dallas . . . Trying to build himself up by lifting weights, but he'd probably be better off eating mashed potatoes for breakfast, lunch and dinner . . . The second-leading all-time scorer at Cleveland State, which tells you all you need to know about that collegiate powerhouse . . . Celtics shipped him to Cleveland in the Scotty Wedman deal . . . Warriors picked him up because they needed a big body to fill space on their bench . . . Played in 72 games, but averaged 3.6 ppg and 2.6 rpg.

Year	Team	G	FG	FG Pct.	FT	FT Pct.	Reb.	Ast.	TP	Avg.
1982-83	Bos.-Clev.	52	76	.420	16	.571	130	18	168	3.2
1983-84	Golden State	72	108	.425	41	.651	184	24	257	3.6
	Totals	124	184	.423	57	.626	314	42	425	3.4

CHRIS ENGLER 25 7-0 240   Center

The not-so-incredible hulk . . . Another one of those non-scoring, non-rebounding reasons why the Warriors missed the playoffs against last year . . . Big, slow midwesterner . . . Does take up a lot of room standing around—and that's what he does best . . . Born March 1, 1959, in Minneapolis . . . Makes his home now in the thriving metropolis of Stillwater, Minn. He's probably the best NBA player in town . . . Played college ball at Wyoming on the same team as other NBA suspects Bill Garnett and Charles Bradley . . . Drafted on the third round by the Warriors in 1982 . . . A big rock-and-roll fan of Bruce Springsteen and The Who . . . If the Warriors get serious about assembling talent, he'll have plenty of time to listen to his record albums . . . Political science major who says he'd like to attend law school. Why not now?

Year	Team	G	FG	FG Pct.	FT	FT Pct.	Reb.	Ast.	TP	Avg.
1982-83	Golden State	54	38	.404	5	.313	104	11	81	1.5
1983-84	Golden State	46	33	.398	14	.609	97	11	80	1.7
	Totals	100	71	.401	19	.487	201	22	161	1.6

JEROME WHITEHEAD 28 6-10 220   Center

Journeyman . . . The word was invented for people like him . . . Never going to be a star, but he's one of those guys who could stick around the league for years because of his size and willingness to work . . . If he doesn't become a big success, it won't be for lack of trying . . . Annually attends Pete Newell's summer camp for big men, trying to improve his skills . . . Born Sept. 30, 1956, in Waukegan, Ill. . . . Played on Marquette's 1977 NCAA championship team, under Al McGuire . . . Drafted by the Buffalo Braves in 1978, he went on to play in Utah, Dallas, Cleveland and San Diego before being traded to Golden State in June for second-round draft pick Jay Murphy . . . Son of a minister . . . Wears goggles just like Kareem, but that's where the similarity ends.

Year	Team	G	FG	FG Pct.	FT	FT Pct.	Reb.	Ast.	TP	Avg.
1978-79	San Diego	31	15	.441	8	.444	50	7	38	1.2
1979-80	S.D.-Utah	50	58	.509	10	.286	167	24	126	2.5
1980-81	Dal.-Clev.-S.D.	48	83	.461	28	.500	214	26	194	4.0
1981-82	San Diego	72	406	.559	184	.763	664	102	996	13.8
1982-83	San Diego	46	164	.536	72	.828	261	42	400	8.7
1983-84	San Diego	70	144	.490	88	.822	245	19	376	5.4
	Totals	317	870	.526	390	.717	1601	220	2130	6.7

TOP ROOKIE

STEVE BURTT 22 6-2 185   Guard

A fine shooter . . . Averaged more than 22 ppg in each of last three years at Iona . . . Shot better than 50 percent after his freshman season and .522 for career . . . Willing to play defense . . . Had solid efforts against NBA players like Doc Rivers and Byron Scott when they were still in school . . . His 2,534 points made him the all-time leading scorer among New York-New Jersey players, unseating Bill Bradley (2,503) . . . Born Nov. 5, 1962, in New York, N.Y.

COACH JOHN BACH: Should have been a Rookie-of-the-Year candidate... Waited a long, long time to get a head coaching job in the NBA... Did a solid job in his first season, keeping his club together with rubber bands and chewing gum for most of the season... But the Warriors simply ran out of gas in the end and finished 37-45... Spent four years as Al Attles' assistant before moving up... Came out of the college ranks, where he spent 10 years at Penn State and 18 at Fordham... Born July 10, 1923, in Brooklyn, N.Y.... Was the oldest rookie coach in the history of the league... Had a one-year playing career with Boston... Most of his life has been basketball... Helped out the legendary Hank Iba with the 1972 Olympic team... An Easterner by birth, but he usually dresses in Western duds nowadays... Pilots small planes and gliders as a hobby.

John Bach was an old pro in first year as pro head coach.

GREATEST FOUL SHOOTER

His style was as distinctive as Kareem Abdul-Jabbar's skyhook and Wilt Chamberlain's dipper dunks. There is the image of Rick Barry at the foul line, bending at the knees and flicking another of his underhanded free throws right into the soft cotton of the net.

He was the best foul shooter the NBA has ever seen. His career percentage of .900 says so, and so do the numbers showing he led the Warriors in each of the eight seasons he played in the Bay Area. He led the league in that category in 1973, 1975, 1976, 1978, 1979 and 1980.

During his four-year career in the ABA, Barry also led that league three times (1969, 1971 and 1972) and his single season mark of .947 in 1979-80 was an NBA record until Calvin Murphy came along and broke it (.958) the next season.

The last of the great underhanders also broke Calvin Murphy's record of 58 in a row when he hit 60 in succession. Murphy eventually reclaimed his record by making 78 straight, but as long as they keep shooting free throws, Barry's name is likely to stay right at the top of the list.

ALL-TIME WARRIOR LEADERS

SEASON

Points: Wilt Chamberlain, 4,029, 1961-62
Assists: Guy Rodgers, 846, 1965-66
Rebounds: Wilt Chamberlain, 2,149, 1960-61

GAME

Points: Wilt Chamberlain, 100 vs. New York, 3/2/62
Assists: Guy Rodgers, 28 vs. St. Louis, 3/14/63
Rebounds: Wilt Chamberlain, 55 vs. Boston, 11/24/60

CAREER

Points: Wilt Chamberlain, 17,783, 1959-65
Assists: Guy Rodgers, 4,845, 1958-70
Rebounds: Nate Thurmond, 12,771, 1963-74

HOUSTON ROCKETS

TEAM DIRECTORY: Chairman: Charlie Thomas; Pres./GM: Ray Patterson; Dir. Pub. Rel.: Jim Foley; Coach: Bill Fitch; Asst. Coaches: Carroll Dawson, Rudy Tomjanovich. Arena: The Summit (16,016). Colors: Red and gold.

SCOUTING REPORT

SHOOTING: There is no overestimating the effect of coach Bill Fitch's fast-break attack on Houston. In only one season, it improved the Rockets from the worst-shooting team in the league to one that made just under 50 percent of its chances. That's because, with great transition players like Ralph Sampson (.523), Rodney McCray (.499) and Lewis Lloyd (.516), the Rockets rank right up there with the Lakers and Celtics when it comes to getting layups and slam dunks. And that number should certainly shoot up this season with the addition of rookie Akeem Olajuwon.

The Rockets can go from one end of the floor to the other as quickly as any team in the league. Their need on offense is a bombs-away outside threat to help loosen things up when the opposition packs in the defense on Ralph and Akeem. Allen Leavell (.477) isn't the answer. Robert Reid (.474) might be. So might ex-rookie Rocket Mitchell Wiggins (.448).

PLAYMAKING: With Sampson and Olajuwon in the lineup, you say a child could do the playmaking. Well, pack your child's suitcase and put him on the next plane to Houston, because the Rockets are most certainly searching for a distributor.

Five years ago Phil Ford would have been the answer. But physical problems have taken the edge off his great skills and have reduced him to a backup. That brings us to Leavell (5.6 assists per game), who the Rockets keep saying is quick and strong-minded. Perhaps he's too strong-minded, because nobody has been able to convince him that a pass inside to Sampson has a higher percentage of succeeding than a Gus Williams-style fast-break jumper from him. Leavell will occasionally bust loose with a big game, but has never shown a desire to make plays consistently. If Fitch can harness him, the Rocket troubles might be over, but that is doubtful. Craig Ehlo will get a look.

DEFENSE: That's Step 2 in the grand scheme of things. Fitch installed the fast-break offense in his first season and intends to devote this year to stopping the other guys from scoring. The Rockets ranked 19th in that category last season (113.7 ppg), but

Rookie of the Year Ralph Sampson will be forward this year.

should improve dramatically with the presence of Olajuwon and his shot-blocking ability in the middle. The easiest way to score against the Rockets this season might be a set shot from halfcourt.

Fitch has changed the Rockets from a passive defensive club to one that will pressure the ball. But they still need plenty of work on their technique since opponents often beat their traps and scored easy hoops. And, lest it be overlooked because of all the offensive fireworks he is likely to produce at forward, Sampson will probably have some difficulty guarding some of the quicker forwards out on the wing.

ROCKET ROSTER

No.	Veteran	Pos.	Ht.	Wt.	Age	Yrs. Pro	College
2	James Bailey	F	6-9	220	27	6	Rutgers
3	Craig Ehlo	G	6-7	185	23	2	Washington State
1	*Phil Ford	G	6-2	186	28	7	North Carolina
11	Major Jones	F	6-9	235	30	6	Albany State (Ga.)
30	*Allen Leavell	G	6-1	170	27	6	Oklahoma City
32	Lewis Lloyd	G	6-6	220	25	4	Drake
22	Rodney McCray	F	6-7	220	23	2	Louisville
33	*Robert Reid	F	6-8	205	29	7	St. Mary's
50	Ralph Sampson	C	7-4	230	24	2	Virginia
20	*Terry Teagle	G	6-5	185	24	3	Baylor
42	*Wally Walker	F	6-8	210	30	9	Virginia
15	Mitchell Wiggins	G	6-4	185	25	2	Florida State

*Free agent unsigned at press time

Rd.	Top Draftees	Sel. No.	Ht.	Wt.	College
1	Akeem Olajuwon	1	7-0	250	Houston
3	Jim Peterson	51	6-10	215	Minnesota
4	Willie Jackson	74	6-6	210	Centenary
5	Al McClain	97	6-1½	180	New Hampshire
7	Joedy Gardner	143	6-4	190	Cal State-Long Beach

REBOUNDING: This is another area of incredible one-year improvement, thanks to Sampson. The Rockets went from being second-worst in the league to ranking fourth overall. Now, it may be difficult for the opposition to get any rebounds at all, with Olajuwon and Sampson in the lineup at the same time. Ralph received a great deal of criticism for not playing close enough to the basket. Yet when the smoke cleared, he had led the entire Western Conference in rebounding with 11.1 rpg. McCray (5.7 rpg) should not be underestimated despite the fact he is only 6-7. He has got a behind the size of Rhode Island that he uses to clear out space and has excellent leaping ability. This will definitely be a strong point.

OUTLOOK: There's a championship in the future for this franchise, but there are still enough holes in the overall picture to prevent the Rockets from blasting off right away. There's the search for the point guard, the need to improve the defense and the time necessary for Sampson and Olajuwon to learn to play together. Still, the Rockets should improve enough to make the playoffs. If not, you can bet that Fitch will be back in Boston—peddling programs at the Garden.

ROCKET PROFILES

RALPH SAMPSON 24 7-4 230   Center

Rookie of the Year by unanimous choice . . . First No. 1 selection in draft to win that honor since Lew Alcindor did it for Milwaukee in 1969-70 . . . Answered critics who said Virginia grad would not be able to respond to constant demands of the pro game . . . Incredibly, he was still attacked for not playing close enough to the basket . . . But he finished as fifth-leading rebounder (11.1 rpg) in the NBA and pulled down most boards (913) of any player in Western Conference . . . Born July 7, 1960, in Harrisonburg, Va. . . . Very mobile, an outstanding leaper and an incredible athlete for such a big man . . . May never develop one shot as consistent as Kareem Abdul-Jabbar's skyhook, but his offensive versatility makes him practically unstoppable . . . Needs to bring up his intensity level in games . . . As far as engaging interviews are concerned, you'd be better off talking to a potted plant.

Year	Team	G	FG	FG Pct.	FT	FT Pct.	Reb.	Ast.	TP	Avg.
1983-84	Houston	82	716	.523	287	.661	913	163	1720	21.0

RODNEY McCRAY 23 6-7 220   Forward

One tough cookie . . . Started slowly in his rookie season after a contract holdout kept him away for almost all of training camp . . . Was out of shape and looked more like "Rodney McMuffin" for the first month or so . . . Once he adapted to the system, he proved that he'll be around for a lot of years . . . Born Aug. 29, 1961, in Mt. Vernon, N.Y. . . . Finished up the year as a starter at small forward, but his future may still be on the other side . . . Improved his outside shooting, but strength is still as a rugged player in traffic and a fearless and tireless rebounder . . . Has great strength and is to be able to go back up the second time for a rebound while everyone else is still coming down from the first jump . . . Quiet, but friendly . . . He'll play defense and is a good complement to Ralph Sampson . . . Brother and former Louisville teammate Scooter plays for Seattle.

Year	Team	G	FG	FG Pct.	FT	FT Pct.	Reb.	Ast.	TP	Avg.
1983-84	Houston	79	335	.499	182	.731	450	176	853	10.8

ROBERT REID 29 6-8 205   Forward

Came back to NBA after year in retirement to pursue his faith in the Pentecostal Church... A thoroughbred, he is at his best when the pace is fast and he can go end to end... Came into the league as an unheralded second-round draft choice out of St. Mary's in San Antonio and has developed into a solid pro... Has capability of exploding on offense on any given night, but still lacks the consistency to move into upper echelon of small forwards... Born Sept. 30, 1955, in Atlanta... The son of a military man, he lived first with his family on the isle of Crete, then in Hawaii, before finally settling down in Shertz, Tex., outside of San Antonio... His mother is a minister in the Pentecostal Church... Has had problems resolving his pro basketball career with his religion in the past, but says he is now committed to the game... Not afraid to roll up his sleeves and play defense, though his rebounding is a bit weak.

Year	Team	G	FG	FG Pct.	FT	FT Pct.	Reb.	Ast.	TP	Avg.
1977-78	Houston	80	261	.455	63	.656	359	121	585	7.3
1978-79	Houston	82	382	.492	131	.704	483	230	895	10.9
1979-80	Houston	76	419	.487	153	.736	441	244	991	13.0
1980-81	Houston	82	536	.482	229	.756	583	344	1301	15.9
1981-82	Houston	77	437	.456	160	.748	511	314	1035	13.4
1983-84	Houston	64	406	.474	81	.659	341	217	895	14.0
	Totals	461	2441	.475	817	.723	2718	1470	5702	12.4

PHIL FORD 28 6-2 186   Guard

Regained respect... After a two-season slide that threatened to end his NBA career, he got a chance to save himself as a free agent with the Rockets and he did... Most of his old magic is gone... He's getting by on his willingness to work and his knowledge of the game... Suffered a serious eye injury in the 1981 playoffs with Kansas City, then was nearly consumed by personal problems... Born Feb. 9, 1956, in Rocky Mount, N.C.... College Player of the Year for North Carolina in 1978 and the No. 2 overall pick in the draft... Started the first 55 games for the Rockets last season, then gave way to Allen

Leavell...Can milk a couple more years out of his career as a reserve.

Year	Team	G	FG	FG Pct.	FT	FT Pct.	Reb.	Ast.	TP	Avg.
1978-79	Kansas City	79	467	.465	326	.813	182	681	1260	15.9
1979-80	Kansas City	82	489	.462	346	.818	172	610	1328	16.2
1980-81	Kansas City	66	424	.478	294	.831	128	580	1153	17.5
1981-82	Kansas City	72	285	.439	136	.819	105	451	713	9.9
1982-83	N.J.-Mil.	77	213	.479	97	.789	103	290	524	6.8
1983-84	Houston	81	236	.502	98	.838	137	410	572	7.1
	Totals	457	2114	.468	1297	.819	827	3022	5550	12.1

LEWIS LLOYD 25 6-6 220   Guard

A late bloomer...Finally given a chance to play full-time after two frustrating seasons with Golden State, this Drake product proved all the talk about his offensive potential wasn't just talk...His style is perfect for coach Bill Fitch's fast-breaking offense...An excellent transition player, he runs the floor well and can finish off the break...Was converted from forward to guard...Born Feb. 22, 1959, in Philadelphia...Attended Overbrook High School, which also produced greats Wilt Chamberlain and Walt Hazzard...Nicknamed "Black Magic" back in Philly and the Bay Area, but has come to be known as "Sweet Lew" in Houston...Not the answer to the Rockets' perimeter shooting needs, but his biggest liability is still his defense...If he can become a better defender, he could turn out to be a steal at the price of only a second-round draft choice.

Year	Team	G	FG	FG Pct.	FT	FT Pct.	Reb.	Ast.	TP	Avg.
1981-82	Golden State	16	25	.556	7	.636	16	6	57	3.6
1982-83	Golden State	73	293	.518	100	.719	260	130	687	9.4
1983-84	Houston	82	610	.516	235	.789	295	321	1458	17.8
	Totals	171	928	.518	342	.763	571	457	2202	12.9

ALLEN LEAVELL 27 6-1 170   Guard

Mercurial...Unfortunately, his game sinks as quickly as it rises...Could probably outrun a cheetah, but often plays out of control and is certainly not the ideal point guard...Would love to go to sleep one night and wake up in the morning as Gus Williams, with the freedom to fire away with his jumper...Born May 27, 1957, in Muncie, Ind....Led the Rockets in assists (459), steals (107) and three-point shots (11-of-71) last season...Improved his field-goal percentage from .415 to .477...Has had a great deal of success considering he entered the league as a fifth-round draft choice out of Oklahoma City...Will play good defense and dive five rows into the stands for a loose ball...But there remain questions about whether he is willing to harness his offense for the benefit of the team.

Year	Team	G	FG	FG Pct.	FT	FT Pct.	Reb.	Ast.	TP	Avg.
1979-80	Houston	77	330	.503	180	.814	184	417	843	10.9
1980-81	Houston	79	258	.471	124	.832	134	384	642	8.1
1981-82	Houston	79	370	.467	115	.852	168	457	864	10.9
1982-83	Houston	79	439	.415	247	.832	195	530	1167	14.8
1983-84	Houston	82	349	.477	238	.832	117	459	947	11.5
	Totals	396	1746	.461	904	.831	798	2247	4463	11.3

MAJOR JONES 30 6-9 235   Forward

The wisecracking member of Jones family ...Used to be Moses Malone's confidant in Houston...Now he just keeps everybody in the locker room loose...Born July 9, 1954, in McGehee, Ark....You'll never see him in the NBA highlight film flying in for a slam dunk or tossing in rainbow jumpers...He's carved out a lengthy NBA career as a blue-collar worker...The kind of player who always looks like he's going to be cut in training camp, then works his tail off to earn a roster spot...Rebounding is his specialty...He and his brothers hold down the top six spots on the Albany State (Ga.) all-time rebounding list.

Year	Team	G	FG	FG Pct.	FT	FT Pct.	Reb.	Ast.	TP	Avg.
1979-80	Houston	82	188	.480	61	.565	381	67	438	5.3
1980-81	Houston	68	117	.464	64	.634	234	41	298	4.4
1981-82	Houston	60	113	.531	42	.545	202	25	268	4.5
1982-83	Houston	60	142	.457	56	.549	263	39	340	5.7
1983-84	Houston	57	70	.538	30	.612	115	28	170	3.0
	Totals	327	630	.485	253	.579	1195	200	1514	4.6

WALLY WALKER 30 6-8 210   Forward

If he was a character in an old-time television series, he'd be Wally from "Leave It To Beaver"...The boy next door...Certainly has his fair share of admirers in the stands in Houston...Started 18 games at small forward, then a reserve for the rest of the season...Obtained from Seattle in 1982 for a second-round draft choice...Born July 18, 1954, in Millersville,

Pa.... Was a star at Virginia long before Ralph Sampson... The fifth overall selection in the 1976 draft, by Portland... Played on the Blazers' championship team as a rookie, then picked up another ring with Seattle in 1978-79... Definitely not a starter, but a model citizen and role player who should stick around for a few more years.

Year	Team	G	FG	FG Pct.	FT	FT Pct.	Reb.	Ast.	TP	Avg.
1976-77	Portland	66	137	.449	67	.670	108	51	341	5.2
1977-78	Port.-Sea.	77	204	.443	75	.625	219	77	483	6.3
1978-79	Seattle	60	168	.490	58	.604	177	69	394	6.6
1979-80	Seattle	70	139	.507	48	.750	170	53	326	4.7
1980-81	Seattle	82	290	.463	109	.645	315	122	689	8.4
1981-82	Houston	70	302	.480	90	.672	305	218	364	9.9
1982-83	Houston	82	362	.449	72	.621	373	199	797	9.7
1983-84	Houston	58	118	.490	6	.333	92	55	244	4.2
	Totals	565	1720	.467	525	.643	1759	844	3968	7.0

TERRY TEAGLE 24 6-5 185   Guard

Potential... Another of those guys who's supposed to have plenty of it... But his production has been disappointing in his first two pro seasons... Was supposed to be long-range bomber the Rockets needed when he was taken in the first round of the 1982 draft... Can stick it from outside occasionally, but does more damage going to the hoop... Born April 10, 1960, in Broaddus, Tex.... A smalltown kid who hasn't been able to adjust to the faster pace of the big city and the pro game... All-time leading scorer in the Southwest Conference for Baylor ... Nice guy, but how long can you wait?

Year	Team	G	FG	FG Pct.	FT	FT Pct.	Reb.	Ast.	TP	Avg.
1982-83	Houston	73	332	.428	87	.696	194	150	761	10.4
1983-84	Houston	68	148	.470	37	.841	78	63	340	5.0
	Totals	141	480	.440	124	.734	272	213	1101	7.8

MITCHELL WIGGINS 25 6-4 185   Guard

Came in August trade for Caldwell Jones... He was the quintessential rookie scoring guard at Houston—explosive but erratic... Drafted in the first round (No. 23 overall) in 1983 draft... Started 40 games and took some heat from fans who wanted to see Reggie Theus instead... Prone to slumps, but has quickness and can make his own shots... Born Sept. 28,

1959, in Lenoir County, N.C....Averaged 12.4 ppg and was third-leading scorer on team...A relatively late bloomer, he was not recruited heavily out of high school and enrolled at McDonnell Junior College in Georgia...After two years at McDonnell, he transferred to Florida State...Played for U.S. National Team in 1982 that finished second in world championships at Cali, Colombia.

Year	Team	G	FG	FG Pct.	FT	FT Pct.	Reb.	Ast.	TP	Avg.
1983-84	Chicago	82	399	.448	213	.742	328	187	1018	12.4

CRAIG EHLO 23 6-7 185 Guard

A project...Holds interesting possibilities as a point guard...Showed potential in training camp, then suffered torn ligaments in his ankle and, following surgery, spent all but the last 10 games of the season on the injured list...Born Aug. 11, 1961, in Lubbock, Tex....Left home to attend Washington State, where he played for two years under George Raveling...Set a school record as a senior with 99 assists...Turned in a couple of heady performances when given a chance to play in the last two weeks of last season...Strictly a long-range prospect.

Year	Team	G	FG	FG Pct.	FT	FT Pct.	Reb.	Ast.	TP	Avg.
1983-84	Houston	7	11	.407	1	1.000	9	6	23	3.3

JAMES BAILEY 27 6-9 220 Forward

Belongs in the Darryl Dawkins Enigma Hall of Fame...Has an incredible body and looks like he should be tearing up NBA...But ever since he was selected sixth overall in the 1979 draft by Seattle, everybody's been waiting for him to play up to the level of his potential...Can be all-world one minute and very ordinary the next...Used as a reserve forward last season, he never developed any consistency...Born May 21, 1957, in Dublin, Ga., but was raised in Westwood, Mass....Was anointed "Jammin' James" at Rutgers and rim-rattling dunks are his specialty...Has a surprisingly good touch from the outside . . . Has tendency to make dumb plays at the worst times . . . Trips over his own desire to succeed . . . Very bad hands.

Year	Team	G	FG	FG Pct.	FT	FT Pct.	Reb.	Ast.	TP	Avg.
1979-80	Seattle	67	122	.450	68	.673	197	28	312	4.7
1980-81	Seattle	82	444	.499	256	.709	607	98	1145	14.0
1981-82	Sea.-N.J.	77	261	.517	137	.612	391	65	659	8.6
1982-83	N.J.-Hou.	75	385	.497	226	.702	474	67	996	13.3
1983-84	Houston	73	254	.491	138	.719	294	79	646	8.8
	Totals	374	1466	.496	825	.688	1963	337	3758	10.0

TOP ROOKIE

AKEEM OLAJUWON 21 7-0 250   Center

"Akeem the Dream" . . . Has been the playing the game for only five years, but was the No. 1 overall pick in draft . . . Already being compared to Bill Russell as a defensive force . . . Runs the floor as well as anyone in the game today . . . Will team with Ralph Sampson . . . Born Jan. 23, 1963, in Lagos, Nigeria . . . An All-American as a junior, he went to the NCAA Final Four three straight times with University of Houston . . . Awesome shot-blocker and strong inside force . . . Averaged 16.9 ppg and 13.7 rpg, then decided to leave school a year early.

COACH BILL FITCH: "Wild Bill" settles in Texas . . . First year in the Western Conference and first year with Ralph Sampson was a humbling experience as Rockets finished at 29-53 . . . But he is used to starting at the bottom, having taken the expansion Cleveland Cavaliers from cellar to a Central Division title . . . There were those who expected the combination of Fitch and Ralph Sampson to have the same dramatic effect as Fitch and Larry Bird, who led the Celtics to 61 victories in his first year in Boston . . . But Celtics were a veteran team composed of quality players. The Rockets had fewer quality players in the supporting cast . . . Born May 19, 1934, in Davenport, Iowa . . . Implemented his fast-breaking style in Houston and, though he didn't produce a whopping win total in his first year, he made the Rockets an exciting team to watch . . . Not much else has changed . . . Still doesn't tolerate lack of effort or laziness . . . Works players 'til they drop from first day of training

camp through last day of the regular season...Was criticized by Sampson for pushing the Rockets too hard...Continues to be the best customer for producers of video tape...His career coaching record is 575-492...Coached Celtics to championship in 1980-81.

Rugged Rodney McCray made it into starting lineup as rookie.

GREATEST FOUL SHOOTER

The streak began Dec. 27, 1980 and didn't end until March 1, 1981. In between, Calvin Murphy made 78 consecutive free throws, establishing an NBA record.

But there was nothing surprising about that. Murphy was always most comfortable at the foul line, where he spent his 13-year professional career proving the skeptics wrong.

Since he was only 5-10, it was easy to underestimate the value of Murphy's shooting and ball-handling talents at the time he left Niagara University, and many teams did just that. But the San Diego Rockets took a gamble and made him a second-round selection in 1970 and rarely has a gamble paid off so well. Murphy played his entire career with the Rockets—moving with the team to Houston in 1971—and finished as the team's all-time leading scorer.

The percentages say that Rick Barry was the best free-throw shooter the Rockets ever had (.941) but he spent just two years in Houston (1978-80). Murphy was consistently outstanding at the line for more than a decade (3,445-of-3,864 for .892) and is ranked No. 2 behind Barry on the NBA's all-time free-throw percentage list. Murphy's 78 in a row is far and away the longest streak in league history. That's why, when the University of Houston team needed help with its free-throw shooting last season, it turned to Murphy. Why not learn from the best?

ALL-TIME ROCKET LEADERS

SEASON

Points: Elvin Hayes, 2,350, 1970-71
Assists: John Lucas, 768, 1977-78
Rebounds: Moses Malone, 1,444, 1978-79

GAME

Points: Calvin Murphy, 57 vs. New Jersey, 3/18/78
Assists: Art Williams, 22 vs. San Francisco, 2/14/70
           Art Williams, 22 vs. Phoenix, 12/28/68
Rebounds: Moses Malone, 37 vs. New Orleans 2/9/79

CAREER

Points: Calvin Murphy, 1,749, 1970-83
Assists: Calvin Murphy, 4,402, 1970-83
Rebounds: Elvin Hayes, 6,974, 1968-72, 1981-84

KANSAS CITY KINGS

TEAM DIRECTORY: Pres./GM: Joe Axelson; Dir. Pub. Rel.: Julie Fie; Coach: Jack McKinney; Asst. Coach: Frank Hamblen. Arena: Kemper Arena (16,770). Colors: Red, white and blue.

SCOUTING REPORT

SHOOTING: This team certainly should shoot better than it did last season. You look at the roster and it's filled with fine offensive talents like Eddie Johnson (.485), Reggie Theus (.419), Mike Woodson (.477) and Larry Drew (.462). Toss in first-round draft choice Otis Thorpe and you've got some guys who can put the ball in the hole with regularity.

The problem here is a very familiar one around the NBA—the absence of a dominating big man to hit high-percentage shots with regularity. Too often, the Kings are forced to rely upon their outside shooting. And everyone knows that if you live by the jumper, you'll also die by it—very early in the spring.

PLAYMAKING: The Kings made Drew a millionaire, so they would have someone capable in charge of the offense. This is his job unless he's hurt or in foul trouble and he does it very well with 7.6 assists per game. Theus can shift over to point guard spot in a pinch, but the Kings will get more mileage out of him by letting Drew set up the play. The Kings are at their best when Drew is doing his waterbug imitation and scooting down the floor on the break. Since new head coach Jack McKinney has had Jerry Sichting running his offense in Indiana the last two seasons he should be delighted with the change.

DEFENSE: The Kings were one of six NBA teams that allowed the opposition to shoot better than 50 percent from the floor last season. That doesn't figure to change much, since they don't have that big shot-blocker in the middle. Joe C. Meriweather has spent 10 years in the league by being adequate and LaSalle Thompson has spent his first two seasons being less than that on offense. He gives up too much height and is still prone to foul trouble. If he worked harder and hustled more, Thompson still might not make the All-Defensive team, but he'd help shore up the defense on a team that needs help.

REBOUNDING: Elevated to full-time status, Thompson has shown that he can go to the boards and get his fair share of rebounds

Larry Drew led Kings in assists and steals.

KING ROSTER

No.	Veteran	Pos.	Ht.	Wt.	Age	Yrs. Pro	College
10	*Don Buse	G	6-4	195	34	13	Evansville
22	Larry Drew	G	6-2	180	26	5	Missouri
8	Eddie Johnson	F	6-7	215	25	4	Illinois
25	Billy Knight	G	6-6	210	32	11	Pittsburgh
50	*Joe C. Meriweather	C-F	6-10	220	31	10	Southern Illinois
40	Larry Micheaux	F	6-9	220	24	2	Houston
20	Ed Nealy	F	6-7	240	24	3	Kansas State
53	Mark Olberding	F	6-9	230	28	10	Minnesota
32	*Dane Suttle	G	6-2	180	23	2	Pepperdine
24	Reggie Theus	G	6-7	205	27	7	Nevada-Las Vegas
41	LaSalle Thompson	C	6-10	245	23	3	Texas
42	Mike Woodson	G	6-5	200	26	5	Indiana

*Free agent unsigned at press time

Rd.	Top Draftees	Sel. No.	Ht.	Wt.	College
1	Otis Thorpe	9	6-9	235	Providence
3	Roosevelt Chapman	54	6-4	200	Dayton
3	Jeff Allen	56	6-10	230	St. John's
4	Carl Henry	80	6-5½	220	Kansas
5	Jim Foster	102	6-8	220	South Carolina

(8.9 rpg). The Kings also picked up Mark Olberding and he did an adequate job (5.5 rpg). Eddie Johnson is one of the best small forwards when it comes to following up his own missed shots and the Kings should benefit from a full season out of the 6-7 Theus, who can go inside, too. The guy who could really help here if he blossoms is second-year man Larry Micheaux. The former "Mr. Mean" loves to knock people down and fight for the ball, but he could never get untracked under former coach Cotton Fitzsimmons.

OUTLOOK: This is a lukewarm basketball town and a lukewarm basketball team. Theus should make the Kings more exciting, but chances are nobody will notice, because the population would rather watch indoor soccer and usually avoids basketball games in droves. That's one of the reasons Fitzsimmons bailed out to San Antonio.

The Kings were the surprise of the league two years ago, winning 45 games, then slumped to 38 wins in 1983-84, but still made the playoffs. That isn't likely to happen this time around, particularly with the rapid improvement of the Houston Rockets. The Kings are a definite candidate for the draft lottery.

KING PROFILES

EDDIE JOHNSON 25 6-7 215   **Forward**

Garbage man... Maybe that's why every other NBA team let him sit at the curb through the first round of the 1981 college draft... Kings finally made him the 29th pick overall and have never regretted it... Has now started 169 straight games... For two straight years, he has led the Kings in scoring... Hit 20-of-64 three-point attempts last season... Loves to mix it up inside... Shows great enthusiasm... Should make the All-Star team one of these days... Born May 1, 1959, in Chicago... Stayed at home to make a name for himself at Illinois, where he set career marks in scoring, rebounding and field-goal percentage... A slow starter, but now he's the cornerstone of the Kings... Finishing work toward his history degree.

Year	Team	G	FG	FG Pct.	FT	FT Pct.	Reb.	Ast.	TP	Avg.
1981-82	Kansas City	74	295	.459	99	.664	322	109	690	9.3
1982-83	Kansas City	82	677	.494	247	.779	501	216	1621	19.8
1983-84	Kansas City	82	753	.485	268	.810	455	296	1794	21.9
	Totals	238	1725	.484	614	.770	1278	621	4105	17.2

LaSALLE THOMPSON 23 6-10 245   **Center**

The kind of guy you want at your side while walking down a dark alley... Forget the brass knuckles, he can do enough damage with his bare hands... Dallas passed him up in the 1982 draft because they didn't think he would be a legitimate NBA center... Has proven otherwise with the Kings... Averaged 10.3 ppg and 8.9 rpg last season... Born June 23, 1961, in Cincinnati... Played under Abe Lemons at Texas, then left school to turn pro after his junior year... Had some personality problems with former coach Cotton Fitzsimmons... Taken fifth overall in the draft by Kings... An avid reader of horror and mystery stories... Keeps pet snakes back home in Cincinnati.

Year	Team	G	FG	FG Pct.	FT	FT Pct.	Reb.	Ast.	TP	Avg.
1982-83	Kansas City	71	147	.512	89	.650	375	33	383	5.4
1983-84	Kansas City	80	333	.523	160	.717	709	86	826	10.3
	Totals	151	480	.519	249	.692	1084	119	1209	8.0

MARK OLBERDING 28 6-9 230   Forward

Another bull in a china shop... Would knock your block off just as soon as look at you... But he has also got a surprisingly good touch from medium range... Spent six years as a bruiser in San Antonio, before spending a season in purgatory with the Chicago Bulls... Kings picked him up on the day of the 1983 draft by shipping guard Ennis Whatley to the Bulls... Added some bulk to the Kings' frontline... Played in all but one game last season... Born April 21, 1956, in Melrose, Minn.... Played for the University of Minnesota in the heyday of Bill Musselman, then followed his coach to the ABA... An original member of "The Bruise Brothers" at San Antonio... Key member of all those divisional championship teams... Despite being one of the league's most physical players, he is also one of the most fun-loving and popular.

Year	Team	G	FG	FG Pct.	FT	FT Pct.	Reb.	Ast.	TP	Avg.
1975-76	S.D.-S.A. (ABA)	81	302	.498	191	.773	530	142	795	9.8
1976-77	San Antonio	82	301	.503	251	.794	449	.119	853	10.4
1977-78	San Antonio	79	231	.481	184	.811	373	131	646	8.2
1978-79	San Antonio	80	261	.474	233	.803	429	211	755	9.4
1979-80	San Antonio	75	291	.478	210	.795	418	327	792	10.6
1980-81	San Antonio	82	348	.508	315	.829	471	277	1012	12.3
1981-82	San Antonio	68	333	.472	273	.808	439	202	941	13.8
1982-83	Chicago	80	251	.481	194	.782	358	131	698	8.7
1983-84	Kansas City	81	249	.494	261	.821	445	192	759	9.4
	Totals	708	2567	.488	2112	.804	3912	1732	7251	10.2

LARRY DREW 26 6-2 180   Guard

Call him "The Landlord"... That's how his teammates referred to him after he signed a lucrative contract that gave him ownership of the Sacramento office building where the Kings' owners have their California headquarters... His return to his hometown has turned around a pro career that had started badly... Detroit drafted him 17th overall in 1980, but he was quickly written out of the Pistons' picture... However, he has blossomed with the Kings, helping the local fans to forget Phil Ford... Born April 2, 1958, in Kansas City... Led the club in assists (558) and steals (121) and was second in scoring, behind Eddie Johnson... Can really spark the Kings when he gets out on the fast break... A decent shooter, he's lightning quick driving to the hoop... Kings gave up only a pair of second-round picks to get this Missouri product... Now about 20 other NBA clubs would like to have him.

Year	Team	G	FG	FG Pct.	FT	FT Pct.	Reb.	Ast.	TP	Avg.
1980-81	Detroit	76	197	.407	106	.797	120	249	504	6.6
1981-82	Kansas City	81	358	.473	150	.794	149	419	874	10.8
1982-83	Kansas City	75	599	.492	310	.820	207	610	1510	20.1
1983-84	Kansas City	73	474	.462	243	.776	146	558	1194	16.4
	Totals	305	1628	.467	809	.799	622	1836	4082	13.4

REGGIE THEUS 27 6-7 205   Guard

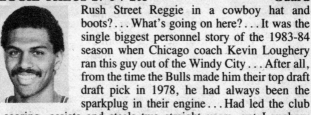

Rush Street Reggie in a cowboy hat and boots?...What's going on here?...It was the single biggest personnel story of the 1983-84 season when Chicago coach Kevin Loughery ran this guy out of the Windy City...After all, from the time the Bulls made him their top draft draft pick in 1978, he had always been the sparkplug in their engine...Had led the club in scoring, assists and steals two straight years, yet Loughery chained him to the bench for the first half of the season...That snapped his four-year string of consecutive games played...Bulls eventually traded him to the Kings for center Steve Johnson and three second-round draft choices in February...Became an instant hit and led the Kings into the playoffs, while Chicago fans booed Johnson every time he stepped onto the floor...Born Oct. 13, 1957, in Inglewood, Cal....Really juiced up the Kings' attack with his ability to run...Attended Nevada-Las Vegas...One of the league's most eligible bachelors....Does some modeling in his spare time.

Year	Team	G	FG	FG Pct.	FT	FT Pct.	Reb.	Ast.	TP	Avg.
1978-79	Chicago	82	537	.480	264	.761	228	429	1338	16.3
1979-80	Chicago	82	566	.483	500	.838	329	515	1660	20.2
1980-81	Chicago	82	543	.495	445	.809	287	426	1549	18.9
1981-82	Chicago	82	560	.469	363	.808	312	476	1508	18.4
1982-83	Chicago	82	749	.478	434	.801	300	484	1953	23.8
1983-84	Chi.-K.C.	61	262	.419	214	.762	129	352	745	12.2
	Totals	471	3217	.475	2220	.803	1585	2682	8753	18.6

BILLY KNIGHT 32 6-6 210   Guard

He's like faulty plumbing—you never know when he's going to be hot or cold...One of the streakiest players in the league today ...Capable of tossing in 40 points one night and not reaching double figures the next...Has spent most of his 10-year pro career with the Indiana Pacers and holds that club's all-time single-game scoring record with 52 points, vs.

San Antonio in 1980...Born June 9, 1952, in Pittsburgh
...Stayed at home and attended Pitt...First-round ABA pick of
the Pacers in 1974...Has frequently been put in the starting
lineup, but rarely stays there for long...Came to the Kings before
the start of the 1983-84 season in a three-team deal that involved
the Knicks...Played in 75 games, started 39 and averaged 12.8
ppg...Gives the Kings a very explosive backcourt...Won the
1981 Players' Association tennis tourney.

Year	Team	G	FG	FG Pct.	FT	FT Pct.	Reb.	Ast.	TP	Avg.
1974-75	Indiana (ABA)	80	580	.534	207	.799	632	168	1371	17.1
1975-76	Indiana (ABA)	70	774	.494	415	.828	708	259	1969	28.1
1976-77	Indiana	78	831	.493	413	.816	582	260	2075	26.6
1977-78	Buffalo	53	457	.494	301	.809	383	161	1215	22.9
1978-79	Boston-Ind.	79	441	.528	249	.841	347	152	1131	14.3
1979-80	Indiana	75	385	.533	212	.809	361	155	986	13.2
1980-81	Indiana	82	546	.533	341	.832	410	157	1436	17.5
1981-82	Indiana	81	378	.495	233	.826	257	118	998	12.3
1982-83	Indiana	80	512	.520	343	.841	324	192	1370	17.1
1983-84	Kansas City	75	358	.491	243	.859	255	160	963	12.8
	Totals	753	5263	.510	2957	.826	4259	1782	13514	17.9

JOE C. MERIWEATHER 31 6-10 220   Center-Forward

Stability, at last...After playing with five different teams in his first five pro seasons, this
Southern Illinois product has spent the last four
establishing a home in Kansas City...Not really
a center and not really a forward...One of
those work-ethic guys who will do what it takes
to help the team and to keep a spot on the
roster...Will never cause defenders to have
nightmares over his offensive capabilities...Born Oct. 26, 1953,
in Phenix City, Ala....Where's the beef? Not on this guy...Chosen
11th overall by Houston in 1975...Then it was on to Atlanta,
New Orleans and New York before plopping down in the midwest
in 1980.

Year	Team	G	FG	FG Pct.	FT	FT Pct.	Reb.	Ast.	TP	Avg.
1975-76	Houston	81	338	.494	154	.644	516	82	830	10.2
1976-77	Atlanta	73	319	.526	182	.714	596	82	820	11.2
1977-78	New Orleans	54	194	.472	87	.654	372	58	475	8.8
1978-79	N.O.-N.Y.	77	242	.484	126	.674	409	79	610	7.9
1979-80	New York	65	252	.528	78	.645	350	66	582	9.0
1980-81	Kansas City	74	206	.496	148	.695	393	77	560	7.6
1981-82	Kansas City	18	47	.516	31	.775	88	17	125	6.9
1982-83	Kansas City	78	258	.570	102	.626	424	64	618	7.9
1983-84	Kansas City	73	193	.532	94	.764	353	51	480	6.6
	Totals	593	2049	.512	1002	.680	3501	576	5100	8.6

MIKE WOODSON 26 6-5 200   **Guard**

Instant offense... After his NBA career got off to a slow start in New York and New Jersey, he has finally found a home with the Kings ...Comes off the bench shooting from the perimeter and has been a fast-acting poison to so many opponents... Drafted No. 12 overall by the Knicks in 1980, he moved across the river to the Nets for half a season... Kings picked him up in exchange for Sam Lacey... Born March 24, 1958, in Indianapolis... Went to Indiana and learned the meaning of hard work and discipline under Bobby Knight... One of a dozen children... Has an explosive first step... How well does he shoot? Ask the Houston Rockets, who watched helplessly as he buried 22-of-24 field-goal attempts against them in February 1983.

Year	Team	G	FG	FG Pct.	FT	FT Pct.	Reb.	Ast.	TP	Avg.
1980-81	New York	81	165	.442	49	.766	97	75	380	4.7
1981-82	N.J.-K.C.	83	538	.503	221	.773	247	222	1304	15.7
1982-83	Kansas City	81	584	.506	298	.790	248	254	1473	18.2
1983-84	Kansas City	71	389	.477	247	.818	175	175	1027	14.5
	Totals	316	1676	.491	815	.792	767	726	4184	13.2

DANE SUTTLE 23 6-2 180   **Guard**

Rookie longshot of the year... Taken on the seventh round as No. 152 overall in 1983... Was the lowest-round pick to earn a spot on an NBA roster... Was virtually squeezed out of playing time in mid-February, when the Kings traded for Reggie Theus... The all-time leading scorer at Pepperdine.... Ranked 14th in the nation in his senior season.... Born Aug. 9, 1961, in Los Angeles... Injuries to other players allowed him to start one time last season... But he's going to have to do something to make a big splash if his pro career is to be extended much longer.

Year	Team	G	FG	FG Pct.	FT	FT Pct.	Reb.	Ast.	TP	Avg.
1983-84	Kansas City	40	109	.509	40	.851	46	46	258	6.5

LARRY MICHEAUX 24 6-9 220   **Forward**

"Mr. Mean"... The silent assassin of the University of Houston's Phi Slama Jama fraternity... Had a difficult time breaking into the rotation as a rookie... Former coach Cotton Fitzsimmons said he did not have an understanding of the game's fundamentals, adding, "His high school and college coaches ought to be shot."... Born March 24, 1960, in Houston... Stayed right at home for his college career and established quite a reputation as a banger and inside scorer... Ranks No. 10 on Cougars' all-time scoring list... Appears slow, but has deceptive quickness... Second-round selection by Chicago in 1983... Traded to Kings for Chris McNealy and a second-round draft choice.

Year	Team	G	FG	FG Pct.	FT	FT Pct.	Reb.	Ast.	TP	Avg.
1983-84	Kansas City	39	49	.544	21	.538	113	19	119	3.1

ED NEALY 24 6-7 240   Forward

You keep wondering what he's doing in the NBA... Well, he's doing all of the fundamental, hard-working things he is asked to do... It was certainly the shocker of the 1982-83 season when he stuck with the Kings as an eighth-round draft choice... Has a decent medium-range shot, but does most of his work on the inside... Has shot better than 56 percent in two pro seasons... Born Feb. 19, 1960, in Pittsburg, Kan.... An Academic All-American at Kansas State... Used to say he was the only player in the NBA whose father drives him to practice... Still lives with his parents... All-state high school star in football... Has the size to be an NFL tight end... Gets chewed up on defense.

Year	Team	G	FG	FG Pct.	FT	FT Pct.	Reb.	Ast.	TP	Avg.
1982-83	Kansas City	82	147	.595	70	.614	485	62	364	4.4
1983-84	Kansas City	71	63	.500	48	.800	222	50	174	2.5
	Totals	153	210	.563	118	.678	707	112	538	3.5

TOP ROOKIE

OTIS THORPE 22 6-9 235   Forward

Played center at Providence... Will be used at the power-forward slot... Can muscle his way inside... No. 2 all-time scorer in Big East (1,625 points) and No. 5 rebounder in Providence history (902)... Born Aug. 5, 1962, in Boynton, Fla.... Named to All-Tournament team at Aloha Classic... Averaged 17.1 ppg and 13.6 rpg last season.

COACH JACK McKINNEY: Still picking up the pieces . . . Five  years after a bicycle accident nearly cost him his life, he is still trying to climb back . . . Was sitting on top of the world as coach of the Lakers at the time of the fall . . . Has now moved on to Kansas City after a four-year stint with the Indiana Pacers . . . Was coaching with his back against the wall in Indy . . . First, there was an absentee owner who wouldn't cough up the money necessary to hang onto talented free agents . . . Then, in his last season with the Pacers, he was expected to work miracles in the won-lost department even though he was without a legitimate center or an honest-to-goodness NBA point guard . . . Named Coach of the Year in 1980-81 . . . Born July 13, 1935, in Chester, Pa. . . . One of the first to come out of the Jack Ramsay School for Coaches . . . Followed Ramsay as the boss at St. Joseph's in Philadelphia, then was Ramsay's assistant at Portland before landing the Laker job . . . Popular and very well-respected around the league . . . Low-key personality will be a direct contrast to previous Kings coach Cotton Fitzsimmons' demeanor . . . Deserves a good break . . . Has overall NBA coaching mark of 134-207.

GREATEST FOUL SHOOTER

He changed uniforms and relocated to different cities so often, it's hard to believe Ron Boone was able to remain so consistent at the foul line.

But the fact is that one of the game's vagabonds, a member of six different teams, was also one of the game's best free-throw shooters, compiling a career percentage of .854 in five NBA seasons and .830 in eight years in the ABA.

Boone is best-known for having the longest consecutive-game streak in pro basketball history. He played in 1,041 straight pro games from Oct. 31, 1968 to Jan. 24, 1981. But since 662 of those games were in the ABA, the NBA does not recognize his record. Instead, Randy Smith (906) is in the NBA books and Boone's mark lives only in the minds of the trivia freaks.

Boone played for the Kings only two seasons (1976-78), but that was long enough for him to become the franchise's all-time best shooter (.848) from the foul line, besting hot shots Jimmy Walker (.845) and Tiny Archibald (.840). Archibald does hold the club record for free throws attempted (2,367) and made (1,989).

ALL-TIME KING LEADERS

SEASON

Points: Nate Archibald, 2,719, 1972-73
Assists: Nate Archibald, 910, 1972-73
Rebounds: Jerry Lucas, 1,688, 1965-66

GAME

Points: Jack Twyman, 59 vs. Minneapolis, 1/15/60
Assists: Phil Ford, 22 vs. Milwaukee, 2/21/79
       Oscar Robertson, 22 vs. New York, 3/5/66
       Oscar Robertson, 22 vs. Syracuse, 10/29/61
Rebounds: Jerry Lucas, 40 vs. Philadelphia, 2/29/64

CAREER

Points: Oscar Robertson, 22,009, 1960-70
Assists: Oscar Robertson, 7,721, 1960-70
Rebounds: Jerry Lucas, 8,831, 1963-69

LOS ANGELES CLIPPERS

TEAM DIRECTORY: Owner: Donald T. Sterling; Pres.: Alan I. Rothenberg; Exec. VP/GM: Carl Scheer; Dir. Pub. Rel.: Scott Carmichael; Coach: Jim Lynam. Arena: Los Angeles Sports Arena (17,500). Colors: Red, white and blue.

Terry Cummings ignited Clippers with 22.9 ppg.

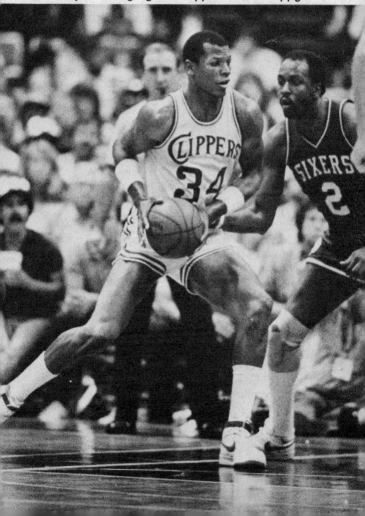

SCOUTING REPORT

SHOOTING: Putting the ball in the basket is one area where the Clippers don't need much help at all, yet it's where they probably helped themselves the most in the college draft. Los Angeles picked Louisville's Lancaster Gordon with the eighth choice overall, then added San Diego State star Michael Cage later in the first round. Gordon, who is from the stable of thoroughbreds trained by Denny Crum, shot better than 50 percent in his college career. Cage was even better, averaging 24.5 ppg and shooting .568.

That pair joins a veteran group of very capable scorers. Center James Donaldson (.596) was second in the league to San Antonio's Artis Gilmore in field-goal percentage last season and part-time wonder Bill Walton (.556) was not far behind. Terry Cummings fell just under the break-even mark (.494) and, while guard Norm Nixon (.462) is not a 50-percent shooter, he can go on hot streaks from the perimeter.

PLAYMAKING: Nixon's the one. That is certainly what Clipper management seemed to be saying on draft day, when they examined their choices and pulled the lever for Gordon. They passed up Cal State-Fullerton's Leon Wood, an excellent playmaker, and that can only be interpreted as a clear endorsement of Stormin' Norman (11.1 assists per game).

Obtained before the start of last season in the trade that sent rookie Byron Scott to the Lakers, Nixon quickly became the heart and soul of the Clippers. He has played on world championship teams and now, with Cage and Gordon around, he has got even more people to set up on offense. The word was that management even consulted Nixon on whether to draft Gordon or Wood and wound up doing just what he said. Craig Hodges is still a capable backup here, but the main burden of the offense is once more in the hands old Savoir Faire.

DEFENSE: Maybe the Clippers wound up in Los Angeles because they were out on the freeway in search of a defense and ended up wandering that far. On paper, this looks like it would be a pretty decent defensive team. But instead, the Clippers hardly knew the meaning of the word, ranking 21st in the league with a yield of 114 ppg last season.

Think about it. They've got the 7-2 Donaldson, the 6-11 Walton and the 6-10 Cummings on the frontline, yet they blocked 90 fewer shots last season than the relatively tiny Denver Nuggets. Of the rookies, Gordon has a solid defensive background, but Cage barely knows that the other end of the floor exists. It's hard

CLIPPER ROSTER

No.	Veteran	Pos.	Ht.	Wt.	Age	Yrs. Pro	College
7	*Michael Brooks	F	6-7	210	26	5	LaSalle
34	Terry Cummings	F	6-9	220	23	3	DePaul
40	James Donaldson	C	7-2	270	27	5	Washington State
24	Craig Hodges	G	6-3	180	24	3	Long Beach State
20	*Greg Kelser	F	6-8	205	27	6	Michigan State
8	Hank McDowell	F	6-9	215	24	4	Memphis State
10	Norm Nixon	G	6-2	175	29	8	Duquesne
7	*Billy McKinney	G	6-0	170	29	7	Northwestern
25	Ricky Pierce	G	6-5	205	25	3	Rice
18	*Derek Smith	G-F	6-6	205	23	3	Louisville
32	Bill Walton	C-F	6-11	225	31	12	UCLA
15	Rory White	F	6-8	210	25	3	South Alabama

*Free agent unsigned at press time

Rd.	Top Draftees	Sel. No.	Ht.	Wt.	College
1	Lancaster Gordon	8	6-3	185	Louisville
1	Michael Cage	14	6-9	225	San Diego State
2	**Jay Murphy	31	6-11	235	Boston College
4	Marc Glass	4	6-3	180	Montana
5	Alonza Allen	73	6-6	190	SW Louisiana

**Drafted by Golden State and traded to Los Angeles

to envision a team coached by Jimmy Lynam—a graduate of the Dr. Jack Ramsay School of Defense—not having an overall team concept and lacking players willing to scrape the skin off their knees.

REBOUNDING: This is another strength that figures to be an even greater strength. With Lynam frequently starting Donaldson (8.4 rpg) and Walton (8.7 rpg) in the frontcourt, the Clippers ranked third in the league in rebounding last season. Now they're adding Cage, who averaged approximately 12 rpg over the course of his college career, and 6-11 rookie Jay Murphy, who was obtained from Golden State in a draft-day trade for Jerome Whitehead. This team can board with the best of them.

OUTLOOK: A year ago, you could look at the Clipper lineup and easily project them into the expanded playoff picture. But in practice, that didn't work out. They once again suffered from the off-again, on-again status of Walton and a porous defense. Now they've added three rookies who should make significant contributions. In their first season in Los Angeles, they will still be the weaker of the two teams in town. But the Clippers should step out of last place in the Pacific Division and a playoff berth is a possibility.

CLIPPER PROFILES

TERRY CUMMINGS 23 6-9 220   Forward

Only doubts about him concern his health . . . Was named Rookie of the Year in 1983 while battling an irregular heartbeat that caused him to collapse during a game . . . Series of tests during offseason eventually pronounced him fit to resume his career and he picked up right where he left off . . . A strong rebounder and aggressive scorer . . . He and New Jersey's Buck Williams are the best two young power forwards in league . . . Born March 15, 1961, in Chicago . . . Starred at DePaul, then turned pro after his junior season . . . An ordained Pentecostal minister . . . Narrowly missed averaging more than 20 points (22.9 ppg) and 10 rebounds (9.6 rpg) for the second straight year . . . If health holds up, he'll be a star for many seasons.

Year	Team	G	FG	FG Pct.	FT	FT Pct.	Reb.	Ast.	TP	Avg.
1982-83	San Diego	70	684	.523	292	.709	744	177	1660	23.7
1983-84	San Diego	81	737	.494	380	.720	777	139	1854	22.9
	Totals	151	1421	.508	672	.715	1521	316	3514	23.3

NORM NIXON 29 6-2 175   Guard

What happened to Magic? Where's Kareem? Where did James Worthy go? Those must have been questions that he asked himself countless times after the trade that sent him from the Lakers to the Clippers for Byron Scott . . . After years of complaining he never got enough of the spotlight with the Lakers, he often found himself the center of attention . . . Also found himself on the losing end many more times than in the past . . . Born Oct. 11, 1955, in Macon, Ga., he attended Macon Southwest High and was given his start by legendary tough-guy coach Don Richardson . . . Second-leading scorer in Duquesne history . . . Selected late in first round of 1977 draft . . . Has always felt unappreciated . . . Clippers felt his leadership could help them to the playoffs last season, but pieces of the puzzle never quite fit . . . Still finished second in NBA to Magic Johnson in assists (11.1 per game)...Calls himself "Savoir Faire."

Year	Team	G	FG	FG Pct.	FT	FT Pct.	Reb.	Ast.	TP	Avg.
1977-78	Los Angeles	81	496	.497	115	.714	239	553	1107	13.7
1978-79	Los Angeles	82	623	.542	158	.775	231	737	1404	17.1
1979-80	Los Angeles	82	624	.516	197	.779	229	642	1446	17.6
1980-81	Los Angeles	79	576	.476	196	.778	232	696	1350	17.1
1981-82	Los Angeles	82	628	.493	181	.808	176	652	1440	17.6
1982-83	Los Angeles	79	533	.475	181	.744	205	566	1191	15.1
1983-84	San Diego	82	587	.462	206	.760	203	914	1391	17.0
	Totals	567	4067	.494	1178	.768	1515	4760	9329	16.5

GREG KELSER 27 6-8 205   Forward

Is he for real or simply lucky to have teamed with Magic Johnson at Michigan State?...In five NBA seasons, he has never justified his status as the fourth player chosen in the 1979 draft by Detroit...Now with his third NBA team, having been shipped south with James Donaldson and Mark Radford in the trade that sent Tom Chambers and Al Wood to Seattle...Born Sept. 17, 1957, in Panama City, Fla....Grew up on the streets of Detroit...Knee problems plagued him in first two years in NBA...Settled down a bit with the Clippers, shooting 51.9 percent...Was effective on fast break...There's still hope, but don't hold your breath waiting for him to make the All-Star team.

Year	Team	G	FG	FG Pct.	FT	FT Pct.	Reb.	Ast.	TP	Avg.
1979-80	Detroit	50	280	.472	146	.719	276	108	709	14.2
1980-81	Detroit	25	120	.421	68	.642	120	45	308	12.3
1981-82	Det.-Sea.	60	116	.428	105	.656	193	57	337	5.6
1982-83	Seattle	80	247	.549	173	.673	403	97	667	8.3
1983-84	San Diego	80	313	.519	250	.702	391	91	878	11.0
	Totals	295	1076	.489	742	.686	1283	398	2899	9.8

BILL WALTON 31 6-11 225   Center-Forward

He was back...Then he wasn't, then he was, then he wasn't...Started season playing on a part-time basis, then was sidelined for several weeks by a hand injury...It's sad to think what "Big Red" might have accomplished if he had been injury-free throughout his career...Shot 55.6 percent from the field, but often appeared tentative on the floor and had trouble playing in second of back-to-back games...Born Nov. 5, 1952, in San Diego...Brilliant and durable player at UCLA, but during his

10-year NBA career, he has been able to play in only 311 of a possible 820 regular-season games... Question is: are Clippers better off hoping he'll come back to full strength or building for the future without him?... Was not as aloof or as critical of teammates last season... In the second half of the season, he played power forward alongside of 7-2 James Donaldson... Was the main cog in the 1976-77 Portland championship team before a series of foot injuries sidelined him and tore apart the potential dynasty.

Year	Team	G	FG	FG Pct.	FT	FT Pct.	Reb.	Ast.	TP	Avg.
1974-75	Portland	35	177	.513	94	.686	441	167	448	12.8
1975-76	Portland	51	345	.471	133	.583	681	220	823	16.1
1976-77	Portland	65	491	.528	228	.697	934	245	1210	18.6
1977-78	Portland	58	460	.522	177	.720	766	291	1097	18.9
1978-79	Portland				Injured					
1979-80	San Diego	14	81	.503	32	.593	126	34	194	13.9
1980-81	San Diego				Injured					
1981-82	San Diego				Injured					
1982-83	San Diego	33	200	.528	65	.536	323	120	465	14.1
1983-84	San Diego	55	288	.556	92	.597	477	183	668	12.1
	Totals	311	2042	.517	821	.650	3748	1260	4905	15.8

MICHAEL BROOKS 26 6-7 210   Forward

Career in jeopardy... Had played in 293 straight games since entering the NBA until suffering a torn anterior cruciate ligament in his right knee, a devastating injury that ended the careers of Billy Cunningham and Doug Collins... Doctors say he may never play again... But he is determined to prove them wrong and says he might even return to action this season... A bit of a puzzle as a pro... Has not lived up to great expectations... Born July 17, 1958, in Philadelphia... Stayed at home to attend LaSalle... Was not expected to be a big scorer in the pros, but sound fundamentals promised a fruitful career ... Instead, he's been mistake-prone and, at times, moody... It may have had something to do with the bad-news characters who were with Clippers during his first couple of pro seasons... After the 1979 Pan Am trials, coach Bobby Knight said, "If I could pick one player in the country to build a team around, it would be Michael Brooks."

Year	Team	G	FG	FG Pct.	FT	FT Pct.	Reb.	Ast.	TP	Avg.
1980-81	San Diego	82	488	.479	226	.706	442	208	1202	14.7
1981-82	San Diego	82	537	.504	202	.757	624	236	1276	15.6
1982-83	San Diego	82	402	.484	193	.697	521	262	1002	12.2
1983-84	San Diego	47	213	.479	104	.689	342	88	530	11.3
	Totals	293	1640	.488	725	.714	1929	794	4010	13.7

RICKY PIERCE 25 6-5 205   Guard

Headed west from Detroit just before the start of the season and found things much more to his liking... Had been a first-round draft choice of the Pistons in 1982, but, after contract hold-out, he reported overweight and could never get out of then-coach Scotty Robertson's dog-house... Clippers picked him up for future considerations... Born Aug. 19, 1959, in Garland, Tex.... Started out at Walla Walla (Wash.) Junior College, then played three years at Rice... Was No. 2 scorer in the NCAA Division I (26.8 ppg) as a senior... Was Rice MVP and All-Southwest Conference for three straight years... U.S. Basketball Writers first-team All-American... A solid perimeter shooter and a heady player... Led the Clippers in free-throw percentage with .861 mark.

Year	Team	G	FG	FG Pct.	FT	FT Pct.	Reb.	Ast.	TP	Avg.
1982-83	Detroit	39	33	.375	18	.563	35	14	85	2.2
1983-84	San Diego	69	268	.470	149	.861	135	60	685	9.9
	Totals	108	301	.457	167	.815	170	74	770	7.1

JAMES DONALDSON 27 7-2 270   Center

A bruiser... Just ask Houston's Ralph Sampson, who was thrown to the floor like a rag doll many times during their five regular-season confrontations... Acquired from Seattle prior to last season along with Greg Kelser... Born Aug. 16, 1957, in Meachem, England... One of handful of NBA players born outside the U.S.... Says his mother is not exactly an avid basketball fan: "It was just recently that she found out Dr. J and Magic Johnson are not the same person."... She also thought he played guard "because I was always guarding somebody." ... Seattle coach Lenny Wilkens eased him into the NBA slowly and he's beginning to pay dividends in San Diego... Fourth-round draft choice in 1979, out of Washington State... Not much of a shot, but when he dunks, the backboard always shakes... A 59.6 percent shooter last season... Engaging personality... A degree in sociology... Darryl Dawkins used to call him "American Tourister" because "his head is as big as a suitcase."

Year	Team	G	FG	FG Pct.	FT	FT Pct.	Reb.	Ast.	TP	Avg.
1980-81	Seattle	68	129	.542	101	.594	309	42	359	5.3
1981-82	Seattle	82	255	.609	151	.629	490	51	661	8.1
1982-83	Seattle	82	289	.583	150	.688	501	97	728	8.9
1983-84	San Diego	82	360	.596	249	.761	649	90	969	11.8
	Totals	314	1033	.588	651	.682	1949	280	2717	8.7

DEREK SMITH 23 6-6 205   Guard-Forward

Another one that got away from Golden State...Continues a long history of players who left the Bay Area and produced elsewhere...Clippers signed him as a free agent before the season and he proved to be very capable, starting 20 games...Born Oct. 1, 1961, in La Grange, Ga....Came out of Denny Crum's stable of thoroughbreds at Louisville...Played on the Cardinals' NCAA championship team with Darrell Griffith in 1980...Never shot less than 54 percent from the field in college and is one of Louisville's top three all-time scorers...Could stick around for a while to haunt the Warriors.

Year	Team	G	FG	FG Pct.	FT	FT Pct.	Reb.	Ast.	TP	Avg.
1982-83	Golden State	27	21	.412	17	.680	38	2	59	2.2
1983-84	San Diego	61	238	.546	123	.755	170	82	600	9.8
	Totals	88	259	.532	140	.745	208	84	659	7.5

CRAIG HODGES 24 6-3 180   Guard

Tailed off...Following a surprising first season in which he was named to the Basketball Digest All-Rookie second team, his level of play dropped off...Had to give up his starting role when Norm Nixon was acquired and since he isn't a good shooter—45.1 percent in two years—he can't provide a spark off the bench...Born June 26, 1960, in Parker Forest, Ill....Played for Long Beach State...Considered a real find when Clippers drafted him on third round...Still thought of highly as a prospect by some around the league.

Year	Team	G	FG	FG Pct.	FT	FT Pct.	Reb.	Ast.	TP	Avg.
1982-83	San Diego	76	318	.452	94	.723	122	275	750	9.9
1983-84	San Diego	76	258	.450	66	.750	86	116	592	7.8
	Totals	152	576	.451	160	.734	208	391	1342	8.8

BILLY McKINNEY 29 6-0 170   Guard

Looks like a cross between Sugar Ray Leonard and Calvin Murphy, but doesn't have the knockout punch or the staying power of either one...Raw speed is what's kept him in the league for six years...This graduate of the Calvin Murphy School of Perpetual Motion can get out and go on the fast break...Also not slow to pack his bags and leave town, considering he's now with his fourth NBA franchise...Born June 5,

1955, in Waukegan, Ill., the birthplace of such NBA greats as Corky Calhoun and Jerome Whitehead...Has been known in the past for the ability to occasionally stick the perimeter shot, but his touch fell off badly last season with the Clippers...His size makes him a defensive liability...Recently married...Played basketball and baseball at Northwestern...Also plays the drums.

Year	Team	G	FG	FG Pct.	FT	FT Pct.	Reb.	Ast.	TP	Avg.
1978-79	Kansas City	78	240	.503	129	.796	85	253	609	7.8
1979-80	Kansas City	76	206	.449	107	.805	86	248	520	6.8
1980-81	Utah-Den.	84	327	.507	162	.862	184	360	818	9.7
1981-82	Denver	81	369	.528	137	.806	142	338	875	10.8
1982-83	Denver	68	266	.487	136	.814	121	288	668	9.8
1983-84	San Diego	80	136	.446	39	.848	54	161	311	3.9
	Totals	467	1544	.493	710	.820	672	1648	3801	8.1

HANK McDOWELL 24 6-9 215   Forward

Travelin' man...Three seasons in the NBA and three teams...But he might stick around the Clipper organization awhile because he doesn't come with a high price tag and he made some fine contributions with more hustle than talent...A fifth-round draft choice of Golden State in 1981...Played part of 1982-83 season for Portland...Born Nov. 13, 1959, in Memphis, Tenn....Played for Memphis State...Doesn't have a big, bruising body, but he'll still go into the lane and fight for rebounds...His musical tastes are strictly rock and roll...Says he'd like to meet the Pope...Was a big fan of Kareem Abdul-Jabbar and Boston Celtics when growing up...Now spends much of his free time involved with photography or gobbling up little alien invaders in video games.

Year	Team	G	FG	FG Pct.	FT	FT Pct.	Reb.	Ast.	TP	Avg.
1981-82	Golden State	30	34	.405	27	.659	100	20	95	3.2
1982-83	G.S.-Port.	56	58	.460	47	.770	119	24	163	2.9
1983-84	San Diego	57	85	.431	38	.679	155	37	208	3.6
	Totals	143	177	.435	112	.709	374	81	466	3.3

TOP ROOKIES

LANCASTER GORDON 22 6-3 185   Guard

Another racehorse from Denny Crum's Louisville stable...Could be a star in the NBA...Will play good defense and is explosive on offense... Born June 24, 1962, in Jackson, Miss.... One of final cuts by 1984 U.S. Olympic team... Owns fine jumper and can go to the boards... Averaged 14.7 ppg on .519 shooting as a senior.

MICHAEL CAGE 22 6-9 225   Forward

Rebounder supreme... Fine inside player... Shot .562 and scored 24.5 ppg as a senior... Some scouts say he is lazy... But if he puts his physical tools to work, he'll be a good one... Born Jan. 28, 1962, in West Memphis, Ark.... Started every game of his four-year college career at San Diego State... High-school teammate of Memphis State's Keith Lee.

COACH JIMMY LYNAM: Hard-nosed, tough street fighter  ... That's the way they raise their guards in Philadelphia and he has that stamp all over him... "Jimmy The Kid"... A little guy, but a big name on the playgrounds and in the gyms of Philly when he was growing up in the '60s... He's always been an overachiever, so it's not surprising that he made it to the big time... Born Sept. 15, 1941, in Philadelphia... The latest product to be cranked out of the coaching factory at St. Joseph's, following in the footsteps of Jack Ramsay, Jack McKinney and Paul Westhead... Played guard at St. Joe's under Ramsay from 1962-64 and was a ball-hawking, defensive leader... Has been guided by Ramsay throughout a coaching career that took him from Fairfield to American and back to St. Joe's before he made the leap to the NBA... Biggest victory at the college level was a nationally televised upset of highly-ranked DePaul in the 1981 NCAA Tournament... Spent two years learning the pro game as an assistant to Ramsay in Portland and then moved to San Diego and put his hustling stamp on the Clippers in his first year, though they finished at 30-52... How energetic is he? Well, he had to have surgery to repair knee damage that resulted from constantly crouching and jumping on the sidelines.

GREATEST FOUL SHOOTER

Forget about the Clippers' rebirth on the West Coast. The greatest free-throw shooter in the franchise's history did not spend his days off at the beach or cruising the local scene in La Jolla.

No, Ernie DiGregorio played for the Clippers back in the days when they were the Buffalo Braves. And he could shoot fouls with the best of them, posting a .906 mark for Buffalo.

How good was he? Well, consider that though he does not have nearly enough attempts (511) to qualify for the NBA's all-time list, DiGregorio's career percentage (.902) was better than all-time leader Rick Barry's (.900).

Since the cross-country move, the Clippers haven't had a consistently fine shooter. In six seasons in San Diego, only Randy Smith led the club in free-throw percentage more than once. The other season leaders were Bobby Smith, Freeman Williams, Charlie Criss and, last season, Ricky Pierce.

ALL-TIME CLIPPER LEADERS

SEASON

Points: Bob McAdoo, 2,831, 1974-75
Assists: Norm Nixon, 914, 1983-84
Rebounds: Elmore Smith, 1,184, 1971-72

GAME

Points: Bob McAdoo, 52 vs. Seattle, 3/17/76
  Bob McAdoo, 52 vs. Boston, 2/22/74
Assists: Ernie DiGregorio, 25 vs. Portland, 1/1/74
Rebounds: Swen Nater, 32 vs. Denver, 12/14/79

CAREER

Points: Randy Smith, 12,735, 1971-79, 1982-83
Assists: Randy Smith, 3,498, 1971-79, 1982-83
Rebounds: Bob McAdoo, 4,229, 1972-76

LOS ANGELES LAKERS

TEAM DIRECTORY: Owner: Jerry Buss; Pres.: Bill Sharman; GM: Jerry West; Dir. Pub. Rel.: Josh Rosenfeld; Coach: Pat Riley; Asst. Coaches: Bill Bertka, Dave Wohl. Arena: The Forum (17,505). Colors: Royal purple and gold.

SCOUTING REPORT

SHOOTING: There's Kareem's skyhook, the Coop-a-loop, the Worthy slama-lama-ding-dong and any one of Magic's mystical moves down the lane. Is it any wonder that the Lakers have led the league in shooting for the last three seasons?

The Lakers don't have an abundance of great perimeter shooters, though Jamaal Wilkes is one. They just get the ball in so close to the basket that they can't miss. Abdul-Jabbar (.576), Johnson (.565), Worthy (.556), Mike McGee (.594), Kurt Rambis (.558), Wilkes (.514) and Cooper (.497) are all money in the bank, especially when they're going for broke on the break. The Boston Celtics proved the Lakers are not the best of teams in a halfcourt offense, but they usually don't have to play that style and, as long as they're running, they're great.

PLAYMAKING: Sure, Magic had his problems in the finals against the Celtics and probably did cost the Lakers an NBA title by making several errors at crucial moments. But, if you were starting an expansion team and needed a point guard, you'd scoop him up faster than you can say "Earvin Johnson." He led the league in assists with 13.1 per game. If there's a weakness in Johnson's passing game, it's that when he's standing still, there seem to be moments of indecision that are not evident when he's playing instinctively on the break. Cooper occasionally runs the show to give Magic a break, but he's not in the same class. Few are.

DEFENSE: The Lakers give up a lot of points, but that's because of the fast pace they like to play. There are plenty of guys on this team who seem to enjoy making the big steal that sets up the transition basket as much as scoring the points themselves. Of course, they can afford to be a little reckless on defense as long as they know Abdul-Jabbar (1.79 blocked shots per game) is back there in the middle, minding the store. He takes his share of criticism, but there aren't many players who want to drive against him when the money's on the line.

The Magic vanished against Boston, but he had a good year.

LAKER ROSTER

No.	Veteran	Pos.	Ht.	Wt.	Age	Yrs. Pro	College
33	Kareem Abdul-Jabbar	C	7-2	235	37	16	UCLA
21	Michael Cooper	G	6-7	170	28	7	New Mexico
00	*Calvin Garrett	G-F	6-7	195	28	5	Oral Roberts
34	*Clay Johnson	G	6-4	185	28	4	Missouri
32	Earvin Johnson	G	6-9	215	25	6	Michigan State
5	*Eddie Jordan	G	6-1	170	29	9	North Carolina
25	Mitch Kupchak	F-C	6-10	230	29	9	North Carolina
11	Bob McAdoo	C-F	6-10	225	33	13	North Carolina
40	Mike McGee	G	6-5	190	25	4	Michigan
41	*Swen Nater	C	6-11	250	34	12	UCLA
31	Kurt Rambis	F	6-8	220	25	4	Santa Clara
4	Byron Scott	G	6-4	202	23	2	Arizona State
35	Larry Spriggs	F	6-7	215	25	4	Howard
52	Jamaal Wilkes	F	6-6	190	31	11	UCLA
42	James Worthy	F	6-9	219	22	3	North Carolina

*Free agent unsigned at press time

Rd.	Top Draftees	Sel. No.	Ht.	Wt.	College
1	Earl Jones	23	6-10	210	District of Columbia
3	George Singleton	69	6-7	210	Furman
4	John Revelli	92	6-8	225	Stanford
5	Lance Berwald	115	6-10	231	N. Dakota State
6	Keith Jones	138	6-1	175	Stanford

Cooper, of course, has made a reputation off his defense, but Wilkes and Rambis are two guys who do the job quietly and effectively. Coach Pat Riley must be emphasizing defense. There have been reports that even Bob McAdoo is playing it.

REBOUNDING: Achilles had his heel and the Lakers have theirs. And because of Los Angeles' weakness on the boards, the 1984 NBA championship banner is hanging from the rafters of Boston Garden. This is just not a team that can handle the constant bumping and banging that characterizes Eastern Conference play. Abdul-Jabbar (7.3 rpg) will retire after this season with the reputation of a passive rebounder. They certainly needed the big, bruising type to give strength to the front line, but instead took the willowy Earl Jones on the first round of the draft. It might prove to be a big mistake.

OUTLOOK: How can you look at a team with all of this talent and say that it's on the way down? It's easy, unless Abdul-Jabbar changes his mind about retiring at age 38. If the big guy walks away, the Lakers will suddenly be a team of greyhounds with nobody anchoring the middle.

At this point, the Lakers are still the cream of the crop in the Western Conference and a good bet to wind up back in the Championship Series for the fourth straight season. But Portland and Houston are coming on strong and the end of the reign could be near.

LAKER PROFILES

KAREEM ABDUL-JABBAR 37 7-2 235   Center

 Shouldn't that be Kareem Abdul-Record, since he holds almost all of them?... Added the big one April 5 of last season in Las Vegas, when a skyhook from the right baseline pushed him past Wilt Chamberlain and into first place on the all-time scoring list... The most potent offensive force in the game today, even at his age... Had a resurgence last season... Of course, he always takes heat when Lakers don't win it all... Born April 16, 1947, in New York City, as Lewis Ferdinand Alcindor... Legend began at Power Memorial High School and was in full bloom at UCLA... Says this will be his final NBA season... Has been named MVP a record six times... Was the No. 1 draft pick of the Milwaukee Bucks in 1969 and led them to the NBA title in 1970-71... Traded to the Lakers in 1975... Trails only Laker general manager Jerry West on the all-time playoff scoring list.

Year	Team	G	FG	FG Pct.	FT	FT Pct.	Reb.	Ast.	TP	Avg.
1969-70	Milwaukee	82	938	.518	485	.653	1190	337	2361	28.8
1970-71	Milwaukee	82	1063	.577	470	.690	1311	272	2596	31.7
1971-72	Milwaukee	81	1159	.574	504	.689	1346	370	2822	34.8
1972-73	Milwaukee	76	982	.554	328	.713	1224	379	2292	30.2
1973-74	Milwaukee	81	948	.539	295	.702	1178	386	2191	27.0
1974-75	Milwaukee	65	812	.513	325	.763	912	264	1949	30.0
1975-76	Los Angeles	82	914	.529	447	.703	1383	413	2275	27.7
1976-77	Los Angeles	82	888	.579	376	.701	1091	319	2152	26.2
1977-78	Los Angeles	62	663	.550	274	.783	801	269	1600	25.8
1978-79	Los Angeles	80	777	.577	349	.736	1025	431	1903	23.8
1979-80	Los Angeles	82	835	.604	364	.765	886	371	2034	24.8
1980-81	Los Angeles	80	836	.574	423	.766	821	272	2095	26.2
1981-82	Los Angeles	76	753	.579	312	.706	659	225	1818	23.9
1982-83	Los Angeles	79	722	.588	278	.749	592	200	1722	21.8
1983-84	Los Angeles	80	716	.578	285	.723	587	211	1717	21.5
	Totals	1170	13006	.560	5515	.717	15005	4719	31527	26.9

EARVIN (MAGIC) JOHNSON 25 6-9 215   Guard

Can he really be so young ... It seems he's been around, doing his Magic tricks, for years ... Changed the entire concept of the point-guard position and is unquestionably the finest passer in the game today ... Unfortunately, he made several critical blunders against Boston in the finals that probably cost Lakers their third NBA championship in five years ... Had another fine regular season ... Can beat you by passing (13.0 assists per game), scoring (17.6 ppg) or rebounding (7.3 rpg) ... The only player in the game he has to look up to is Larry Bird ... Born Aug. 14, 1959, in Lansing, Mich.... Led his high-school team to a state championship and Michigan State to the NCAA crown in 1979 ... Left school after his junior year and the Lakers claimed him with the No. 1 pick in the draft... Rest is history ... His 42-point, 15-rebound, seven-assist, three-steal performance against Philadelphia in Game 6 of the 1980 finals was probably the best in NBA playoff history.

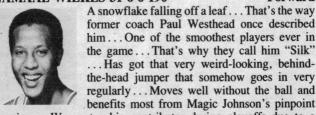

Year	Team	G	FG	FG Pct.	FT	FT Pct.	Reb.	Ast.	TP	Avg.
1979-80	Los Angeles	77	503	.530	374	.810	596	563	1387	18.0
1980-81	Los Angeles	37	312	.532	171	.760	320	317	798	21.6
1981-82	Los Angeles	78	556	.537	329	.760	751	743	1447	18.6
1982-83	Los Angeles	79	511	.548	304	.800	683	829	1326	16.8
1983-84	Los Angeles	67	441	.565	290	.810	491	875	1178	17.6
	Totals	338	2323	.542	1468	.790	2841	3327	6136	18.2

JAMAAL WILKES 31 6-6 190   Forward

A snowflake falling off a leaf ... That's the way former coach Paul Westhead once described him ... One of the smoothest players ever in the game ... That's why they call him "Silk" ... Has got that very weird-looking, behind-the-head jumper that somehow goes in very regularly ... Moves well without the ball and benefits most from Magic Johnson's pinpoint passing ... Was not a big contributor during playoffs due to a gastrointestinal illness ... Born May 2, 1953, in Berkeley, Cal., as Jackson Keith Wilkes ... Raised in Ventura and starred with Bill Walton on two NCAA title teams at UCLA ... Excellent defensive player ... Son of a minister ... Has hit 50 percent or better from the field six years in a row ... Taken on the first round (No. 11) by Golden State in 1974 and won a title there while winning Rookie-of-the-Year Award ... Signed as a free agent by the Lakers in 1977 ... His 37-point effort in Game 6 of 1980 NBA finals is probably the most underrated effort in playoff history. That's because Magic Johnson had 42 that night.

Year	Team	G	FG	FG Pct.	FT	FT Pct.	Reb.	Ast.	TP	Avg.
1974-75	Golden State	82	502	.442	160	.734	671	183	1164	14.2
1975-76	Golden State	82	617	.463	227	.772	720	167	1461	17.5
1976-77	Golden State	76	548	.478	247	.797	578	211	1343	17.7
1977-78	Los Angeles	51	277	.440	106	.716	380	182	660	12.9
1978-79	Los Angeles	82	626	.504	272	.751	609	227	1524	18.6
1979-80	Los Angeles	82	726	.535	189	.808	525	250	1644	20.0
1980-81	Los Angeles	81	786	.526	254	.758	435	235	1827	22.6
1981-82	Los Angeles	82	744	.525	246	.732	393	143	1734	21.1
1982-83	Los Angeles	80	684	.530	203	.757	343	182	1571	19.6
1983-84	Los Angeles	75	542	.514	208	.743	340	214	1294	17.3
	Totals	713	6052	.500	2112	.758	4994	1994	14222	18.4

JAMES WORTHY 23 6-9 219   Forward

If Kurt Rambis is Clark Kent, then this guy is Superman... Has already been labeled the next Dr. J... It is certainly hard to argue after the way he swooped and swirled and soared against the Boston Celtics in the NBA Championship Series... Absolutely devastating on the fast break... Can block shots, hit the jumper and dunk with the best of them... Shot 55.6 percent from the field... Has a good jumper... Born Feb. 27, 1961, in Gastonia, N.C.... Played on Dean Smith's only NCAA championship team at North Carolina in 1982 and made the steal that sealed the victory over Georgetown... Perfectly suited to the Laker fast-break philosophy... Will star for years to come.

Year	Team	G	FG	FG Pct.	FT	FT Pct.	Reb.	Ast.	TP	Avg.
1982-83	Los Angeles	77	447	.579	138	.624	399	132	1033	13.4
1983-84	Los Angeles	82	495	.556	195	.759	515	207	1185	14.5
	Totals	159	942	.567	333	.697	914	339	2218	13.9

KURT RAMBIS 25 6-8 220   Forward

The Clark Kent look... Rambis Youth... They became the latest Hollywood fads when he signed with the Lakers in 1981... Has proven valuable in three seasons of doing the banging and dirty work under the boards... Smart enough and enough of a hustler to get down the floor and finish off the fast break with passes from Magic Johnson... Born Feb. 25, 1958, in Cupertino, Cal.... Played college ball at Santa Clara... The Knicks, who have been looking for a power forward ever since, drafted him on the third round in 1980 and promptly cut him... Played one season in Greece, then returned to earn a spot with the Lakers and won an NBA title in his first year in the league . . . Now every team wants a player just like him . . . Can be found at the beach . . . First name is Darrell . . . Kurt is his middle name.

Year	Team	G	FG	FG Pct.	FT	FT Pct.	Reb.	Ast.	TP	Avg.
1981-82	Los Angeles	64	118	.518	59	.504	348	56	295	4.6
1982-83	Los Angeles	78	235	.569	114	.687	531	90	584	7.5
1983-84	Los Angeles	47	63	.558	42	.636	266	34	168	3.6
	Totals	189	416	.551	215	.616	1145	180	1047	5.5

MICHAEL COOPER 28 6-7 170   Guard

Coop-a-loops and slam dunks are his trademarks . . . Became a starter last season after Norm Nixon was traded . . . That may have actually made him less effective . . . Was devastating when he came off the bench like a bolt of lightning . . . Not a jump-shooter, but he led the club in three-pointers (38-of-121 for 31.4 percent), which he shoots like set shots . . . Born April 15, 1956, in Los Angeles . . . Wiry fellow who can leap through the roof of the Forum, but that doesn't mean he isn't willing to mix it up on the inside . . . A steal by the Lakers on the third round of 1978 draft out of New Mexico . . . His game is way up there in the stratosphere and so is his head, according to some observers.

Year	Team	G	FG	FG Pct.	FT	FT Pct.	Reb.	Ast.	TP	Avg.
1978-79	Los Angeles	3	3	.500	0	.000	0	0	6	2.0
1979-80	Los Angeles	82	303	.524	111	.776	229	221	722	8.8
1980-81	Los Angeles	81	321	.491	117	.785	336	232	763	9.4
1981-82	Los Angeles	76	383	.517	139	.813	269	230	907	11.9
1982-83	Los Angeles	82	266	.535	102	.785	274	315	639	7.8
1983-84	Los Angeles	82	273	.497	155	.838	262	482	739	9.0
	Totals	406	1549	.512	624	.802	1370	1580	3776	9.3

BOB McADOO 33 6-10 225   Center-Forward

"Big Mac" has made it all the way back . . . Has found a home the last three seasons and is likely to finish his career with the Lakers . . . Probably deserves it after all the years of turmoil and bouncing around from Buffalo to New York to Boston to Detroit to New Jersey . . . Gives the Lakers the outside shooting they need and has been known to carry the offensive burden for long stretches . . . Born Sept. 25, 1951, in Greensboro, N.C. . . . Spent two years at Vincennes Junior College, then one year under Dean

Smith at North Carolina...Started his NBA career with Buffalo in 1972 and led league in scoring for three straight years, from 1974-76...The bottom fell out after he was traded to Knicks in 1976-77 and he became an unwanted gypsy until Lakers signed him in 1981...Now he is appreciated again.

Year	Team	G	FG	FG Pct.	FT	FT Pct.	Reb.	Ast.	TP	Avg.
1972-73	Buffalo	80	585	.452	271	.774	728	139	1441	18.0
1973-74	Buffalo	74	901	.574	459	.793	1117	170	2261	30.6
1974-75	Buffalo	82	1095	.512	641	.805	1155	179	2831	34.5
1975-76	Buffalo	78	934	.487	559	.762	965	315	2427	31.1
1976-77	Buf.-N.Y. Knicks	72	740	.512	381	.738	926	205	1861	25.8
1977-78	New York	79	814	.520	469	.727	1010	298	2097	26.5
1978-79	N.Y.-Bos.	60	596	.529	295	.656	520	168	1487	24.8
1979-80	Detroit	58	492	.480	235	.730	467	200	1222	21.1
1980-81	Det.-N.J.	16	68	.433	29	.707	67	30	165	10.3
1981-82	Los Angeles	41	151	.458	90	.714	159	32	392	9.6
1982-83	Los Angeles	47	292	.520	119	.730	247	39	703	15.0
1983-84	Los Angeles	70	352	.471	212	.803	289	74	916	13.1
	Totals	757	7020	.503	3760	.754	7650	1849	17803	23.5

MITCH KUPCHAK 30 6-10 230   Forward-Center

"The Kup" is back...After playing just 26 games in two years due to torn knee ligaments, he has rehabilitated himself to the point where he saw playing time in 36 games in 1983-84...Should be in there competing for playing time this year...A banger...Very aggressive rebounder who can be useful to Lakers...That's why Dr. Jerry Buss signed him to a seven-year, $5.6-million contract in the first place...Has also had back problems...Born May 24, 1954, in Hicksville, N.Y....Was ACC Player of the Year at North Carolina in 1976...Played on the gold medal-winning 1976 Olympic team in Montreal...A first-round draft choice of Bullets in 1976...Named to the All-Rookie team...Joined the Lakers in 1981 in trade for Jim Chones, Brad Holland and two draft choices.

Year	Team	G	FG	FG Pct.	FT	FT Pct.	Reb.	Ast.	TP	Avg.
1976-77	Washington	82	341	.572	170	.691	494	62	852	10.4
1977-78	Washington	67	393	.512	280	.697	460	71	1066	15.9
1978-79	Washington	66	369	.539	223	.743	430	88	961	14.6
1979-80	Washington	40	67	.419	52	.693	105	16	186	4.7
1980-81	Washington	82	392	.525	240	.706	569	62	1024	12.5
1981-82	Los Angeles	26	153	.573	65	.663	210	33	371	14.3
1982-83	Los Angeles					Injured				
1983-84	Los Angeles	34	41	.380	22	.647	87	7	104	3.1
	Totals	397	1756	.527	1052	.704	2355	339	4564	11.5

MIKE McGEE 25 6-5 190   Guard

A late bloomer... Was given an opportunity to start 45 games last season and he proved he does belong... Can fill it up from outside ... Nicknamed "Little Mac"... Lost his starting job in the NBA Championship Series when Laker coach Pat Riley went with James Worthy for height... Has never complained about his plight... Just keeps on working... Born July 29, 1959, in Tyler, Tex., and grew up in Omaha, Neb.... Set a new Big Ten scoring record during his college career at Michigan... Drafted on the first round by the Lakers in 1981.

Year	Team	G	FG	FG Pct.	FT	FT Pct.	Reb.	Ast.	TP	Avg.
1981-82	Los Angeles	39	80	.465	31	.585	49	16	191	4.9
1982-83	Los Angeles	39	69	.423	17	.739	53	26	156	4.0
1983-84	Los Angeles	77	347	.594	61	.540	193	81	757	9.8
	Totals	155	496	.539	109	.577	295	123	1104	7.1

SWEN NATER 34 6-11 250   Center

At last, a winner again... Though Lakers came up short in the NBA Championship Series, he was still far better off than in the previous five seasons in San Diego... Came back from knee problems and played roughly 10 minutes a game as a backup to Kareem Abdul-Jabbar... That must have been a familiar feeling, since he played the same role behind Bill Walton on two NCAA title-winners at UCLA... Born Jan. 14, 1950, in Denhelder, The Netherlands... Hardly The Flying Dutchman... Big and slow, but knows all the tricks... Played for three different ABA teams before joining Milwaukee in 1976... Also spent one year in Buffalo... Led league in rebounding in 1980 and was runnerup the next two years.

Year	Team	G	FG	FG Pct.	FT	FT Pct.	Reb.	Ast.	TP	Avg.
1973-74	Va.-S.A. (ABA).....	79	467	.552	180	.709	998	129	1114	14.1
1974-75	S.A. (ABA)	78	495	.542	185	.752	1279	97	1175	15.1
1975-76	N.Y.-Va. (ABA).....	76	320	.492	108	.697	766	55	748	9.8
1976-77	Milwaukee........	72	383	.528	172	.754	865	108	938	13.0
1977-78	Buffalo..........	78	501	.504	208	.765	1029	216	1210	15.5
1978-79	San Diego........	79	357	.569	132	.800	701	140	846	10.7
1979-80	San Diego........	81	443	.554	196	.718	1216	233	1082	13.4
1980-81	San Diego........	82	517	.553	244	.795	1017	199	1278	15.6
1981-82	San Diego........	21	101	.577	59	.747	192	30	262	12.5
1982-83	San Diego........	7	6	.300	4	1.000	13	1	16	2.3
1983-84	Los Angeles	69	124	.490	63	.692	264	27	311	4.5
	Totals	722	3714	.535	1551	.748	8340	1235	8980	12.4

CALVIN GARRETT 28 6-7 195   Guard-Forward

Another end-of-the-bench hustler... The Lakers signed him as a free agent in September 1983 after watching him in the Southern California Summer League... Less than three years before, he was in the starting lineup of the Houston Rockets when they played Boston in the NBA finals... Solid defensive player, but not much of an offensive threat... Born July 11, 1956, in Parsons, Tenn.... Started college at Austin Peay, then transferred to Oral Roberts... Drafted on the third round by Chicago in 1979... Still the second-leading scorer in Oral Roberts history... Very close friend of Moses Malone... Says his favorite pre-game meal is soup, ice cream and soda pop.

Year	Team	G	FG	FG Pct.	FT	FT Pct.	Reb.	Ast.	TP	Avg.
1980-81	Houston	70	188	.453	50	.806	264	132	427	6.1
1981-82	Houston	51	105	.434	17	.654	94	76	230	4.5
1982-83	Houston	4	4	.364	2	1.000	7	3	10	2.5
1983-84	Los Angeles	41	78	.513	30	.769	71	31	188	4.6
	Totals	166	375	.457	99	.767	436	242	885	5.2

LARRY SPRIGGS 25 6-7 215   Forward

Chews nails... Rough and tough, but doesn't have enough polish to be a regular in the NBA... Lakers were his third team in three years as a pro... Made club work hard in practice... If he had been another two or three inches taller he'd be feared around the league... A real banger... Born Sept. 8, 1959, in Cheverly, Md.... Attended San Jacinto Junior College and Howard.... A fourth-round draft pick by Houston in 1981... Yo-yoed between Rockets and the CBA for two seasons, before Houston let him go in 1982... Played nine games with Chicago... Earned a spot with Lakers on the basis of his Southern California Summer League play.

Year	Team	G	FG	FG Pct.	FT	FT Pct.	Reb.	Ast.	TP	Avg.
1981-82	Houston	4	7	.636	0	.000	6	4	14	3.5
1982-83	Chicago	9	8	.400	5	.714	9	3	21	2.3
1983-84	Los Angeles	38	44	.537	36	.720	61	30	124	3.3
	Totals	51	59	.522	41	.695	76	37	159	3.1

BYRON SCOTT 23 6-4 202   Guard

Great Scott...Lakers thought so much of this young prospect, they traded veteran Norm Nixon to San Diego for him and Swen Nater...Has got the bloodlines of a thoroughbred and should fit into the Laker stable...A very good perimeter shooter...It took time to gain confidence in his game as a rookie...Started 49 games ...Quick and has exceptional leaping ability...Born March 28, 1961, in Ogden, Utah, but grew up in Inglewood, Cal....Tremendous offensive talent...Left Arizona State after junior season...First guard and first undergraduate taken in the 1983 draft, as the No. 4 overall pick by San Diego...When Clippers couldn't sign him, Lakers moved in and made the deal...They won't regret it.

Year	Team	G	FG	FG Pct.	FT	FT Pct.	Reb.	Ast.	TP	Avg.
1983-84	Los Angeles	74	334	.484	112	.806	164	177	788	10.6

TOP ROOKIE

EARL JONES 22 6-10 210   Center

Could be a sleeper...Was highly rated coming out of high school...But there are questions about him after spending college career at University of District of Columbia, an NCAA Division II school...Might not be able to take the pounding or play on the inside...Not shy on offense...Very cocky about his ability...Scored 28.6 ppg and had 9.7 rpg, but those numbers were posted against questionable competition.

COACH PAT RILEY: Voted Coach of the Year by *Gentleman's*

Quarterly...His reputation revolves around his very stylish wardrobe...Often overlooked is fact that he's a darn fine coach...Has shown the right around of firmness and restraint to guide the talented Lakers into the NBA finals three years in a row...Born March 20, 1945, in Rome, N.Y....Grew up as a tough street kid, contrary to his current Hollywood image...Starred at Kentucky under Adolph Rupp...Was the first draft choice of the 1967 expansion San Diego Rockets...That began a nine-year pro career that was never spectacular and included stops in Phoenix and Los Angeles... Was also drafted by the NFL Dallas Cowboys... Took an unusual road to the head coaching job... Was working as Chick Hearn's color commentator when then-coach Jack McKinney was seriously injured in a bicycle accident. Interim boss Paul Westhead hired him as an assistant. Two seasons later, Westhead was fired and Riley moved up... One of the best young coaches in the game... Overall NBA coaching mark is 162-73.

James Worthy proved worthy in championship competition.

GREATEST FOUL SHOOTER

How do you choose just one?

Do you reach back into the Minneapolis days and single out George Mikan? Or do you go to the statistics that rank Jerry West and Elgin Baylor as No. 1 and No. 2 in the club record books in free throws made and free throws attempted? Or do you stick strictly to the percentages, which rank Cazzie Russell (.877), Ron Boone (.852) and Stu Lantz (.849) as the top three foul shooters to wear the Laker uniform?

One thing you can do for certain is to leave out Wilton Norman Chamberlain, who distinguished himself at the foul line only with a long history of ineptitude.

Well, purists may argue, but it says here that longevity counts for something. And on that basis, the nod goes to West, whose percentage of .814 on 7,160-of-8,801 over 14 seasons is the best in Laker history.

ALL-TIME LAKER LEADERS

SEASON

Points: Elgin Baylor, 2,538, 1960-61
Assists: Earvin (Magic) Johnson, 875, 1983-84
Rebounds: Wilt Chamberlain, 1,712, 1968-69

GAME

Points: Elgin Baylor, 71 vs. New York, 11/15/60
Assists: Jerry West, 23 vs. Philadelphia, 2/1/67
        Earvin (Magic) Johnson, 23 vs. Seattle, 2/21/84
Rebounds: Wilt Chamberlain, 42 vs. Boston, 3/7/69

CAREER

Points: Jerry West, 25,192, 1960-74
Assists: Jerry West, 6,238, 1960-74
Rebounds: Elgin Baylor, 11,463, 1958-72

PHOENIX SUNS

TEAM DIRECTORY: Chairman: Richard Bloch; Pres.: Donald Pitt; VPs: Donald Diamond, Marvin Meyer, Lawrence Kartiganer; Exec. VP/GM: Jerry Colangelo; Dir. Pub. Rel.: Tom Ambrose; Coach: John MacLeod; Asst. Coaches: John Wetzel, Al Bianchi. Arena: Veterans Memorial Coliseum (14,660). Colors: Purple, orange and copper.

Larry Nance left foes with severe case of Sun-burn.

SCOUTING REPORT

SHOOTING: The only thing hotter than the weather in the Valley of the Sun is this bunch. If NBA Slam-Dunk champion Larry Nance (.576) isn't throwing down one of his whirlybird shots, then Walter Davis (.512) is launching one of his ICBMs from the outskirts of Flagstaff. Among the starting five, only forward Maurice Lucas didn't make half of his shots last season and he was no slouch at .497.

Kyle Macy (.501) has classic form on his shots from the outside and it looks like center James Edwards (.536) might finally be ready to prove that he's worth at least part of that hefty $700,000-per-year salary. The Suns have made the adjustment from a run-and-shoot team to a pound-away-on-the-inside offense and it hasn't taken away from their ability to put the ball in the basket.

PLAYMAKING: Macy (4.3 assists per game) inherited the playmaker's job last season after Dennis Johnson was shipped to Boston, but coach John MacLeod was never really happy with his performance and was always searching for an alternative. Rookie Rod Foster had his chances and occasionally excelled, but proved far too inconsistent, despite his blinding speed.

The playmaking void was evident in the drafting of Colorado flash Jay Humphries. He's a good penetrator who can dish the ball off. Humphries also possesses a 35-inch vertical leap, which means that he's probably the only guy capable of handing the ball to the skywalking Nance somewhere above the rim.

DEFENSE: They used to be real soft touches out in the desert. But that was before the arrival of Lucas the Enforcer, who taught them how to use parts of the anatomy like the elbow and the knee. Now the Suns are one of the Western Conference's most physical teams. Nance (2.11 blocked shots per game) and Alvan Adams are both excellent shot-blockers and Davis will make more than his share of big defensive plays by using his great speed. Edwards is getting a little better in this area, but the 7-0 center was still only fourth on the team in rejections and that doesn't say much for him as an intimidator. The big boost to the defense should be Humphries, who is quick and isn't afraid to get his nose bloodied.

REBOUNDING: Ouch! This is where the Suns are really hurting. They ranked 20th in the NBA in this department, but somehow were still among the final four teams alive in the playoffs. Nance (8.2 rpg) and Lucas (9.7 rpg) both pulled the wagon, but too often

SUN ROSTER

No.	Veteran	Pos.	Ht.	Wt.	Age	Yrs. Pro	College
33	Alvan Adams	C	6-9	218	30	10	Oklahoma
6	Walter Davis	G	6-6	205	30	8	North Carolina
53	James Edwards	C	7-0	235	28	8	Washington
10	Rod Foster	G	6-1	160	24	2	UCLA
20	*Maurice Lucas	F	6-9	235	32	11	Marquette
4	Kyle Macy	G	6-3	190	27	5	Kentucky
22	Larry Nance	F	6-10	215	25	4	Clemson
32	Charles Pittman	F	6-7	229	26	3	Maryland
8	Ricky Robey	C-F	6-11	240	28	7	Kentucky
7	Mike Sanders	F	6-6	210	24	3	UCLA
14	Alvin Scott	F	6-7	219	29	8	Oral Roberts

*Free agent unsigned at press time

Rd.	Top Draftees	Sel. No.	Ht.	Wt.	College
1	Jay Humphries	13	6-3	182	Colorado
2	Charles Jones	36	6-8	215	Louisville
3	Murray Jarman	59	6-5	210	Clemson
4	Jeff Collins	82	6-2	175	Nevada-Las Vegas
5	Bill Flye	105	6-9½	220	Richmond

Edwards (4.8 rpg) was dead weight riding in the back. Maybe that's why Darryl Dawkins wishes Edwards was back in the Eastern Conference, so he'd have somebody to dominate on the boards again. Denver guard T.R. Dunn is a much better rebounder than the Phoenix big guy.

The 6-3 Humphries is a leaper, but he's not going to help very much in this department. Maybe management would like to explain that Dennis Johnson-for-Rick Robey trade again. Weren't the Suns supposed to be getting a very physical player who would help them out considerably on the boards?

OUTLOOK: Early last season, there were whispers of discontent and rumors that MacLeod had finally worn out his welcome. So, of course, the Suns finished strong and took the Lakers all the way to the sixth game in the conference finals.

You can take shots at MacLeod's system, but it has worked consistently. If he ever had a dominating big man, the Suns just might break through and go all the way. But alas, they have Edwards in the middle. And that's why a return to the Western Conference finals would be an incredible feat.

SUN PROFILES

WALTER DAVIS 30 6-6 205   Guard

The Roadrunner... Neither Wily Coyote nor any NBA player can catch him... Some observers wonder if he would have become one of the all-time greats if he had been left at forward... But he hasn't done badly at guard, leading Phoenix in scoring and making the All-Star team once again last season... Posts up the small guards and runs past the big ones... Born Sept. 9, 1954, in Pineville, N.C.... One of the many sleek machines that rolled off Dean Smith's assembly line at North Carolina... Youngest of 13 children... Played on the gold-medal-winning 1976 Olympic team... Coming off the worst-shooting season (.512) of his seven-year career... Can be absolutely spectacular... The only thing missing from his game is a mean streak... Just too nice a guy for his own good sometimes.

Year	Team	G	FG	FG Pct.	FT	FT Pct.	Reb.	Ast.	TP	Avg.
1977-78	Phoenix	81	786	.526	387	.830	484	273	1959	24.2
1978-79	Phoenix	79	764	.561	340	.831	373	339	1868	23.6
1979-80	Phoenix	75	657	.563	299	.819	272	337	1613	21.5
1980-81	Phoenix	78	593	.539	209	.836	200	302	1402	18.0
1981-82	Phoenix	55	350	.523	91	.820	103	162	794	14.4
1982-83	Phoenix	80	665	.516	184	.818	197	397	1521	19.0
1983-84	Phoenix	78	652	.512	233	.863	202	429	1557	20.0
	Totals	526	4467	.535	1743	.832	1831	2239	10714	20.4

LARRY NANCE 25 6-10 215   Forward

"Flash-Nance" ... "Slambassador" ... "The High-Atollah of Slamola"... Those are just a few of the titles he earned after besting Julius Erving in the finals of the NBA Slam Dunk Contest at last year's All-Star Game... There are helicopters that can't hover as long as this guy... The sky is the limit after just three years in the pros... Nobody thought this Clemson product would have this kind of impact when the Suns stole him with the 20th pick in 1981... Born Feb. 12, 1959, in Anderson, S.C.... Goes from end to end as well as anybody in the game today... His numerous slam dunks and layups resulted in a .576 shooting percentage last season... An awesome shot-blocker... Second on the Clemson all-time rebounding list, behind Tree Rollins... Finally stepped into the spotlight with his victory in the Slam Dunk Contest... Now everybody knows his name.

Year	Team	G	FG	FG Pct.	FT	FT Pct.	Reb.	Ast.	TP	Avg.
1981-82	Phoenix	80	227	.521	75	.641	256	82	529	6.6
1982-83	Phoenix	82	588	.550	193	.672	710	197	1370	16.7
1983-84	Phoenix	82	601	.576	249	.707	678	214	1451	17.7
	Totals	244	1416	.556	517	.684	1644	493	3350	13.7

MAURICE LUCAS 32 6-9 235   Forward

The Bouncer...The Enforcer...Mr. Muscle...Call him what you want, but do it with a smile on your face...One of the guys who brought the power forward position into vogue when he was helping Portland win an NBA title in 1976-77...Still plays the same way today...Still has that nice touch from the outside, too...Was instrumental in the Suns' success in the playoffs last season...Born Feb. 18, 1952, in Pittsburgh...Wears a constant scowl during games, but is actually very pleasant off the court...One of the league's best interviews...Left Marquette early and played with St. Louis and Kentucky in the ABA, before Portland picked him up in the dispersal draft...Was traded to New Jersey for Calvin Natt in 1980 and then made a one-year stop in New York...Has played the last two years in Phoenix...Don't mess with him.

Year	Team	G	FG	FG Pct.	FT	FT Pct.	Reb.	Ast.	TP	Avg.
1974-75	St. Louis (ABA)	80	438	.467	180	.786	816	287	1058	13.2
1975-76	St.L.-Ky. (ABA)	86	620	.461	217	.767	970	224	1460	17.0
1976-77	Portland	79	632	.466	335	.765	899	229	1599	20.2
1977-78	Portland	68	453	.458	207	.767	621	173	1113	16.4
1978-79	Portland	69	568	.470	270	.783	716	215	1406	20.4
1979-80	Port.-N.J.	63	371	.456	179	.749	537	208	923	14.7
1980-81	New Jersey	68	404	.484	191	.752	575	173	999	14.7
1981-82	New York	80	505	.504	253	.725	903	179	1263	15.8
1982-83	Phoenix	77	495	.474	278	.781	799	219	1269	16.5
1983-84	Phoenix	75	451	.497	293	.765	725	203	1195	15.9
	Totals	745	4937	.473	2403	.764	7561	2110	12285	16.5

KYLE MACY 27 6-3 190   Guard

The boy next door...Mom, apple pie and Kyle...Many people look down their noses at him because of his All-American image...But he has always done the job, particularly in the playoffs last spring...Can hit the outside jumper and doesn't mind contact...In fact, for a little guy, he throws one of the meanest elbows in the league...Born April 9, 1957, in Kendalville, Ind....Played for his dad during high school in Peru, Ind. and was named Mr. Basketball...Started at Purdue, transferred to Kentucky and was a starter on the 1978 Wildcat NCAA title team, along with Suns teammate Rick Robey . . . Phoenix is always talking about trading him . . . Plays the tenor sax.

Year	Team	G	FG	FG Pct.	FT	FT Pct.	Reb.	Ast.	TP	Avg.
1980-81	Phoenix	82	272	.511	107	.899	132	160	663	8.1
1981-82	Phoenix	82	486	.514	152	.899	261	384	1163	14.2
1982-83	Phoenix	82	328	.517	129	.872	165	278	808	9.9
1983-84	Phoenix	82	357	.501	95	.833	186	353	832	10.1
	Totals	328	1443	.511	483	.878	744	1175	3466	10.6

JAMES EDWARDS 28 7-0 235   Center

The $700,000 mistake . . . Yes, he finally came around and had a decent season for the Suns, but he's still stealing money every time he gets paid . . . One of the few people in the NBA who is happy that owner Ted Stepien passed through Cleveland . . . Born Nov. 22, 1955, in Seattle . . . Attended Washington . . . A third-round draft pick of the Lakers in 1977 . . . Had played for three-plus seasons in Indiana before Stepien made him a millionaire with his ridiculous free-agent offer . . . Suns picked him up in February 1982 for Jeff Cook and a third-round draft choice . . . Finally showed signs of playing like a pro in the second half of the year . . . But he's still a creampuff on the inside.

Year	Team	G	FG	FG Pct.	FT	FT Pct.	Reb.	Ast.	TP	Avg.
1977-78	L.A.-Ind.	83	495	.453	272	.646	615	85	1252	15.2
1978-79	Indiana	82	534	.501	298	.676	693	92	1366	16.7
1979-80	Indiana	82	528	.512	231	.681	578	127	1287	15.7
1980-81	Indiana	81	511	.509	244	.703	571	212	1266	15.6
1981-82	Cleveland	77	528	.511	232	.684	581	123	1288	16.7
1982-83	Clev.-Pho.	31	128	.487	69	.639	155	40	325	10.5
1983-84	Phoenix	72	438	.536	183	.720	348	184	1059	14.7
	Totals	508	3162	.501	1529	.680	3541	863	7853	15.5

ALVAN ADAMS 30 6-9 218   Center

Is he an architect or a basketball player? . . . His heart would probably say the former, but fiscal sense says he'll stick with hoops for a couple more years . . . Has been criticized for not appearing to care very much . . . But he has adjusted to his role of coming off the bench as a backup to James Edwards . . . Still one of the finest passing centers in the game today . . . One of the underrated dunkers in the league, too . . . Born July 19, 1954, in Lawrence, Kan. . . . Played at Oklahoma under Suns' coach John MacLeod . . . There were all sorts of great things projected when Phoenix reached the NBA Championship Series in his rookie year . . . The plain and simple fact is he's too small to take a team all the way... Working toward a degree in historical architecture and likes to restore old houses.

Year	Team	G	FG	FG Pct.	FT	FT Pct.	Reb.	Ast.	TP	Avg.
1975-76	Phoenix	80	629	.469	261	.735	727	450	1519	19.0
1976-77	Phoenix	72	522	.474	252	.754	652	322	1296	18.0
1977-78	Phoenix	70	434	.485	214	.730	565	225	1082	15.5
1978-79	Phoenix	77	569	.530	231	.799	705	360	1369	17.8
1979-80	Phoenix	75	465	.531	188	.797	609	322	1118	14.9
1980-81	Phoenix	75	458	.526	199	.768	546	344	1115	14.9
1981-82	Phoenix	79	507	.494	182	.781	586	356	1196	15.1
1982-83	Phoenix	80	477	.486	180	.829	548	376	1135	14.2
1983-84	Phoenix	70	269	.462	132	.825	319	219	670	9.6
	Totals	678	4330	.495	1839	.774	5257	2974	10500	15.5

MIKE SANDERS 24 6-6 210   Forward

One of those guys who will have plenty of addresses if he stays in the league... There just isn't much call for a forward his size who doesn't do anything exceptionally well... Was a member, along with Phoenix teammate Rod Foster, of the UCLA team that lost the NCAA title game to Louisville in 1980... Did a fine defensive job on seven-footer Joe Barry Carroll in that tourney... Born May 7, 1960, in Vilidia, La.... Taken on the fourth round by Kansas City in 1982... Cut by KC in training camp... Spent 26 games in his rookie year with San Antonio... Caught on again with the Suns last year... You'll probably be able to keep track of him by following the CBA.

Year	Team	G	FG	FG Pct.	FT	FT Pct.	Reb.	Ast.	TP	Avg.
1982-83	San Antonio	26	76	.484	31	.721	94	19	183	7.0
1983-84	Phoenix	50	97	.478	29	.690	103	44	223	4.5
	Totals	76	173	.481	60	.706	197	63	406	5.3

RICK ROBEY 28 6-11 240   Center-Forward

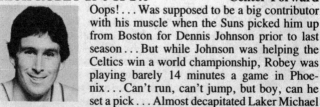

Oops!... Was supposed to be a big contributor with his muscle when the Suns picked him up from Boston for Dennis Johnson prior to last season... But while Johnson was helping the Celtics win a world championship, Robey was playing barely 14 minutes a game in Phoenix... Can't run, can't jump, but boy, can he set a pick... Almost decapitated Laker Michael Cooper in the playoffs... Has had his share of injury problems in the last two seasons... When he's healthy, he loves to get into the paint and mix it up... Born Jan. 30, 1956, in Coral Gables, Fla.... Owns and raises thoroughbred race horses... But also spends much of his free time out on the golf course or throwing down a few brews . . . Was a key figure on Kentucky's 1978 NCAA championship team.

Year	Team	G	FG	FG Pct.	FT	FT Pct.	Reb.	Ast.	TP	Avg.
1978-79	Ind.-Bos.	79	322	.478	174	.777	513	132	818	10.4
1979-80	Boston	82	379	.521	184	.684	530	92	942	11.5
1980-81	Boston	82	298	.545	144	.574	390	126	740	9.0
1981-82	Boston	80	185	.493	84	.535	295	68	454	5.7
1982-83	Boston	59	100	.467	45	.577	219	65	245	4.2
1983-84	Phoenix	61	140	.545	61	.693	198	65	342	5.6
	Totals	443	1424	.510	692	.649	2145	548	3541	8.0

ALVIN SCOTT 29 6-7 219   Forward

There was a time when he could hang in the air like a hummingbird . . . Now he's put on plenty of weight and isn't nearly as spectacular . . . Strictly a deep sub, playing about 10 minutes a game . . . No threat as a shooter . . . Fills the lanes on the break and gives the starters a rest . . . Born Sept. 14, 1955, in Cleveland, Tenn. . . . Has turned meager talent into a seven-year pro career, all with Phoenix . . . Played at Oral Roberts and made the Suns as a seventh-round draft choice in 1977 . . . His brother Terry is still an assistant at ORU.

Year	Team	G	FG	FG Pct.	FT	FT Pct.	Reb.	Ast.	TP	Avg.
1977-78	Phoenix	81	180	.488	132	.691	357	88	492	6.1
1978-79	Phoenix	81	212	.535	120	.714	360	126	544	6.7
1979-80	Phoenix	79	127	.422	95	.779	228	98	350	4.4
1980-81	Phoenix	82	173	.497	97	.764	268	114	444	5.4
1981-82	Phoenix	81	189	.497	108	.730	294	149	486	6.0
1982-83	Phoenix	81	124	.479	81	.736	224	97	329	4.1
1983-84	Phoenix	65	55	.444	56	.778	100	48	167	2.6
	Totals	550	1060	.487	689	.735	1831	720	2812	5.1

ROD FOSTER 24 6-1 160   Guard

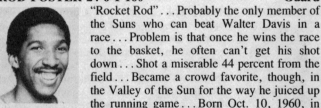

"Rocket Rod" . . . Probably the only member of the Suns who can beat Walter Davis in a race . . . Problem is that once he wins the race to the basket, he often can't get his shot down . . . Shot a miserable 44 percent from the field . . . Became a crowd favorite, though, in the Valley of the Sun for the way he juiced up the running game . . . Born Oct. 10, 1960, in New Britain, Conn. . . . Was a prep All-American and went to UCLA, where he starred in the backcourt . . . Bruins went to the Final Four in his freshman year and then he sagged. Maybe he was a victim of his own early hype . . . Must get his game under control . . . Started 34 times as a rookie, but only consistency will get him more time in coach John MacLeod's rotation.

Year	Team	G	FG	FG Pct.	FT	FT Pct.	Reb.	Ast.	TP	Avg.
1983-84	Phoenix	80	260	.448	122	.787	120	172	664	8.3

CHARLES PITTMAN 26 6-7 229 — Forward

Nothing flashy . . . Has kept his job by putting his nose to the grindstone and working at it . . . Doesn't have much size, but is willing to go strong to the boards . . . Usually one of the first two forwards off the bench . . . His shooting percentage (.603) was so high because he rarely shoots from more than a couple of feet away . . . Born March 23, 1958, in Rocky Mount, N.C. . . . Went to junior college in California, then toiled under Lefty Driesell at Maryland . . . The only boy among nine children in his family . . . Maybe that's how he learned to keep battling for what is his . . . Drafted on the third round by Phoenix in 1982 . . . Was cut in training camp, but returned for the last 28 games after playing with Billings, Mont. of the CBA.

Year	Team	G	FG	FG Pct.	FT	FT Pct.	Reb.	Ast.	TP	Avg.
1982-83	Phoenix	28	19	.475	25	.676	31	7	63	2.3
1983-84	Phoenix	69	126	.603	69	.683	214	70	321	4.7
	Totals	97	145	.582	94	.681	245	77	384	4.0

TOP ROOKIE

JAY HUMPHRIES 22 6-3 182 — Guard

Inconsistent at Colorado . . . Great physical skills, including a 35-inch vertical leap . . . Had a fine showing at the Aloha Classic . . . Can run an offense and is a standout defender . . . Born Oct. 17, 1962, in Inglewood, Cal. . . . Named to All-Big Eight second team . . . Will compete for jobs of Kyle Macy and Rod Foster . . . Averaged 15.4 ppg and shot .509 as senior.

COACH JOHN MacLEOD: If you spend too much time in one place, they're bound to start picking you apart . . . That almost happened to him last season, his 11th with the Suns . . . His club struggled and didn't reach the .500 mark until well after the All-Star break . . . But the Suns surprised everyone by extending the Lakers to six games in the Western Conference finals, vindicating their coach . . . He's a cross between a college professor and a fashion model, but he isn't a bad coach at all . . . Some of his players say that he worries too much about distributing minutes and doesn't go with the hot hand...Every coach should have such problems...Born Oct. 3, 1937, in New Albany, Ind....Led Oklahoma to two NIT bids in six years before making the jump to the NBA...Has led the Suns to the playoffs eight times in nine years and Phoenix has posted seven straight winning records...NBA coaching mark is 489-413...Was one of the first to make the successful transition from the college to the pro ranks...Was once a sparring partner for boxer Jimmy Ellis, but wised up...Had a promising baseball career ended when he suffered an arm injury tossing balls at an Altoona, Pa., amusement park...Definitely has stood the test of time.

All-Star Walter Davis topped the Suns in scoring.

GREATEST FOUL SHOOTER

Call out the FBI. Assemble a grand jury for an investigation. There's got to be something fishy going on, because Kyle Macy made only 83.3 percent of his free throws last season.

If you don't think that's cause for alarm, you haven't been paying very much attention to the Phoenix Suns, because Macy standing at the foul line is as much a sure thing as the temperature in the Arizona desert hitting 100 in August.

Dribble. Shoot. Swish. Dribble. Shoot. Swish. Chalk up two more for Macy and the Suns.

But during 1983-84, something came over Macy—maybe it was the moon or the tides or something involving his astrological sign—and he surrendered his team leader's status to Walter Davis, no slouch himself at .863.

But maybe it's not such a tragedy. After all, Macy did lead the club in free throws from 1980-83. And you wouldn't want to hang a guy for a career mark of .878, would you?

Of course not. And with the game on the line, Kyle Macy still is the shooter Phoenix would want on the line.

ALL-TIME SUN LEADERS

SEASON

Points: Charlie Scott, 2,048, 1972-73
Assists: Gail Goodrich, 605, 1969-70
Rebounds: Paul Silas, 1,015, 1970-71

GAME

Points: Paul Westphal, 49 vs. Detroit, 2/21/80
Assists: Gail Goodrich, 19 vs. Philadelphia, 10/22/69
Rebounds: Paul Silas, 27 vs. Cincinnati, 1/18/71

CAREER

Points: Dick Van Arsdale, 12,060, 1968-77
Assists: Alvan Adams, 2,974, 1975-84
Rebounds: Alvan Adams, 5,257, 1975-84

PORTLAND TRAIL BLAZERS

TEAM DIRECTORY: Chairman: Lawrence Weinberg; Exec. VP: Harry Glickman; Dir. Pub. Rel.: John White; Coach: Jack Ramsay; Asst. Coaches: Bucky Buckwalter and Rick Adelman. Arena: Memorial Coliseum (12,666). Colors: Red, black and white.

SCOUTING REPORT

SHOOTING: Most of these guys shoot the basketball as well as Dr. Jack Ramsay jumps rope, which is very well. How many other teams could give up their best percentage shooter in Calvin Natt (.583), a guy who scored 16.2 ppg, and be completely happy?

The Blazers have to be delighted with the three-for-one deal that sent Natt, Wayne Cooper and Lafayette Lever to Denver. That's because in return they got scoring machine Kiki Vandeweghe. Kiki scored 29.4 ppg, the third-highest mark in the league, and should be just as devastating in Ramsay's offense, which will definitely provide him with his share of open shots.

And Vandeweghe (.558) won't lack accomplished company. Do you want twisting, back-door layups mixed with over-the-top rainbows? Well, then turn to Jim Paxson (.514). How about some muscle moves and medium-range jumpers? Try Kenny Carr (.564). Looking for shots from the wing? Call on Mychal Thompson (.524). And let's not forget Kentucky grad Sam Bowie, the second player picked in the draft and a potent scorer before missing two years with a shin injury. If Bowie's shooting touch comes all the way back, there may not be any rebounds for anyone to get.

PLAYMAKING: Ramsay is so confident Darnell Valentine can run his offense that he put Lever—a promising young point guard—into the package for Vandeweghe. Lever and Valentine (5.8 assists per game) had split the point-guard duties almost equally the last two seasons and it became apparent that the approach was retarding the progress of both players. Now Valentine knows that the job is his and should be able to play much more aggressively.

Thompson is also a good passer and, for all of the attention he gets for moving without the ball, so is Paxson. But the biggest addition again is Bowie. He is a student of the game and plays the high post a lot like Bill Walton did in his glory days with Portland. Bowie may not have to score much to be the final piece in the Blazers' puzzle. Ramsay will get the most out of him.

DEFENSE: Let's just say that the concept isn't totally foreign to them, but they are certainly not fluent in the language. The

Ex-Nugget Kiki Vandeweghe brings 29.4-ppg mark to Portland.

problem has been one of size. Cooper and Thompson were always just too small to provide enough inside defense. But that should change with the 7-1 Bowie roaming the middle and swatting away shots.

Natt, a power forward trapped inside the body of a small forward, did not provide much opposition at his position. That will not change much, since Kiki is not a practitioner of the art of

TRAIL BLAZER ROSTER

No.	Veteran	Pos.	Ht.	Wt.	Age	Yrs. Pro	College
34	Kenny Carr	F	6-7	230	29	8	NC State
22	Clyde Drexler	F-G	6-7	210	22	2	Houston
24	Audie Norris	C-F	6-9	230	23	3	Jackson State
4	*Jim Paxson	G	6-6	200	27	6	Dayton
54	Tom Piotrowski	C	7-1	240	24	2	LaSalle
43	Mychal Thompson	F	6-10	226	29	7	Minnesota
14	Darnell Valentine	G	6-2	185	25	4	Kansas
55	Kiki Vandeweghe	F	6-8	220	26	5	UCLA
31	Peter Verhoeven	F	6-9	214	25	4	Fresno State

*Free agent unsigned at press time

Rd.	Top Draftees	Sel. No.	Ht.	Wt.	College
1	Sam Bowie	2	7-1	235	Kentucky
1	Bernard Thompson	19	6-6½	207	Fresno State
2	Victor Fleming	26	6-5	195	Xavier (Ohio)
2	Steve Colter	33	6-3	165	New Mexico State
2	Jerome Kersey	46	6-7	220	Longwood

defense. But the sleeper here could be rookie forward Bernard Thompson. He spent four years learning how to belly up at Fresno State, generally regarded as the best defensive club in college basketball. The Blazers are capable of creating problems when they employ their press. And Paxson, the complete player, also gets the job done here.

REBOUNDING: They ranked in the bottom half of the league last season and Bowie will not be able to change that all by himself. He is going to need help and that will have to come from the likes of the laid-back Thompson (8.7 rpg). Carr (7.8 rpg) isn't afraid to put in an honest day's work on the boards and is usually quite effective on the inside.

OUTLOOK: With Kareem Abdul-Jabbar getting ready to hang up his skyhook in Los Angeles, the question might be whether it will be the Trail Blazers or the Rockets who inherit the Western Conference throne in the future. The Rockets are coming on, but Portland is ahead in the building process at this point.

If Bowie comes on to have a very strong year, Portland could make a very serious run at the Lakers in the Pacific Division. The Blazers have all the pieces now and need only maturity.

TRAIL BLAZER PROFILES

KIKI VANDEWEGHE 26 6-8 220   Forward

Blockbuster sent this guy from Denver to Portland for Calvin Natt, Lafayette Lever, Wayne Cooper and two future draft picks...After all, the son of former New York Knick Ernie Vandeweghe has become one of the brightest new stars in the league...Very few people thought he would develop into such an offensive force...But whether he is pulling up to shoot a 20-footer or making one of those back-door moves, he's like money in the bank...Former UCLA star was the NBA's third-leading scorer last season...Could be even more devastating in Jack Ramsay's system, if rookie center Sam Bowie plays well...Born Aug. 1, 1958, in Weisbaden, West Germany...Raised in Southern California, but minus the tan...A workaholic, he's always looking to improve his game...Drafted on the first round in 1980 by Dallas, but refused to play there...Traded to Denver, where he starred for three seasons...A two-time All-Star in three pro seasons...Buys and sells antique cars.

Year	Team	G	FG	FG Pct.	FT	FT Pct.	Reb.	Ast.	TP	Avg.
1980-81	Denver	51	229	.426	130	.818	270	94	588	11.5
1981-82	Denver	82	706	.560	347	.857	461	247	1760	21.5
1982-83	Denver	82	841	.547	489	.875	437	203	2186	26.7
1983-84	Denver	78	895	.558	494	.852	373	238	2295	29.4
	Totals	293	2671	.541	1460	.857	1541	782	6829	23.3

KENNY CARR 29 6-7 230   Forward

Has found a home—and the fact that the Trail Blazers traded Calvin Natt in the off-season means he's going to stay...Spent the early part of his NBA career packing and unpacking and trying to live down a reputation as a bad seed...Played in Los Angeles, Cleveland and Detroit before landing in Portland in 1982, just before the trade deadline...Jack Ramsay seems to have found the secret to motivating him...Born Aug. 15, 1955, in Washington, D.C....Has had some rather famous teammates...Played with Adrian Dantley at DeMatha High School and joined David Thompson at N.C. State...Plucked on the first round by the Lakers in 1977, but was never able to get any playing time . . . Has a real fear of flying, which has got to make life in the NBA difficult.

Year	Team	G	FG	FG Pct.	FT	FT Pct.	Reb.	Ast.	TP	Avg.
1977-78	Los Angeles	52	134	.444	55	.647	208	26	323	6.2
1978-79	Los Angeles	72	225	.500	83	.606	292	60	533	7.4
1979-80	L.A.-Clev.	79	378	.492	173	.658	588	77	929	11.8
1980-81	Cleveland	81	469	.511	292	.714	835	192	1230	15.2
1981-82	Clev.-Det.	74	348	.503	198	.656	531	86	895	12.1
1982-83	Portland	82	362	.505	255	.697	589	116	981	12.0
1983-84	Portland	82	518	.561	247	.673	642	157	1283	15.6
	Totals	522	2434	.510	1303	.675	3685	714	6174	11.8

JIM PAXSON 27 6-6 200　　　　　　　　　　Guard

Perpetual motion . . . John Havlicek reincarnate . . . One of the finest off guards in the league in just five years . . . Always moving without the ball . . . Will slip in the back door to catch a pass for a layup or toss in a long jumper over your head . . . Born July 9, 1957, in Kettering, Ohio . . . Father Jim played with Minneapolis and Cincinnati in the late '50s . . . Brother John is keeping the family tradition alive as a 1983 first-round draft choice of San Antonio . . . Played at Dayton and was a first-round pick of the Trail Blazers in 1979 . . . They knew he'd be good, but not this good . . . Former Blazer Dave Twardzik calls Paxson "exactly what Jack Ramsay wants all five players to be."

Year	Team	G	FG	FG Pct.	FT	FT Pct.	Reb.	Ast.	TP	Avg.
1979-80	Portland	72	189	.411	64	.711	109	144	443	6.2
1980-81	Portland	79	585	.536	182	.734	211	299	1354	17.1
1981-82	Portland	82	662	.526	220	.767	221	276	1552	18.9
1982-83	Portland	81	682	.515	388	.812	174	231	1756	21.7
1983-84	Portland	81	680	.514	345	.841	173	251	1722	21.3
	Totals	395	2798	.513	1199	.792	888	1201	6827	17.3

MYCHAL THOMPSON 29 6-10 226　　　　　Forward

Had to spend some time in the pivot last season, which isn't his idea of fun . . . Now that Sam Bowie is coming aboard, he'll be much happier and much more effective at forward . . . Born Jan. 30, 1955, in Nassau, The Bahamas and spends time there during the off-season . . . Maybe it's those island breezes that have made him such a laid-back individual . . . Has caught some flack about not being emotional enough . . . Admits he's not intense . . . Grew up in Miami and that's where he gave up his early interests in cricket, softball and soccer to pursue basketball...Went from the sunny climes of the south to play college ball at Minnesota...First pick overall in the 1978 draft, making him the first foreign-born player to be taken No. 1.

Year	Team	G	FG	FG Pct.	FT	FT Pct.	Reb.	Ast.	TP	Avg.
1978-79	Portland	73	460	.490	154	.572	604	176	1074	14.7
1979-80	Portland				Injured					
1980-81	Portland	79	569	.494	207	.641	686	284	1345	17.0
1981-82	Portland	79	681	.523	280	.628	921	319	1642	20.8
1982-83	Portland	80	505	.489	249	.621	753	380	1259	15.7
1983-84	Portland	79	487	.524	266	.667	688	308	1240	15.7
	Totals	390	2702	.505	1156	.629	3652	1467	6560	16.8

DARNELL VALENTINE 25 6-2 185   Guard

The job is his...Spent the last two seasons splitting the point-guard duties with Lafayette Lever...But Lever has been traded, so now the offense is in his capable hands...A fine passer and a hard-nosed defensive player...Had some injury problems during three-year NBA career...Born Feb. 3, 1959, in Chicago ...Made a big name as an All-American at Kansas...Blazers jumped on him in the first round in 1981...Played on the 1980 Olympic team...If he develops a consistent jumper, he's got All-Star potential.

Year	Team	G	FG	FG Pct.	FT	FT Pct.	Reb.	Ast.	TP	Avg.
1981-82	Portland	82	187	.413	152	.760	149	270	526	6.4
1982-83	Portland	47	209	.454	169	.793	117	293	587	12.5
1983-84	Portland	68	251	.447	194	.789	127	395	696	10.2
	Totals	197	647	.439	515	.781	393	958	1809	9.2

AUDIE NORRIS 23 6-9 230   Center-Forward

Doesn't have an abundance of talent, but gets the most from it...Skills are limited to scoring on the inside and rebounding...Would probably knock his grandmother into the stands if it meant getting a loose ball...Probably couldn't guard his grandmother, though...Born Dec. 18, 1960, in Jackson, Miss....A second-round draft choice in 1982...Was cut in training camp, then returned halfway through the year...Got just one start in 79 games last season for the Blazers...Improved his shooting to .504...Attended Jackson State...Can have a long career as a role player and designated banger.

Year	Team	G	FG	FG Pct.	FT	FT Pct.	Reb.	Ast.	TP	Avg.
1982-83	Portland	30	26	.413	14	.467	69	24	66	2.2
1983-84	Portland	79	124	.504	104	.698	257	76	352	4.5
	Totals	109	150	.485	118	.659	326	100	418	3.8

CLYDE DREXLER 22 6-7 210   Forward-Guard

Dunk you very much... The archduke of slam-dunking Phi Slama Jama at the University of Houston... Has got the raw talent to be a real star—the speed, the size and the leaping ability... If he can pull the whole game together, he could be a Dr. J type on the fast break... "Clyde The Glide"... Born June 22, 1962, in New Orleans... Grew up in Houston and went to college just a few miles from his home... Was the first Cougar player to score 1,000 points, grab 900 rebounds and dish out 300 assists in a career... Reported late to training camp and, as a result, got off to a slow start... Looked jittery at times... His outside shot needs a great deal of work... But he's got all the tools and should blossom in Portland's running game... Says he'd like to meet Lola Falana. Who wouldn't?

Year	Team	G	FG	FG Pct.	FT	FT Pct.	Reb.	Ast.	TP	Avg.
1983-84	Portland	82	252	.451	123	.728	235	153	628	7.7

TOM PIOTROWSKI 24 7-1 240   Center

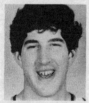

A project... That's what they call guys like this... They also call guys like this tall and that's why he managed to win a spot on the roster... As Utah coach Frank Layden says, "You can't coach height."... Well, Jack Ramsay is quite a coach if he can make this guy a legitimate NBA player... He's slow and not very aggressive... Born Oct. 17, 1960, in Chester County, Pa.... Could barely walk and chew gum when he played as a freshman at LaSalle... By the end of his four years, he could walk and chew gum... Not much else.

Year	Team	G	FG	FG Pct.	FT	FT Pct.	Reb.	Ast.	TP	Avg.
1983-84	Portland	18	12	.462	6	1.000	16	5	30	1.7

PETER VERHOEVEN 25 6-9 214   Forward

A hustler and a banger who has stuck around for three years by—what else?—hustling and banging... Strictly bench filler and practice fodder... A fourth-round draft choice of the Blazers in 1981... Born Feb. 15, 1959, in Hanford, Cal.... Played for Fresno State team that was ranked No. 1 in the nation on defense... Erupted on Christmas night 1981 against Seattle, with 28 points and 12 rebounds... That will probably happen again sometime after the next sighting of Haley's Comet

...Doesn't like the hectic NBA travel schedule or city life...Wants to be a farmer when his playing career is done.

Year	Team	G	FG	FG Pct.	FT	FT Pct.	Reb.	Ast.	TP	Avg.
1981-82	Portland	71	149	.503	51	.708	254	52	349	4.9
1982-83	Portland	48	87	.509	21	.677	96	32	195	4.1
1983-84	Portland	43	50	.500	17	.680	61	20	117	2.7
	Totals	162	286	.504	89	.695	411	104	661	4.1

TOP ROOKIES

SAM BOWIE 23 7-1 235   Center
A thoroughbred...Returned to college action for senior season after sitting out two years with stress fracture of left shinbone ...If he can stay healthy, he'll be one of the great ones...Born March 17, 1961, in Lebanon, Pa....Highly recruited as a prep star...Showed flashes of brilliance at Kentucky...Intelligent ...Excellent high-post passer out of Bill Walton mold...Averaged 10.5 ppg and 9.2 rpg in comeback campaign.

BERNARD THOMPSON 22 6-6½ 207   Forward
Averaged 15.7 ppg as a senior at Fresno State, but is more known for his hard-nosed defense...Led the Bulldogs to NIT title in 1983...Plays very aggressively and could contribute to Blazers off the bench...Born Aug. 30, 1962, in Phoenix...Set school record with .577 shooting in four years.

COACH JACK RAMSAY: What can you say about a middle-aged man who jumps rope, jogs and rides a bicycle?...Well, don't challenge him to a race...Has very few challengers in the coaching profession..."Dr. Jack"...Considered by many as the best in the business...The teacher of other NBA coaches, including Jack McKinney, Paul Westhead and Jimmy Lynam ...Born Feb. 21, 1925, in Philadelphia... That's where the legend began...His St. Joseph's teams were famous for their hustle and for pulling off big upsets...Made the jump to the pros with the 76ers, then went on to Buffalo...Moved to Portland in 1976-77 and took the Blazers all the way to the NBA title...Has given up the wild sport coats and crazy plaid pants of the early days...Doesn't kick over as many chairs, either...Played in the old Eastern League from 1949-55

...Ranks first in victories (703) among active coaches and trails only Red Auerbach (938) on the all-time list... Overall NBA mark is 703-609.

GREATEST FOUL SHOOTER

The world champion Portland Trail Blazers of 1976-77 had so many finely tuned parts. There was Maurice Lucas holding down the fort at the power forward spot, Bob Gross playing solid defense on the other side, Lionel Hollins playing like a silver streak in the backcourt and Bill Walton orchestrating things in the middle.

The other guard was Dave Twardzik, fresh from four seasons with the ABA Virginia Squires and the final piece of the puzzle in the starting lineup. He was also the Blazers' all-time best foul shooter.

Twardzik shot fouls at an .842 clip in the championship season and set the club mark of .873 two years later. He played only four seasons with the Blazers (1976-80), before a back injury forced him off the court and put him behind the microphone. He retired with a career percentage of .823.

ALL-TIME TRAIL BLAZER LEADERS

SEASON

Points: Geoff Petrie, 2,031, 1970-71
Assists: Kelvin Ransey, 555, 1981-82
           Kelvin Ransey, 555, 1980-81
Rebounds: Lloyd Neal, 967, 1972-73

GAME

Points: Geoff Petrie, 51 vs. Houston, 2/16/73
        Geoff Petrie, 51 vs. Houston, 1/20/73
Assists: Rick Adelman, 17 vs. Cleveland, 11/19/71
Rebounds: Sidney Wicks, 27 vs. Los Angeles, 2/26/75

CAREER

Points: Geoff Petrie, 9,732, 1970-76
Assists: Geoff Petrie, 1,647, 1970-76
Rebounds: Sidney Wicks, 4,086, 1971-76

SAN ANTONIO SPURS

TEAM DIRECTORY: Pres.: Angelo Drossos; GM: Bob Bass; Dir. Pub. Rel.: Wayne Witt; Coach: Cotton Fitzsimmons; Asst. Coaches: Scotty Robertson, Gary Fitzsimmons. Arena: HemisFair Arena (15,693). Colors: Silver, black and white.

As long as George Gervin's around, it'll be Ice Age in NBA.

SCOUTING REPORT

SHOOTING: The object of the game is to put the ball into the basket, isn't it? That's the philosophy they've always preached in San Antonio and that's the style of play that has made the Spurs one of the NBA's highest-scoring and most entertaining teams. If George (Iceman) Gervin (.490) doesn't get you, then Mike Mitchell (.488) will. Or perhaps Artis Gilmore (.631) or Johnny Moore (.446) will do the damage. It's second nature to the Spurs, like sitting by the Riverwalk and sipping margaritas. And there's no evidence any of them will slow down this season.

For the first time since entering the NBA in 1976-77, San Antonio is coming off a year in which it failed to make the playoffs. But that fact and the presence of new head coach Cotton Fitzsimmons won't change the basic fabric of this club. Get the ball off the boards, get it down the floor and put up a shot. The Spurs don't mess around.

PLAYMAKING: The Spurs figured they were taking a gamble when they resurrected the career of veteran John Lucas last season, but it turned about to be the best thing that happened to the club all season. Moore was out with an injury and Lucas stepped right in. Now the Spurs have themselves two very capable players who can keep the pressure on the defense with their constant wheeling and dealing. Lucas ranked third in assists in the NBA last season (10.7 per game) and Moore was fourth (9.6 per game). There is obviously no weakness here.

DEFENSE: If you wonder why the Spurs made Arkansas' Alvin Robertson their top pick in the draft, you need only look at his defensive reputation and the Spurs' stats from last year, when they gave up more than 120 ppg. Defense is one of the Fitzsimmons' favorite things and it's the thing he's going to have to improve most.

The addition of Robertson—the outstanding defensive player at the Aloha Classic—will allow the Spurs to employ more presses and traps. But if they are going to improve greatly, they're going to have to get more aggressive play out of frontline people like Gilmore (2.06 blocked shots per game) and Mitchell.

Gene Banks shows a willingness to try at the defensive end, but doesn't have great instincts and loses his man too frequently. Just ask Purvis Short or Bernard King, who racked up 52 and 50 points respectively while being guarded by Banks last season. And don't even bother to mention defense to Gervin. You can't teach an old dog new tricks.

SPUR ROSTER

No.	Veteran	Pos.	Ht.	Wt.	Age	Yrs. Pro	College
20	Gene Banks	F	6-8	223	25	4	Duke
10	*Ron Brewer	G	6-4	180	29	7	Arkansas
44	George Gervin	G	6-8	185	32	13	Eastern Michigan
53	Artis Gilmore	C	7-2	260	35	14	Jacksonville
42	Edgar Jones	F-C	6-10	225	28	5	Nevada-Reno
15	*John Lucas	G	6-3	175	31	9	Maryland
31	Mark McNamara	C	7-1	240	25	3	UC-Berkeley
34	Mike Mitchell	F	6-7	215	28	7	Auburn
00	Johnny Moore	G	6-3	175	26	5	Texas
4	John Paxson	G	6-2	185	24	2	Notre Dame
11	Fred Roberts	F	6-10	220	24	2	Brigham Young
25	Brant Widener	F	6-10	240	24	2	William & Mary

*Free agent unsigned at press time

Rd.	Top Draftees	Sel. No.	Ht.	Wt.	College
1	Alvin Robertson	7	6-3	190	Arkansas
3	Joe Binion	57	6-8½	215	North Carolina A&T
4	John Devereaux	78	6-8	228	Ohio
4	Ozell Jones	90	6-11	220	Cal State-Fullerton
5	Eric Richardson	100	6-3	180	Alabama

REBOUNDING: For those believers in the philosophy that rebounding wins games, check out the Spurs. They were the second-best boarding team in the entire league last season and it didn't do them a lick of good. The cast is the same this time around and you can be sure that the Spurs will be right at the forefront when it comes to crashing the glass.

Gilmore (10.3 rpg) uses his massive body to get position, while Mitchell (7.2 rpg) and Banks (7.3 rpg) prefer the kamikaze approach of diving into a crowd. Gervin uses those pointy elbows and his height advantage to pick up plenty of offensive rebounds. And then there's Edgar Jones, who lives among the planets anyway.

OUTLOOK: They were due to take a fall last season, but the Spurs' climb back to respectability might be longer than they think. Key cogs in the machine such as Gervin and Gilmore are getting up there in age and the Spurs don't have anybody in the wings.

Many observers think that Robertson has the potential to be a star. But his presence is not likely to be enough to restore the Spurs to the top of the Midwest Division, which used to be their permanent residence. The rest of the Midwest has improved too much and the Spurs should consider themselves lucky just to return to the playoffs.

SPUR PROFILES

GEORGE GERVIN 32 6-8 185   Guard

"Ice"... That's all you have to say to identify the most prolific scoring guard in the history of the game... Sure, he's getting up in age. Sure, he's run up and down the floor thousands of times. But if your life depended on somebody making an 18-foot jumper, you'd surely want him to shoot it... There were whispers during last season that he was beginning to slip off his pedestal, but his 25.9-ppg average didn't support that theory... Captain and heart and soul of the Spurs... It's a crying shame he hasn't won an NBA title... Born April 27, 1952, in Detroit... His story was cliche-ridden tale of growing up in the streets and developing his incredible game by shooting at a bushel basket nailed to a pole... Bounced out of Eastern Michigan after one year for fighting and headed back to the streets... ABA Virginia Squires discovered him in the semipro ranks in Detroit ... Then his legend began to grow... He's a four-time NBA scoring champ who finished sixth in the league last season.

Year	Team	G	FG	FG Pct.	FT	FT Pct.	Reb.	Ast.	TP	Avg.
1972-73	Virginia (ABA)	30	161	.472	96	.814	128	34	424	14.1
1973-74	Va.-S.A.(ABA)	74	672	.471	378	.815	624	142	1730	23.4
1974-75	San Antonio (ABA)	84	784	.474	380	.830	697	207	1965	23.4
1975-76	San Antonio (ABA)	81	706	.499	342	.857	546	201	1768	21.9
1976-77	San Antonio	82	726	.544	443	.833	454	238	1895	23.1
1977-78	San Antonio	82	864	.536	504	.830	420	302	2232	27.2
1978-79	San Antonio	80	947	.541	471	.826	400	219	2365	29.6
1979-80	San Antonio	78	1024	.528	505	.852	403	202	2585	33.1
1980-81	San Antonio	82	850	.492	512	.826	419	260	2221	27.1
1981-82	San Antonio	79	993	.500	555	.864	392	187	2551	32.3
1982-83	San Antonio	78	757	.487	517	.853	357	264	2043	26.2
1983-84	San Antonio	76	765	.490	427	.842	313	220	1967	25.9
	Totals	906	9249	.505	5130	.839	5135	2476	23746	26.2

ARTIS GILMORE 35 7-2 260   Center

"A-Train" was derailed... Suffered a broken cheekbone and orbital blowout fracture when hit with an elbow late in the season. That forced him to miss 18 games and all but wiped out the Spurs' chances of sneaking into the playoffs... Still stands tall and strong in the middle... Led the league in field-goal percentage (.631) again... Born Sept. 21, 1949, in Chipley, Fla.... Has enjoyed two seasons in a more relaxed atmosphere in San Antonio after being asked to carry too much of the load in Chicago...Obtained from the Bulls for Mark Olberding and Dave Corzine...A very friendly giant, but don't mess with him on the floor. He's regarded by most as the strongest player in the NBA...Started college career at Gardner-Webb, then rose to national prominence by leading Jacksonville to Final Four ...Starred for the Kentucky Colonels in the ABA and won a title there...Has not had that luck in NBA...The league's all-time best percentage shooter...Wants respect...."No matter what I do, most people will always call me a loser," he says...Avid scuba diver.

Year	Team	G	FG	FG Pct.	FT	FT Pct.	Reb.	Ast.	TP	Avg.
1971-72	Kentucky (ABA)	84	806	.598	391	.646	1491	230	2003	23.8
1972-73	Kentucky (ABA)	84	687	.559	368	.643	1476	295	1743	20.9
1973-74	Kentucky (ABA)	84	621	.494	326	.667	1538	329	1568	18.7
1974-75	Kentucky (ABA)	84	784	.580	412	.696	1361	208	1081	23.1
1975-76	Kentucky (ABA)	84	773	.552	521	.682	1303	211	2067	24.6
1976-77	Chicago	82	570	.522	387	.660	1070	199	1527	18.6
1977-78	Chicago	82	704	.559	471	.704	1071	263	1879	22.9
1978-79	Chicago	82	753	.575	434	.739	1043	274	1940	23.7
1979-80	Chicago	48	305	.595	245	.712	432	133	855	17.8
1980-81	Chicago	82	547	.670	375	.705	828	172	1469	17.9
1981-82	Chicago	82	546	.652	424	.768	835	136	1517	18.5
1982-83	San Antonio	82	556	.626	367	.740	984	126	1479	18.0
1983-84	San Antonio	64	351	.631	280	.718	662	70	982	15.3
	Totals	1024	8003	.577	5001	.697	14094	2646	21010	20.5

GENE BANKS 25 6-8 223   Forward

How could a guy this size ever come to be known as "Tinkerbell?" You ask him... Actually, the nickname came from his days at West Philadelphia High, when he first showed incredible agility and light-footed moves... Could benefit from an extra inch or two, since he plays power forward...But he gets by nonetheless and is fearless on the offensive boards...Not much of a perimeter shooter...He'll run all day on the break...Born May 15, 1959, in Philadelphia...Was the most sought-after prep player in the nation and went on to help Duke reach Final Four in his freshman season...Spurs were fortunate to get him on the second round of the 1981 draft...Never going to be an All-Star, but the blue-collar workers rarely are...He's a winner...Says he'd like to be the governor of Pennsylvania some day.

Year	Team	G	FG	FG Pct.	FT	FT Pct.	Reb.	Ast.	TP	Avg.
1981-82	San Antonio	80	311	.477	145	.684	411	147	767	9.6
1982-83	San Antonio	81	505	.550	196	.705	612	279	1206	14.9
1983-84	San Antonio	80	424	.568	200	.741	582	254	1049	13.1
	Totals	241	1240	.535	541	.712	1605	680	3022	12.5

MIKE MITCHELL 28 6-7 215   Forward

Mr. Consistency... For nearly three years he's been the other bullet in the Spurs' double-barreled attack... An outstanding post-up player down on the baseline, he'll also kill you with the long, long jumper... After fighting for respect during his first three years in Cleveland, he has come into his own in San Antonio... After an excellent playoff performance against Lakers in 1983, he got big contract from the Spurs... Outstanding in the transition game... Can go high to get key rebounds ... Born Jan. 1, 1956, in Atlanta... Set the school scoring and rebounding records at Auburn... Was labeled a bad seed in Cleveland, but has shown no evidence of that with the Spurs... Will play hurt... Two sprained ankles did not keep him out of starting lineup for most of last two months of season... Sews and designs some of his own clothes.

Year	Team	G	FG	FG Pct.	FT	FT Pct.	Reb.	Ast.	TP	Avg.
1978-79	Cleveland	80	362	.513	131	.736	329	60	855	10.7
1979-80	Cleveland	82	775	.523	270	.787	591	93	1820	22.2
1980-81	Cleveland	82	853	.476	302	.784	502	139	2012	24.5
1981-82	Clev.-S.A.	84	753	.510	220	.728	540	82	1726	20.5
1982-83	San Antonio	80	686	.511	219	.758	537	98	1591	19.9
1983-84	San Antonio	79	779	.488	275	.779	570	93	1839	23.3
	Totals	487	4208	.501	1417	.766	3119	565	9843	20.2

JOHN LUCAS 31 6-3 175   Guard

The Comeback Kid... There are very few around the NBA who ever thought they'd see this guy back in the league, let alone playing as well as he did last season with the Spurs... His career and life had virtually fallen apart after several run-ins with drugs... But he got his act back together and was given another chance by Spurs' GM Bob Bass after Johnny Moore was sidelined by injuries... Talk about taking advantage of an opportunity... Stepped in as starting point guard and finished fourth in the league in assists (10.7)... Born Oct. 31, 1953, in Durham, N.C.... His parents are both high school principals and his early life was a fantasy... Standout high school basketball and tennis player... First-round draft choice out of Maryland... Excelled with the Houston Rockets... Sent to Golden State as compensation for the free-agent signing of Ricky Barry and the walls began tumbling down... Played for Washington before slipping out of the league in 1982... Asked about late-season pressure of trying for the playoffs: "That's not pressure. Pressure is not having a job and having my daughter tell me she's hungry." . . . Wonderful story of putting it all back together . . . Once was the doubles partner of tennis transsexual Renee Richards.

Year	Team	G	FG	FG Pct.	FT	FT Pct.	Reb.	Ast.	TP	Avg.
1976-77	Houston	82	388	.477	135	.789	219	463	911	11.1
1977-78	Houston	82	412	.435	193	.772	255	768	1017	12.4
1978-79	Golden State	82	530	.462	264	.822	247	762	1324	16.1
1979-80	Golden State	80	388	.467	222	.768	220	602	1010	12.6
1980-81	Golden State	66	222	.439	107	.738	154	464	555	8.4
1981-82	Washington	79	263	.426	138	.784	166	551	666	8.4
1982-83	Washington	35	62	.473	21	.500	29	102	145	4.1
1983-84	San Antonio	63	275	.462	120	.764	180	673	689	10.9
	Totals	569	2540	.455	1200	.774	1470	4385	6317	11.1

JOHNNY MOORE 26 6-3 175   Guard

The guy who wouldn't quit . . . After having being cut by the Spurs as a rookie, he returned to win a spot in the starting lineup, so you knew that a few injuries early last season wouldn't stop him . . . Led the NBA in assists in 1981-82, but has become a better all-around player since then . . . Perimeter shooting has gone from atrocious to outstanding . . . Great speed . . . Doug Moe was the coach who cut him in 1979 . . . Texas alumnus went back to the gym and put his nose to the grindstone until he improved his game . . . Teamed up with John Lucas last season to form the best one-two assist punch in the league . . . Ranked fifth in assists while Lucas was fourth . . . Born March 3, 1958, in Altoona, Pa. . . . Claims he's a dyed-in-the-wool Texan.

Year	Team	G	FG	FG Pct.	FT	FT Pct.	Reb.	Ast.	TP	Avg.
1980-81	San Antonio	82	249	.479	105	.610	196	373	604	7.4
1981-82	San Antonio	79	309	.463	122	.670	275	741	741	9.4
1982-83	San Antonio	77	394	.468	148	.744	277	753	941	12.2
1983-84	San Antonio	59	231	.446	105	.755	178	566	595	10.1
	Totals	297	1183	.465	480	.694	926	2454	2881	9.7

EDGAR JONES 28 6-10 225   Forward-Center

What's tall, gangly, looks like a jack o'lantern and can jump through the roof? . . . If you've seen this guy play in either New Jersey, Detroit or San Antonio, you don't have to think twice . . . One of the most prolific and awesome slam dunkers in the game—despite his poor showing at the NBA Slam Dunk Contest—he makes you want to jump out of your seat when he swoops in and rattles the rim . . . Great leaper . . . But something funny happened last season—he developed consistency and made some solid contributions to Spurs... Started several games when Artis Gilmore was sidelined with injuries... Born June 17, 1956, in Fort Rucker, Ala.... Taken on the second round by New Jersey in 1980, then shipped to Motown before finding a home in heart of Texas... CBA Rookie of the Year in 1980... Legend says he decided to attend Nevada-Reno, then showed up the first day of school in office of Jerry Tarkanian at Nevada-Las Vegas, ready to play. Tark had to give him directions to Reno.

Year	Team	G	FG	FG Pct.	FT	FT Pct.	Reb.	Ast.	TP	Avg.
1980-81	New Jersey	60	189	.529	146	.670	263	43	524	8.7
1981-82	Detroit	48	142	.548	90	.698	207	40	375	7.8
1982-83	Det.-S.A.	77	237	.495	201	.703	448	89	677	8.8
1983-84	San Antonio	81	322	.500	176	.727	449	85	826	10.2
	Totals	266	890	.512	613	.701	1367	257	2402	9.0

FRED ROBERTS 24 6-10 220   Forward

A banger... Midway through the season he shaved off his beard, but that didn't make him any less rugged under the boards... This rookie was not afraid to mix it up with anybody and that may have been a result of playing one year of pro ball in Italy... Born Aug. 14, 1960, in Provo, Utah... Spurs picked him up from New Jersey along with a second-round draft choice and cash in return for giving up their rights to coach Stan Albeck... Ironically, Albeck is one who liked him so much when coach was still in San Antonio, but never got a chance to coach him in New Jersey... Attended Brigham Young and was originally a second-round pick by Milwaukee in 1982... Went to the Nets with Mickey Johnson for Phil Ford... Not much of an offensive threat... A hustler who works hard and gives up his body in order to get a rebound... You've got to like him.

Year	Team	G	FG	FG Pct.	FT	FT Pct.	Reb.	Ast.	TP	Avg.
1983-84	San Antonio	79	214	.536	144	.837	304	98	573	7.3

RON BREWER 29 6-4 180   Guard

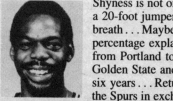

Shyness is not one of his faults... He'll put up a 20-foot jumper almost as often as he takes a breath... Maybe that plus his .461 shooting percentage explains why he's bounced around from Portland to San Antonio to Cleveland to Golden State and back to San Antonio in only six years... Returned for his second stint with the Spurs in exchange for a 1985 second-round draft choice and cash... Born Sept. 16, 1955, in Fort Smith, Ark.... Seemed destined for stardom in the NBA after an All-

American career at Arkansas, where he teamed with Sidney Moncrief and Marvin Delph...Drafted by Portland, but quickly fell into disfavor with coach Jack Ramsay...Has shown an ability to light up the scoreboard at all stops along the way, but has also demonstrated some poor judgment about when to shoot...Good speed.

Year	Team	G	FG	FG Pct.	FT	FT Pct.	Reb.	Ast.	TP	Avg.
1978-79	Portland	81	434	.494	210	.820	229	165	1078	13.3
1979-80	Portland	82	548	.464	184	.840	214	216	1286	15.7
1980-81	Port.-S.A.	75	275	.436	91	.798	86	148	642	8.6
1981-82	S.A.-Clev.	72	569	.477	211	.812	161	188	1357	18.8
1982-83	Clev.-G.S.	74	344	.426	142	.835	144	96	837	11.3
1983-84	G.S.-S.A.	53	179	.444	52	.776	63	50	413	7.8
	Totals	437	2349	.461	890	.820	897	863	5613	12.8

MARK McNAMARA 25 7-1 240   Center

As an NBA center, he'd make a good actor...In fact, he has acting experience...Spent a summer as stand-in for actor who played Chewbacca in *Return of the Jedi*...On the basketball floor, he isn't much more than stand-in, either...Gets his time when Artis Gilmore and Edgar Jones are either hurt or tired...Born June 8, 1959, in San Jose, Cal....Drafted in first round by the Philadelphia 76ers in 1982 and got himself a world championship ring by just sitting on the bench...Spurs picked him up early last season for a second-round pick in 1986...Played first two years of college ball at Santa Clara, then transferred to California...Joined Lew Alcindor and Bill Walton as only players in Pac-10 history to lead conference in scoring, rebounding and field-goal percentage...Led nation as a senior by shooting .702...Doesn't shoot from very far out...Reportedly collects snakes, but he denied that last year.

Year	Team	G	FG	FG Pct.	FT	FT Pct.	Reb.	Ast.	TP	Avg.
1982-83	Philadelphia	36	29	.453	20	.444	76	7	78	2.2
1983-84	San Antonio	70	157	.621	74	.471	317	31	388	5.5
	Totals	106	186	.587	94	.465	393	38	466	4.4

JOHN PAXSON 24 6-2 185   Guard

Brutal baptism...Learned the hard way what it's like to play contract hardball with Spurs' president Angelo Drossos...Played only 458 minutes all season, so no one really knows whether he can cut it in the league...Born Sept. 29, 1960, in Dayton, Ohio...Lacks the height of brother Jim, an All-Star for Portland...But after he had completed an outstanding college career at Notre Dame, there were those who said he's the best in the family...Dad was a pro in Cincinnati and Minneapolis...Excellent shooter and knows how to run the offense...Defense is questionable...Was a two-time Academic All-American.

TOP ROOKIE

ALVIN ROBERTSON 22 6-3 190   **Guard**
The lineal descendant of talented guards Sidney Moncrief and Darrell Walker at Arkansas...Excellent defensive player... Standout playmaker...Born July 22, 1962, in Cleveland... Member of 1984 U.S. Olympic team...An overachiever ...Always hustling...Averaged 15.5 ppg and 5.9 assists per game last season.

COACH COTTON FITZSIMMONS: The little guy moves into another big job...Is only 5-7, but he was just the right size for coaching vacancy with Spurs... Moves on to San Antonio after spending six years with the Kansas City Kings...It comes as no surprise, because he's been unhappy with the lack of support his teams received in KC the last few years, when Kings were often outdrawn by an indoor soccer team... His clubs advanced to the playoffs in three of the last four seasons, but Kings were obviously overmatched in the first round last season and were swept by Lakers...But 1983-84 was a big season for Cotton...Notched his 500th NBA win March 1 at Houston and now takes a 13-year pro record of 512-546 to Texas...Born Oct. 7, 1931, in Bowling Green, Mo....Small-college All-American at Hannibal-LaGrange Junior College and Midwestern University...Started coaching at Kansas State alongside Tex Winter...This will be his fifth stop in the NBA, following stints in Phoenix, Atlanta, Buffalo and Kansas City...His inspirational leadership should be just what sagging Spurs need after disappointing season...Always gets the most out of his players...Inducted into Missouri Sports Hall of Fame in 1982.

GREATEST FOUL SHOOTER

Why should it be a surprise? After all, he's as much a part of San Antonio as the Alamo. And doesn't he spend more time shooting the ball than any of the other Spurs?

Naturally, the guy the Spurs go to when things get tough or when the money is on the line is the best free-throw shooter in club history. George Gervin. Who else?

The Iceman is as cool at the line as he is making one of those running one-handers in traffic. He's led San Antonio in foul shooting for the last three seasons and four times in his 11 years with the Spurs. Gervin's .842 mark last season gave him an .839 career percentage.

Though the former Captain Late, James Silas, enjoyed his glory days as the Spurs' top man at the line—leading the team in six seasons with an overall percentage of .854 for San Antonio—Gervin, as usual, has been just a little bit better with a percentage of .857 as a Spur.

It goes without saying that Gervin holds the club record in free throws attempted (5,667) and made (4,859), but he also owns the mark for most made in one game with 18, against Philadelphia in 1979 and against Kansas City in 1983.

ALL-TIME SPUR LEADERS

SEASON

Points: George Gervin, 2,585, 1979-80
Assists: Johnny Moore, 762, 1981-82
Rebounds: Swen Nater, 1,279, 1974-75

GAME

Points: George Gervin, 63 vs. New Orleans, 4/9/78
Assists: John Lucas, 24 vs. Denver, 4/15/84
Rebounds: Manny Leaks, 35 vs. Kentucky, 11/27/70

CAREER

Points: George Gervin, 22,078, 1974-84
Assists: Johnny Moore, 2,454, 1980-84
Rebounds: George Gervin, 4,607, 1974-84

SEATTLE SUPERSONICS

TEAM DIRECTORY: Chairman: Barry Ackerly; GM/VP: Les Habegger; Dir. Pub. Rel.: Rick Moxley; Coach/Dir. Player Personnel: Lenny Wilkens. Arena: Kingdome (40,192). Colors: Green and yellow.

SCOUTING REPORT

SHOOTING: You wake up one day and the magic is gone. That's what seems to have happened to the Sonics, who were NBA champions only six seasons ago. What was once a very potent offensive machine is now in need of a complete overhaul.

Gus Williams' snowbird layups and rainbow jumpers are gone to Washington in the three-way deal that brought rookie center Tim McCormick and veteran guard Ricky Sobers to the Northwest. Jack Sikma (.499) is about the only offensive weapon the Sonics know they can count on every night heading into the season.

The rest of the cast is suspect. Tom Chambers (.499) can be brilliant one night and dreadful the next and Al Wood (.494) is strictly a streak shooter. Danny Vranes couldn't hit two-of-three 10-footers if his life depended on it and then the picture really starts to fall apart. What will be the next tragedy to befall David Thompson? And can second-year man Jon Sundvold (.445) regain his deadly shooting touch after being in and out of the lineup last year like a yo-yo? This is a team that is going to scramble desperately on offense.

PLAYMAKING: There is a new era being ushered in here with the departure of Williams. Even when he was going through one of his cold streaks as a shooter, Williams always ran the offense well. Sobers (4.7 assists per game) will now perform most of those duties and is nowhere near as effective as Williams in the transition game.

DEFENSE: This is just one more area where the Sonics are going to be struggling to find a team concept and identity—and one more way they're going to miss Gus. Williams was third in the league in steals last season with 2.36 per game, and always seemed to be headed down the floor for one of his breakaway layups.

Sobers is a capable defender and is a couple of inches taller than Williams, but Wood has not thrown very many defensive blankets over the opposition since coming into the league. They'll be expecting some big things out of McCormick, who made a

Jack Sikma, playing every game, topped Sonics with 19.1 ppg.

SONIC ROSTER

No.	Veteran	Pos.	Ht.	Wt.	Age	Yrs. Pro	College
32	*Fred Brown	G	6-3	185	36	14	Iowa
24	Tom Chambers	C	6-11	225	25	4	Utah
51	Reggie King	F	6-6	244	27	6	Alabama
21	Scooter McCray	F	6-8	209	24	2	Louisville
43	Jack Sikma	C	6-11	230	28	8	Illinois Wesleyan
14	Ricky Sobers	G	6-3	198	31	10	Nevada-Las Vegas
20	Jon Sunvold	G	6-1	170	23	2	Missouri
44	David Thompson	G	6-4	195	30	10	NC State
23	Danny Vranes	F	6-7	210	26	4	Utah
4	Al Wood	G	6-6	193	26	4	North Carolina

*Free agent unsigned at press time

Rd.	Top Draftees	Sel. No.	Ht.	Wt.	College
1	**Tim McCormick	11	6-11	240	Michigan
2	Cory Blackwell	28	6-5	210	Wisconsin
2	Danny Young	39	6-3	170	Wake Forest
3	Terry Williams	52	6-8	210	Alabama
4	Jeff Jenkins	83	6-8	205	Xavier (Ohio)

**Picked by Cleveland, traded to Bullets, then traded to Sonics

strong showing at the U.S. Olympic trials and is regarded by many as a sleeper. He is a good shot-blocker and the Sonics will need all of those talents.

REBOUNDING: Once more, Sikma (11.1 rpg) can be counted on to give up his body every night to fight and scratch and claw for any rebound that is within reach. Vranes has excellent leaping ability and doesn't mind belting an opponent if it means getting the ball off the boards. But McCormick is going to have to contribute heavily here if the Sonics are going to hold their own. Chambers (6.5 rpg) can be an effective rebounder when he wants to, which isn't often enough for a player with his physical attributes.

OUTLOOK: The front office felt it was time to make major changes after the Sonics were eliminated by Dallas in the first round of the playoffs. The Sonics had to do it sooner or later, but are likely to suffer for it in the short run. Williams was too large a part of the offense not to be missed. The glory days of the franchise are but a memory and, come springtime, the playoffs might be, too.

SONIC PROFILES

JACK SIKMA 28 6-11 230   Center

Mr. Consistency... Much has changed from the championship days of yesteryear in Seattle, but this guy certainly hasn't... Has missed just seven games due to injury in seven pro seasons ... Leaves his heart and soul out on the floor with every game... Of course, the back-stepping, reverse-pivot jumper is his trademark... But he's a hustler and bruiser and has the scars on his face to prove it... Born Nov. 14, 1955, in Kankakee, Ill.... Traded in his Prince Valiant hairstyle for an Orphan Annie perm several seasons ago and usually curls opponents' hair with his play... The cornerstone of the franchise... Former GM Zollie Volchok once said he wouldn't trade Sikma for the reincarnation of Marilyn Monroe in his bedroom. This guy is good or Zollie has lost his marbles... First-round draft choice out of tiny Illinois-Wesleyan in 1977.

Year	Team	G	FG	FG Pct.	FT	FT Pct.	Reb.	Ast.	TP	Avg.
1977-78	Seattle	82	342	.455	192	.777	678	134	876	10.7
1978-79	Seattle	82	476	.460	329	.814	1013	261	1281	15.6
1979-80	Seattle	82	470	.475	235	.805	908	279	1175	14.3
1980-81	Seattle	82	595	.454	340	.823	852	248	1530	18.7
1981-82	Seattle	82	581	.479	447	.855	1038	277	1611	19.6
1982-83	Seattle	75	484	.464	400	.837	858	233	1368	18.2
1983-84	Seattle	82	576	.499	411	.856	911	327	1563	19.1
	Totals	567	3524	.470	2354	.830	6258	1759	9404	16.6

RICKY SOBERS 31 6-3 198   Guard

Went coast to coast on draft day when Bullets traded him with rookie Tim McCormick for Gus Williams... Love him, hate him, you can't ignore him... Not shy... Will take the shot, whether it's there or not... Hoisted up 111 three-point field-goal attempts, making 29 of them ... Was Washington's second-leading scorer (15.6 ppg), but hit only 45.6 percent of his shots... A physical player who can overwhelm smaller guards on defense... In chronic foul trouble, he was disqualified 10 times... Can't leave him alone... Hit 83.7 percent of his foul shots... Born Jan. 15, 1953, in the Bronx, N.Y.... Started 81 games... Hurt Bullets in playoffs with subpar performances against Boston... Led team with 117 steals... Signed in midseason of 1982-83 as a free agent and felt right at home with Bullet coach

Gene Shue's home for the wayward...Sonics are his fifth pro team since leaving Nevada-Las Vegas.

Year	Team	G	FG	FG Pct.	FT	FT Pct.	Reb.	Ast.	TP	Avg.
1975-76	Phoenix	78	280	.449	158	.823	259	215	718	9.2
1976-77	Phoenix	79	414	.496	243	.841	234	238	1071	13.6
1977-78	Indiana	79	553	.453	330	.825	327	584	1436	18.2
1978-79	Indiana	81	553	.463	298	.882	301	450	1404	17.3
1979-80	Chicago	82	470	.469	200	.837	242	426	1161	14.2
1980-81	Chicago	71	355	.462	231	.935	144	284	958	13.5
1981-82	Chicago	80	363	.453	195	.768	142	301	940	11.8
1982-83	Washington	41	234	.438	154	.832	102	218	645	15.7
1983-84	Washington	81	508	.456	221	.837	179	377	1266	15.6
	Totals	672	3730	.461	2030	.843	1930	3093	9599	14.3

TOM CHAMBERS 25 6-11 225   Center

Looks like a choirboy, but it's usually the opposition that sings complaints about his rough style of play and liberal tossing of elbows... Tough to figure out...Has all the skills and physical tools to be a fine one...But the word is that the demons inside his head have held him back more than anything else...After making him their top pick in 1981, the San Diego Clippers gave up on him after two up-and-down seasons...Was shipped north to the rain country in the deal for James Donaldson and Greg Kelser...Born June 21, 1959, in Ogden, Utah and attended University of Utah...Has the boyish good looks to be a member of the Osmond family...But he'd probably have no reservations about hitting Marie in the cheek with an elbow if it meant getting a rebound...Can be a strong inside player and has decent range from the perimeter...All indications are that he should be a solid player for a long time...He's married, girls, and has a family.

Year	Team	G	FG	FG Pct.	FT	FT Pct.	Reb.	Ast.	TP	Avg.
1981-82	San Diego	81	554	.525	284	.620	561	146	1392	17.2
1982-83	San Diego	79	519	.472	353	.723	519	192	1391	17.6
1983-84	Seattle	82	554	.499	375	.800	532	133	1483	18.1
	Totals	242	1627	.498	1012	.715	1612	471	4266	17.6

AL WOOD 26 6-6 193   Guard

Coach Lenny Wilkens wanted him badly in Seattle when he came out of college in 1981 ...Finally made it to the Sonics after two years, when he came north from San Diego with Tom Chambers in the trade for James Donaldson and Greg Kelser...Another product of Dean Smith's factory at North Carolina...Was the rave of the NCAA tournament and Atlanta made him the No. 4 pick in the entire draft . . . Hawks caught flak for giving up too quickly and shipping him to San Diego in his rookie season . . . They may have been right . . . Has made the transition from small forward to big guard, but there's still something missing from his game . . . It's doubtful any team could win a championship with him in the starting lineup . . . Can hit the open shot from the perimeter . . . Born June 2, 1958, in Grey, Ga. . . . Willing to work. Once walked five miles in a snowstorm to get to a game in Atlanta . . . Still catches heat from his teammates about those Dumbolike ears that flap in the wind.

Year	Team	G	FG	FG Pct.	FT	FT Pct.	Reb.	Ast.	TP	Avg.
1981-82	Atl.-S.D.	48	179	.470	93	.782	134	58	454	9.5
1982-83	San Diego	76	343	.464	124	.770	236	134	825	10.9
1983-84	Seattle	81	467	.494	223	.823	275	166	1160	14.3
	Totals	205	989	.479	440	.799	645	358	2439	11.9

DAVID THOMPSON 30 6-4 195   Guard

Disco David . . . Had the kind of year he'd like to forget . . . Couldn't come to terms on a contract until the middle of the season . . . Played in just 19 games—and played well—before going dancing with his teammates at Studio 54 on a road trip to New York . . . Court case is still pending, so no one is commenting. But what is known for sure is that he fell down a flight of stairs and tore ligaments in his knee, finishing him for the season . . . Certainly didn't need more problems . . . Went through drug rehab program and suffered from many rumors about his personal life in the two previous years, forcing a trade from Denver in 1982 . . . Born June 13, 1954, in Shelby, N.C. . . . Two-time College Player of the Year at North Carolina State . . . Recent past seems to have overshadowed his earlier greatness . . . How quickly everyone seems to have forgotten that this guy was in Dr. J's class as a gravity-defying skywalker in his early pro years . . . Now he's just looking to regain lost respect . . . Scored 73 points in final game of the 1978 season for Denver.

Year	Team	G	FG	FG Pct.	FT	FT Pct.	Reb.	Ast.	TP	Avg.
1975-76	Denver (ABA)	83	807	.515	541	.794	525	308	2158	26.0
1976-77	Denver	82	824	.507	477	.766	334	337	2125	25.9
1977-78	Denver	80	826	.521	520	.778	390	362	2172	27.2
1978-79	Denver	76	693	.512	439	.753	274	225	1825	24.0
1979-80	Denver	39	289	.468	254	.758	174	124	839	21.5
1980-81	Denver	77	734	.506	489	.795	287	231	1967	25.5
1981-82	Denver	61	313	.486	276	.814	148	117	906	14.9
1982-83	Seattle	75	445	.481	298	.784	270	222	1190	15.9
1983-84	Seattle	19	89	.539	62	.849	44	13	240	12.6
	Totals	592	5020	.505	3356	.781	2446	1939	13422	22.7

FRED BROWN 36 6-3 185   Guard

"Downtown"... An ageless wonder... Sure, he's lost some speed and quickness since the early days... But he can still drill those three-pointers from anywhere on the floor... Playing his 13th season, he had one of the finest shooting years (.510) of his career... Born July 7, 1948, in Milwaukee, where he grew up with John Johnson, who later became a teammate on the Sonics' championship team in 1979... Very active in local charities and very popular in the community... Buys 200 tickets to every game to give away... Iowa product has spent his entire career with the Sonics... Will move into the front office when his playing career is through... A class act all the way.

Year	Team	G	FG	FG Pct.	FT	FT Pct.	Reb.	Ast.	TP	Avg.
1971-72	Seattle	33	59	.328	22	.759	37	60	140	4.2
1972-73	Seattle	79	471	.455	121	.818	318	438	1063	13.5
1973-74	Seattle	82	578	.471	195	.863	401	414	1351	16.5
1974-75	Seattle	81	737	.480	226	.831	343	284	1700	21.0
1975-76	Seattle	76	742	.488	273	.869	317	207	1757	23.1
1976-77	Seattle	72	534	.479	168	.884	232	176	1236	17.2
1977-78	Seattle	72	508	.488	176	.898	188	240	1192	16.6
1978-79	Seattle	77	446	.469	183	.888	172	260	1075	14.0
1979-80	Seattle	80	404	.479	113	.837	155	174	960	12.0
1980-81	Seattle	78	505	.488	173	.832	175	233	1206	15.5
1981-82	Seattle	82	393	.455	111	.860	140	238	922	11.2
1982-83	Seattle	80	371	.520	58	.806	97	242	814	10.2
1983-84	Seattle	71	258	.510	77	.895	62	194	602	8.5
	Totals	963	6006	.478	1896	.858	2637	3160	14018	14.6

REGGIE KING 27 6-6 244   Forward

Talk about your one-year wonders... A couple of decent playoff series with Kansas City against Phoenix and Houston in 1981 had everybody talking about this guy as the next great power forward of the '80s... Baloney... If anything, he's been overrated since he came out of Alabama so highly regarded in 1979... Now he's overweight, out of shape and lucky to be in the league... Born Feb. 14, 1957, in Birmingham, Ala.... Stayed at home for his college career and became an All-American ... Plays a power forward's game, but can't really bang with the big guys because he can't jump and doesn't have their size... A first-round pick (18th overall) of Kings in 1979, but he blossomed only that one spring on national television... Averaged only 8.2 ppg and shot only .442 in first year with the Sonics... Had a shot as a starter for 42 games, but showed he can't get the job done... Has been around for five years, but don't expect him to survive for many more years.

Year	Team	G	FG	FG Pct.	FT	FT Pct.	Reb.	Ast.	TP	Avg.
1979-80	Kansas City	82	257	.515	159	.726	566	106	673	8.2
1980-81	Kansas City	81	472	.544	264	.684	786	122	1208	14.9
1981-82	Kansas City	80	383	.509	201	.705	523	173	967	12.1
1982-83	Kansas City	58	104	.462	73	.760	240	58	281	4.8
1983-84	Seattle	77	233	.520	136	.660	470	179	602	7.8
	Totals	378	1449	.519	833	.699	2585	638	3731	9.9

DANNY VRANES 26 6-7 210   Forward

OK, who wants to take the responsibility for drafting this guy so high?... Sure, he's a nice player, a great leaper and a hustler... But No. 5 overall in the 1981 draft was absolutely ridiculous... Usually shoots better than 50 percent from the field—mostly from short range but averages about eight points a game... Move him three feet from the hoop and his offense is nonexistent... Born Oct. 29, 1958, in Salt Lake City, Utah... A product of the University of Utah... A cousin of former NBA player Jeff Judkins... Another one of those guys who will smile, look innocent and then belt you in the mouth with an elbow under the basket... Maybe that's why the Sonics have been reluctant to admit they made a big, big mistake.

Year	Team	G	FG	FG Pct.	FT	FT Pct.	Reb.	Ast.	TP	Avg.
1981-82	Seattle	77	143	.546	89	.601	198	56	375	4.9
1982-83	Seattle	82	226	.527	115	.550	425	120	567	6.9
1983-84	Seattle	80	258	.521	153	.648	395	132	669	8.4
	Totals	239	627	.529	357	.602	1018	308	1611	6.7

JON SUNVOLD 23 6-1 170   Guard

Hoo boy, did he prove the experts wrong... Was thought to be too small and too slow to be able to survive in the league... Lenny Wilkens and the Sonics took a lot of heat for making him their No. 1 draft choice in 1983... Wound up scoring only 6.9 ppg and shooting .445 from the field, but much of that wasn't his fault... Had a good start, then lost his playing time when

David Thompson returned after contract dispute...When Thompson was hurt late in the season, he had lost his sharpness...A deadly accurate bomber who'll be able to eventually fill the role of Freddie Brown...Smart, heady, knows the game...Weakness is lack of size that makes playing defense difficult...Born July 2, 1961, in Sioux Falls, S.D....Second-leading scorer in Missouri history...There's definitely a place for him in the league.

Year	Team	G	FG	FG Pct.	FT	FT Pct.	Reb.	Ast.	TP	Avg.
1983-84	Seattle	73	217	.445	64	.889	91	239	507	6.9

SCOOTER McCRAY 24 6-8 209   Forward

He and Rockets' Rodney were the first brother combination to enter the NBA in the same season since Tom and Dick Van Arsdale...He's a year older than Rodney and admits that his younger brother is actually the better player ...Knee injury forced him to sit out a year in college at Louisville...Not a great offensive threat (.388 from the field)...He'll have to get by with hustle on the defense and intensity in going to the boards in order to stick around in the NBA...Born Feb. 8, 1960, in Mt. Vernon, N.Y....His real first name is Carlton...Mother gave him the nickname that has stuck all his life when he was a baby. She used to call him "my little Scooter Pie."

Year	Team	G	FG	FG Pct.	FT	FT Pct.	Reb.	Ast.	TP	Avg.
1983-84	Seattle	47	47	.388	35	.700	115	44	129	2.7

TOP ROOKIE

TIM McCORMICK 22 6-11 240   Center-Forward

Drafted No. 11 overall by Cleveland and Sonics got him from Bullets along with Ricky Sobers in three-team deal that sent Gus Williams to Washington...Career at Michigan peaked with strong showing in NIT...Was named MVP with 28 points in victory over Notre Dame...A hustler...Could be a sleeper...A finalist for a spot on the Olympic team, but didn't make final cut...Born March 10, 1962, in Clarkston, Mich....Averaged 12.1 ppg and 5.9 rpg as senior.

COACH LENNY WILKENS: New member of the 500-win club... Came through a tumultuous season with a career total of 522 victories against 440 losses... But the joyous days of winning championships and nearly filling the huge Kingdome are past... His team now has to fight for respectability around the league and in its hometown... His act is wearing thin... Nobody really expected big things from the Sonics last season, so it was not a surprise when they didn't deliver... The most galling aspect of the season was the way it ended: the Sonics blew a six-point lead in the final 32 seconds of regulation, then lost in overtime to Dallas in the first round of the playoffs... Born Oct. 28, 1937, in Brooklyn, N.Y.... Was a standout guard at Providence, then enjoyed an NBA career that saw him wind up as the second-leading all-time assist man, behind Oscar Robertson... NBA career included stops in St. Louis, Atlanta, Seattle, Portland and Cleveland... One of the last of the player-coaches in Seattle and Portland... Failed in his first go-round as the Sonics' coach, but then returned 23 games into the 1977-78 season and took the team to the finals... In 1978-79, Seattle won it all... Not a screamer out of the Hubie Brown mold, but not one of the NBA's fun guys, either.

GREATEST FOUL SHOOTER

He has made an entire career and a name for himself by tossing in bombs from "Downtown," so it stands to reason that Fred Brown can hit with high accuracy from a mere 15 feet away, at the foul line.

Actually, the SuperSonics have long been a good free-throw shooting team. From Dick Snyder to Spencer Haywood to Lenny Wilkens to Jack Sikma, so many of the big names who have worn the green and gold have been 75 percent shooters from the stripe. Sikma was ranked among the top 10 in the NBA last season with an .856 mark. But even though Brown did not have enough attempts to qualify (77-of-86 for .896), he was a shade better, maintaining the level of consistency that has made him one of the game's great pure shooters.

Brown had a stranglehold on the Sonics' lead from 1975-79, but since then he has had to fight it out with the younger generation.

Still, when you look back at the long list of accomplishments in a wonderful career, you can note that Brown remains the best foul shooter the Sonics have ever had with a mark of .857.

ALL-TIME SUPERSONIC LEADERS

SEASON

Points: Spencer Haywood, 2,251, 1972-73
Assists: Lenny Wilkens, 766, 1971-72
Rebounds: Jack Sikma, 1,038, 1981-82

GAME

Points: Fred Brown, 58 vs. Golden State, 3/23/74
Assists: Gus Williams, 20 vs. Dallas, 12/9/83
Rebounds: Jim Fox, 30 vs. Los Angeles, 12/26/73

CAREER

Points: Fred Brown, 14,018, 1971-84
Assists: Fred Brown, 3,160, 1971-84
Rebounds: Jack Sikma, 6,258, 1977-84

UTAH JAZZ

TEAM DIRECTORY: Pres.: Sam Battistone; GM/Coach: Frank Layden; Exec. VP: Dave Checketts; VP-Dir. Las Vegas operation: Dave Fredman; Dir. Pub. Rel.: Bill Kreifeldt; Asst. Coaches: Scott Layden, Phil Johnson. Arenas: Salt Palace (12,143), Salt Lake City, and Thomas and Mack Center (18,500), Las Vegas. Colors: Purple, gold and green.

Jazzy Adrian Dantley topped NBA with 30.6 ppg.

SCOUTING REPORT

SHOOTING: There are only a couple of first-class shooters on this club, but, fortunately for the Jazz, they do most of the shooting. Adrian Dantley's .558 mark from the field was particularly amazing when you consider he was the league's leading scorer (30.6 ppg) and took 1,438 shots last season. Dantley has always been virtually unstoppable inside but, while working to rehabilitate his right wrist from surgery, he greatly improved his touch from the perimeter. There's no place on the floor from which it's safe to let him shoot—and that goes double for the foul line, where he hit 85.9 percent of his 946 chances.

The Mr. Outside of the attack is Darrell Griffith (.490), The Mad Bomber. Griffith's 91 three-point field goals were more than any other team made last year. Last year's rookie surprise Thurl Bailey showed that he can score consistently on the inside and also possesses a very nice from medium range. Of course, supersub John Drew (.479) has never been known to be shy, but he's a streaky shooter who can catch fire and burn you. Rickey Green's best shot is a breakaway layup and he got enough of them to post a .486 mark.

PLAYMAKING: Color it Green. The little CBA refugee has finally established himself as one of the best in the league and is coming off his first appearance in the NBA All-Star Game. Green looks like Carl Lewis when he sprints from end to end on the break and is the sparkplug of the offense with 9.2 assists per game. The problem last season was that Green had to play too many minutes, because there wasn't any depth at his position.

That's what prompted GM-coach Frank Layden to surprise everybody by taking unheralded John Stockton of Gonzaga with his first-round draft choice. He is another of those guys who gained attention at the U.S. Olympic trials with his intelligence and willingness to work. He is a good penetrator who can dish it off and should relieve Green of some of the burden.

DEFENSE: Height is what makes 7-3½ center Mark Eaton a defensive force. He couldn't leap over a dime, but by simply gaining the proper position, holding his ground and raising his arms, Eaton led the NBA in blocked shots with 4.28 per game last season. Dantley is learning more about defense, while Bailey was solid in his rookie season. The Jazz are also solid in the backcourt, where Green, who led the league with 2.65 steals per game, and Griffith can intercept balls in the passing lanes.

JAZZ ROSTER

No.	Veteran	Pos.	Ht.	Wt.	Age	Yrs. Pro	College
11	*Mitchell Anderson	F	6-8	195	24	3	Bradley
41	Thurl Bailey	F	6-11	215	23	2	NC State
33	Tom Boswell	F	6-7	225	31	7	South Carolina
4	Adrian Dantley	F	6-5	210	28	9	Notre Dame
20	*John Drew	F	6-6	205	30	11	Gardner-Webb
53	Mark Eaton	C	7-3½	290	27	3	UCLA
31	Jerry Eaves	G	6-3	185	25	3	Louisville
14	Rickey Green	G	6-0	170	30	7	Michigan
35	Darrell Griffith	G	6-4	190	26	5	Louisville
20	Bob Hansen	G	6-6	205	23	2	Iowa
44	*Rich Kelley	C	7-0	240	31	10	Stanford
45	*Jeff Wilkins	F-C	6-10	240	29	5	Illinois State

*Free agent unsigned at press time

Rd.	Top Draftees	Sel. No.	Ht.	Wt.	College
1	John Stockton	16	6-1	175	Gonzaga
3	David Pope	62	6-7½	210	Norfolk State
4	Jim Rowinski	86	6-8	240	Purdue
5	Marcus Gaither	108	6-4	190	Fairleigh Dickinson
6	Chris Harrison	132	6-8	230	West Virginia Wesleyan

REBOUNDING: There is no Moses Malone-type, rebounding-eating monster here, but they all have a sense of their responsibility on the boards and hit them hard as a unit. Eaton (7.3 rpg) led the way last season, but Utah had five different players pull down more than 445 rebounds. Dantley, of course, is the leader on the offensive glass, where he puts his own rare misses right back in the hole. Green will sneak through the tall timber to come up with a key rebound from time to time.

OUTLOOK: Even if they do manage to repeat as Midwest Division champs, the Jazz will never be able to recapture the magic that was part of the best season in the history of the franchise. Everything went their way, even the race with Dallas during the final weeks of the regular season.

Utah will not be overlooked by the experts who tabbed them for last in the division last year. The Jazz are likely to be fighting it out again with the Mavericks, but it's going to be difficult for Utah to improve on last year's 45-37 record. And once more, the Jazz will be no real threat in the playoffs.

JAZZ PROFILES

ADRIAN DANTLEY 28 6-5 210   Forward

A.D. is back . . . After missing most of 1982-83 with torn ligaments in his right wrist, he led league in scoring (30.6 ppg), free throws attempted (946) and free-throws made (813) . . . Named Comeback Player of the Year . . . Everybody always said he was too slow and too small to be considered among the greats . . . Now he's finally getting his recognition as an unstoppable offensive force . . . Born Feb. 28, 1956, in Washington, D.C. . . . The legend began to grow at DeMatha High, where he played with Kenny Carr . . . Went to Notre Dame, where he seemed to gather almost as many critics as points . . . Acquired reputation as a ballhog . . . Kicked around from Buffalo to Indiana to Los Angeles before finally finding a home in Utah . . . Now you'd probably have to use explosives to blast him out of a Jazz uniform.

Year	Team	G	FG	FG Pct.	FT	FT Pct.	Reb.	Ast.	TP	Avg.
1976-77	Buffalo	77	544	.520	476	.818	587	144	1564	20.3
1977-78	Ind.-L.A.	79	578	.512	541	.796	620	253	1697	21.5
1978-79	Los Angeles	60	374	.510	292	.854	342	138	1040	17.3
1979-80	Utah	68	730	.576	443	.842	516	191	1903	28.0
1980-81	Utah	80	909	.559	632	.806	509	322	2452	30.7
1981-82	Utah	81	904	.570	648	.792	514	324	2457	30.3
1982-83	Utah	22	233	.580	210	.847	140	105	676	30.7
1983-84	Utah	79	802	.558	813	.859	448	310	2418	30.6
	Totals	546	5074	.550	4055	.823	3676	1787	14207	26.0

RICKEY GREEN 30 6-0 170   Guard

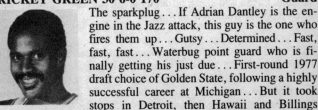

The sparkplug . . . If Adrian Dantley is the engine in the Jazz attack, this guy is the one who fires them up . . . Gutsy . . . Determined . . . Fast, fast, fast . . . Waterbug point guard who is finally getting his just due . . . First-round 1977 draft choice of Golden State, following a highly successful career at Michigan . . . But it took stops in Detroit, then Hawaii and Billings of the CBA before he was able to catch on with Jazz . . . Born Aug. 18, 1954, in Chicago . . . Led league in steals (2.65 per game) and was sixth in assists (9.2 per game) last season . . . One of the best in business at getting the ball into the hands of the scorers . . . Has some offensive punch himself and will burn you if left alone to scoot around... Used to be a scorer, breaking Bob McAdoo's records at Vincennes Junior College.

Year	Team	G	FG	FG Pct.	FT	FT Pct.	Reb.	Ast.	TP	Avg.
1977-78	Golden State	76	143	.381	54	.600	116	149	340	4.5
1978-79	Detroit	27	67	.379	45	.672	40	63	179	6.6
1980-81	Utah	47	176	.481	70	.722	116	235	422	9.0
1981-82	Utah	81	500	.493	202	.765	243	630	1202	14.8
1982-83	Utah	78	464	.493	185	.797	223	697	1115	14.3
1983-84	Utah	81	439	.486	192	.821	230	748	1072	13.2
	Totals	390	1789	.473	748	.760	968	2522	4330	11.1

DARRELL GRIFFITH 26 6-4 190   Guard

The former "Dr. Dunkenstein"... Now he's more like Dr. Strangelove, because of his fascination with the bomb... Led NBA in three-point field-goal accuracy (.361) in 1983-84... His 91 bombs were more than any other entire team scored... Still capable of wowing the crowd with sensational dunks on the break... Probably would have a much higher profile if he played outside of Salt Lake City. But then, who wouldn't?... Had to do some ball-handling chores last season as backup to Rickey Green... Born June 1, 1958, in Louisville, Ky.... Bluegrass State is still his offseason home... The most highly-recruited prep player in the nation at Male H.S.... Led Louisville to the NCAA title in 1980... Taken second in the draft, ahead of Kevin McHale.

Year	Team	G	FG	FG Pct.	FT	FT Pct.	Reb.	Ast.	TP	Avg.
1980-81	Utah	81	716	.464	229	.716	288	194	1671	20.6
1981-82	Utah	80	689	.482	189	.697	305	187	1582	19.8
1982-83	Utah	77	752	.484	167	.679	304	270	1709	22.2
1983-84	Utah	82	697	.490	151	.696	338	283	1636	20.0
	Totals	320	2854	.480	736	.698	1235	934	6598	20.6

JOHN DREW 30 6-6 205   Forward

The story continues... Should have been the NBA Comeback Player of the Year in 1982-83, when he overcame a drug addiction to put the pieces of his career together... Showed that he's determined to stay straight... Highest-scoring reserve (17.7 ppg) in league last season... Plays like he's enjoying it again... Will never receive praise from Hubie Brown for his defense, but he is certainly trying... Born Sept. 30, 1954, in Vredenburg, Ala.... Came to Utah with Freeman Williams for

Dominique Wilkins in controversial 1982 trade... Promptly admitted he had a drug problem and didn't play until the last 44 games of the season... But he has been a key cog in Jazz machine... Played at Gardner-Webb... Second-round 1974 pick by Atlanta... Hubie used him as his whipping boy... Once claimed he was as good as Dr. J, only didn't get the ink... No way.

Year	Team	G	FG	FG Pct.	FT	FT Pct.	Reb.	Ast.	TP	Avg.
1974-75	Atlanta	78	527	.428	388	.713	836	138	1442	18.5
1975-76	Atlanta	77	586	.502	488	.744	660	150	1660	21.8
1976-77	Atlanta	74	689	.487	412	.714	675	133	1790	24.2
1977-78	Atlanta	70	593	.480	437	.760	511	141	1623	23.2
1978-79	Atlanta	79	650	.473	495	.731	522	119	1795	22.7
1979-80	Atlanta	80	535	.453	489	.757	471	101	1559	19.5
1980-81	Atlanta	67	500	.456	454	.787	383	79	1454	21.7
1981-82	Atlanta	70	465	.486	364	.741	375	96	1298	18.5
1982-83	Utah	44	318	.474	296	.755	235	97	932	21.2
1983-84	Utah	81	511	.479	402	.778	338	135	1430	17.7
	Totals	720	5374	.471	4225	.748	5006	1189	14983	20.8

THURL BAILEY 23 6-11 215   Forward

"Thurl the Pearl"... There was some question about whether this finesse player who doesn't particularly enjoy contact would be a real success in the NBA... But he answered critics with a splendid season and made the All-Rookie team... A good shooter from up to 15 feet ... Also proved he can be a capable rebounder... Despite his size, he has the moves of a small forward... No. 7 pick overall in 1983 draft... Born April 7, 1961, in Washington, D.C.... First member of North Carolina State's 1983 NCAA championship team to be drafted... Wants to be a radio-TV announcer... Plans probably won't be realized until after a long pro career... Served as a congressional page one summer.

Year	Team	G	FG	FG Pct.	FT	FT Pct.	Reb.	Ast.	TP	Avg.
1983-84	Utah	81	302	.512	88	.752	464	129	692	8.5

JERRY EAVES 25 6-3 185   Guard

Another of "The Doctors of Dunk"... Played with Jazz teammate Darrell Griffith on 1980 Louisville club that won the NCAA title ... Used as a backup to point guard Rickey Green... Born Feb. 8, 1959, in Louisville, Ky., and still lives there in off-season... Ranks among Louisville's top 20 all-time scorers, but is really not an offensive threat in NBA... Will have to survive on hustle ... Working to complete degree requirements in business marketing ... Most noteworthy thing he did last season was to paste a patch of hair back onto his scalp after it had been inadvertently cut off during a haircut. Patch fell out and onto the floor during a game in Phoenix, nearly prompting a call to the exterminator ... Shaved his head at halftime.

Year	Team	G	FG	FG Pct.	FT	FT Pct.	Reb.	Ast.	TP	Avg.
1982-83	Utah	82	280	.487	200	.810	122	210	761	9.3
1983-84	Utah	80	132	.451	92	.697	85	200	356	4.5
	Totals	162	412	.475	292	.770	207	410	1117	6.9

TOM BOSWELL 31 6-7 225   Forward

Returned from abroad ... Signed with the Jazz as a free agent after playing previous year in Italy ... Last stint in NBA had been in 1979-80, with Utah ... Strictly a body to use in practice and to fill up all of the seats on the bench ... Born Oct. 2, 1953, in Montgomery, Ala., he now lives in Denver ... College career began at South Carolina State and ended at South Carolina ... First-round 1975 draft pick of Boston ... Spent three years with the Celtics.

Year	Team	G	FG	FG Pct.	FT	FT Pct.	Reb.	Ast.	TP	Avg.
1975-76	Boston	35	41	.441	14	.583	71	16	96	2.7
1976-77	Boston	70	175	.515	96	.711	306	85	446	6.7
1977-78	Boston	65	185	.518	93	.756	288	71	453	7.1
1778-79	Denver	79	321	.532	198	.697	538	242	840	10.6
1979-80	Den.-Utah	79	346	.564	206	.755	442	161	903	11.4
1983-84	Utah	38	28	.538	21	.762	64	16	73	1.9
	Totals	366	1096	.518	628	717	1709	591	2821	7.7

JEFF WILKINS 29 6-10 240   Forward-Center

A vagabond ... Guys like him used to make up the entire Jazz roster ... That's why Utah was always mired at bottom of standings until last season ... Born March 9, 1955, in Chicago, and lives in Calumet City, Ill., in offseason ... Is not shy about putting up jumper ... Doesn't know much about defense and doesn't play it ... Was the basketball version of Phileas Fogg, touring the world before catching on with the Jazz in 1980 ... Has taken the ball to the hoop in such exotic places as Billings (Mont.), Turkey, Hawaii, Cuba, Argentina and the Philippines.

Year	Team	G	FG	FG Pct.	FT	FT Pct.	Reb.	Ast.	TP	Avg.
1980-81	Utah	56	117	.450	27	.675	274	40	261	4.7
1981-82	Utah	82	314	.437	137	.778	611	90	765	9.3
1982-83	Utah	81	389	.477	156	.780	596	132	934	11.5
1983-84	Utah	81	249	.479	134	.736	455	73	632	7.8
	Totals	300	1069	.462	454	.759	1935	335	2592	8.6

MITCHELL ANDERSON 24 6-8 195   Forward

Resembles comedian Jimmy (J.J.) Walker, but he's really no joke...Doesn't get much playing time and that probably has to do with having Adrian Dantley and John Drew ahead of him...Capable of getting hot and scoring points in bunches off the bench...Shooting (.423) was way off last season...Born Sept. 23, 1960, in Chicago...All-time leading scorer at Bradley...Drafted on the second round by Philadelphia in 1982, then was released early in the season...Got his big break with the Jazz when Dantley suffered a wrist injury and Anthony Roberts flunked a physical.

Year	Team	G	FG	FG Pct.	FT	FT Pct.	Reb.	Ast.	TP	Avg.
1982-83	Phil.-Utah	65	190	.501	100	.571	294	67	480	7.4
1983-84	Utah	48	55	.423	12	.414	63	22	122	2.5
	Totals	113	245	.481	112	.549	357	89	602	5.3

MARK EATON 27 7-3½ 290   Center

You can't coach height...That's why Utah coach Frank Layden said when he signed this unheralded UCLA bench-warmer to a four-year, guaranteed contract...Layden was right—he has turned into an honest-to-goodness defensive stopper...Led the league in blocked shots with 4.28 per game...Imagine how many he'd block if he could jump...Born Jan. 24, 1957, in Inglewood, Cal....Was famous for being the world's tallest auto mechanic until a friend convinced him to attend Cypress Junior College...From there, it was on to the UCLA bench for two years until Utah made him a fourth-round 1982 pick...Has contended from the start that he was not 7-4 and finally proved it by allowing teammates to measure him... An incredible hulk who will continue to get better.

Year	Team	G	FG	FG Pct.	FT	FT Pct.	Reb.	Ast.	TP	Avg.
1982-83	Utah	81	146	.414	59	.656	462	112	351	4.3
1983-84	Utah	82	194	.466	73	.593	595	113	461	5.6
	Totals	163	340	.442	132	.620	1057	225	812	5.0

RICH KELLEY 31 7-0 240   Center

If Frank Layden is the NBA's version of Henny Youngman, then this guy is George Carlin ...The center of the counter-culture... Very adequate backup pivot who is better known for his ability to go one-on-one in an interview... Born March 23, 1953, in San Mateo, Cal.... Was weird before the rest of California... Seventh pick overall in 1975 draft by New Orleans Jazz, so this is his second go-round with the franchise... Has also spent time with New Jersey, Phoenix and Denver... Was a teammate of Mike Bratz at Stanford... Holds a degree in psychology... Likes to travel... Likes most everything.

Year	Team	G	FG	FG Pct.	FT	FT Pct.	Reb.	Ast.	TP	Avg.
1975-76	New Orleans	75	184	.485	159	.776	528	155	527	7.0
1976-77	New Orleans	76	184	.477	156	.792	587	208	524	6.9
1977-78	New Orleans	82	304	.505	225	.779	759	233	833	10.2
1978-79	New Orleans	80	440	.506	373	.814	1026	285	1253	15.7
1979-80	N.J.-Phoe.	80	229	.473	244	.787	515	178	702	8.8
1980-81	Phoenix	81	196	.506	175	.758	441	282	567	7.0
1981-82	Phoenix	81	236	.467	167	.749	497	293	639	7.9
1982-83	Den.-Utah	70	130	.444	142	.811	404	138	402	5.7
1983-84	Utah	75	132	.500	124	.765	490	157	388	5.2
	Totals	700	2035	.488	1765	.784	5247	1929	5835	8.3

BOB HANSEN 23 6-6 205   Guard

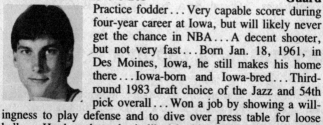

Practice fodder... Very capable scorer during four-year career at Iowa, but will likely never get the chance in NBA... A decent shooter, but not very fast... Born Jan. 18, 1961, in Des Moines, Iowa, he still makes his home there... Iowa-born and Iowa-bred... Third-round 1983 draft choice of the Jazz and 54th pick overall... Won a job by showing a willingness to play defense and to dive over press table for loose balls... Hard worker who is liked by his teammates... Likes to play tennis.

Year	Team	G	FG	FG Pct.	FT	FT Pct.	Reb.	Ast.	TP	Avg.
1983-84	Utah	55	65	.448	18	.643	48	44	148	2.7

TOP ROOKIE

JOHN STOCKTON 22 6-1 175   **Guard**

A surprise pick to many...Will be used as backup at point
...Attracted attention at the Olympic trials, raising his stock
...A gutsy player...Smart...Can run an offense...Will stick
the outside shot...Born March 26, 1962, in Spokane, Wash.
...Averaged 20.9 ppg his senior year at Gonzaga and shot .577
from field.

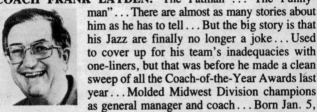

COACH FRANK LAYDEN: "The Fatman"..."The Funny-
man"...There are almost as many stories about
him as he has to tell...But the big story is that
his Jazz are finally no longer a joke...Used
to cover up for his team's inadequacies with
one-liners, but that was before he made a clean
sweep of all the Coach-of-the-Year Awards last
year...Molded Midwest Division champions
as general manager and coach...Born Jan. 5,
1932, in Brooklyn, N.Y....True to his East Coast roots, but has
become the hit of Salt Lake City...One of the most popular after-
dinner speakers in sports...Was college roommate of Knick coach
Hubie Brown at Niagara...Was Calvin Murphy's college coach
at Niagara, then broke into the NBA as the director of player
personnel with the Atlanta Hawks...Became GM of the New
Orleans Jazz in 1979 and took over dual roles when the club moved
to Utah...Received plenty of criticism for trading away potential
all-stars...Now he's everybody's hero...Never turns down second helpings...Overall NBA coaching record is 92-134.

GREATEST FOUL SHOOTER

After bouncing around from Buffalo to Indiana to Los Angeles,
Adrian Dantley has finally found a home with the Utah Jazz. He
has also found a second home—at the foul line.

Everybody in the league will tell you that A.D. lives there. He
was there 946 times last season. That's more often than many
players have gone to the line in their entire careers.

And, hoo boy, does Dantley make opponents pay once he gets

there. He takes his good old time. He bounces the ball, eyes the basket, rolls the ball back into his arms, caresses it and, usually, stabs it right into the net.

Dantley ranked sixth in the NBA with his .859 percentage last season and has a lifetime mark of .823. But he should be placed in a special category all his own, because when it comes to getting to the foul line, nobody does it better than Dantley, who has taken 4,926 free throws during his eight-year pro career.

ALL-TIME JAZZ LEADERS

SEASON

Points: Adrian Dantley, 2,457, 1981-82
Assists: Rickey Green, 748, 1983-84
Rebounds: Len Robinson, 1,288, 1977-78

GAME

Points: Pete Maravich, 68 vs. New York, 2/25/77
Assists: Rickey Green, 20 vs Atlanta, 2/14/84
Rebounds: Len Robinson, 27 vs. Los Angeles, 11/11/77

CAREER

Points: Adrian Dantley, 9,816, 1979-84
Assists: Rickey Green, 2,310, 1980-84
Rebounds: Rich Kelley, 3,622, 1975-79, 1982-84

1984 NBA COLLEGE DRAFT

Sel. No.	Team	Name	College	Ht.
FIRST ROUND				
1.	Houston	Akeem Olajuwon	Houston	7-0
2.	Portland (from Indiana)	Sam Bowie	Kentucky	7-1
3.	Chicago	Michael Jordan	North Carolina	6-6
4.	Dallas (from Cleveland)	Sam Perkins	North Carolina	6-9
5.	Philadelphia (from Clippers)	Charles Barkley	Auburn	6-7
6.	Washington	Melvin Turpin	Kentucky	6-11
7.	San Antonio	Alvin Robertson	Arkansas	6-4
8.	Clippers (from Golden State)	Lancaster Gordon	Louisville	6-3
9.	Kansas City	Otis Thorpe	Providence	6-9
10.	Philadelphia (from Denver)	Leon Wood	Cal. St.-Fullerton	6-3
11.	Atlanta	Kevin Willis	Michigan St.	7-0
12.	Cleveland	Tim McCormick	Michigan	6-11
13.	Phoenix	Jay Humphries	Colorado	6-3
14.	Clippers (from Seattle)	Michael Cage	San Diego St.	6-9
15.	Dallas	Terry Stansbury	Temple	6-5
16.	Utah	John Stockton	Gonzaga	6-1
17.	New Jersey	Jeff Turner	Vanderbilt	6-9
18.	Indiana (from New York)	Vern Fleming	Georgia	6-5
19.	Portland	Bernard Thompson	Fresno St.	6-6½
20.	Detroit	Tony Campbell	Ohio St.	6-7
21.	Milwaukee	Kenny Fields	UCLA	6-7
22.	Philadelphia	Tom Sewell	Lamar	6-5
23.	Los Angeles	Earl Jones	District of Columbia	6-10
24.	Boston	Michael Young	Houston	6-7
SECOND ROUND				
25.	Indiana	Devin Durrant	Brigham Young	6-7
26.	Portland (from Chicago via Indiana)	Victor Fleming	Xavier (Ohio)	6-5
27.	Cleveland	Ron Anderson	Fresno St.	6-7
28.	Seattle (from Houston)	Cory Blackwell	Wisconsin	6-6
29.	Indiana (from Clippers via Philadelphia)	Stuart Gray	UCLA	7-0
30.	Golden State (from Washington)	Steve Burtt	Iona	6-2
31.	Golden State	Jay Murphy	Boston College	6-11
32.	Detroit (from San Antonio)	Eric Turner	Michigan	6-3
33.	Portland (from Denver)	Steve Colter	New Mexico St.	6-3
34.	Washington (from Kansas City via Detroit and Atlanta)	Tony Costner	St. Joseph's	6-9½
35.	Golden State (from Atlanta)	Othell Wilson	Virgina	6-0
36.	Phoenix	Charles Jones	Louisville	6-8
37.	Chicago (from Seattle via Atlanta and Kansas City)	Ben Coleman	Maryland	6-9
38.	Dallas	Charles Sitton	Oregon St.	6-9
39.	Seattle (from New Jersey)	Danny Young	Wake Forest	6-3
40.	Dallas (from Utah)	Anthony Teachey	Wake Forest	6-9
41.	Dallas (from New York via New Jersey)	Tom Sluby	Notre Dame	6-4
42.	Denver (from Portland)	Willie White	Tenn.-Chattanooga	6-3
43.	Chicago (from Detroit via Indiana and Kansas City)	Greg Wiltjer	Victoria (B.C.)	6-11
44.	Washington (from Milwaukee)	Fred Reynolds	Texas-El Paso	6-7
45.	Golden State (from Phil.)	Gary Plummer	Boston University	6-9

Kentucky's Sam Bowie was picked second overall by Portland.

Sel. No.	Team	Name	College	Ht.
46.	Portland (from Los Angeles)	Jerome Kersey	Longwood	6-7
47.	Boston	Ronnie Williams	Florida	6-8

THIRD ROUND

Sel. No.	Team	Name	College	Ht.
48.	Philadelphia (from Indiana)	James Banks	Georgia	6-6
49.	Chicago	Tim Dillon	Northern Illinois	6-8
50.	Cleveland	Ben McDonald	Cal. St.-Irvine	6-8½
51.	Houston	Jim Peterson	Minnesota	6-10
52.	Seattle (from Clippers)	Terry Williams	Alabama	6-8
53.	Washington	Ricky Ross	Tulsa	6-6
54.	Kansas City (from San Antonio)	Roosevelt Chapman	Dayton	6-4
55.	Golden State	Lewis Jackson	Alabama St.	6-6
56.	Kansas City	Jeff Allen	St. John's	6-10
57.	San Antonio (from Denver)	Jeff Binion	North Carolina A&T	6-8½
58.	Atlanta	Bobby Parks	Memphis St.	6-5
59.	Phoenix	Murray Jarman	Clemson	6-5
60.	Cleveland (from Seattle)	Leonard Mitchell	Louisiana St.	6-7
61.	Dallas	Jeff Cross	Maine	6-10
62.	Utah	David Pope	Norfolk St.	6-7½
63.	New Jersey	Yommy Sangodeyi	Sam Houston St.	6-9
64.	New York	Curtis Green	Southern Mississippi	6-1
65.	Portland	Tim Kearney	West Virginia	6-11
66.	Detroit	Kevin Springman	St. Joseph's	6-10
67.	Milwaukee	Vernon Delancy	Florida	6-5
68.	Philadelphia	Butch Graves	Yale	6-3
69.	Los Angeles	George Singleton	Furman	6-7½
70.	Boston	Rick Carlisle	Virginia	6-5

FOURTH ROUND

Sel. No.	Team	Name	College	Ht.
71.	Indiana	Ralph Jackson	UCLA	6-1½
72.	Chicago	Melvin Johnson	NC-Charlotte	6-9
73.	Cleveland	Art Aaron	Northwestern	6-7
74.	Houston	Willie Jackson	Centenary	6-5
75.	Clippers	Marc Glass	Montana	6-3
76.	Washington	Jim Grandholm	South Florida	7-0
77.	Chicago (from Golden State)	Mark Halsel	Northeastern	6-5½
78.	San Antonio	John Devereaux	Ohio	6-8
79.	Denver	Karl Tilleman	Calgary (Canada)	6-2
80.	Kansas City	Carl Henry	Kansas	6-5½
81.	Atlanta	Dickie Beal	Kentucky	5-10
82.	Phoenix	Jeff Collins	Nevada-Las Vegas	6-2
83.	Seattle	Jeff Jenkins	Xavier (Ohio)	6-8
84.	Dallas	John Horrocks	North Texas St.	7-0
85.	New Jersey	Hank Cornley	Illinois St.	6-7
86.	Utah	Jim Rowinski	Purdue	6-8
87.	New York	Bob Thornton	Cal.-Irvine	6-10
88.	Portland	Brett Applegate	Brigham Young	6-7½
89.	Detroit	Philip Smith	New Mexico	5-10
90.	San Antonio (from Milwaukee)	Ozell Jones	Cal. St.-Fullerton	6-11
91.	Philadelphia	Earl Harrison	Morehead St.	6-7
92.	Los Angeles	John Revelli	Stanford	6-8½
93.	Boston	Kevin Mullin	Princeton	6-5

FIFTH ROUND

Sel. No.	Team	Name	College	Ht.
94.	Indiana	Gene Smith	Georgetown	6-2
95.	Chicago	Lamont Robinson	Lamar	6-2

*North Carolina's Michael Jordan, left, and Sam Perkins were
third (Chicago) and fourth (Dallas) first-rounders.*

Sel. No.	Team	Name	College	Ht.
96.	Cleveland	Vince Hinchen	Boise State	6-4½
97.	Houston	Al McClain	New Hampshire	6-1½
98.	Clippers	Alonza Allen	SW Louisiana	6-6
99.	Washington	Colin Irish	Bowling Green	6-6
100.	San Antonio	Eric Richardson	Alabama	6-3
101.	Golden State	Steve Bartek	Doane College	6-8
102.	Kansas City	Jim Foster	South Carolina	6-8
103.	Denver	Prince Bridges	Missouri	6-1½
104.	Atlanta	Terry Martin	NE Louisiana	6-9
105.	Phoenix	Bill Flye	Richmond	6-9½
106.	Seattle	Ely Pasquale	Victoria (B.C.)	6-1
107.	Dallas	Dave Williams	Illinois-Chicago	7-2
108.	Utah	Marcus Gaither	Fairleigh-Dickinson	6-5
109.	New Jersey	Michael Gerren	South Alabama	6-6
110.	Golden State (from New York)	Scott McCollum	Pepperdine	6-9
111.	Portland	Mike Whitmarsh	San Diego	6-7
112.	Detroit	Rick Doyle	Texas-San Antonio	6-10
113.	Milwaukee	Ernie Floyd	Holy Cross	6-8
114.	Philadelphia	Dan Federman	Tennessee	6-10
115.	Los Angeles	Lance Berwald	North Dakota St.	6-10
116.	Boston	Todd Orlando	Bentley	6-10

SIXTH ROUND

117.	Indiana	Clyde Vaughan	Pittsburgh	6-4
118.	Chicago	Jeff Tipton	Morehead St.	6-11
119.	Cleveland	Matt Doherty	North Carolina	6-7½
120.	Milwaukee (from Houston)	McKinley Singleton	Alabama-Birmingham	6-5
121.	Clippers	Phillip Haynes	Memphis St.	6-3
122.	Washington	Blaise Bugajeski	Illinois Wesleyan	6-4

Kentucky's Mel Turpin wound up in Cleveland via Washington.

Sel. No.	Team	Name	College	Ht.
123.	Golden State	Tony Martin	Wyoming	6-6
124.	San Antonio	Dion Brown	SW Louisiana	6-7
125.	Denver	Willie Burton	Tennessee	6-7
126.	Kansas City	Bruce Vanley	Tulsa	6-9½
127.	Atlanta	Jim Master	Kentucky	6-4½
128.	Phoenix	Herman Veal	Maryland	6-6
129.	Seattle	Graylin Warner	SW Louisiana	6-7½
130.	Dallas	LaVerne Evans	Marshall	6-3½
131.	New Jersey	Oscar Schmidt	Brazil	6-8
132.	Utah	Chris Harrison	West Va. Wesleyan	6-8
133.	New York	Eddie Wilkins	Gardner-Webb	6-10
134.	Portland	Lance Ball	Western Oregon	6-10
135.	Detroit	Rennie Bailey	Louisiana Tech	6-4
136.	Milwaukee	Mike Reddick	Stetson	6-8
137.	Philadelphia	Gary Springer	Iona	6-6½
138.	Los Angeles	Keith Jones	Stanford	6-1½
139.	Boston	Steve Carfino	Iowa	6-2

SEVENTH ROUND

Sel. No.	Team	Name	College	Ht.
140.	Indiana	Kenton Edelin	Virginia	6-8
141.	Chicago	Butch Hays	California	6-3
142.	Cleveland	Joe Jakubick	Akron	6-5
143.	Houston	Joedy Gardner	Cal. St.-Long Beach	6-4
144.	Clippers	David Brantley	Oregon	6-6
145.	Washington	Tim Garrett	New Mexico	6-7
146.	San Antonio	Michael Pitts	California	6-11
147.	Golden State	Cliff Higgins	Cal. St.-Northridge	6-6
148.	Kansas City	Chipper Harris	Robert Morris	6-1
149.	Denver	Mark Simpson	Catawba	6-8
150.	Atlanta	Vince Martello	Florida St.	6-6
151.	Phoenix	Raymond Crenshaw	Oklahoma St.	6-6½
152.	Seattle	Gary Gatewood	Oregon	6-3
153.	Dallas	George Turner	Cal.-Irvine	6-2
154.	Utah	Bob Evans	Southern Utah St.	7-1
155.	New Jersey	Sean Kerins	Syracuse	6-8
156.	New York	Ken Bannister	St. Augustine (NC)	6-9
157.	Portland	Victor Anger	Pepperdine	6-8
158.	Detroit	Barry Francisco	Bloomsburg St.	6-5
159.	Milwaukee	Tony William	Florida St.	6-1
160.	Philadelphia	Rich Congo	Drexel	6-7
161.	Los Angeles	Richard Haenisch	Chaminade (Hawaii)	6-6
162.	Boston	Mark Van Valkenburg	Farmingham St.	6-6

EIGHTH ROUND

Sel. No.	Team	Name	College	Ht.
163.	Indiana	Tom Heitz	Kentucky	6-9
164.	Chicago	Brett Crawford	U.S. International	6-7
165.	Cleveland	Elliot Beard	Oberlin	6-1
166.	Houston	Greg Wolff	Angelo St.	6-7
167.	Clippers	Jim McLoughlin	Temple	6-4
168.	Washington	Darryl Odom	West Va. Wesleyan	6-4
169.	Golden State	Paul Brozovich	Nevada-Las Vegas	6-10
170.	San Antonio	Danny Tarkanian	Nevada-Las Vegas	6-2
171.	Denver	Bill Wendlandt	Texas	6-7
172.	Kansas City	Nate Rollins	Fort Hays State	6-7
173.	Atlanta	Robert Brown	LIU	6-0
174.	Phoenix	Mark Fothergill	Maryland	6-9
175.	Seattle	Jerry McMillan	DePaul	6-4
176.	Dallas	Leroy Sutton	Arkansas	6-6
177.	New Jersey	Chris Winans	Utah	6-8

San Antonio made Arkansas' Alvin Robertson seventh pick.

Cal State-Fullerton's Leon Wood was a 76er first-rounder.

Sel. No.	Team	Name	College	Ht.
178.	Utah	Eric Booker	Nevada-Las Vegas	6-4
179.	New York	Ricky Tunstall	Youngstown State	7-0
180.	Portland	Steve Flint	Cal.-San Diego	6-8
181.	Detroit	Dale Roberts	Appalachian State	6-9
182.	Milwaukee	Brad Jergenson	South Carolina	6-8
183.	Philadelphia	Frank Dobbs	Villanova	6-4
	Los Angeles	Pass		
184.	Boston	Champ Godboldt	Holy Cross	6-4

NINTH ROUND

Sel. No.	Team	Name	College	Ht.
185.	Indiana	Brian Martin	Kansas	6-9
186.	Chicago	Calvin Pierce	Oklahoma	6-6
187.	Cleveland	John Shimko	Xavier (Ohio)	6-4½
188.	Houston	Bill Coon	Presbyterian (S.C.)	6-9
189.	Clippers	Dave Schultz	Westmont	6-3
190.	Washington	Mike Emanuel	Pembroke St.	6-5
191.	San Antonio	Melvin Roseboro	St. Mary's (Tex.)	6-5
192.	Golden State	Mitchell Arnold	Fresno St.	6-4
193.	Kansas City	Greg Turner	Auburn	6-7
194.	Denver	Cecil Exum	North Carolina	6-6
195.	Atlanta	Fred Brown	Georgetown	6-5
196.	Phoenix	Buddy Cox	Bellarmine	6-7
197.	Seattle	Mike Williams	Idaho St.	6-8
198.	Dallas	John Tudor	Louisiana State	6-6
199.	Utah	Kelly Knight	Kansas	6-7½
200.	New Jersey	Billy Ryan	Princeton	6-3
201.	New York	Marc Marotta	Marquette	6-6
202.	Portland	Dennis Black	Portland	6-7½
203.	Detroit	Ben Tower	Michigan St.	6-8
204.	Milwaukee	Edwin Green	Massachusetts	6-7
205.	Philadelphia	Michael Mitchell	Drexel	6-9
	Los Angeles	Pass		
206.	Boston	Joe Dixon	Merrimack	6-5

TENTH ROUND

Sel. No.	Team	Name	College	Ht.
207.	Indiana	Gary Carver	Western Kentucky	6-6
208.	Chicago	Carl Lewis	Houston	6-1
209.	Cleveland	Darrell Space	Northeast Illinois	6-4
210.	Houston	Robert Turner	Canisius	6-3
211.	Clippers	Dick Mumma	Penn St.	6-10
212.	Washington	Glynn Myrick	Stetson	6-3
213.	Golden State	Tim Bell	Cal.-Riverside	6-7
214.	San Antonio	Frank Rodriguez	New Mexico St.	6-7
215.	Denver	Dexter Bailey	Xavier (Ohio)	6-4
216.	Kansas City	Victor Coleman	NW Missouri St.	6-5
217.	Atlanta	Doug Mills	Hofstra	6-1
218.	Phoenix	Ezra Hill	Liberty Baptist	6-1
219.	Seattle	Greg Brandon	Creighton	6-7
220.	Dallas	Napoleon Johnson	Grambling	6-7
221.	New Jersey	Phil Jamison	St. Peter's	6-1
222.	Utah	Mike Curran	Niagara	6-3
223.	New York	Mike Henderson	C.W. Post	6-9
224.	Portland	Randy Dunn	George Fox	6-5
225.	Detroit	Dan Pelekoudas	Michigan	6-1
226.	Milwaukee	Mike Toomer	Florida A&M	6-9½
227.	Philadelphia	Martin Clark	Boston College	6-8
	Los Angeles	Pass		
228.	Boston	Dan Trant	Clark	6-2

Temple's Terry Stansbury got a first-round call from Dallas.

1983-84
NATIONAL BASKETBALL ASSOCIATION

FINAL STANDINGS

EASTERN CONFERENCE

Atlantic Division	Won	Lost	Pct.
Boston	62	20	.756
Philadelphia	52	30	.634
New York	47	35	.573
New Jersey	45	37	.549
Washington	35	47	.427

Central Division	Won	Lost	Pct.
Milwaukee	50	32	.610
Detroit	49	33	.598
Atlanta	40	42	.488
Cleveland	28	54	.341
Chicago	27	55	.329
Indiana	26	56	.317

WESTERN CONFERENCE

Midwest Division	Won	Lost	Pct.
Utah	45	37	.549
Dallas	43	39	.524
Denver	38	44	.463
Kansas City	38	44	.463
San Antonio	37	45	.451
Houston	29	53	.354

Pacific Division	Won	Lost	Pct.
Los Angeles	54	28	.659
Portland	48	34	.585
Seattle	42	40	.512
Phoenix	41	41	.500
Golden State	37	45	.451
San Diego	30	52	.366

CHAMPION: Boston

Champ Celtics' Larry Bird was regular-season and playoff MVP.

INDIVIDUAL HIGHS

Most Minutes Played, Season: 3,034, Ruland, Washington
Most Points, Game: 57, Short, Golden State vs. San Antonio, 1/7
Most Field Goals Made, Game: 24, Short, Golden State vs. San Antonio, 1/7
Most 3-Point Field Goals Made, Game: 4, Cooper, Los Angeles vs. Philadelphia, 3/7;
Bratz, Golden State vs. Utah, 3/15;
Ellis, Dallas at Philadelphia, 3/30;
Griffith, Utah at Dallas, 4/7;
Griffith, Utah vs. Denver, 4/10;
Ellis, Dallas at Golden State, 4/15
Most Free Throws Made, Game: 28, Dantley, Utah vs. Houston, 1/4
Most Rebounds, Game: 27, Malone, Philadelphia vs. Boston, 3/25 (2 OT);
24, Ruland, Washington vs. Houston, 2/7
Most Offensive Rebounds, Game: 15, Malone, Philadelphia vs. Boston, 3/25 (2 OT)
12, Thompson, Kansas City vs. Houston, 11/5;
Smith, Golden State at Indiana, 11/25
Most Defensive Rebounds, Game: 19, Williams, New Jersey vs. Detroit, 1/21
Most Offensive Rebounds, Season: 355, Williams, New Jersey
Most Defensive Rebounds, Season: 686, Sikma, Seattle
Most Assists, Game: 24, Lucas, San Antonio vs. Denver, 4/15
Most Blocked Shots, Game: 13, Dawkins, New Jersey vs. Philadelphia, 11/5;
Sampson, Houston at Chicago, 12/9 (OT)
Most Steals, Game: 9, Cook, New Jersey vs. Portland, 12/3
Most Personal Fouls, Season: 386, Dawkins, New Jersey
Most Games Disqualified, Season: 22, Dawkins, New Jersey

INDIVIDUAL SCORING LEADERS
Minimum 70 games or 1,400 points

	G	FG	FT	Pts.	Avg.
Dantley, Utah	79	802	813	2418	30.6
Aguirre, Dallas	79	925	465	2330	29.5
Vandeweghe, Denver	78	895	494	2295	29.4
English, Denver	82	907	352	2167	26.4
King, New York	77	795	437	2027	26.3
Gervin, San Antonio	76	765	427	1967	25.9
Bird, Boston	79	758	374	1908	24.2
Mitchell, San Antonio	79	779	275	1839	23.3
Cummings, San Diego	81	737	380	1854	22.9
Short, Golden State	79	714	353	1803	22.8
Malone, Philadelphia	71	532	545	1609	22.7
Erving, Philadelphia	77	678	364	1727	22.4
Blackman, Dallas	81	721	372	1815	22.4
Free, Cleveland	75	626	395	1669	22.3
Ruland, Washington	75	599	466	1665	22.2
Johnson, E., Kansas City	82	753	268	1794	21.9
Wilkins, Atlanta	81	684	382	1750	21.6
Abdul-Jabbar, Los Angeles	80	716	285	1717	21.5
Thomas, Detroit	82	669	388	1748	21.3
Tripucka, Detroit	76	595	426	1618	21.3

All-around Rolando Blackman averaged 22.4 ppg for Dallas.

REBOUND LEADERS
Minimum 70 games or 800 rebounds

	G	Off.	Def.	Tot.	Avg.
Malone, Philadelphia	71	352	598	950	13.4
Williams, New Jersey	81	355	645	1000	12.3
Ruland, Washington	75	265	657	922	12.3
Laimbeer, Detroit	82	329	674	1003	12.2
Sampson, Houston	82	293	620	913	11.1
Sikma, Seattle	82	225	686	911	11.1
Parish, Boston	80	243	614	857	10.7
Robinson, Cleveland	73	156	597	753	10.3
Greenwood, Chicago	78	214	572	786	10.1
Bird, Boston	79	181	615	796	10.1

FIELD-GOAL LEADERS
Minimum 300 FG Made

	FG	FGA	Pct.
Gilmore, S.A.	351	556	.631
Donaldson, S.D.	360	604	.596
McGee, L.A.	347	584	.594
Dawkins, N.J.	507	855	.593
Natt, Port.	500	857	.583
Ruland, Wash.	599	1035	.579
Abdul-Jabbar, L.A.	716	1238	.578
Nance, Phoe.	601	1044	.576
Lanier, Mil.	392	685	.572
King, N.Y.	795	1391	.572

3-POINT FIELD-GOAL LEADERS
Minimum 25 Made

	FG	FGA	Pct.
Griffith, Utah	91	252	.361
Evans, Den.	32	89	.360
Moore, S.A.	28	87	.322
Cooper, L.A.	38	121	.314
Williams, N.Y.	25	81	.309
Sobers, Wash.	29	111	.261

FREE-THROW LEADERS
Minimum 125 FT Made

	FT	FTA	Pct.
Bird, Bos.	374	421	.888
Long, Det.	243	275	.884
Laimbeer, Det.	316	365	.866
Davis, Phoe.	233	270	.863
Pierce, S. D.	149	173	.861
Dantley, Utah.	813	946	.859
Knight, K.C.	243	283	.859
Sikma, Sea.	411	480	.856
Vandeweghe, Den.	494	580	.852
Johnson, Bos.	281	330	.852

ASSISTS LEADERS
Minimum 70 games or 400 assists

	G	A	Avg.
Johnson, L.A.	67	875	13.1
Nixon, S.D.	82	914	11.1
Thomas, Det.	82	914	11.1
Lucas, S.A.	63	673	10.7
Moore, S.A.	59	566	9.6
Green, Utah.	81	748	9.2
Williams, Sea.	80	675	8.4
Whatley, Chi.	80	662	8.3
Drew, K.C.	73	558	7.6
Davis, Dall.	81	561	6.9

Utah's Darrell Griffith led NBA in 3-point field goals.

STEALS LEADERS Minimum 70 games or 125 steals			
	G	St.	Avg.
Green,Utah	81	215	2.65
Thomas, Det......	82	204	2.49
Williams, Sea.	80	189	2.36
Cheeks, Phil..	75	171	2.28
Johnson, L.A.	67	150	2.24
Dunn, Den.	80	173	2.16
Williams, N.Y.	76	162	2.13
Cook, N.J.	82	164	2.00
Conner, G.S.......	82	162	1.98
Erving, Phil.......	77	141	1.83

BLOCKED-SHOTS LEADERS Minimum 70 games or 100 blocked shots			
	G	Blk.	Avg.
Eaton, Utah	82	351	4.28
Rollins, Atl.	77	277	3.60
Sampson, Hou.	82	197	2.40
Nance, Phoe......	82	173	2.11
Gilmore, S.A.......	64	132	2.06
Hinson, Clev.......	80	145	1.81
Thompson, K.C....	80	145	1.81
Erving, Phil........	77	139	1.81
Abdul-Jabbar, L.A.	80	143	1.79
Carroll, G.S.......	80	142	1.78

ALL-TIME NBA RECORDS

INDIVIDUAL
Single Game
Most Points: 100, Wilt Chamberlain, Philadelphia vs New York, at Hershey, Pa., Mar. 2, 1962

Most FG Attempted: 63, Wilt Chamberlain, Philadelphia vs New York, at Hershey, Pa., Mar. 2, 1962

Most FG Made: 36, Wilt Chamberlain, Philadelphia vs New York, at Hershey, Pa., Mar. 2, 1962

Most Consecutive FG Made: 18, Wilt Chamberlain, San Francisco vs New York, at Boston, Nov. 27, 1963; Wilt Chamberlain, Philadelphia vs Baltimore, at Pittsburgh, Feb. 24, 1967

Most FT Attempted: 34, Wilt Chamberlain, Philadelphia vs St. Louis, at Philadelphia, Feb. 22, 1962

Most FT Made: 28, Wilt Chamberlain, Philadelphia vs New York, at Hershey, Pa., Mar. 2, 1962; Adrian Dantley, Utah vs Houston at Las Vegas, Nev., Jan. 4, 1984

Most Consecutive FT Made: 19, Bob Pettit, St. Louis vs Boston, at Boston, Nov. 22, 1961; Bill Cartwright, New York vs Kansas City, Nov. 17, 1981

Most FT Missed: 22, Wilt Chamberlain, Philadelphia vs Seattle, at Boston, Dec. 1, 1967

Most Assists: 29, Kevin Porter, New Jersey vs Houston at N.J., Feb. 24, 1978

Most Personal Fouls: 8, Don Otten, Tri-Cities at Sheboygan, Nov. 24, 1949

Season
Most Points: 4,029, Wilt Chamberlain, Philadelphia, 1961-62

Highest Average: 50.4, Wilt Chamberlain, Philadelphia, 1961-62

Most FG Attempted: 3,159, Wilt Chamberlain, Philadelphia, 1961-62

Most FG Made: 1,597, Wilt Chamberlain, Philadelphia, 1961-62

Most 3-Pt. FG Attempted: 239, Brian Taylor, San Diego, 1979-80

Most 3-Pt. FG Made: 73, Rick Barry, Houston, 1979-80; Don Buse, Indiana, 1981-82

Highest FG Percentage: .727, Wilt Chamberlain, Los Angeles, 1972-73

Highest 3-Pt. FG Percentage: .443, Fred Brown, Seattle, 1979-80

Most FT Attempted: 1,363, Wilt Chamberlain, Philadelphia, 1961-62

Elvin Hayes retired with NBA record 50,000 minutes played.

Most FT Made: 840, Jerry West, Los Angeles, 1965-66
Highest FT Percentage: .958, Calvin Murphy, Houston, 1980-81
Most Rebounds: 2,149, Wilt Chamberlain, Philadelphia, 1960-61
Most Assists: 1,099, Kevin Porter, Detroit, 1978-79
Most Personal Fouls: 386, Darryl Dawkins, New Jersey, 1983-84
Most Disqualifications: 26, Don Meineke, Fort Wayne, 1952-53

Career

Most Points Scored: 31,527, Kareem Abdul-Jabbar, Milwaukee Bucks and Los Angeles Lakers, 1970-84

Highest Scoring Average: 30.1, Wilt Chamberlain, 1960-73

Most FG Attempted: 24,272, Elvin Hayes, San Diego, Washington and Houston, 1969-84

Most FG Made: 13,006, Kareem Abdul-Jabbar, 1970-84

Highest FG Percentage: .593, Artis Gilmore, Chicago and San Antonio, 1976-83

Most FT Attempted: 11,862, Wilt Chamberlain, 1960-73

Most FT Made: 7,694, Oscar Robertson, Cincinnati and Milwaukee, 1961-74

Highest FT Percentage: .900, Rick Barry, San Francisco and Golden State Warriors, Houston, 1965-67, 1972-80

Most Rebounds: 23,924, Wilt Chamberlain, 1960-73

Most Assists: 9,887, Oscar Robertson, 1961-74

Most Minutes: 50,000, Elvin Hayes, San Diego, Washington and Houston, 1969-84

Most Games: 1,303, Elvin Hayes, 1969-84

Most Personal Fouls: 4,193, Elvin Hayes, 1969-84

Most Times Disqualified: 127, Vern Mikkelsen, Minneapolis, 1950-59

TEAM RECORDS
Single Game

Most Points, One Team: 173, Boston, vs Minneapolis at Boston, Feb. 27, 1959; 186, Detroit vs Denver, Dec. 13, 1983 (3 overtimes)

Most Points, Two Teams: 318, Denver 163 vs San Antonio 155, Jan. 11, 1984; 370, Detroit 186 vs Denver 184, Dec. 13, 1983 (3 overtimes)

Most FG Attempted, One Team: 153, Philadelphia, vs Los Angeles at Philadelphia (3 overtimes), Dec. 8, 1961

Most FG Attempted, Two Teams: 291, Philadelphia 153, Los Angeles 138 at Philadelphia (3 overtimes), Dec. 8, 1961

Most FG Made, One Team: 72, Boston, vs Minneapolis at Boston, Feb. 27, 1959; 74, Denver at Detroit, Dec. 13, 1983 (3 overtimes)

Most FG Made, Two Teams: 142, Detroit 74 at Denver, 68, Dec. 13, 1983 (3 overtimes)

Most FT Attempted, One Team: 86, Syracuse, vs Anderson at Syracuse (5 overtimes), Nov. 24, 1949

Most FT Attempted, Two Teams: 160, Syracuse 86, Anderson 74 at Syracuse (5 overtimes), Nov. 24, 1949

Most FT Made, One Team: 59, Syracuse, vs Anderson at Syracuse (5 overtimes), Nov. 24, 1949

Most FT Made, Two Teams: 116, Syracuse 59, Anderson 57 at Syracuse (5 overtimes), Nov. 24, 1949

Most Rebounds, One Team: 109, Boston, vs Detroit at Boston, Dec. 24, 1960

Most Rebounds, Two Teams: 188, Philadelphia 98 vs Los Angeles 90, Dec. 8, 1961 (3 overtimes)

Most Assists, One Team: 53, Milwaukee vs Detroit, Dec. 26, 1978

Most Assists, Two Teams: 88, Phoenix 47, San Diego 41 at Tucson, Ariz., Mar. 15, 1969

Most Assists, Two Teams, OT: 89, Detroit 48, Cleveland 41 at Cleveland, Mar. 28, 1973

Most Personal Fouls, One Team: 66, Anderson, at Syracuse (5 overtimes), Nov. 24, 1949

Most Personal Fouls, Two Teams: 122, Anderson 66, Syracuse 56 at Syracuse (5 overtimes), Nov. 24, 1949

Most Disqualifications, One Team: 8, Syracuse, vs Baltimore at Syracuse (1 overtime), Nov. 15, 1952

Most Disqualifications, Two Teams: 13, Syracuse 8, Baltimore 5 at Syracuse (1 overtime), Nov. 15, 1952

Most Points in a Losing Game: 184, Denver vs Detroit, Dec. 13, 1983 (3 overtimes)

Widest Point Spread: 63, Los Angeles 162, Golden State 99 at Los Angeles, Mar. 19, 1972

Most Consecutive Points in a Game: 24, Philadelphia, vs Baltimore, Mar. 20, 1966

Season

Most Games Won: 69, Los Angeles, 1971-72

Most Games Lost: 73, Philadelphia, 1972-73

Longest Winning Streak: 33, Los Angeles, Nov. 5, 1971 to Jan. 7, 1972

Longest Losing Streak: 20, Philadelphia, Jan. 9, 1973 to Feb. 11, 1973

Most Points Scored: 10,731, Denver, 1981-82

Most Points Allowed: 10,328, Denver, 1981-82

Highest Scoring Average: 126.5, Denver, 1981-82

Highest Average, Points Allowed: 126.0, Denver, 1981-82

Most FG Attempted: 9,295, Boston, 1960-61

Most FG Made: 3,980, Denver, 1981-82

Highest FG Percentage: .529, Los Angeles, 1979-80

Most FT Attempted: 3,411, Philadelphia, 1966-67

Most FT Made: 2,434, Phoenix, 1969-70

Highest FT Percentage: .821, KC-Omaha, 1974-75

Most Rebounds: 6,131, Boston, 1960-61

Most Assists: 2,562, Milwaukee, 1978-79

NBA SCORING CHAMPIONS

Season	Pts./Avg.	Top Scorer	Team
1946-47	1389	Joe Fulks	Philadelphia
1947-48	1007	Max Zaslofsky	Chicago
1948-49	1698	George Mikan	Minneapolis
1949-50	1865	George Mikan	Minneapolis
1950-51	1932	George Mikan	Minneapolis
1951-52	1674	Paul Arizin	Philadelphia
1952-53	1564	Neil Johnston	Philadelphia
1953-54	1759	Neil Johnston	Philadelphia
1954-55	1631	Neil Johnston	Philadelphia
1955-56	1849	Bob Pettit	St. Louis
1956-57	1817	Paul Arizin	Philadelphia
1957-58	2001	George Yardley	Detroit
1958-59	2105	Bob Pettit	St. Louis
1959-60	2707	Wilt Chamberlain	Philadelphia
1960-61	3033	Wilt Chamberlain	Philadelphia
1961-62	4029	Wilt Chamberlain	Philadelphia
1962-63	3586	Wilt Chamberlain	San Francisco
1963-64	2948	Wilt Chamberlain	San Francisco
1964-65	2534	Wilt Chamberlain	San Fran.-Phila.
1965-66	2649	Wilt Chamberlain	Philadelphia
1966-67	2775	Rick Barry	San Francisco
1967-68	2142	Dave Bing	Detroit
1968-69	2327	Elvin Hayes	San Diego
1969-70	*31.2	Jerry West	Los Angeles
1970-71	*31.7	Lew Alcindor	Milwaukee
1971-72	*34.8	K. Abdul-Jabbar	Milwaukee
1972-73	*34.0	Nate Archibald	K.C.-Omaha
1973-74	*30.6	Bob McAdoo	Buffalo
1974-75	*34.5	Bob McAdoo	Buffalo
1975-76	*31.1	Bob McAdoo	Buffalo
1976-77	*31.1	Pete Maravich	New Orleans
1977-78	*27.2	George Gervin	San Antonio
1978-79	*29.6	George Gervin	San Antonio
1979-80	*33.1	George Gervin	San Antonio
1980-81	*30.7	Adrian Dantley	Utah
1981-82	*32.3	George Gervin	San Antonio
1982-83	*28.4	Alex English	Denver
1983-84	*30.6	Adrian Dantley	Utah

*Scoring title based on best average with at least 70 games played

MOST VALUABLE PLAYER

1955-56 Bob Pettit, St. Louis
1956-57 Bob Cousy, Boston
1957-58 Bill Russell, Boston
1958-59 Bob Pettit, St. Louis
1959-60 Wilt Chamberlain, Philadelphia
1960-61 Bill Russell, Boston
1961-62 Bill Russell, Boston
1962-63 Bill Russell, Boston
1963-64 Oscar Robertson, Cincinnati
1964-65 Bill Russell, Boston
1965-66 Wilt Chamberlain, Philadelphia
1966-67 Wilt Chamberlain, Philadelphia
1967-68 Wilt Chamberlain, Philadelphia
1968-69 Wes Unseld, Baltimore
1969-70 Willis Reed, New York

1970-71 Lew Alcindor, Milwaukee
1971-72 Kareem Abdul-Jabbar, Milwaukee
1972-73 Dave Cowens, Boston
1973-74 Kareem Abdul-Jabbar, Milwaukee
1974-75 Bob McAdoo, Buffalo
1975-76 Kareem Abdul-Jabbar, L.A.
1976-77 Kareem Abdul-Jabbar, L.A.
1977-78 Bill Walton, Portland
1978-79 Moses Malone, Houston
1979-80 Kareem Abdul-Jabbar, L.A.
1980-81 Julius Erving, Philadelphia
1981-82 Moses Malone, Houston
1982-83 Moses Malone, Philadelphia
1983-84 Larry Bird, Boston

ROOKIE OF THE YEAR

1952-53 Don Meineke, Fort Wayne
1953-54 Ray Felix, Baltimore
1954-55 Bob Pettit, Milwaukee
1955-56 Maurice Stokes, Rochester
1956-57 Tom Heinsohn, Boston
1957-58 Woody Sauldsberry, Philadelphia
1958-59 Elgin Baylor, Minneapolis
1959-60 Wilt Chamberlain, Philadelphia
1960-61 Oscar Robertson, Cincinnati
1961-62 Walt Bellamy, Chicago
1962-63 Terry Dischinger, Chicago
1963-64 Jerry Lucas, Cincinnati
1964-65 Willis Reed, New York
1965-66 Rick Barry, San Francisco
1966-67 Dave Bing, Detroit
1967-68 Earl Monroe, Baltimore
1968-69 Wes Unseld, Baltimore

1969-70 Lew Alcindor, Milwaukee
1970-71 Dave Cowens, Boston
        Geoff Petrie, Portland
1971-72 Sidney Wicks, Portland
1972-73 Bob McAdoo, Buffalo
1973-74 Ernie DiGregorio, Buffalo
1974-75 Keith Wilkes, Golden State
1975-76 Alvan Adams, Phoenix
1976-77 Adrian Dantley, Buffalo
1977-78 Walter Davis, Phoenix
1978-79 Phil Ford, Kansas City
1979-80 Larry Bird, Boston
1980-81 Darrell Griffith, Utah
1981-82 Buck Williams, New Jersey
1982-83 Terry Cummings, San Diego
1983-84 Ralph Sampson, Houston

COACH OF THE YEAR

1962-63 Harry Gallatin, St. Louis
1963-64 Alex Hannum, San Francisco
1964-65 Red Auerbach, Boston
1965-66 Dolph Schayes, Philadelphia
1966-67 Johnny Kerr, Chicago
1967-68 Richie Guerin, St. Louis
1968-69 Gene Shue, Baltimore
1969-70 Red Holzman, New York
1970-71 Dick Motta, Chicago
1971-72 Bill Sharman, Los Angeles
1972-73 Tom Heinsohn, Boston

1973-74 Ray Scott, Detroit
1974-75 Phil Johnson, Kansas City-Omaha
1975-76 Bill Fitch, Cleveland
1976-77 Tom Nissalke, Houston
1977-78 Hubie Brown, Atlanta
1978-79 Cotton Fitzsimmons, Kansas City
1979-80 Bill Fitch, Boston
1980-81 Jack McKinney, Indiana
1981-82 Gene Shue, Washington
1982-83 Don Nelson, Milwaukee
1983-84 Frank Layden, Utah

Utah's Frank Layden was voted NBA Coach of the Year.

NBA CHAMPIONS

Season	Champion	Eastern Division			Western Division	
		W.	L.		W.	L.	
1946-47	Philadelphia	49	11	Washington	39	22	Chicago
1947-48	Baltimore	27	21	Philadelphia	29	19	St. Louis
1948-49	Minneapolis	38	22	Washington	45	15	Rochester
1949-50	Minneapolis	51	13	Syracuse	39	25	Indianap.*
1950-51	Rochester	40	26	Philadelphia	44	24	Minneapolis
1951-52	Minneapolis	40	26	Syracuse	41	25	Rochester
1952-53	Minneapolis	47	23	New York	48	22	Minneapolis
1953-54	Minneapolis	44	28	New York	46	26	Minneapolis
1954-55	Syracuse	43	29	Syracuse	43	29	Ft. Wayne
1955-56	Philadelphia	45	27	Philadelphia	37	35	Ft. Wayne
1956-57	Boston	44	28	Boston	34	38	StL-Mpl-FtW
1957-58	St. Louis	49	23	Boston	41	31	St. Louis
1958-59	Boston	52	20	Boston	49	23	St. Louis
1959-60	Boston	59	16	Boston	46	29	St. Louis
1960-61	Boston	57	22	Boston	51	28	St. Louis
1961-62	Boston	60	20	Boston	54	26	Los Angeles
1962-63	Boston	58	22	Boston	53	27	Los Angeles
1963-64	Boston	59	21	Boston	48	32	San Fran.
1964-65	Boston	62	18	Boston	49	31	Los Angeles
1965-66	Boston	55	25	Boston	45	35	Los Angeles
1966-67	Philadelphia	68	13	Philadelphia	44	37	San Fran.
1967-68	Boston	62	20	Philadelphia	56	26	St. Louis
1968-69	Boston	57	25	Baltimore	55	27	Los Angeles
1969-70	New York	60	22	New York	48	34	Atlanta
1970-71	Milwaukee	42	40	Baltimore	66	16	Milwaukee
1971-72	Los Angeles	48	34	New York	69	13	Los Angeles
1972-73	New York	57	25	New York	60	22	Los Angeles
1973-74	Boston	56	26	Boston	59	23	Milwaukee
1974-75	Golden State	60	22	Washington	48	34	Golden State
1975-76	Boston	54	28	Boston	42	40	Phoenix
1976-77	Portland	50	32	Philadelphia	49	33	Portland
1977-78	Washington	44	38	Washington	47	35	Seattle
1978-79	Seattle	54	28	Washington	52	30	Seattle
1979-80	Los Angeles	61	21	Boston	60	22	Los Angeles
1980-81	Boston	62	20	Boston	57	25	Phoenix
1981-82	Los Angeles	57	25	Philadelphia	58	24	Los Angeles
1982-83	Philadelphia	65	17	Philadelphia	53	29	Los Angeles
1983-84	Boston	62	20	Boston	54	28	Los Angeles

*1949-50 Central Division Champ: Minneapolis and Rochester tied 51-17.

NBA TV/Radio Roundup

NATIONAL TELEVISION
CBS will again carry national telecasts of NBA games, with Dick Stockton doing the play-by-play. WTBS, the cable television network, will produce 55 regular-season and 20 playoff games.

ATLANTA HAWKS
John Sterling and Charlie Criss call the shots on WTBS (Channel 17) and WCNN radio (680).

BOSTON CELTICS
The Celtics can be seen on WBZ (Channel 4) and SportsChannel and heard on WRKO (680). Gil Santos and Bob Cousy handle the TV chores while it's Mike Gorman and Tom Heinsohn on Sports-Channel. Johnny Most and Glenn Ordway form the radio team.

CHICAGO BULLS
Jim Durham is the voice of the Bulls on WIND radio (560). Milo Hamilton goes behind the mike for WGN-TV (Channel 9), while Bill Hazen and Johnny Kerr work cable games on SportsVision.

CLEVELAND CAVALIERS
Joe Tait follows the action on radio station WWWE (1100). Announcers for WUAB-TV (Channel 43) were to be chosen.

DALLAS MAVERICKS
Dave Barnett does the play-by-play on WBAP radio (820). The Mavs' television outlet is KXAS-TV (Channel 5).

DENVER NUGGETS
Jeff Kingery and Bob Martin describe the action on KOA radio (850), while Jim Conrad, Al Albert and Irv Brown do the honors on KWGN-TV (Channel 2).

DETROIT PISTONS
George Blaha does double duty, calling the shots on CKLW radio (800) and WKBD-TV (Channel 50).

GOLDEN STATE WARRIORS
Warriors action is carried over KBHK-TV (Channel 44), with Ted Robinson behind the mike. KCBS radio (740) airs all games.

Gus Williams (1) will be wearing a Bullet uniform this year.

HOUSTON ROCKETS

Gene Peterson calls 'em on KPRC radio (950) and Greg Lucas on KTXH (Channel 20).

INDIANA PACERS

Marty Brennaman does it on WTTV-TV (Channel 4) and Bob Lamey follows the action on WIBC radio (1070).

KANSAS CITY KINGS

The Kings are carried over KCMO radio (810) and KEKR-TV (Channel 62). An announcing team had not been selected at press time.

LOS ANGELES CLIPPERS

Radio and TV plans were not determined at press time.

LOS ANGELES LAKERS

Chick Hearn and Keith Erickson are back to call the shots on KLAC radio (570) and KHJ-TV (Channel 9).

MILWAUKEE BUCKS

Jon McGlocklin and Jim Irwin share radio duties on WTMJ radio (620), while Eddie Doucette and McGlocklin handle television on WVTV (Channel 18).

NEW JERSEY NETS

Steve Albert and Bill Raftery are behind the mike for WOR-TV (Channel 9) and are joined by Bob Goldsholl on SportsChannel. Mel Proctor and Mike DiTomasso are the radio voices for WNBC (660).

NEW YORK KNICKS

Marv Albert and Butch Beard call the action on WOR-TV (Channel 9), while Beard and Jim Karvellas handle games for MSG Cable. Albert and John Andariese work the radio side.

PHILADELPHIA 76ERS

The 76ers are carried by WFIL radio (560) and WPHL-TV (Channel 17), with Neil Funk and John Nash describing the action.

PHOENIX SUNS

Al McCoy does the play-by-play for KTAR radio (620), and gets help from Dick Van Arsdale on KPNX-TV (Channel 12). George Allen and Van Arsdale call the shots for American Cable TV.

PORTLAND TRAIL BLAZERS

KEX radio (1190) is the home of the Blazers, with Bill Schonely and Dave Twarzik at the mike. The TV outlet is KOIN (Channel 6), with Steve Jones and Larry Steele announcing.

SAN ANTONIO SPURS

Announcers were yet to be named for WOAI radio (1200) and Rogers Cable (Channel 7) at press time.

SEATTLE SUPERSONICS

Bob Blackburn is the radio voice of the Sonics on KIRO (710), while Wayne Cody handles TV duties for KIRO-TV (Channel 7). Jimmy Jones and Jim Marsh call the shots on the Sonics' Super-Channel cable network.

UTAH JAZZ

Rod Hundley is the voice of the Jazz. Radio and TV outlets were not yet announced at press time.

WASHINGTON BULLETS

The Bullets can be heard on WTOP radio (1500), with Frank Daly handling play-by-play. Mike Patrick and a partner who was unnamed at press time will describe the action for WDCA-TV (Channel 20).

Official 1984-85 NBA Schedule

SUBJECT TO CHANGE

*Afternoon Game
**Site to be selected

Fri Oct 26
Atl at NJ
Cle at Phil
Bos at Det
Wash at Chi
Phoe at GS
Utah at Sea

Sat Oct 27
Det at NY
Phil at Atl
NJ at Cle
Wash at Ind
Chi at Mil
*Hou at Dal
LAL at SA
Port at KC
GS at Den
LAC at Utah

Sun Oct 28
LAL at Dal
Phoe at Sea

Mon Oct 29
Mil at Chi

Tue Oct 30
Phil at NJ
Atl at Wash
Cle at Det
Dal at Hou
Den at SA
Chi at KC
NY at Utah
LAC at Phoe
GS at LAL
Sea at Port

Wed Oct 31
NJ at Bos
Dal at Ind
Wash at Mil

Thu Nov 1
Det at Atl
Hou at KC
Chi at Den
Port at Phoe
NY at LAC
SA at GS
LAL at Sea

Fri Nov 2
Det at Bos
Dal at Phil
Mil at Wash

Ind at Cle
Sea vs Utah
   in LV
SA at LAL

Sat Nov 3
Ind at NJ
Wash at Atl
Cle at Mil
Phoe at Dal
NY at Hou
Den at KC
Port at LAC
Utah at GS

Sun Nov 4
NY at SA
Port at LAL

Mon Nov 5
Det at Cle
Den at LAC

Tue Nov 6
NY at Dal
KC at Hou
Sea at SA
Den at LAL
Phoe at Port

Wed Nov 7
LAC at Bos
Wash at NJ
Ind at Phil
Chi at Det
Atl at Mil
SA at Utah

Thu Nov 8
Chi at NY
LAC at Wash
Atl at Dal
Sea at Hou
Port at Den
Cle at Phoe
LAL at GS

Fri Nov 9
Phil at Bos
KC at NJ
Ind at Mil
GS at Utah
LAL at Port

Sat Nov 10
KC at NY

Bos at Wash
Mil at Det
Chi at Ind
Sea at Dal
LAC at Hou
Cle at SA
Utah at Den
Atl at Phoe

Sun Nov 11
NJ at LAL
GS at Port

Mon Nov 12
Bos at Ind
Dal at Utah

Tue Nov 13
Wash at NY
Mil at Atl
SA at Chi
Cle at Hou
Phoe at Den
NJ at LAC
Dal at Port
GS at Sea

Wed Nov 14
NY at Bos
Det at Phil
SA at Wash
Hou at Ind
NJ at Phoe

Thu Nov 15
Cle at Atl
Bos at Chi
Mil at LAC
Dal at GS
Utah at Port

Fri Nov 16
NY at Wash
Phil at Det
SA at Ind
Hou at Den
Mil at Phoe
KC at LAL
Port at Sea

Sat Nov 17
Cle at NY
Ind at Atl
Phil at Chi
Det at SA
SA at Hou

Phoe at Utah
KC at LAC
NJ at GS

Sun Nov 18
Mil at LAL
LAC at Port
NJ at Sea

Mon Nov 19
Ind at Chi

Tue Nov 20
GS at NY
Wash at Phil
Mil at Dal
Det at Hou
Utah at KC
Phoe at LAL
NJ at Port
Den at Sea

Wed Nov 21
GS at Bos
KC at Wash
Utah vs Atl
   in NO
NY at Cle
Phil at Ind
Chi at Mil
Det at SA
LAL at Phoe
Den at LAC

Fri Nov 23
Wash at Bos
GS at Cle
NY at Det
KC at Ind
Hou at Utah
Phil at Phoe
Chi at Sea

Sat Nov 24
Ind at NY
Det at Wash
NJ at Atl
GS at Mil
Hou at Dal
Utah at SA
Bos at KC
Phil at Den
LAL at LAC
Chi at Port

Sun Nov 25
Atl at Cle

Phoe at Utah
KC at LAC
NJ at GS

Tue Nov 27
Atl at NY
Phil at Wash
Port at Cle
Mil at Ind
Bos at Dal
Hou at SA
LAC at Den
Utah at Phoe
Chi at GS
KC at Sea

Wed Nov 28
NY at NJ
Ind at Phil
Mil vs Atl
   in NO
Port at Det
Bos at Hou
LAL at Utah
Sea at LAC

Thu Nov 29
Cle at Wash
Dal at SA
Chi at Phoe
KC at GS

Fri Nov 30
Ind at NJ
Port at Phil
Hou at Atl
Wash at Det
NY at Mil
Sea at Dal
Den at Utah
Chi at LAC
KC at LAL

Sat Dec 1
Port at NY
Mil at Wash
Bos at Cle
Det at Ind
Sea at Hou
LAC at SA
Utah at Den
GS at Phoe

Sun Dec 2
Cle at Bos
NJ at Phil
Chi at LAL

Phoe at LAC
Sea at LAL

Mon Dec 3
Phoe at Sea

Tue Dec 4
Den at NY
LAL at Cle
Bos at Det
NJ at Chi
LAC at Hou
Atl at SA
Utah at GS
Phoe at Port

Wed Dec 5
Den at Bos
LAL at NJ
Mil at Phil
LAC at Dal
Atl at KC

Thu Dec 6
Dal at NY
Ind at Wash
Det at Mil
Sea at Utah
Hou at GS
SA at Port

Fri Dec 7
LAL at Phil
LAC at Atl
Den at Det
NY at Chi
KC at Phoe
SA at Sea

Sat Dec 8
Bos at NJ
LAL at Wash
Den at Cle
Dal at Chi
Ind at Mil
Phoe at GS
Hou at Port

Sun Dec 9
Atl at Bos
NY at Phil
KC vs Utah
  in LV
SA at LAC
Hou at Sea

Mon Dec 10
Atl at Ind

Tue Dec 11
NJ vs Bos
  in Hart
Phil at NY
Utah at Wash
Mil at Cle
Det at Chi
SA at KC
Port at Den
Hou at Phoe
LAC at GS

Wed Dec 12
Mil at NJ
Bos at Phil
Cle at Atl
  in NO
Chi at Det
KC at Dal
Den at SA
GS at LAL

Thu Dec 13
Utah at NY
Atl at Hou
Wash at Phoe
Port at LAC
LAL at Sea

Fri Dec 14
Utah at Bos
Chi at NJ
Ind at Det
Phil at Mil
SA at Dal
KC at Den
Port at GS

Sat Dec 15
Bos at Atl
NY at Cle
NJ at Ind
Phil at Chi
Dal at Hou
Phoe at SA
Sea at KC
Wash at LAC

Sun Dec 16
Utah at Mil
Sea at Den
GS at LAC
Wash at LAL

Tue Dec 18
Bos at NY
NJ at Wash
LAL at Atl
SA at Cle
Utah at Ind
Hou at Chi
Dal at Mil
Phoe at KC
Den at GS
Port at Sea

Wed Dec 19
Mil at Bos
Wash at NJ
SA at Phil
LAL at Hou
Det at Den
Sea at LAC

Thu Dec 20
Cle at NY
Chi vs Atl
  in NO

Det at Utah
KC at Port

Fri Dec 21
Ind at Bos
SA at NJ
Mil at Phil
NY at Wash
Dal at Den
Phoe at LAL
Sea at GS

Sat Dec 22
NJ at Phil
Wash at Atl
Cle at Ind
Bos at Chi
SA at Mil
Den at Hou
Det at KC
Dal at Utah
Port at Phoe
LAC at Sea

Tue Dec 25
NJ at NY
Atl at Cle
*Phil at Det
GS at Port

Wed Dec 26
Det at NJ
*Ind at Wash
NY vs Atl
  in NO
Hou at Mil
LAC at Dal
SA at Den
KC at Utah
Bos at Phoe
Sea at LAL

Thu Dec 27
Cle at Chi
Port at SA
Hou at KC
Bos at LAC
GS at Sea

Fri Dec 28
NY at NJ
Atl at Wash
Det at Ind
LAL at Den
Phil at Utah
Dal at Phoe

Sat Dec 29
Wash at NY
Mil at Cle
NJ at Det
Atl at Chi
Utah at Dal
Port at Hou
Bos at SA
Ind at KC
LAC at LAL
Phil at GS

Den vs Sea
  in Tacoma

Sun Dec 30
Bos at Mil
Phoe at LAC

Tue Jan 1
Ind at Utah
Phil at Port

Wed Jan 2
Bos at NJ
Chi at Atl
Cle at Det
Phoe at KC
Hou at Den
Phil at Sea

Thu Jan 3
Wash at Cle
LAC at Mil
Dal at SA
Ind at GS
Sea at Port

Fri Jan 4
NY at Bos
Phoe at NJ
Atl at Det
Mil at Chi
LAC at KC
Den at Utah
Port at LAL

Sat Jan 5
Chi at NY
Det at Wash
NJ at Atl
Phoe at Cle
Phil at Mil
KC at Dal
LAC at Den
Hou at GS
Ind at Sea

Sun Jan 6
Hou vs Utah
  in LV
SA at LAL
Ind at Port

Mon Jan 7
Bos at NY
Phoe at Phil
GS at KC
Utah at LAC
Dal at Sea

Tue Jan 8
NJ at Cle
Wash at Mil
KC at Hou
GS at SA
Den at LAL
Dal at Port

Wed Jan 9
Chi at Bos
Det at Phil
Mil at Ind
NY at Den
Sea at Phoe

Thu Jan 10
Dal at KC
Utah at LAL
Sea at GS

Fri Jan 11
Wash at Bos
Atl at NJ
Hou at Phil
Ind at Det
NY at Chi
Cle at Mil
LAL at Dal
Port at SA
KC at Den
LAC at Phoe

Sat Jan 12
Bos at Atl
Chi at Cle
NY at Ind
Utah at Phoe
LAC at GS

Sun Jan 13
*Hou at NJ
*Phil at Wash
*LAL at Det
*Den at Mil
*Port at Dal
*KC at Sea

Mon Jan 14
Wash at Cle
Den at Chi

Tue Jan 15
Phil at NY
Atl at Ind
LAL at Mil
Utah at SA
Cle at KC
Dal at GS
Hou at Port
LAC vs Sea
  in Tacoma

Wed Jan 16
LAL at Bos
Chi at NJ
Atl at Phil
GS at Den
Wash at Utah
Dal at Phoe
Hou at LAC

Thu Jan 17
Det at NY
Cle at Chi
SA at KC

Fri Jan 18
Sea at Atl
Bos at Ind
NJ at Mil
Wash at Den
Port at Utah
Hou at Phoe
Dal at LAL

Sat Jan 19
Det at NJ
Atl at NY
Sea at Cle
Chi at Ind
Utah at Hou
Phoe at SA
Wash at KC
Dal at LAC
LAL at GS
Den at Port

Sun Jan 20
*Phil at Bos

Mon Jan 21
GS at Ind

Tue Jan 22
Sea at NY
GS at Wash
Det vs Atl
in NO
Phil at Cle
Port at Chi
Phoe at Hou
KC at SA
NJ at Utah
LAC at LAL

Wed Jan 23
Sea at Bos
Phoe at Atl
Port at Ind
SA at Dal

Thu Jan 24
Dal at Wash
GS at Det
Mil at KC
NJ at Den
Cle at Utah

Fri Jan 25
Ind at Bos
Sea at Chi
SA at Hou
Phil at LAL

Sat Jan 26
Ind at NY
Phoe at Wash
Sea at Det
Atl at Chi
NJ at Dal
Mil at Hou
GS at KC
Cle at Den

LAL at Utah
Phil at LAC

Sun Jan 27
*Port at Bos
Mil at SA

Mon Jan 28
LAC at NY
Phil at Dal
NJ at Hou
Den at Utah

Tue Jan 29
Det vs Bos
in Hart
Ind vs Atl
in NO
LAC at Cle
KC at Chi
NJ at SA
Phoe at Den
Mil at GS
LAL at Port

Wed Jan 30
Bos at Phil
Chi at Wash
KC at Det
Cle at Ind
NY at Phoe
Hou at LAL

Thu Jan 31
LAC at NJ
Dal at Den
Port at GS
SA at Sea

Fri Feb 1
KC at Bos
Chi at Phil
Cle at Atl
Wash at Ind
Utah at Dal
NY at LAL
SA at Port
Mil at Sea

Sat Feb 2
*Phil at NJ
Bos at Wash
KC at Cle
Atl at Det
Den at Hou
SA at Utah
LAL at LAC
NY at GS
Mil at Port

Sun Feb 3
Den at Dal
Sea at Phoe
Ind at LAL

Mon Feb 4
Atl at Phil

Cle at Wash
Det at Mil
GS at SA
Ind at LAC

Tue Feb 5
Dal vs Atl
in NO
NJ at Det
Bos at Chi
LAL at Hou
SA at KC
Den at Phoe
Utah at Port
NY at Sea

Wed Feb 6
Cle at Bos
Mil at NJ
Wash at Phil
GS at Dal
Sea at Den

Thu Feb 7
Det at Wash
Chi at Cle
Atl at Mil
GS at Hou
LAC at SA
Utah at KC
Ind at Phoe
NY at Port

Sun Feb 10
*All-Star Game
in Indianapolis

Tue Feb 12
Dal at Cle
Phil at Ind
Det at Chi
NJ at Mil
Phoe at Hou
KC at SA
Atl at Den
LAC at LAL
Utah at GS
Bos at Port
Wash at Sea

Wed Feb 13
Cle at NJ
NY at Phil
Dal at Det
Atl at Utah
GS at LAC

Thu Feb 14
Hou at NY
Mil at Ind
Phoe at SA
Den at KC
Bos at Sea

Fri Feb 15
Det at NJ
Cle at Phil

Ind at Chi
Phoe at Dal
SA at Den
LAC at Utah
Atl at LAL
Bos at GS
Wash at Port

Sat Feb 16
NJ at NY
Hou at Cle
Phil at Det
KC at Sea

Sun Feb 17
*Phoe at Ind
*Chi at Mil
Atl at LAC
*Bos at LAL
*Wash at GS
KC at Port

Mon Feb 18
*Phil at Cle
Phoe at Det
Bos at Utah
SA at LAC

Tue Feb 19
Mil at NY
GS at Atl
LAL at Chi
Dal at Hou
Port at KC

Wed Feb 20
Utah at NJ
GS at Phil
Mil at Det
Cle at Ind
Port at Dal
Wash at SA
Bos at Den
Hou at Phoe
Sea at LAC

Thu Feb 21
LAL at KC

Fri Feb 22
Chi vs Bos
in Hart
GS at NJ
Det at Phil
NY at Atl
Utah at Cle
LAL at Ind
Wash at Dal
Port at Hou
SA at Phoe
Den at Sea

Sat Feb 23
Mil at Cle
NJ at Det
GS at Chi

Wash at Hou
Dal at KC

Sun Feb 24
*LAL at NY
*Utah at Phil
*Bos at Ind
*Port at SA
*Phoe at Den
*LAC at Sea

Tue Feb 26
SA at NY
Den at Atl
Cle at Chi
Phil at Mil
Utah at Dal
Phoe at KC
Hou at LAL
Sea at GS
LAC at Port

Wed Feb 27
SA at Bos
Atl at NJ
Den at Wash
Chi at Det
NY at Ind
Mil at Utah
Hou at LAC

Thu Feb 28
Phil at KC
LAL at Phoe
Port at GS
Cle vs Sea
in Tacoma

Fri Mar 1
Atl at Bos
NJ at Wash
SA at Det
NY at Chi
Den at Dal
Hou at Utah
Cle at Port

Sat Mar 2
Wash at NY
SA at Atl
Sea at Ind
LAL at Dal
Mil at Den
KC at Phoe
LAC at GS

Sun Mar 3
*Det at Bos
NJ at Chi
*Phil at Hou
KC at LAC
Utah at Port

Mon Mar 4
Mil at Det
Phil at SA
Dal at Phoe
Cle at GS

Tue Mar 5
Bos at NY
Port vs Atl
  in NO
Wash at Chi
Sea at Mil
Ind at Dal
NJ at KC
Hou at Den

Wed Mar 6
Chi at NY
Sea at NJ
Atl at Phil
Port at Wash
NY at Det
Utah at Hou
Ind at SA
Cle at LAC
GS at LAL

Thu Mar 7
Den at KC
SA at Phoe

Fri Mar 8
Dal at Bos
Port at NJ
Sea at Phil
Utah at Det
LAC at Chi
KC at Mil
Ind at Hou

Sat Mar 9
*Phil at NY
Sea at Wash
Det at Atl
Utah at Chi
Hou at SA
Ind at Den
GS at Phoe
Cle at LAL

Sun Mar 10
*Dal at NJ
Port at Mil
*LAC at KC

Mon Mar 11
Chi at Wash
Mil at Atl
Ind at Cle
LAC at Det
Sea at Dal

Tue Mar 12
Phoe at NY
Bos vs Atl
  in NO
NJ at Ind
Det at Chi
Den at Hou
Port at KC
Utah at LAL
SA at GS

Wed Mar 13
Phoe at Bos
Wash at NJ
LAC at Phil
Cle at Mil
KC at Dal
LAL vs Utah
  in LV

Thu Mar 14
Chi at NY
Hou at Det
LAC at Ind
Atl at GS
SA at Sea

Fri Mar 15
NY at Phil
Hou at Wash
Bos at Cle
Phoe at Chi
Den at Dal
KC at Utah
SA at LAL
GS at Port

Sat Mar 16
Ind at NY
NJ at Phil
Wash at Det
Phoe at Mil
Cle at Dal
LAL at LAC
Atl at Sea

Sun Mar 17
*Hou at Bos
*Ind at NJ
Mil at Chi
*Den at SA
*Utah at KC
GS at LAC
Atl at Port

Mon Mar 18
Dal at Den
GS at Utah
Det at Sea

Tue Mar 19
Wash vs Atl
  in NO
Phil at Cle
NJ at Mil
SA at Dal
Chi at Hou
LAL at Phoe
Det at Port

Wed Mar 20
Mil at Bos
Cle at NJ
KC at Phil
NY at Wash
Den at Ind
Chi at SA

Utah at LAC
GS at Sea

Thu Mar 21
Port at Phoe
Det at GS

Fri Mar 22
Cle at Bos
Den at NJ
Mil at Phil
KC at Atl
NY at Ind
LAL at Hou
Dal at SA
Utah at Sea

Sat Mar 23
Bos at Wash
Atl at Cle
Ind at Mil
Chi at Dal
NY at KC
Phoe at GS
LAC at Port

Sun Mar 24
*Den at Phil
*Sea at SA
Chi vs Utah
  in LV
Det at LAL

Mon Mar 25
NY at Mil
Sea at KC
Port at LAC

Tue Mar 26
Mil at Wash
NJ vs Atl
  in NO
NY at Cle
Ind at Chi
GS at Dal
KC at Hou
Utah at Den
Det at Phoe
LAL at Port

Wed Mar 27
Bos at NJ
Wash at Phil
Atl at Ind
GS at SA
Dal at Utah
Det at LAC
LAL at Sea

Thu Mar 28
Mil at NY
Chi at Cle
KC at Den
Phoe at LAC

Fri Mar 29
Phil at Bos

NJ at Wash
Atl at Det
GS at Hou
SA at Utah
Dal at LAL
Port at Sea '

Sat Mar 30
NJ at NY
*Ind at Cle
Bos at Det
Phil at Chi
Atl at Mil
Utah at Hou
GS at KC
Port at Den
LAC at Phoe

Sun Mar 31
Wash at Ind
SA at LAC
Phoe at LAL

Mon Apr 1
Hou at Sea

Tue Apr 2
Phil at Atl
Wash at Cle
Det at Ind
NJ at Chi
Bos at Mil
LAL at Den
Sea at Phoe
Dal at GS
Hou at Port

Wed Apr 3
Ind at Bos
NY at NJ
Cle at Phil
Chi at Wash
LAL at SA
KC at LAC

Thu Apr 4
Atl at NY
Det at Mil
Sea at Utah
Den at Phoe
Hou at GS

Fri Apr 5
Wash at Bos
Chi at Phil
Cle at Det
LAC at Dal
SA at Den
KC at LAL
Sea at Port

Sat Apr 6
Mil at NJ
Cle at Wash
Chi at Atl
Phil at Ind
Hou at Dal

Phoe at Utah
KC at GS

Sun Apr 7
*NY at Bos
Hou at SA
GS at Den
*Port at LAL

Mon Apr 8
Chi at Ind
**Phoe vs Sea

Tue Apr 9
Det at NY
Bos at Phil
Atl at Wash
NJ at Cle
SA at Hou
Dal at KC
LAC vs Utah
  in LV
Den at LAL
Phoe at Port

Wed Apr 10
Phil at NJ
NY at Atl
Ind at Det
Wash at Mil
Den at LAC

Thu Apr 11
Bos at Cle
Hou at KC
Port at Utah
LAL at GS
**Dal vs Sea

Fri Apr 12
Mil at Bos
Cle at NY
Ind at Phil
Wash at Det
Atl at Chi
LAC at Hou
KC at SA
Utah at Phoe
Sea at LAL
Dal at Port

Sat Apr 13
Chi at NJ
Phil at Wash
Ind at Atl
NY at Mil
Den at GS

Sun Apr 14
*NJ at Bos
*Det at Cle
Sea at Hou
*Utah at SA
*LAL at KC
GS at Phoe
Dal at LAC
Den at Port